A Dangerous Grace

Read Irwin Myers

PublishAmerica
Baltimore

© 2007 by Read Irwin Myers.
All rights reserved. No part of this book may be reproduced, stored in a retrieval system or transmitted in any form or by any means without the prior written permission of the publishers, except by a reviewer who may quote brief passages in a review to be printed in a newspaper, magazine or journal.

First printing

ISBN: 1-4241-6511-3 (softcover)
ISBN: 978-1-4489-6401-7 (hardcover)
PUBLISHED BY PUBLISHAMERICA, LLLP
www.publishamerica.com
Baltimore

Printed in the United States of America

Table of Contents

Introduction 7

Chapter One: A London Landmark 9
Chapter Two: Why Bother? 18
Chapter Three: Discovering Real Grace 46
Chapter Four: Glimpses of Glorious Grace 60
Chapter Five: Once More—with Heart! 110
Chapter Six: The Five Keys of Grace 141
Chapter Seven: Decisive Destinies Discovered 164
Chapter Eight: The Grace Paradigm 175
Chapter Nine: The Savage Christian 199
Chapter Ten: Blood-Blind Believers 221
Chapter Eleven: Mark the Sky 244
Chapter Twelve: The God Mind 253
Chapter Thirteen: Warning: Danger Ahead! 266
Chapter Fourteen: The First and Second Voice 276
Chapter Fifteen: Truth in Tension with Truth 288

Epilogue 301
Bibliography 307
Works Cited 311

Introduction

"How much more will those who receive God's abundant provision of grace...reign in life?" (Romans 5:17).

   Romans 5:17 sets the standard of life God has promised every Christian believer. It is about absolute possibility. It defines the means by which the true Christian life is discovered and lived. It is by discovering the practical implication of these few words that the body of Christ can discover its true and supernatural identity. If believers miss what God is saying to us in these few cryptic words, what it means to be truly Christian remains a mystery. It is only as one discovers what it means to receive the abundant provision of grace that one reigns in life. To the degree a believer learns to receive of abundant grace is the degree to which that believer rises above the soulish, carnal world and discovers what it means to "reign in life." And what is the contemporary reality?
   "Well, we are not into grace right now." An evangelist friend had recommended to a pastor that I be invited to minister in his fellowship. In speaking with the pastor he inquired as to the message I'd bring to his congregation. I indicated that my core message centered in grace. After our conversation his response was precisely as quoted.
   While ministering in the southern United States I was invited to speak at a church of some three thousand people. After five days of ministering on the grace of Christ one of the two senior pastors came to me in the parking lot and said, "You may not know it but this teaching on grace has saved our ministry and our church."
   Over more than thirty five years of ministry I've met hundreds of pastors. In conversation with them they have asked me what I would minister on if they invited me to come to their churches. Now get this! Only three have asked me to come and minister solely on the grace of Christ. Two of the three were in the third world.

Repeatedly I have asked Christians and whole congregations to give me the biblical definition of grace with its references. To date not one has given the definition of grace as found plainly in the pages of Scripture. God has given us the core definition of grace three times. None use the term "unmerited favor."

If the individual believer, the family, or the body of Christ, are to be fully what God intends them to be then grace must become a functional reality. Apart from functional grace we will never be the salt and light Christ intends us to be. For grace to be found in its functional dimension it must first be understood. Functional grace can only rest on a clear knowledge of its biblical definition.

What I have written in the following pages is intended to be an introduction to a biblical definition of grace and how grace is designed to function in the lives of believers, the body of Christ, and human culture. I have endeavored to provide the hungry believer with some initial insights into the prevailing covenant of Christ; that is HIS grace! If we do not understand grace it cannot be said that we accurately understand either Christ's covenant or the New Testament. Following on then, to the degree that grace is not understood is the degree to which man is left with nothing more than some form of pragmatic religion. It is my hope, imperfect as this book may be, that some will find in these pages a place to begin their own pursuit of His glorious grace.

Chapter One
A London Landmark

It was only a short walk from the Barbican underground station to a plaque set next to the sidewalk. Most people would walk past this spot and never notice the plaque commemorating an event that bore significant impact on Western history. It was at this spot on the 24th of May, 1738, that John Wesley encountered the grace of God. He later wrote in his own words that he "felt his heart strangely warmed." On that day in history, grace bore its transforming impact on the very nature of a radical sinner. The plaque goes on to note the following: "This experience of grace…was the beginning of…Methodism."

Wesley correctly understood the substance of what God had ministered into his life.

Four significant things about this plaque caught my attention. The first thing was that his *heart* had been deeply affected and changed by God the Holy Spirit, and the whole direction of his life was changed. His motivations, priorities, ideals, and life itself were radically altered. There was a sovereign invasion of his heart by the sovereign God.

The second thing that leapt out at me as I stood on the sidewalk staring at the plaque was the observation that what had happened to Wesley's heart was an experience of grace. Grace became a functional force and by it, his heart was transformed. Wesley, in describing this event, used two words: *strangely* and *warmed*. The conversion of the human heart by a sovereign intervention of God may indeed seem strange. It is totally contrary to all that is strictly of human passion. To go from the pub and the party to prayer and the power of God cannot be easily appreciated by those who are strangers to the grace of God. It cannot be said that grace has been received if the heart is not subsequently driven by an upward and passionate inclination. It is by grace that a heart previously cold and indifferent toward God now burns with a passion satisfied only by an ever-increasing intimacy with God.

The third thing that impacted me was the phrase, "was the beginning." Where else can Christian experience begin? Where else could the heart become capable of such a profound revolution that through one individual the world should find its way out of darkness? Experiential grace is the place where the necessary elements of the kingdom of God find their beginning. Until the church of Christ finds its heart "strangely warmed," the kingdom of God cannot come into our congregations or upon our cultures and the world around us will not be impacted in the necessary measure.

The fourth thing that settled upon me was that this experience was the beginning of Methodism. It was surely this but it was significantly more than the beginning of a church movement. This beginning of grace in the heart of a single man not only affected a personal *regeneration*, it flowed far beyond the personal dimension to impact the surrounding culture with *revival* and the subsequent influences of *reformation*. Don't slip past these three R's too quickly! Methodism became an expression of Christianity that was relevant to the world and the culture of mankind. The nature of grace unleashed cannot be ignored by cultures gripped in the mire of paganism. It is grace unleashed in a single human heart that goes to the "uttermost parts of the world." Wesley's experience of grace did not stop with another man sitting quietly in a pew: it penetrated to even the smallest hamlet of the known world. There was such a driving passion in the heart of one man that tens of thousands fell under the wonder of saving grace. As grace entered the hearts of men, the dark faces of societies in the grip of human degradation were changed. Grace is the only substance in the universe that has the power to radically transform the human heart and its inherent passions, so that only a changed world can satisfy its aims.

We, as believers, may very well pray for revival and work for the transformation of human societal conditions with no significant impact. *If grace does not first have its total and significant work in our minds and hearts, then grace in its potential to transform cannot find its way into the mainstream of human culture and need.*

Standing on the sidewalk beside that historic Ebenezer, I prayed with a friend. "As grace once streamed into the tiny crevice of a human heart, resulting in the manifestation of an immense and personal God, so Heavenly Father, in your love and mercy for a lost humanity, let the measures of grace seep through the crevice of my finite heart. This so that in some measure hope, redemption, beauty, purity of love and the like might be descriptive of our present generations." I could see a flood of God's magnificent grace flowing into hearts of individuals around the world, carrying with it the life characteristic of his *living water*. Wishful thinking, an overactive imagination, or perhaps a prophetic vision? Only time will tell.

This much is absolute: grace is the only saving mechanism for man in the universe, "for by grace are you saved." (Ephesians 2:8). Nothing else saves. If we do not come to God via the grace gate, then salvation remains a possibility, not a possession. It strikes me that the kind of grace addressed in this verse has significantly broader implications than many allow. The breadth and depth of this verse is magnificent. Here the Holy Spirit declares that by functional grace we are saved. Saved from what? Oh, yes, saved from sin. Praise God! However, for many that is where this verse stops. We look back to a moment in time when grace came into our hearts and we gave our lives to Christ as though that was all grace was meant to do. Looking carefully at this declaration of heaven opens significantly broader possibilities because the statement, "For by grace are you saved..." raises the question, "Saved from what?" Grace not only saved us from sin in a past tense, it saves us from our present sin and will prove sufficient to do so tomorrow. When grace becomes operative by faith, it liberates us wherever we need freedom. Make the list as long as you want! Grace can save us from destructive habits, addictions, failing marriages, poverty, depression, shattered relationships, anger and fear. Grace not only serves as a mechanism to save us *from* eternal annihilation and the whole spectrum of human adversity, it functions to save us by bringing us *into* the positive realities of the kingdom of God. What do you need to be brought out of, or conversely, brought into? Find grace and you will find it to be sufficient; it will make meeting your need possible. You fill in the blanks:

"For by grace I am saved from _____
by faith, that not of myself; it is the gift of God."

A ship coming into harbor must necessarily come by way of the prescribed channel. The captain must not only know about the channel, he must use it! Grace is that gateway into the gifts of God. Through Christ, God has set the passageway before mankind, and grace is the *only* passageway into the manifold riches of God! Reflecting on the state of human culture, with the imposition of hateful humanism, are we wide of the mark in presuming that God's grace is sufficient? If one Man came into the world, "full of grace" and that one Man changed human history, can we not conclude that grace remains as his legacy and is still sufficient? Fullness of grace was sufficient for a man named Stephen who lived through that grace and adjunct faith, a life characteristic of signs, wonders, and miracles. The infant church, full of grace, faced the task of overcoming evil with good, and grace proved sufficient for the survival of the church to this day. Grace pierced the rock hard heart of a man on his murderous journey to Damascus, and history was never to be the same. There are many names along with the Wesleys' that could be listed here who acted to change their world once grace had truly penetrated their hearts. History took a turn for the better, and a true concept of freedom was laid in the foundation of human society. Apart from functional grace, no message of freedom can be extended to heal the human spirit or bond the human family.

What do I mean by "functional grace?" Simply this: grace must be more than a Christian doctrine, more than a nice religious word that we pay dutiful homage to, and more than an ethereal word we use in our hymnology. If grace had not become a functional agent of empowerment, then salvation could not become experiential. If believers are to experience increasing administrations of God in life, then grace must be that functional agent, because without it, the Christian life is diminished, and the New Man is incapacitated. As the doctrine of grace becomes experience, we learn practically what it means to "grow in grace" (II Peter 4:18).

Grace must not only have its initial work in converting us, but be permitted continual working. Only grace can affect the core nature of what we are as fallen man. This change becomes manifest in what motivates us. This is reflected in the quality of our relationships and the miracle of a harnessed tongue, compelled by the beauty of holy passions and evidenced in giving and forgiving. Tongues that once cursed now minister grace. Listen to the conversations in the different spheres of the church and our words betray our confession. "For out of the overflow of the heart the mouth speaks" (Mt. 12:34). The heart, still stone, manifests itself in words that stone. The heart "strangely warmed" manifests a flood of grace that saves, lifts, and impels men to the greatness of their inherent, godly potential. It is only as this wondrous flood of grace renews the heart that the possibility for revival followed by a second reformation exists. Surely we have prayed for revival. Books have been written as to why revival "tarries." Revival, among a number of things, does mean that large numbers of people find Christ as Savior. People on the streets and in our neighborhoods find a desire for God springing up in their hearts. What previously they were callous to, they now must have as if driven by the thirst of dying men. Why does revival "tarry"? Daring the wrath of many more knowledgeable, revival is held off because of the absence of grace. Until believers find the reality of functional grace at work in their own hearts and minds, revival will not come in the kingdom dimension that we all desire. There is no substitute for the flood of grace. Fasting and prayer cannot substitute for grace. Finances in abundance cannot bring about revival that transforms lives, towns, nations, laws, and governments. In the absence of grace, the experience of revival cannot come into our cultures. Tears, faith, preaching, or longing for such a move of God will not bring the needed revival our countries must have if any vestige of freedom is to be left to our children. *There is no substitute for functional grace!* The measure in which we miss grace becomes the measure in which the world will miss God. Conversely, the measure in which the world is missing God demonstrates to some degree the measure the believing church is missing grace. Put these two words together: Grace-Revival. In the words of the old jingle, "You can't have one without the other!" Mankind outside Christ lives in a graceless reality.

On one occasion while in London I had occasion to speak to an individual who claimed to be a Buddhist. In the course of conversation, this individual asked why I thought Christianity to be valid over all other world religions. The answer for me was simple: grace. No other system of religion or human philosophy articulates grace or offers a mediated redemption based solely and purely on the grounds of grace. In fact, grace is contrary to the human intellectual process. The more someone is educated in worldly logic the more illogical a grace-based redemption appears. The most educated can then be in danger of being the most foolish. Knowledge of any sort potentially carries its own poison. Knowledge puffs up (I Corinthians 8:1), but God gives grace to the humble (I Peter 5:5). Grace is contrary to what men perceive as logical; it is revolutionary!

Grace can even have about it the appearance of being repugnant. For example, in late 1997 the world was made aware of a young lady in Texas who was to be put to death for killing a man with a pickaxe. "Good people," those who understand good apart from grace, might think, "I have lived a good life. At least I've never been anywhere near as bad as this woman who committed murder was. Are you telling me that she is going to heaven while I am going to hell? If that's true, then God is not fair!" This reasoning often takes another form: "Is God going to send people to hell who have never heard of Christ? If that is what God is like then I want no part of him!"

Scripture addresses this problem by noting in various places that God's way of thinking is contrary to man's way of thinking. The wisdom of God is foolishness to man. Grace, once it has pierced the human heart, is designed to radically alter the way one thinks. God says in Jeremiah 31:33, "This is the covenant I will make with the house of Israel.... I will put my law in their minds." Christ died to put into force the new covenant referred to here—the covenant of grace. Those so impacted by grace are expected to think with radically different thought patterns and principles. This new way of thinking is intended to produce a people who live and operate in complete contradiction to a world in the grip of gracelessness. The man outside grace thinks we've gone mad!

What started out as a beautiful Saturday afternoon in a small Irish town called Omah became a day of shocking tragedy. The IRA detonated a bomb killing some twenty-eight people and wounding many more. With a couple of exceptions, the dead and wounded were Irish people killed and wounded by Irish people. Many of the dead were young school children. Wives, mothers, friends, visitors all lay dead under the blow of graceless animosity. The bombers, in the face of total community outrage, offered a pathetic apology saying they did not mean to kill people. To set off a bomb of this size and then to suggest they did not mean to kill people demonstrates their own profound lack of "sensibility," or ability to sense the impact of their own deeds. Murder and mayhem, to the graceless mind of the terrorist, is logical and even necessary. There is no ability in graceless hearts to feel beyond their own selfish need or to think beyond their own twisted logic. The deadness in the graceless life is so complete that it has no capacity to "sense" its own horror or the horror inflicted on others. It is indeed "senseless."

Consider the Nazis. Consider the abortionists and the proponents of abortion. Even those activists who blow up clinics and kill doctors in the name of God and Justice have missed the meaning of grace! To kill innocent people makes sense only to the people without sense—that is, people without a God-induced mindset.

With this new mindset a remarkable and otherworldly wisdom manifests. I think sometimes that this other and higher wisdom can only truly manifest out of long and painful tragedy. Such was the case in Ireland. Fathers, mothers, husbands, and wives of the dead in Omah demonstrated this otherworldly attitude of mind. They were not in the streets screaming for blood and vengeance. Through long and painful years of tragedy, the Irish psyche manifested something contrary to the natural mind: in quiet pain at the tragic loss of loved ones, people gathered in the streets of Ireland forgiving the murderous terrorists and praying for them. Ireland stood still on the streets of its own land. There were no faces hidden behind masks or screams for vengeance; instead, the acute awareness manifested that unless forgiveness was allowed to flow in their hearts to heal and temper, they would be bound into an endless cycle of violence.

We need to reflect seriously as to what caused this kind of corporate response to such outrageous savagery. Forgiveness has its distinctive roots in Christianity. It is specifically a fruit of functional grace. Whatever extent Christianity operates in that land revealed itself that day, for out of long years of murder, violence, and tragedy arose awareness that unless people walk in a manifestation of grace evidenced by forgiveness, lives would remain forever bound to the hearts and violence of evildoers and past betrayals. The scene on the streets in Ireland showed a people reaching out for the release found only in grace. The false logic system characteristic of the natural mind of man was forcefully brought into subjection to a higher principle of life—forgiveness. This fruit of grace is the only route to a life free from the hateful heart of the terrorist. Tears of forgiveness instead of screams of hate are the only route to the healing of the broken heart and a broken world!

As I watched the pictures of the public memorial service on the streets of Omah, I could not keep my mind from turning to other scenes where innocent people had died. We've all watched what takes place on the streets in Islamic cities where the death of innocents (and the not-so innocent) has occurred. No manifestation of grace can be seen! Why? There is no grace in Islam. In the absence of grace, cries of "Jihad!" fill the air. The streets fill with people in a rage burning flags and firing off guns. Hate binds the heart to perennial horror. Those whose religion offers no grace are forever locked into a cycle of savage violence and a quenchless thirst for vengeance that never loosens its grip on the heart and is borne in generation after generation. Unless grace comes on the scene, nothing but annihilation of one party by another can break the cycle. In the absence of grace, death is the only closure. A Christianity steeped in grace brings closure that allows life, forgiveness and freedom to prevail: a Christianity void of grace carries with it the same violent passions characteristic of any other religious system. Herein lies the explanation of the violence that has characterized the history of a Christianity reduced to nothing more than a set of religious regulations and empty liturgy, where God bears the blame for everything from the Crusades to personal atrocities committed by individuals claiming God's sanction over their actions.

READ IRWIN MYERS

Mankind can only break free of past desolations and violence by forcing our unwilling minds and hearts through the narrow gate of grace. The world in its gracelessness has a right to come to the real church of Christ and dip into the clear waters of grace. If grace is not made available to the world by the church, then the world has no place to turn and has no hope for peace or release from its self-inflicted pain. Grace is the great antidote to all demonic poison. Indeed, if the world made a trek to the local church and placed its dipper of need into the waters running there, would they be refreshed by the clean, life-giving waters of another Kingdom, or would the waters they drink taste all too much like the bitter waters from which they long to turn? Would they find a people who respond out of grace to hurts and injury, extending genuine forgiveness and offering relational reconciliation, or a place of harsh words, criticisms, rejection, slander, divisions, and broken relationships? We all know what kind of water the world *should* drink at the fountain of the church, but what they should drink and what they would *actually* drink are most often two different things. It seems that we are content for this sullied reality to continue. Rather than confront and rectify the gracelessness manifest in the body of Christ, we continue to wound and reject, all the while declaring we are a loving community!

This tyranny of conflict, division, and relational devastation so characteristic of the body of Christ never ceases to amaze me. Tragically, behind the outward façade of many churches, there is a dark side of humanity manifest that few seem willing to confront. I have seen it in the fellowships I've pastored and continue to face it firsthand. In many places I have asked a series of questions that go something like this: "How many of you have been wounded in church?" Invariably, heads nod. Then I ask, "How many of you would agree that the church is one of the hardest places to survive long term?" Agreement is almost universal. If you haven't been shot in your local church yet, just hang around a while—it's coming. What should surprise us is not that this dark side exists, but rather our reluctance to confront it, expose it, and remove it from our midst!

Yes, this is uncomfortable, but you cannot heal something you refuse to acknowledge. Some even get angry when this aspect of church life is exposed. Perhaps we need to make a journey in our spirits to that plaque in London asking the Father to "strangely warm our hearts." Interestingly enough, that warming of Wesley's heart lasted a lifetime. A fresh experience of grace could be the beginning of a move of God that touches the heart of our lost generations. Perhaps reflecting on the quiet people in the streets of Omah may cause us to seek our Father for a fresh outpouring of grace that we can then extend to one another in our churches. If they could gather to pray for and forgive the likes of such men and women, how much more must we, as believers, find His grace so that the church can offer the world—and each other—a last taste of grace that sweetens, heals, forgives, loves and offers life!

Yet grace is so easily and rationally missed. The heart finds responding to the possibility of grace a great endeavor. Great in the effort the heart must expend against its own lower inclinations and great in the possibilities unlocked should this endeavor be undertaken. What is this great endeavor? For believers to become effective administrators of grace to one another so that the world in turn can draw upon this abundant provision. If the reality of functional grace is not operative in our own relationships, then we have nothing but religion to offer the world. Such a religion is no better than any other if we have missed the effectual working of grace. Grace will indeed bother the inclinations of any heart that has settled only for an outward expression of Christian religion. The perplexity is this: if we have missed effectual grace, then we won't readily recognize it when we settle for a religious form of Christianity. What happens then? In the name of our brand of Christianity, others who identify themselves with Christ—but not our particular brand—become the targets of our doctrinal missiles. If you do not see "it" as I see "it" then the mandate to love one another somehow becomes nothing more than a non-binding proposition. Preference and opinion replace the high and hard call of grace. What is the evidence and result of missed grace? Some of the world's most trivial battles are fought out in the church with a notorious savagery. I'm sure we've all been privy to fights over the color of a carpet, whether pews are better than chairs, or the value of paint over wallpaper.

Do we leave our confession like this, or are we bound by truth to find the resolution grace can interpose? Dare we refuse such a journey? A changed world is the ultimate fruit of a great grace discovered. A signpost on a sidewalk in London bears evidence of such discovery, as does the history of the early church. Perhaps if the church of the present age finds grace in such measure, an eternal signpost may be found on some high road in heaven.

Chapter Two
Why Bother?

The phone rang one day with a pastor inviting me to come minister in his church. He said a mutual friend had recommended me, asked about my availability and the kinds of topics I preferred to minister on. "Wow!" I thought, "What an opportunity!" I told him that the most significant thing I could do to strengthen his church would be to minister on grace. There was a rather pronounced pause. Having had this experience on numerous occasions, I knew he was trying to find some nice, religious way of saying this didn't interest him. He said he'd speak to his leadership and get back to me. I was not surprised when a few weeks later I received a letter from him indicating that grace did not fit into their ministry agenda at this time. This has often typified the response I encounter to the subject of grace. Somehow it does not rank high on our teaching agendas.

Every time I've ever heard a message on grace—and I mean *without fail*—the speaker begins with some grace scripture and shortly thereafter delineates grace in terms of something else. Grace gets defined as love, forgiveness, mercy, faith, truth and on one occasion grace was even declared to be the anointing. It seems that we intend to speak of grace, but end up speaking on some other topic, calling it "grace." Perhaps it should be observed here that love is love, not grace; forgiveness is forgiveness, not grace; mercy is mercy, not grace; faith is faith, not grace; truth is truth, not grace. Granted, all these and more relate to and flow out of grace, but they are not grace. What seems to be important is that believers come to understand what grace is, how it is appropriated and what it produces.

Another time, again upon the recommendation of a mutual friend, I once met two pastors in the southern states who invited me to come to their church of over 2,000 people to speak on grace. I had never before had a pastor invite me to minister solely on grace. I spoke five times from a Wednesday through a Sunday morning on some introductory concepts of grace. After the Sunday morning services I was invited to lunch with the husband-and-wife ministry team. Before I left, the wife came to me in the parking lot of the restaurant and thanked me with the following words: "You may not know it, but with these teachings on grace you have saved our church and our ministry." Profound words from a ministry team of long-term effectiveness! Let me be clear here: I did not and cannot save anyone's church or ministry. Grace on the other hand—well, that is what grace does best: it saves! In reality, the more grace flows, the greater the demand placed on our faith and, as we couple faith with grace, God's redemptive power increases.

There are literally thousands of pastors struggling in their churches, wounded to the core, wondering about their call, hardening their hearts to people just to stay in their calling and perplexed by the almost impossible complexities they face in their churches. Numerous wives pay an even greater price while standing with their husbands in ministry. Countless numbers of ministers who have been ministering faithfully over a period of time have not had the kind of growth and corporate unity they desire. It is as though they have come to an impasse. While "the ministry" ought to be an inexpressible joy, for many it becomes exquisitely difficult. The answer lies in finding *functional grace*. No, grace does not abolish the presence of demonic warfare nor does it eradicate the carnal attitudes every minister will encounter. Instead, grace enables constancy in ministry and the maintenance of intimacy with the Holy Spirit in the midst of the struggle.

It is important to note that grace is not just for one particular brand of evangelical Christianity. Grace is the necessary ingredient for *any* successful expression of the Christian faith. An authentic Christian community cannot be realized until effectual grace characterizes the minds and hearts of those in that community. As believers, we must all learn what it means to "receive the abundant provision of grace" (Romans 5:17). Whether you are a fundamentalist, a conservative evangelical, a Pentecostal, a neo-Pentecostal, a charismatic, or even a neo-charismatic, God's grace must be something we actively *receive*. Until grace affects our perception of reality, we will have significant difficulty in successfully getting our eyes off those in that other "brand" of Christianity and onto a lost world for whom Christ died. In the absence of grace, one group will find it necessary to correct and rebuke another of a different evangelical persuasion. One pastor will feel compelled to leave the substance of the Gospel in order to correct another pastor. One Christian will find it necessary to set their pastor straight or send a letter of rebuke to that television minister or Christian writer, frequently stamping it with the phrase, "I judge you in love," as though God endorses their spirit of condemnation. A severe gracelessness then characterizes what biblically is supposed to be the grace community.

The best way for a "grace awakening" to come to the believing church is through leadership that has experienced the transforming power of effectual grace. Grace ideally should flow from the leadership to those led. Perhaps this is naive, for the effectual working of grace would necessitate change of a radical nature. Grace is dangerous in that the institution will suffer: it cannot precede or take first place over grace. Some of what has been held dear will have to go the way of the dinosaur. This does not entail the abolition of truth, but a refining of our beliefs reflected in the expression of genuine love for all believers. The biblical injunction to "walk in love" applies to all of us in Christ, not just to those who agree with our particular brand of Christianity.

In World War I, a kind of stalemate existed between the Allied forces and the German troops. The trenches were dug; between them lay no man's land. With both sides sniping at one another if someone dared show his head, venturing out of the trench meant you were immediately dead. Historically, denominational attitudes are similar: my group gives me medals for polishing off that other infidel believer. The triumph of "my" brand of Christianity somehow is more important than the life of the person I just shot, and I get promoted as a warrior in the noble defense of Christianity. In the wars between Christian tribes, the matter of honoring one another as instructed in Romans 12:10 is overlooked. It seems we forget that only the blood of Christ makes any of us innocent. Grace-powered love alone will carry us joyfully beyond our own borders to discover the hidden treasure in others of different practice but similar conviction. If we continue to miss the grace of God, the feuds frequently fought with great intensity in the pew of the local assembly will continue and peace will be reduced to a religious euphemism. If grace does not characterize our motives and agendas, we come to the place where we are gracelessly killing other believers in the name of truth—not truth as it is, but truth as we define it.

Grace is a key attribute of God that, by the Spirit, must characterize the community of believers if our nations are to ever find the light of a relevant hope in the face of the complex human dilemma. Apart from manifest grace in the church, our efforts, no matter how sincere, can never succeed in the necessary measure. *We were neither designed nor meant to succeed apart from functional grace!*

In some measure, this sets the stage for considering why we should bother to come to grips with grace: what it is, how it functions, how to receive it, and its impact on us as believers in a world that has no answer except the one we are supposed to offer. We must heave against the carnal heart's hostility and endure the Spirit's discipline to find grace in abundance. Whatever one thinks of this author or of the peculiar expressions other believers use in their worship and service to God, the truth is this: *we all need to find more of the reality and fruit of grace in our own lives and attitudes. The fate of the world rests on such discovery.*

So why bother? Here are a few reasons why I have found the grace chase both profitable and necessary.

One: Grace stands as the core of Christ's covenant with men.

Ask believers today what grace is and they will tell you that it is "unmerited favor." Ask them to explain what that means substantially or, for example, how it works in lives to enable supernatural unity in the body of Christ and few have a clear, functional, appreciation of covenantal grace.

Grace is the substance God gives to his people as His response to abounding sin. Certainly God has extended something to us unearned that is granted as a "favor," but in specific terms, what is that favor? There must be more to our understanding of grace than the term "unmerited favor." Romans 6:14-16 tells us we are not under the law, but under grace—not as a license to sin, but as power to obey. Is it possible for anyone to claim to understand the New Testament while not having a thorough understanding of grace? How can we become "ministers of grace" if we do not understand what grace is and how it works?

Two: A covenant not understood is a covenant not kept.

As believers, we have been brought into the covenant of grace and are therefore expected to live within the parameters of that covenant. How can believers be expected to live within a set of boundaries if they do not understand what those boundaries are? How can we know that we are living within the new covenant if we don't understand what grace is and what terms it sets out for us to live by? Ignorance is no excuse for failing the high and hard call of grace.

Three: Christian experience cannot transcend the degree of functional grace operative in one's life and faith.

The New Testament makes it clear that we can be "full" of grace. In John 1:14, Christ is declared to have been "full" of grace. Acts 6:8 describes Stephen as being "full" of grace. On the other hand, believers can "miss the grace of God." In Hebrews 12:15, the inspired author places the responsibility not to miss grace directly upon the believer, which sets an implied responsibility upon those who minister. This raises the possibility that grace is not automatically dispensed from heaven, suggesting that our concept of "unmerited favor" may in fact be a misnomer. In II Corinthians 6:1 the apostle Paul writes, "…we urge you not to receive God's grace in vain." So, we can be full of grace, we can miss grace, and we can even receive the grace of God in vain.

We can limit the degree to which grace flows in our lives. Believers need to discover what it means to be full of grace and need to be given criteria by which they can discern in what measure grace is being missed, received in vain or responded to! Yes, we can persevere in spite of a lack of knowledge of grace, but the effectiveness of faith is frustrated proportionally: what we should be and attain is missed relative to the measure of grace effectively at work in our lives and congregations.

Four: Grace is the only mechanism in the universe that has the capacity to radically alter the human heart.

In 1984, an interview of Pope John Paul II appeared in *Time Magazine*. Journalist Lance Morrow talked to the Pope about his visit to the prison where his would-be assassin was consigned and was so moved by the Pope's response that he noted in his article, "There will be no escape from wars, hunger, misery, racism, the violation of human rights or silent missiles—if our hearts are not changed" (33). Truly, the heart must be changed if the authentic Christian is to appear before a world full of death and disaster. "Tender-hearted and easily entreated" desperately needs to become the mark and attitude of the Christian community. If our hearts have not been changed, what do we have to offer in the way of hope to the world?

Consider God's description of the new covenant he purposed to establish through Christ in Jeremiah 31:33: "This is the covenant I will make…. I will put my law in their minds and write it on their *hearts*." In Ezekiel 36:26, God declares of the covenant he would later make with man: "I will give you a new *heart*." Note that it is not a modification of the *old* heart, but God significantly and specifically says a *new* heart. Whose heart is transplanted into the human breast? His! II Corinthians 3:3 says we are an epistle of Christ, "written not with ink…on tablets of stone, but on tablets of flesh, that is, of the heart." This provision of grace, spoken of several times in other scriptures, fundamentally transforms the nature and ruling passions in the human heart since the pre-conversion heart is "desperately wicked and deceitful above all things" (Jeremiah 17:9). We cannot enter into the things of the New Covenant if the implantation of the new heart has not taken place.

With the implantation of the new heart, the core nature of man is changed and a paradigm shift occurs, affecting his whole life. Grace working moves the individual into a whole new and other dimension of life and reality. The passions, motivations, desires, and attitudes now become a demonstration of the heavenly nature of Christ. "If any man be in Christ he is a new creature," (II Corinthians 5:17) works to transform the individual in Christ so he becomes a different person, and a different likeness appears. This new heart is capable of receiving and responding to God-placed desires. When God says in Psalms 37:4, "He will give you the desires of your heart," he has no obligation to satisfy the carnal demands man would place upon him. The heart becomes an open receptacle where he implants his kingdom desires (the things he wants for me), which translate to a manifestation of God's redemptive love to a lost humanity. This puts an end to the concept of "now I get my pink Rolls Royce." If *God* writes a pink Rolls on my heart, fine, but it has no place when it is born out of my own unregenerate ambition. Glory, power, and control are attractive to the carnal man. We need to put down our fleshly cravings, come to Him with an open heart and give him the time and opportunity to put into our hearts the eternal equivalent of the carnal counterfeit. Hearts that come to God hungry for the desires he wants to implant are the open hearts he can use. Suddenly and supernaturally a shift takes place, and we begin the process of putting on the "new man." A number of spiritual realities can now be manifest.

Five: Grace imparts the capacity to walk in love.

The Father's heart is the only heart that naturally has the capacity to love. Scripture sets an impossible standard when it directs us to walk in love, unless we have the "new heart." Apart from the Father's heart, our lives will be marked by struggle: husbands will struggle to love their wives, wives will struggle to submit to their husbands, and Christians will struggle to walk in unity with other Christians. It is only as the Holy Spirit of Grace deposits the substance of the Father's heart in us that the community of believers can find the power to love one another. The great witness of the church is not in our proclamation but in the demonstration of love. Bypass loving one another and our proclamation lacks authenticity. It is only by a supernaturally powered love that the believing community can move into and maintain unity. Skip empowered love and unity remains a theological concept after which men strive in their own strength, only to fail. Skip "unity" and the world will have a significant problem in knowing the God that sent Christ into the world. It is only as the new heart becomes functional in our relationships that we become credible witnesses of Christ. We can invite the world to receive Christ when we have not yet manifested relationships that testify of a heavenly kingdom, but the relational devastation in the church testifies against us. Remember the question asked in chapter one: "Do you think the church has proven to be a most difficult place to survive long-term?" How do *you* answer that question? If the church is so hard to live in, then why should people in the world, with all their relational difficulties, come into the church? How soon before they are targeted for verbal and emotional destruction? Are you uncomfortable yet? Yes, we can skip this because it makes us uncomfortable and threatens our establishment, but to ignore this lack of functional grace in the local church rips the heart out of our message to the world! Authentic Christianity must become a genuine manifestation of loving relationships operating out of a supernatural power. If we fail in this we are left with an inadequate and self-defeating confession. There may well be the presence of truth but it will be a truth apart from grace. "Full of grace" precedes "full of truth," and truth must find its temper in grace. Otherwise truth kills! Grace, therefore, is the only provision in the universe that has the power to solve the relational chaos in the church. It is only as believers learn to practically live out of the heart of the Father that we can hang in there with one another, and that in a loving way! Want the bottom line here? We ain't there yet!

Six: Grace tames the tongue.

James 3:8 notes, "No man can tame the tongue. It is a restless evil, full of deadly poison." Yes it is true; no man can tame the tongue, but this does not mean the tongue cannot be tamed. For example, Proverbs 10:11 declares that,

"The mouth of the righteous is a fountain of life." How is hell to be silenced and the destructive power of the tongue brought under control? Through the implantation and release of the Father's heart, which ignites the passion of the Father's heart for others. Instead of operating out of the natural heart, new life motivations flow from a divine source with a manifestation of divine power. Life takes on the hue of heaven, and the radical man is manifest in distinct ways. The outflow of that reality typifies our vocabulary and characterizes the very motivations driving us as believers. We move beyond human passion into supernatural expressions of loving acceptance toward one another, and the community of Christ becomes God's living demonstration of hope to an otherwise hopeless world.

Grace clearly implies that as believers we have been recipients of the Father's heart but what so often is coming out of the mouth is anything but a manifestation of the Father's heart. Any time spent in the church reveals speech that betrays the heart of God and only proves that the human heart cannot love. It invariably comes to the place where it has no ability in and of itself to cover. It believes its own conclusion, and that conclusion flows out of the mouth in all its destructive force. More church ministries die under the destructive tongues of their own adherents than by the covert strategies of hell. Believers do demonic work as demons happily stand by in agreement! James puts it like this: "If anyone considers himself religious and yet does not keep a tight rein on his tongue, he deceives himself and his religion is worthless" (James 1:26). Go back to Matthew 12:7: "For by your words you will be acquitted, and by your words you will be condemned." Somehow we do not take God seriously when he tells us that we are going to give account for every idle word we've spoken (Matthew 12:36-37).

The reality is this: the unconverted human heart has no capacity in and of itself to cover. More accurately, it feeds on the very thing that should be covered. Luke 6:45 declares that, "Out of the heart the mouth speaks." Clearly we can know what is in the heart by the kinds of words that come out of the mouth. It's easy to deliberate over the kinds of words that we hear in the assembly of the local church, but how about the words that come out of your mouth? How do you speak to your spouse, your children, your parents, or your pastor? How do you speak of your church or of others who believe in Christ but exercise their faith differently than you do? Do we build one another up or tear one another down? Are we expert in what is wrong with this or that person or thing in the body of Christ? Do we minister a love that effectually covers and offers encouragement? It seems we've forgotten

Proverbs 17:17 that declares, "A friend loves at all times, and a brother is born for adversity." In truth the one who is a friend loves you in the worst times, a brother is proven to be a brother only when the going gets really tough, and failure proves you are human! You see, "love will cover a multitude of sins" (I Peter 4:8) because that is love's primary function!

Destructive language among believers is nothing short of hell's cursing. That same passage in James 3 says that the untamed tongue, "corrupts the whole person, sets the whole course of his life on fire, and is itself set on fire by hell." The flapping of untamed tongues defies our confession that we are Christian and corrupts the local church, sets its whole course on fire, and that fire is itself a fire set by hell. Again, James says that, "out of the same mouth come praise and cursing." We profess to be Christian and curse other believers. Cursing is not just taking the Lord's name in vain or using bad language. Cursing means we pronounce declarations against other individuals that demonic spirits can perform. Now, note the very next phrase, "My *brothers*, this should not be." When we speak, our sole purpose should be to speak into the needs of others to build them up according to their need. Whatever we say must benefit those who listen to us. Paul, in Ephesians 4:29 (KJV), directs us to minister grace to one another, saying, "Let no corrupt word proceed out of your mouth, but what is good for necessary edification, that it may impart grace to the hearers." Ask the congregation in any church if they are Bible believers, and the answer is a resounding, "Yes!" But does our believing include accountability to what the Holy Spirit is directing in Ephesians? Yet such denigration is rampant among those who should be brothers and sisters in Christ. Amazing how easily we violate the royal law when speaking of our churches, pastors, fellow believers, and even our bosses, co-workers, neighbors, and others in the world.

The reality of the tragedy that is occurring in the body of Christ should stun us into heartbroken silence and repentance. It's not the other guy. We have to examine *ourselves*. Some among us may stop, ponder what our words reflect of the heart, and fall on our knees in utter sorrow and genuine repentance. But we cannot simply determine that from now on we are going to do better. It's not by works—a self-determined effort to improve performance—lest any should boast. This matter was not meant for you to settle and correct on your own. Recognition of the problem is meant to drive you to God. When we begin to face our own failure of speech, the place to begin is, "Grace, oh God, give me grace!" A broken heart and a soul found locked in the grip of wrong speech may well shout its anguish to a loving God;

then mercy can find its true dominion and authority over the carnal impulse toward judgment. If we are not changed in our speech and thus in our churches, how do we dare plead for revival or expect mercy when we who have received mercy offer none to those we target with our non-grace words?

At this point I want to express a caution: Do not show up at the next communion service in your church if your words do not minister grace to those in need. Who are those around you who need your grace-full words? Perhaps the very ones who have let out your life's blood! Hmm! Sounds a bit like real discipleship, a bit like dying daily, like losing your life so as to find it. No one can be considered genuinely "new" if left to struggle in Christian things without the new heart. In ourselves, we are not big enough, nor can we love enough, but we trade in our smallness and weakness so that *his* strength may be *perfected* in us! What are the results? We are enabled supernaturally to come out on the high ground of grace-oriented speech. The biblical standard to which the world cannot attain is achieved. Our words demonstrate a kingdom not of this world. Man of another sort is made manifest in a graceless world, and God is glorified in us!

Seven: Grace is the foundational component for success in our lives.

Several years ago I was in London, England and had a very frustrating experience. It was November, and I had been invited to minister in a church. I was to take the underground (subway) to a certain tube station, and there a member of the pastor's staff would pick me up. I arrived a bit early and stood outside in a cold drizzle. I'd caught a cold a few days earlier and was already feeling miserable as the cold seeped into my bones. The longer I stood there the more miserable I felt. My toes were going numb, and I was losing the edge of my spiritual keenness. I stood there for an hour and fifteen minutes, and no one showed. Finally I gave up and made the return trip to where I was staying. Needless to say, I was not a happy camper. I worked on improving my attitude and phoned the pastor the next day inquiring as to what might have happened. He seemed mystified. He had sent a man to pick me up at the station. What could have gone wrong? I then asked him if he had described me to the man who had come to pick me up. Had he told him what I would be wearing and that I was carrying a Bible in a brown leather case? No, he had not. The question I then asked was, "How was this man to identify me if he had not been given criteria by which to pick me out of the crowd?"

Scripture records in Genesis 6:8 that Noah found grace. Could you find grace? If someone asked you to make a trip down to a busy airport and pick up a friend named Grace, what would you need if you were to succeed? She'd be there to be found, but could you pick her out? There is something that you must absolutely have: you must know something about what Grace looks like, or you will not be able to find her. She could walk right past you or be standing next to you, but without a description you would not recognize her. On the other hand, if you were given a picture you could pick her out of a crowd of a thousand people coming through the gate and approach her confidently, knowing fully that you have found the right "Grace."

    Whenever God wants to initiate his plan for our lives he always does so by sending grace our way. If grace is what God gives out at the throne, what is he putting into our hands? If we do not know what grace is, how it works, or in what forms it comes, how can we use it or know when we've missed it? If we want to succeed in our lives, families, jobs, finances, churches, and ministries, then we must recognize some of the distinguishing characteristics of grace. For example, let's say you have a problem with your car, and you take it to a mechanic. He looks at your car, tells you what the problem is, goes to the parts department, and hands you a weird-looking gizmo with the statement, "Just install this and your problems are solved." You look at the part and don't have the foggiest idea what it is for, where it goes, or how it works, and you remain perplexed. Even though you now have the thing that will fix it, your problem remains a problem. When it comes to your car, you can pay the mechanic to put the part in for you, but when it comes to plugging grace into your own life, you are the only mechanic on the scene! Ignorance will never fix what needs fixing. At this point, it really helps if you have a functional relationship with the Holy Spirit. He is the helper you need. So here's the question: do you want it fixed or not? If we can't fix our own dilemmas how can we offer to fix the world's? Let's go and find Gracie. She's out there waiting for you to find her. Her feet may be cold from a long wait, but she won't be in an ugly mood when we find her. After all, her name is Grace! Why bother? Well, the truth is, Grace is a singularly lovely lady and an indispensable guide in the whole scheme of biblical revelation.

Eight: The discovery of functional grace is the only means by which fear loses its destructive torment in our lives.

    Whether we know it or not, fear torments many who know Christ as their Savior. Almost universally, we know the declaration of I John 4:18: "Perfect love casts out fear.... He that is perfected in love has no fear," but many are tormented by fears of an innumerable variety. Fear of old age, heights, diseases, poverty, rejection, bugs, tiny spaces, man, authority, death, and countless other phobias afflict us today. We can deal with the demons that administer fear and have some success. We certainly need to confront and remove such demonic presences. However, the job is not yet done. Perfect love must be experienced if people are to be genuinely fear-free.

How do we come to experience the inward reality of a perfect love so vibrant that fear loses its place in us? When I receive the gift of the new heart, there dwells within me the reality of perfect love, and what is characteristic of the Father's nature becomes an inherent possibility. That means we can plug into the very nature and passions natural to the heart of God! It is not something that *I* do; it is something that *love* does. *I* do not cast out fear; *perfect love* casts out fear and puts an end to torment. There is no fear in the heart of God, only love, thus that perfect love becomes the inward warrior that takes fear by the scruff of the neck and "casts" it out. If fear is defeated in the heart, *fear is defeated!* The love of the Father becomes so experientially real that fear, in fact, loses its foothold in us, and we experience what it means to be fear free. It does not mean that some experiences won't occur where fear would try to come in, but as those occasions occur, the overwhelming magnitude of the Father's love for us eclipses any feeble attempt by the enemy to get us to believe we are outside the protective embrace of that love. There is nothing it can grasp to assert its presence or power. Reading from left to right it looks like this:

GRACE ➜ THE NEW HEART ➜ PERFECT LOVE = FREEDOM FROM FEAR!

A Personal Discovery

Several years ago, I was awakened in the pre-dawn hours by a severe pain that gripped the left side of my chest and ran down my left arm. It was painful to move or even breathe. About four in the afternoon, I decided I should go to a medical clinic because the pain had not subsided. The nurse at the desk asked me what was I there for and I told her I thought I was having a heart attack. At first she looked incredulous, I guess because I looked so cool. There was no fear in my heart. She looked at me for a minute and then decided that I was telling her the truth. She immediately slipped down a hall and a moment later a doctor came rushing out. He took me into one of his examining rooms, put me on a bed and began to listen to my heart. His face took on a look of alarm, "Don't move!" he ordered. He called to his nurse and said, "Get an ambulance, this man is having a heart attack!" Still, there was no fear.

I was rushed to the emergency room of the local hospital. I was lifted onto a bed, with doctors and nurses rushing around. My right arm was hanging over the side of the bed where a nurse was monitoring my pulse and blood pressure. I began to black out, and that nurse began to almost shout, "We're losing him, we're losing him!" The only thing I was mindful of as blackness settled in upon me was an incredible surge of joy. Wondering if this was what it is like to die, I thought to myself, "What a gas!"

The blackness started to recede a bit, and a nurse, patting my left arm, asked, "How are you doing Mr. Myers?" Everything in me wanted to laugh and say, "Would you believe super-good?" but I figured they might think I was hysterical. To my amazement, in the whole experience there was not a shred of fear. What was the other side of this experience?

My wife was at home in a state of panic and tears. Suddenly she heard the Holy Spirit tell her to look at Psalm 91:14-16. She turned there as she sat in the living room and read, "'Because he loves me,' says the Lord, 'I will rescue him; I will protect him for he acknowledges my name. He will call upon me, and I will answer him.'" Instantly, Sharon knew that there was nothing to worry about. Fear left her, and she knew the power of the Father's love that cast out the fear that had gripped her only seconds before. The doctors did five tests and were apparently convinced that when I was admitted I had been having a heart attack. The next morning, however, there was no pain, no evidence of heart damage and no evidence of having ever had a heart attack. They simply came and said, "We don't know what happened, but you can go home."

Perfect love cast out fear. Torment did not have its way! Instead of fear, what I had experienced was a near-irrepressible joy, and the fear that had gripped my wife was instantly "cast" out. Bless His holy name! Beloved, you do not have to remain a prisoner of fear and torment. You do not even have to fear death, for death is swallowed up in victory! God has said, "I will give you a new heart." Go to him, ask for it, and keep on asking for it. Seek it and keep on seeking it. Knock and keep on knocking, and it will be given to you. It is the Father's will to give you that "new heart" that knows no fear!

Nine: Grace is the only means by which true, biblical holiness can be attained.

There is an inextricable relationship between the working of grace and the kind of holiness that is acceptable to God. I cannot make myself holy in any case. God alone, by the administrations of the Holy Spirit, makes me holy. In the history of the church, both past and present, so much has been passed off for holiness that if a hundred people were asked to define the essential nature of holiness, there would be a hundred definitions. What does a holy person look or act like? Any accurate definition or understanding of holiness cannot be arrived at outside the implications of grace. *The grace gate must be used if we hope to become holy in terms that God considers holy.*

The pursuit of genuine holiness is mandatory. God is holy, and we are enjoined to be holy even as he is holy (I Peter 1:16). After all, we have been given nothing less than the *Holy* Spirit. The first letter to the Corinthians speaks specifically of the need for being holy. Ephesians 1:4 declares, "For he chose us in him before the creation of the world to be holy and blameless in his sight." In verse six of the same chapter, grace pops into the picture: "To the praise of his glorious grace, which he has freely given us in the One he loves." Holiness can only occur within the context of grace. The parameters of holiness no longer exist within a set of laws, but within the new covenant. Holiness now has to do with things like the death and resurrection of Christ, faith in his shed blood, and what the Holy Spirit now ministers within the heart of believers. A radical departure has occurred. Holiness is not someone living up to some visible standard or set of rules devised by religion or held by some community. Arbitrary regulations regarding hairstyle or proper Sunday attire cease to be the standard by which holiness is measured. Conversely, holiness cannot be measured by how well someone lives up to some arbitrary set of standards.

I was once made personally aware of one occasion where a man was an elder in an evangelical church for years, but on certain nights of the month he participated in a local coven, taking his daughter with him, where she was ritualistically abused. Oh, yes—he met the carnal standards of holiness so well that he served as an elder, but his true loyalties lay with the prince of darkness. Many times what passes for holiness is nothing more than conformity to standards set by the community, and if anyone does not keep the rigid set of rules, they are subjected to group censure. If they still refuse to conform, a vicious ostracism follows. In fact no one even has the right to raise questions as to the logic of this rule or that—just conform or face the consequences!

How many of the people sitting in our churches—evangelical, Pentecostal or charismatic, really have a genuine appreciation of what it means to be holy? As believers, we tend to judge one another's apparent state of holiness by outward appearance. "They are such a lovely couple. After twenty-five years of marriage they still walk into church every Sunday holding hands, and he always puts his arm around her when they sit together. What a positive model for our church!" But what goes on in the home behind closed doors could be anything but a loving marriage: he secretly is hooked on pornography, she holds him at ransom with her body, they sleep in separate rooms, living separate lives under the same roof, both claiming allegiance to Christ. It is for the sake of their reputation, status in the church, and acceptance as leaders in the church that they maintain the outward facade of a happy marriage. This could very well be as far as holiness really goes in much of the contemporary Christian community. Francis Schaeffer has some substantial things to say in this regard in his book, *True Spirituality.* I rather suspect that true holiness would blow most of our community standards right out of the water. We may very well not know true holiness in a person if we saw it, simply because holiness has so often been reduced to nothing more than the keeping of standards indigenous to "our" church group.

Was Christ holy? Every church member would say, "Absolutely!" Yet he violated all the standards set by the religious community of his day. He went where you weren't supposed to go, did what you weren't supposed to do. He "worked" on the Sabbath, associated with questionable people, and even treated the known and accepted standards with contempt. Christ was holy; he was full of grace; yet death was the only thing Christ was considered worthy of, according to the prevailing standards of holiness. Perhaps Christ was putting his finger on the nature of true holiness when he said, "Anyone who is angry with his brother will be subject to judgment," and then, "anyone who looks at a woman lustfully has already committed adultery with her in his heart." We may be able to maintain the keeping of some outward set of standards, but what about that inward reality that no one sees? What goes on in the heart is the only true measure of holiness. As such, only God can really see holiness with certainty. He is the only one who has the ability to look into the heart and know what lies there.

If the believing church is to truly discover and experience authentic holiness, then it can only be found by coming via the grace gate. This much is as true today as it was in Christ's day: those who discover and live in true holiness may very well find themselves outcast from the religious city of evangelical circles because grace and rigid religious standards cannot peacefully cohabit. Grace exterminates religion! Why should we bother with the pursuit of grace? It is the only gateway by which we as believers can satisfy a holy God.

Ten: The gate leading to the power of God is functional grace.

There is a significant need for a radical increase of spiritual power in the body of Christ. Christ declared in Acts 1:8 that power would characterize the Christian life, "when the Holy Spirit comes on you." Christ himself was first full of grace before he demonstrated the power of God. If we as believers want to experience the power of the Spirit, we must come by the grace gate. Do not reach first for power; reach first for grace! Acts 6:8 notes that Stephen was "a man full of God's grace and power." The same verse tells us he "did great wonders and miraculous signs." Scripture is incredibly precise: grace necessarily precedes power. Bill Gothard defines grace as desire and power, but if you don't know what it is to receive grace, how do you find the power that is released within the context of grace?

Grace is the gateway into the power and provisions of God's kingdom. Paul declares that he became a servant of the gospel of God's grace evidenced by the working of God's power. II Peter 1:2 sets grace first in order and then notes in verse 3 that it is through His divine power that we have received "everything pertaining to life and godliness." Grace first, then power, and in that order. In Hebrews 4:16 we are directed to come boldly to the throne of grace. Once there God gives us grace, which he expects us to use so that our needs are met by the subsequent release of power.

Ephesians 2:8 sets out the same scenario: "For by grace you have been saved." The power of God operated in us only as we first responded to the grace of God. "To as many as received...to them gave he power." (John 1:12). The power God uses to save us does not precede his grace. The operation and receipt of grace preceded the flow of saving power. (This will become clearer as we deal with the nature of grace in a later chapter.) If the believer of today wishes to manifest the power of the kingdom of God then he must first deal with what it means to be "full" of grace. The early church was a supernatural church, and it is recorded that "great grace was upon them all" (Acts 4:33). The more grace believers learn to "receive," the more the supernatural power of God will be manifest. Any absence of power can be traced back directly to some absence of grace. Why should we bother to come to grips with the nature of functional grace? Simply put, because the human dilemma demands of us the demonstration of a power not of this world.

Eleven: Whenever the power of the Holy Spirit manifests, God's glory is manifest.

Glory cannot be separated from power. This reason is an extension of the Grace/Power principle. Note how the Lord's Prayer ends: "For thine is the kingdom, the power, and the glory" (Matthew 6:13). In Psalm 63:2, David says, "I have seen you in the sanctuary and beheld your power and glory." Paul points out that Christ is able to do immeasurably more than all we ask or imagine, according to His *power* and that as this *power* is working in us His *glory* is manifest in the church (Ephesians 3:20-21). We have "the light of the knowledge of the glory of God…in earthen vessels…to show that this all-surpassing power is from God" (II Corinthians 4:6-7). Christ's final appearing will be with "great power and glory" (Matthew 24:30).

This relationship between power and glory can be illustrated in an Old Testament passage. In Exodus 16:7, God says the following: "In the morning you will see the glory of the Lord." The very next morning the manna appeared. The manna was the manifestation of the glory of the Lord. Implicit in the manifestation of that glory was first the necessity of power. In these closing days of grace, God is intent upon restoring his glory to the church. That glory will make God visible in many and unusual ways as He releases his power in the lives of those who will receive the abundant provision of grace. The whole equation then looks like this:

GRACE: **the Gateway into God's**   **POWER**
POWER: **the Gateway into God's**   **GLORY**

or

GRACE   ➜   **POWER**   ➜   **GLORY.**

To glorify God is to make Him visible in the natural realm. It is as believers recover functional grace that God will restore his glory to the church. If believers want the glory of God to characterize their lives, then they must come via the grace gate.

A statement heard frequently in the body of Christ is that we must be careful to give him all the glory. Now I realize that Isaiah 48:11 the Lord declares, "I will not yield my glory to another." However, Christ declares something altogether different under grace. Under Law, God will not share his glory, but in the New Covenant, Christ himself declares: "I have given them the glory that you gave me" (John 17:22). If we want our churches to be characterized by the glory of God, then there must be, as one writer put it, a "grace awakening" (Swindoll). Whatever our denominational identities, grace is the prerequisite for us all if we would have God manifest himself through us to the world!

The pattern of Grace to Power to Glory is implicit throughout scripture. Christ was full of grace and was raised from the dead by the working of mighty power. Glory was manifest; God was visible and known to be God by that power. Consider the raising of Lazarus: the Word of God's *grace* led to *power* with the result that *glory* was made visible to those watching. Exodus 19:16-19 depicts Moses assembling the people of Israel before the mountain inhabited by the Lord. It is really difficult to argue the non-existence of God in the face of dense smoke, lightening, booming thunder, an unseen trumpet sounding louder and louder and the ground under your feet trembling violently. In the presence of such glory, it is probably not even a good idea to argue for God's non-existence. Why bother with the pursuit of understanding grace in practical terms? Because God made visible to an unbelieving world in such ways will restore God's glory to the believing church. Surely such a reality in the church would make the effort to recover grace worthwhile!

Twelve: Grace is the only means by which believers can experience the effectual working of faith.

We must find the grace gate that leads to a life of genuine faith. When the Holy Spirit begins to impart grace to our hearts, that impartation requires a faith response if grace is to be received. Conversely, if faith is to be properly taught, then it must be in the context of grace. Simplified it looks like this: Grace puts a demand on us for Faith

READ IRWIN MYERS

Faith Must Be a Response to Grace

This principle is outlined in Ephesians 2:8: "For by grace are you saved through faith." This has been touched on earlier, but let's go a bit further. If we are to discover a legitimate faith that can move the mountain obstacles in our lives, churches and nations, then an understanding of how grace and faith are interrelated is essential. You can't have one without the other. Consider: could you have been saved by faith if grace had not become operative first? Or is it possible for an individual to be saved by grace alone, apart from the operation of faith?

Look at it this way: if grace is to be in anyway effective, it requires faith as a functional reality. Historically, it seems that we have played one concept against the other. Some that say we are saved by faith, that it's all of man; others that we are saved by grace alone, that it's all of God. Scripture indicates that it is not one or the other but both—*all of God requiring all of man*. To be saved, grace and faith must both have their joint work. For example, healing cannot be said to be all by faith. Do you know a lot about faith and still find that what you have had faith for is still not manifesting? Well, when we apply Ephesians 2:8 to healing, it reads, "For by grace am I saved *from disease* by faith." The two work together to produce the desired results. If the believer is to discover the effective power of faith then the understanding and practice of faith must be rooted in the grace of God. To teach one or the other exclusively is to teach only half of what needs to be understood. I may determine to teach that prosperity is the direct result of faith, but the desired fruit will not become widespread. Much of the church will remain paupers in the middle of incredible wealth. Neither can it be taught that all you have to get is the "all grace" of II Corinthians 9:8 to be prosperous. It seems we want to make prosperity simple when it is anything but simple. There is an inextricable bond between grace and faith. It will only be as we learn how these two truths work in conjunction with one another that we can expect to work the "greater works" of John 14:12. The reality is this: when we, by the Spirit, begin to move in the grace of God by faith, we will discover that we can be saved from any circumstance. Have you had a lot of teaching on faith? Praise the Lord. We surely need to thank God for the incredibly rich teachings we have had on faith, but what depth of teaching have you had on grace? The reality is that when the two spiritual commodities of grace and faith come together, there is an explosion of spiritual power. *Faith operates on the fuel of grace.* Think of your salvation. Grace came, you responded by faith, and an explosion of power was released. You were no longer a child of the evil one. Instantly you became a child of God. One moment you were headed toward hell, and then an explosion of power, flowing out of the grace-faith counterparts and your eternal destiny was radically changed! This power is known as "dunamis." This change in life is somewhat like a baseball flying in at ninety-five miles an hour, hitting the bat, and flying off in the opposite direction even faster! Why should believers make the effort to become acquainted with grace? Because by doing so the effectiveness of our faith can be ignited to bring us into dimensions of supernatural power! This is a power that transforms our own lives, our spiritual experiences, our ministries, churches and our impact on a desperate world. Apart from functional grace that is kissed by heart faith, mankind is left with a form of godliness and nothing more. Christianity devoid of relevant, functional grace is no Christianity at all! Lip service to grace is nothing but religious death.

Thirteen: Grace is the way into your miracle.

There are problems in every life. No one can live life apart from the crushing impact of need. We all need something, and most need it urgently. As eyes fall on these pages, believer and unbeliever alike are doubtless faced with some impossible set of circumstances. Many, however, live most of their lives chained to that set of impossible circumstances. The only solution lies in discovering functional grace imparted into our lives by the Spirit of God. "Let us then approach the throne of grace with confidence so that we may receive mercy and find grace *to help us* in our time of need," (Hebrews 4:16). There are a number of things stated here that should cause us to become thirsty for grace in its functional reality. Let's look at the four progressive things that happen here:

1. We approach boldly the throne of grace.
2. When we do, God always extends mercy.
3. Then he gives us one thing: grace.
4. Found in that grace is power that meets our need.

Now, we need to understand that at the throne, God imparts only one thing in the context of this verse: *grace*. Every person who reads these lines can look into their own lives and find some place where they need God's help. We do not go the throne of grace and discover that God solves all our problems. We are charged with the responsibility of administering that grace if we are to have the need met. Many in contemporary Christianity have not thought through what the Holy Spirit is saying in this verse. Grace is not some sort of magic wand we can wave, and presto! Grace requires an operative stewardship on our part. God gives us something he has called grace. We are then held accountable for discovering how that grace works to meet our needs. There is a fundamental sense in which grace dispensed at the throne requires its own revelation. When it is understood what grace is requiring of the recipient, immediately one is called to faith. Once given, grace does not function automatically: it demands the operation of faith for it to meet a specific need. There seems to be a deep propensity among believers to think that if they get grace from God then all their problems will be solved. This is nothing short of a "magic" mentality and has nothing to do with biblical Christianity.

Some get past the "magic" mentality only to go directly to a "miracle" mentality: "I go to the throne, God gives me grace, and praise the Lord, I've got my miracle." There *is* miracle grace, but in the context of this and other verses, grace given at the throne does not imply, "I've got my miracle breakthrough!" Why? God is not inclined to extend *miracles* as a way of solving life's problems just to make life easy and problem free. The reality is that if people receive a miracle today they will need another miracle tomorrow, and an unhealthy dependence on God for miracles becomes a way of life. Again: God is not into *magic*; he is interested in *maturity*. There is a sense in which miracles demand nothing of me in the way of character growth, and a lifestyle is established of going from crisis to crisis, instead of from glory to glory. Consequently, we never come to the spiritual maturity God intends because miracles become the focus of seeking God rather than relationship. It is easier to let God, who is well able, meet my needs via miracles than to understand that he wants me to grow up, learn how to receive his abundant provision of grace, live by faith, and thus *reign in life!* Grace places an inherent demand upon the recipient for spiritual growth and a gaining of spiritual insight into the supernatural lifestyle. Saying these things is not to imply that miracles have ceased or are not necessary. They easily and inherently follow the application of grace insight and are manifestly necessary if we are to effectively propagate the purposes of God in the earth.

Paul, in II Corinthians 12, went to the throne of grace three times asking God to solve his problem. What was God's response to the Apostle of Grace?

In everyday terminology, God said, "Grow up, Paul. Stop asking me to solve your problem and practice what you preach. If you will discover practically what my grace is and how to apply it, you will find help that meets the need." If you as a believer will learn what sufficient grace means in practical terms, you will discover what "my strength made perfect in your weakness," means. What a concept! Stop and think about this for a bit: *God's omnipotence perfectly expressed in one's weakness = the awesome result of grace!*

This is all the result of God's extending to finite humanity the privilege of participating in the incredible diversity of his grace! There is no stinginess in the heart of God, even if it appears that He is making grace hard to find and experience. More accurately, this is characteristic of the immensity of God's heart wanting to lift the feeble human spirit into an increasing parity with himself, treating us as sons and daughters. Not that we are equal, but grace allows us to participate in something of his divine nature. An intimate acquaintance develops. When God gives us a measure of grace designed to meet some need in our lives, he is requiring, among other things, the activation of faith in some regard. We find life marked by a profusion of need, and as these needs abound we go boldly to the throne of grace. On every occasion God gives us grace of a particular design such that, once unlocked, has the power to meet the need, which we in turn must learn to apply. Over the course of many trips to the throne a pattern is established. We come to understand in practical terms what scripture means when it directs us in II Peter 4:18 to "grow in grace."

By way of observation, note that grace and glory appear together here: the recurring working of grace makes it evident that something supernatural is taking place in a person's life, and God is glorified. Grace so experienced by numbers of individuals in specific congregations can only mean the ever-increasing glory of God in congregations. Grace is the gate to glory and to a spiritual, supernatural reality in our personal relationship with the Father. It is as believers discover corporately what it means to appropriate grace functionally, that God can restore His glory to His church. God's glory cannot be restored to a church that does not know how to manifest maturity through the progressive appropriations of grace. The directive to "grow in grace" is not optional: it is the imperative of Christian living! Growth must take place within the context of grace. Grace demands of us spiritual maturity as the heirs of God! In His love, God can settle for nothing less. It is thus that we discover the grace gate to maturity. Can anyone be considered mature if they have not experienced the progressive appropriations inherent in the working of grace? Yes, these kinds of questions may be prickly, and I'm not poking just to make you uncomfortable. Think instead of the sweet benefit of discovering this path of grace!

Reason Fourteen: Only a faith response to grace can release the supernatural working of the gifts.

I considered avoiding what is dealt with here so as not to lose some whose lives might be enriched by the appropriation of grace, however, there is a significant application that would be missed if I did. The intent is not to be controversial, and I would like to think that those who would disagree with me would nonetheless press on in the pursuit of grace.

I came into the pastorate directly from a small consulting company in downtown Toronto. My wife and I had come to know Christ some eight years earlier and had been taught to believe the cessationist view regarding the gifts of the Spirit as recorded in I Corinthians 12 (that they have ceased to function in the church), and I personally held the position that if people spoke in tongues they were demon possessed. I had believed the general teaching I'd received. We had been in the pastoral ministry only a couple of years and had no idea how much in over our heads we were. We had simply known the call of Christ to ministry and had obeyed. I knew I needed a lot of help from God.

While kneeling at my living room chair quietly doing my best to pray, I suddenly found my mouth making weird sounds. For a few unguarded moments this strange occurrence flowed, and I was stunned by what was happening. Within moments I realized that I was speaking in tongues. I sat back on the floor of my living room and the thought that ran wildly through my mind was "Oh, my God, I'm possessed!" It may seem funny to some, but for me at that moment it was almost terrifying.

Sitting on the floor I had another strange experience. I heard words flowing into my head, and I knew the voice to be that of the Lord saying, "Come now let us reason together," followed by a series of questions something like this. "To whom were you praying? Whose servant are you? Who redeemed you? Were you not saved by faith in the blood of Christ? So do you really think the Devil can push all this aside and take possession of one I have redeemed?"

Within moments, an understanding of what was happening lay fixed in my heart. What I had just experienced was not the Devil, it was a legitimate experience with clear biblical authority. That tongues had not passed away as

I had believed was almost more than I could take in! Then came another bombshell: if tongues were a legitimate work of the Holy Spirit, then the other gifts of the Spirit must be available and legitimate expressions of Christian faith! I have to tell you I spent a bit of time sitting on the floor of my living room that morning. When I got up I had no theology on the gifts. I just knew they were still operative and available.

Since that time I have experienced the Holy Spirit minister healing, miracles, wisdom, knowledge, faith, prophesy, tongues, interpretation of tongues and on occasion discerning of spirits. Romans 12:6 makes an absolute statement: "We have different gifts, according to the grace given us." Immediately afterward, Paul encourages the operation of the gift of prophesy. The gift of prophecy is not a skill that is learned, enabling a person to preach really well. There is an outright gift that comes into the life of the believer sovereignly by the Holy Spirit and finds its validity in the context of the grace of God. In I Peter 4:10, the biblical standard is set. Every believer is to use whatever gift he has *received* (as opposed to *"developed"*) to administer grace in its various forms. These gifts are directly rooted in the grace of God. To be ministering in the gifts is to be faithful! Peter makes it clear that when believers use the gifts, which are operated in us by the Spirit, they are ministering the grace of God to others. If we hold to a cessationist view of the gifts, then we find ourselves holding to a view that limits the provisions that lie in the grace of God and further, have taken a position that forbids any ministry of grace that operates through them to the church and the world. That is Peter's message to the believer. Again, a gift is *not* something learned, it is *not* a talent: it is something deposited into the life by the Holy Spirit and activated by the faith of the believer.

I have been privileged to minister in a wide variety of churches, and of those who would declare that all the gifts of the Spirit are available for use today, the number of believers effectively functioning in any of the gifts beyond tongues and sometimes interpretation is disheartening. It seems we have gotten as far as tongues and no further. Oh, yes, prophecy is for today—but very few Spirit-filled believers have grown into mature expressions of the prophetic.

The reality is this: every gift listed in I Corinthians 12 is declared to be the work of the Holy Spirit: "The same God works all of them in all men" (v. 6), and "All these are the work of one and the same Spirit" (v. 11). When the Holy Spirit goes to work, inexorably he will manifest or work, wisdom, knowledge, faith, healing, miracles, prophesy, discerning, tongues, and/or interpretation of tongues. If we legitimately want to pray for a moving of the Holy Spirit, then we must know we are praying that he will go to work in our lives and churches. Well, when the Holy Spirit starts to work, what does he work? All of the above, and that just as He sees fit. If we pray for a moving of the Spirit and then deny that he works such things as wisdom, knowledge, miracles, healing, and prophecy, we are just wasting our time in a religious activity. We cannot say, "Holy Spirit, we really want you to move in our midst, but we don't believe and therefore cannot allow the manifestation of wisdom, knowledge, faith, or healing." What an incredible contradiction! If we want the Holy Spirit to work in our midst then we cannot forbid the gifts he manifests and that scripture defines as the very means by which He works.

Christ declared that "these things shall you do and greater" (John 14:12). Many of the works Christ did are manifestations of the gifts of the Spirit. Now really, do we think that we can do the "greater works" if we do not have the Spirit doing his work in our lives, when Christ himself depended on the Holy Spirit for the manifestation of supernatural power? Is it at all conceivable that it is possible to manifest a supernatural kingdom apart from the "work" of the Holy Spirit? This appears to me to be nothing less that presumptive arrogance! The facts are these:

When believers flow in the works of the Holy Spirit they are ministering God's grace.
If we do not flow in the works of the Spirit, then in that measure we fail to minister God's grace.
If we deny these works of the Spirit, then we are forbidding the ministry of God's grace.

Why should we bother to get a grip on grace? We must understand that when believers come into the functional reality of grace, one of the results will be the administering of the gifts of the Spirit to our generation. As believers learn to flow in the grace of God, our churches will become places where the gifts of the Spirit will bring forth the manifest power of God. If we want to move past tongues into greater expressions of the Spirit's gifts, then we need to get a grip on grace. The gifts manifest as a result of grace. (For detailed biblical perspective on the gifts of the Spirit see my second book on grace, *The Grace Deficit.*)

Reason Fifteen: Grace is the only way to fulfill the demand the world is placing upon the body of Christ.

In light of scriptures, the body of Christ is supposed to be a supernatural organism in the earth bearing witness to the invisible kingdom of God. Paul declares in I Corinthians 2 that he went up to Corinth in demonstration of the Spirit's power. His intent was that those saved in that city should have a faith that rested on the power of God as opposed to the wisdom of man's words. Clearly, Christ's intent as evidenced in Acts 1:8 was that believers filled with the Holy Spirit should live lives characterized by supernatural power. In Luke 24:49, Christ directs the apostles to wait in Jerusalem until they are endued with power. Perhaps we should note here that when power fell, it didn't just fall on the apostles, it fell on *all* the believers who were present. This power is not just for the few. It is for every believer who will reach out for it. Now let me be clear: this word power does not refer to a power rooted in the ability or skill of a man. This word refers to a release of power that comes into the life by a direct act of the Holy Spirit.

In Acts 14:3, Paul and Barnabas were in a place called Iconium where the Lord "confirmed the message of grace by enabling them to do miraculous signs and wonders." In a world that has, for the most part, rejected Christ and the moral principles of scripture, we will never get their attention if we do not come into greater manifestations of the power of God. By this I mean the manifest working of miracles, signs, and wonders. I Corinthians 4:20 says, "The kingdom of God is not a matter of talk but of power." The "kingdom of God" has got to be more than a theology. What's the point here? Unless we actually discover how grace is meant to function, the body of Christ will never become the instrument of God's power in the earth as He intended. There is a direct link between grace and power in scripture. Jesus Christ came into the earth full of grace, and his life and ministry give full demonstration of the power of God. Stephen was a man full of grace, and an inherent characteristic of his testimony was the manifest power of God. "Great grace was upon them all," is the description given of the early church. We only have to look at the record to find a church that was characterized by a power that changed the world. Scripture makes it clear that the believer is to put on the likeness of Christ. The various injunctions that direct this conformity to Christ are numerous, and they cannot simply be limited to character qualities. If we are to really *be* like Christ then we must be like him in *all* respects, one of those being the manifest power of God. If we really care about our world and about the world our children will inherit from us then responsible believers must recognize that there is an undeniable demand being placed upon us for the demonstration of God's power. The key to this power presently lies hidden in the mystery of grace.

Want an illustration? Imagine a well-maintained 747 airliner. The necessary support systems are in place, and the cabin is full of people nicely seated, having paid the fee for the privilege of sitting there. The only reasonable expectation in the minds of those sitting on that jet is that it has the power to fly. If that plane is powerless, it is nothing but a useless piece of junk. Imagine paying your money to sit in an aircraft, knowing it is going nowhere because it has no power to do what it is designed to do! Those who pay to sit in such a craft can only be seen as ridiculous. The truth is absolute: power, and I mean supernatural, miracle power, is essential if the body of Christ is to be credible in the earth. The key to that power lies hidden in a discovery of grace. Christ was the incarnate, living, eternal Word, yet even for Christ there was an accreditation that God considered necessary. Acts 2:22 tells us Jesus was "a Man attested by God to you by miracles, wonders, and signs which God did through Him in your midst." I would suggest that if God considered it necessary to authenticate Christ with such demonstrations of power, then we need nothing less. Have we settled for less? The release of such power comes to authenticate the message of grace. The pursuit of grace is therefore worth the trouble of stretching our minds and spiritual paradigms.

A Closing Consideration

Human history is full of the imposition of one form of tyranny or another upon mankind. Anthropology studies man's cultures and the references the people within that culture make toward God. Should the age of grace be extended into the future to any considerable degree, anthropologists may well look with wonder at the period of history in which biblical values held consensus among the historic western democracies. Looking at the incredible shift away from the biblical values that lie at the foundation of historic western democracies, those anthropologists may well look at the loss of those values in amazement. They may wonder how values that allowed amazing degrees of individual freedom while propagating a power that allowed for individualized self-government were lost. The age in which the values of scripture and the influence of grace on those historic democracies will only appear as a blip on the screen of human history. In the absence of grace, every culture must degenerate into ever-increasing anarchy and tyranny. The call and challenge to answer tomorrow's questions lies with the present generation of believers. Both the early church and the leaders of the Reformation discovered the necessary grace and power to mark the history of succeeding generations. Recall Wesley's comment regarding the discovery of grace as quoted in the first chapter. Should the age of grace continue, what will future anthropologists discover of the values this present generation of believers lived by or died for? It is time for a new generation of believers to discover the grace and power of God so as to mark the future of ensuing generations. Success or failure is the challenge that lies before the present generation of believers!

Chapter Three
Discovering Real Grace

Grace that works beyond our initial salvation experience can only be learned when the Holy Spirit undertakes to teach us in the theater of our own disasters and failures. Simply reading a book or attending a seminar on the subject will do little to change a person's life without the life circumstances God chooses to use as the context for such teaching. While this may prove very unpleasant—indeed, even excruciatingly painful—if people really want to come to a functional appreciation of God's grace in their lives, that understanding will almost always be discovered in the darkest experiences of life. Somehow, in the pit of darkness, the beauty and reality of grace majestically begins to grip and transform the human spirit. There is no sterile highway to a genuine understanding and experience of present and glorious grace. I say this to offer hope to those whose paths are leading through the valley of the shadow of death to people who have "lost their faith," ministers who have been driven from their calling, those in deep straits of stress in life, business, or family, those in oppressive depression, and generally those who wonder, "Where is God?" Such people are the prime candidates for the stirrings of grace. Certainly grace works its wonderful presence in the lives of the joyful believers experiencing the blessings that life in Christ has to offer, but significantly, it is also for those whose only reality is darkness and despair. Grace is sufficient for every individual, from the lowest ebb of life to those on the cutting edge of what Christ is doing in the earth. However, it often appears that if someone knows the manifold riches of grace in the high places of life, that person will first have discovered the sufficiency of grace while staring down some black hole of human dismay.

The intensity of human pain varies according to what one may be experiencing. We as onlookers tend to regard what another person is struggling with as somehow less gut wrenching when compared to our own adversities. Every person's pain seems to be the ultimate in suffering. But whatever darkness is encountered, genuine Christianity (versus the religious brand) offers what no other religion or lack thereof can offer—*grace*. Cling to your humanism if you will, and you cling to adversity alone.

A Graceless Existence

Sir Charles Chaplin expressed his humanist philosophy through a little man in comic adversities. His movies depict this little man falling down stairs, caught in a revolving door, nearly being trampled by runaway horses, or being thrown around in a car careening out of control. Several generations have laughed at this little comic without really understanding what he was saying about the human condition. In his silent movies he depicted his view of the human condition: man caught in a universe, a passionless machine that has no awareness of his existence or pain. The machine grinds on, and the man in the picture is a victim caught in the accidents and uncertainties of human existence.

Several years ago I happened to catch a TV interview with him. At the time of this interview, Mr. Chapman was in his eighties and in a wheelchair. The interviewer described him as an icon. In contemporary understanding an icon is a person known in much of the civilized world. (Frank Sinatra, for example, would be considered as an icon.) The dictionary, however, gives a substantially different slant on what the interviewer was asking. The dictionary defines an icon as a person who breaks images, or makes attacks upon cherished beliefs. Mr. Chapman depicted humanity as a creature that is simply caught in an unfeeling machine. He attacks the belief that there is a personal God who is in control, making concepts such as hope, illusionary.

At one point, the interviewer asked, "Sir Charles, what is it like to be an icon to the whole world?" Mr. Chapman was quiet for a moment. His answer was direct and pointed only to ultimate despair when he said, "I am lonely." The interviewer looked perplexed. His answer seemed to make no sense. How could he be lonely? He had his family around him, lived in the lap of luxury, and knew the best people in English society. Lonely? The truth is that no matter what form it takes, atheism leaves man without a personal God and no recourse from that extreme reality, abandoning us as victims of a terrible existence. *The absence of a functional grace is the ultimate adversity among the living.* What did Sir Charles understand of his atheistic assumption? Simply put, there is no personality behind the universe to make it a personal place. We are a wretched bit of conscious being hanging meaninglessly in a meaningless universe, going nowhere but oblivion. There is no other voice beyond the ramblings of men, nothing to break an endless terrible silence. Life is merely existence apart from a personal God. There is no knowledge that the possibility of grace even exists. Those of us who were trained to believe in the humanistic concept of reality can be most difficult to persuade, but once persuaded can be most joyful. Perhaps this is what C. S. Lewis was communicating when he wrote *Surprised by Joy,* which is the record of his own discovery that the universe had a Person and Personality behind it upon which he could base an understanding of himself as man. He was known, created, and loved by an awesomely powerful Creator who had given him a present and eternal destiny.

What C. S. Lewis had in fact discovered was that the Christian, no matter the tragedy experienced, is never alone. The reality of God's presence, love, and oversight in the midst of great darkness is brought to bear on our consciousness by the impartation of grace. Grace is a tangible substance God gives that invades our darkness. What a wonderful discovery! Mr. Lewis discovered what Sir Charles had missed: he discovered that God and grace could actually alter the inward reality of blackness and despair that plagues man apart from God. Grace proves sufficient even when outward circumstances remain unchanged. Grace floods perceptively into the broken heart and transforms the inward consciousness so that man becomes aware of God's presence, love, hope, meaning, and strength.

A Radical Invasion

I once had occasion to meet and pray with a minister in England who had been pastoring in a church for twenty-five years. I knew nothing about his circumstance the night I met him. After most of the people had gone home, I felt led to pray with him. I spoke prophetically to him naming specific things with which he had been struggling. I was surprised when he suddenly fell to the floor in a ball, uttering loud groans. After some minutes he got up to go home, but invited me to visit him the next morning before I left for London.

On the visit next morning, he recounted to me the events that bore on the previous evening. He had made his decision to resign from the ministry. He was totally worn down to the place where he wasn't sure he even wanted to have anything to do with either church or believers. His testimony was that as I spoke, the Spirit answered a series of questions he'd been asking The Lord for two years. Then he found himself on the floor making loud groans. When he got up from the floor, all the discouragement, fatigue, and the desire to quit had completely left him. He told me that he felt like he was brand new, as though he was just starting out in ministry. I visited him a year later, and the joy and desire to serve had not left him. He told me then that he'd had gone to a church board meeting following that evening encounter with the Lord, and one of his board members looked at him as he walked into the room and said, "It's good to have you back, pastor!" The man had no idea as to what had happened. He just saw a renewed countenance. Hey, pastor, let me say there's refreshing at the Spirit's fountain of grace sufficient for your deepest need and the cry heard only before the throne!

That is what grace can do. It can work in such a way as to literally transform the inward reality of the human heart. This in turn renews us to keep on keeping on. After more than thirty years in ministry I have become acutely aware that there are deep rivers of pain in the body of Christ. These rivers touch us at every level, from the most prominent leaders to the most inconspicuous individual in the back row of the church. In II Corinthians 12:9, there is a wonderful declaration made by Christ himself, "My grace is sufficient for you," and human extremity is where the Holy Spirit most often shows up to manifest this magnificent truth. The English pastor found that a touch of grace applied by the Holy Spirit transforms the inner reality and hence the outward capability. Grace is indigenous only to genuine Christianity. It has the capacity to take an apparent loser, written off by others, and transform the inward heart so that he or she is empowered to rise above the circumstance and pain. Grace at work in the heart cannot be defeated.

Grace confounds the mind. Whenever grace comes in, the carnal mind grovels in its thirst for supremacy; however, grace speeds you past the carnal ramblings of the mind to the transformation of your spirit under direction of the Holy Spirit (Galatians 6:18). The mind, being limited to the soul realm, can only stand outside what is going on in the spirit realm and scream its carnal insistence that it be allowed to understand. If it doesn't scream, it will bleat because it is not being consulted.

We cannot let experience dictate what truth is: experience must conform to scripture and to the Spirit of truth, for what God teaches will never contradict biblical truth. Conversely, truth must not be manipulated so as to prohibit genuine, Holy Spirit-directed experience. Grace is designed to intertwine with daily life experiences. What insight I have gained into grace has come through the teaching of the Holy Spirit in the theater of real discouragement and in the context of my own struggle for a genuine reality in God: this is not stuff extracted from commentaries. Although I was not aware of them at the time the events were taking place, the lessons God led me through can be broken down into four stages.

Stage One: A Confrontation with the Word

We had been in the ministry some seven years and had seen numbers of people give their lives to the Lord over that span of time. However, there were individuals in my congregation who, in most precise terms, hated me. They were born again but had become extremely hostile toward me. (Anyone who has functioned in a pastoral position for any length of time will know about such hostility coming their way.) I'd listened to their criticisms and had even asked they write them down for me. I'd gone to their homes to pick up the lists and sat quietly as they went through their complaints. I'd spent time in my office meditating on what they were saying and asking the Lord to show me how to respond and where I needed to change. The criticisms were sharp and cut deep into my heart. I felt discouraged and isolated from many in the congregation. It was a Monday morning, and I had driven to the bank to make the deposit of the Sunday offerings. As I sat there beside the bank staring at the brick wall, I said to God, "Lord, if what these folks are saying is true then I have to question my own intellectual integrity. Am I sane or insane?" This was no joke. I was struggling with my own sanity. I knew that I had not been called to the ministry because I was so capable: if anything, my inabilities and weaknesses cried out daily: "What do you think you are doing? Who do you think you are? You've made a dreadful mistake!"

Stage Two: The Necessary Leap of Faith and a Period of Silence

Then the Spirit spoke in a very quiet way, "You have to believe what I have said about you in my Word." There was nothing else, and I heard it only once. Having no better idea, I simply acknowledged, "Okay, Lord, what your Word says about me I will believe," and slipped into the bank still feeling dejected.

A few days later I was reading through II Corinthians 2 and came to verse fourteen: "But thanks be to God, who always leads us in triumphal procession in Christ." Instantly, I remembered what the Spirit had dropped into my heart a few days earlier. My first thought was, "Surely something is amiss. Be *thankful*? God had *always* led *me* in triumphal procession? God help the world! "Lord," I said, "if this is triumphal procession, please don't show me defeat." I sat there pondering how what I was going through could be construed as triumphal in any way. Everything in my mind screamed, "What utter nonsense! Well, that can't possibly apply to you."

Then something started to creep into my thoughts. Right there on the pages of scripture, God was saying one thing and my mind was screaming the exact opposite. Next shock: only one of us could be right! If this was true, then somehow what to me appeared disastrous was, in fact, God leading me in triumphal procession! Men were shouting all kinds of graceless words at me, and I had basically concluded that they were right. Then God showed up and said something radically different about both my circumstance and myself. I knew that somehow I had accepted an incorrect perception of my reality, that the myriad criticisms against me were wrong (at *least* in the way they'd been delivered), and the people who believed those things about me were wrong. Honestly, I have to admit that I surrendered grudgingly. I didn't understand how I was wrong, or how the criticisms or the critics were wrong. All I knew was that God had been leading me triumphantly and that I was to be thankful.

"Okay, Lord," I said, beginning to praise him. *This was the leap of faith!* Everything in my mind screamed, "Now you really *are* out of your mind!" I didn't realize it, but that was in fact the truth: I was out of my mind and going into the spirit realm where God is God. I took my mind to task and spoke inwardly to it: "Mind, I order you to think these biblical thoughts: 'now thanks be unto God who always leads me in triumphal procession.'" Like meat through a meat grinder, I forced my mind to repeat the truth of God's Word and surrender its own, wrong conclusion: I was not a disaster and I was being led in total victory. My mind suddenly went quiet, and it was as if something in my heart said, "There now, that's better." For several weeks, although I could not understand *how* I was being led in triumphal procession, I just accepted it as being the truth in my life and ministry. God knew better than I did. Jesus was Lord, not my mind. I went into a place of inner peace, even though the attitudes of those people in my church remained just as hostile as ever. This was *the period of silence*. There was no explanation, only a decision to believe God. It was a few weeks later when I heard the Holy Spirit ask, "Would you like to know how you are being led in triumphal procession?" I was an ardent listener!

Stage Three: Understanding "Triumphal Procession"

In the next few moments it was as though the Spirit took me on a tour of every adversity, every criticism, every crushing word, every act of rejection, every hardened face, every inner sense of having been wounded and every thing that had gone wrong. Then came startling words: "Son, do you not know that you are mighty in your faith? Your acts of faith have been noted, and you are known in heaven as an overcomer!" I was stunned. All I'd wanted to do was throw in the towel. How, by any criteria, could these things be true? Then came the explanation (which, by the way, is true for every believer): "You have been in many situations and faced numerous assaults against your life and ministry." This much I already knew. "Although you have been engaged in many disheartening, crushing situations, you refused to give up. In every single instance of assault and warfare with the powers of darkness you never surrendered your faith. Nothing has plucked you out of my hand. You know who your Savior is, and that I love you. In the face of every adversity and betrayal, you have chosen to keep believing." As these thoughts flooded my mind and soul, I was reminded of I John 5:4, "This is the victory that has overcome the world, even our faith." Faith had done its work and on every occasion when I had come under hell's assault I had won. Had I even once *really* surrendered my faith, I would no longer have been in the ministry or even following God.

Now, why am I sharing this? Every reader who knows Christ has come under real and heavy assault. The truth our Father wants you to get hold of is this: although you have been through countless adversities and trials, you have fought the good fight of faith, and your faith has stood the test. Oh, yes, you may have been dazed, bloodied, and knocked to the carpet a dozen times, but when the next challenge to your faith came, you showed up to fight. Satan wants you to think that because you've been wounded, you've lost. That's a lie. Pummeled by circumstance, betrayal, discouragement, criticism, and self-doubt, you still believe in Christ, believe you are destined to stand before the throne, and know that there is a mansion in heaven with your name on it! The issue is that you still believe—and the truth is, Satan has been driven from the theater of your faith every time he has shown up! "This is our victory…even our faith" (I John 5:4). You are not a wimp, a loser, or a failure. Whether you are aware of it or not, you are known as an overcomer, marching victorious before heaven and hell. Had you really lost even once in the struggle of faith, you would not be reading these lines. Are you getting this? *Every single time Satan has lost, and you have won!*

It was as this unfolded in my heart and mind that I began to rejoice. God had so moved in my life that by the measure of faith he'd given me I was indeed being led—always and on every occasion—in triumphal procession. So are you, saint! Then came the first direct revelation the Spirit gave me regarding grace: He showed me how my weaknesses qualified me to be a minister of grace.

Stage Four—A Revelation of Grace, Perfected Strength

Think about this phrase, "My strength is made perfect in your weakness." How does this work? In II Corinthians 12:9 God is speaking about his strength and power. Ask yourself, how strong, how powerful is he? Oh, yes, he's omnipotent, but what does this mean? Can anyone ever appreciate the limitless power of God? Then add this to the equation: God states that this limitless strength is *perfected*, made *perfect*. Now mull over what it means that his limitless strength can be made perfect. But it goes on! Imagine God's limitless strength finding perfect opportunity *in your life*. Where does it find its opportunity? *In your weakness!* The process by which His limitless strength is to be perfected in life, God calls grace. Grace is how God's strength is made perfect. This is what is inferred when he says, "My grace is sufficient for you." There I was. I had just understood that faith had won the day and was now understanding God's perspective on my weaknesses, my struggles, my disappointments.

Not too long after my first revelation of being led in triumphal procession, one of the members of my congregation confronted me, looked into my eyes across a table, and said, "You are the worst example of a preacher I have ever met. I wouldn't even hire you to dig ditches." What a downer! I carried this feeling away from the conversation, feeling unequal to the task to which God had called me, but the Spirit reminded me of the words of Paul in II Corinthians 2:16: "And who is equal to such a task?"

"Well, Paul," I thought, "you got that right!" Then a Holy Spirit thing happened. I looked down at my open Bible and saw II Corinthians 3:5: "Not that we are competent to claim anything for ourselves, but our competence comes from God. He has made us competent as ministers of a new covenant." There it was! I was *not* competent in myself. I *wasn't* equal to the task of being a minister of grace. But right there on the page I was being told that God had, *past tense*, made me a competent minister of the new covenant, a competent minister of—you guessed it—grace!

Once again I was confronted with the Word of God over the word of men and my own mind. The phrase, "You have to believe what God says about you in his Word," flashed through my mind. I knew God had to be right. The Word had to be given its place of authority and supremacy in my thought life. I didn't understand; I just acknowledged it to be so. Again there was a period of silence. I just believed that no matter what, God had made me a competent minister of His grace covenant.

A few weeks later the Spirit said quietly in my heart, "Would you like to know how and why you have been made a competent minister of grace?" Again, I couldn't wait for the explanation. "I did not call you to the ministry because you were so strong. I choose the weak and beggarly things to confound the wise. You are exactly what I need to demonstrate my grace to others." I still did not understand. While the Spirit didn't speak in linear words, the essence of what unfolded in my mind was this:

"You have made numerous mistakes; you have not understood what was happening on many occasions; your attitudes, motives, insights have all demonstrated how weak you are, but I have shown you and enabled you to keep on keeping on despite your weaknesses and failures. You have been called to minister grace. I have shown you that my grace is made sufficient for you by finding in your weaknesses opportunity to demonstrate my strength perfectly. The weaknesses that men use to write you off are the very instruments I use to demonstrate my strength. When you are weak then I am strong, and you become a competent minister of my grace. How do you suppose you have been able to keep on in the face of all these trials, criticisms and inadequacies? I have been giving you strength to minister despite your weaknesses. People can easily see your weaknesses, but in your life-style you have shown that there is a way to persevere even in weakness. Their conclusion, if they have eyes to see what I am doing, would not be to reject you but to take courage. The people in your congregation can look at you and see a weak struggling human being who just keeps on trusting, believing, and ministering."

This was demonstrated for me one Sunday morning when a young man came up to me after the service. He had only recently given his life to Christ. As he approached me he had the most discouraged look on his face. He walked up to me and in very sad tones said. "Pastor, I just can't make it as a Christian." I was really concerned for him and asked him why. He told me he had gone to a Bible study the evening before. During the course of the evening he had shared with the group that he had a real struggle with lust. The leader of the group had been shocked at such transparency and rebuked him. The rebuke indicated that he could never be a Christian if he struggled with lust. He was devastated! As he stood before me, his whole countenance seemed to droop. I looked at him rather incredulously and said, "Do you think you are the only man who contends with lust?" His eyes jerked upward and he looked into my face. "You mean…you mean…you?" My answer, "Well, what do you think? If someone believes in Christ, does God somehow turn them into eunuchs and take away the natural sex drive?" A look of astonishment crossed his face, then relief, then joy followed by these words, "Well, if you can make it, Pastor, so can I!" He turned to go, his whole demeanor changed, strengthened by shared weakness. This took place in 1975 and he's still pressing on in a triumphal faith. Grace sufficient!

God ministers strength through our willingness to be transparently, vulnerably weak. Why in our weakness? Because it is there that human effort can't hope to cope, and we finally admit our inadequacy. If, in that moment of brokenness, we humbly submit to God instead of crawling off to nurse our pain (or worse yet, accept our pain as an unchangeable facet of our personality), it is then that God's grace can be demonstrated in its sufficiency. In being transparently weak we find God's strength coming into our own hearts. We can then become channels through which His strength flows into the hearts and lives of others who are struggling with their own sense of failure and humanity. By sharing our weaknesses as we persevere, others can look at our lives and see how we persist in the faith and they can take heart. Grace is given and flows only through the humble. The God-generated ability to endure is an overt demonstration of God's functional grace in our lives. This demonstration of keeping on despite our brokenness glorifies an invisible God, making him visible. Just consider what scripture says about weakness. It is as though Paul rubs it in when he declares in II Corinthians 12:9, "I will therefore boast all the more gladly about my weaknesses, *so that Christ's power might rest on me*" [emphasis added.] I wonder how many churches would hire a minister who came to an interview and all he did was boast about his weaknesses, not just *speak* of his weaknesses but *boast* about them gladly! How many believers understand God's grace route to his power? The route is found in exposed weaknesses rather than hiding them or denying them.

Hebrews 11 lists the names of those who became God's chief instruments of power to their generation. Note that in every case, God chose not the strong and competent, but the weak. Verse 34 sets out the place we all must begin, "whose weakness was turned to strength." In Judges 6:15, Gideon can only see his abject weakness in the face of an angelic visitation. Israel has been stripped of her power and is subject to the totalitarian power of the Midianites. Gideon recounted how he came from the weakest clan of the weakest tribe, and of all his family he was the weakest member. How easily the weak are disdained by those who in their ignorant arrogance operate outside this amazing principle of grace! The sad truth is that many church groups operate outside this principle of wisdom and, even if they were to be confronted with this truth about weakness, would reject it. How many of us would go out to hire someone to lead our church that ranked himself as the weakest individual on the ladder of possibilities? Yet I Corinthians 1:28 states clearly the principle upon which God operates—he chooses the weak and beggarly things of the world to confound the wise.

Are you weak? Wonderful! Grace is God's provision for the weak! You are a prime candidate for the grace expressions of the Holy Spirit. It is really difficult to be proud of our weaknesses and failures because they are downright humiliating, and that's the point! God gives grace to the *humble*. Paul didn't boast about his intellect, missionary journeys, education, or great revelations; he boasted about his weaknesses. He understood a paradigm of ministry that revolved around weakness versus strength. *Weakness is a prime principle that must be understood by those who would desire the power of God to rest upon their ministry.*

People become competent ministers of the new covenant of grace, not so much by what they preach or by education, but by discovering the place weakness holds in their own lives before God. There is a transparency about their lives that makes them easy targets for criticism. People may wonder, "What in the world is he/she doing in the ministry? What keeps them going?" It can't be seen because it's something the Spirit does in the heart. Somehow, he or she finds strength to persevere in the faith—they just never quit. The ministry of grace is much more one of *demonstration* than *proclamation*. In the very face of overt weakness and corporate criticism, somehow the individual keeps on keeping on, and people continue receiving a supernatural touch. A grace proclamation is authenticated by the demonstration of strength that comes from God expressing his strength in weakness, and a lifestyle not of this world is manifest. What then is being witnessed is a weak individual manifesting the perfect strength of God!

One of the greatest challenges the minister of grace faces is not allowing their personal weaknesses and failures to drive them from their calling. Many of the current paradigms of ministry do not allow weakness. Those in ministry must play to their strengths. Ministers are evaluated on their strengths and the organization they are called to minister in demands there be no evidence of brokenness. Interesting that grace was made available to humanity through brokenness. Even our theologies legislate that we cannot be discouraged, stressed out, ready to quit, wounded or isolated. We dare not share our struggles and failures with other ministers or with our congregations. We have believed a false theology that causes us to live in denial. "I'm doing great! I know nothing but victory! My faith is up to the challenge, glory!" But in reality we are hiding our own fatigue, struggling alone with the pressure the ministry has puts on the marriage. "No one knows I can't keep my mind off Mrs. So-and-So. They don't need to know that the family is falling apart." Those thoughts of finding a motel room and getting stone drunk or even of committing suicide are battles fought fearfully alone. In the business of doing God's business, we dare not let anyone know our quiet tears. Questions like, "What would happen if the leadership of my denomination or congregation really knew how bad I'm feeling?" or, "What would they do to me if they really knew what happened to me?" The answer in many instances would be clear: "You're history, baby!" The revelation of real personal struggles means the end of the association. Rather than be real, transparent, and find that God's strength can be found in weakness, we live a lie before our ministry group and congregation, trying to keep up the standard at any cost. Isolated and desperate, the minister thinks, "But I'm the leader. I'm not allowed to be anything but strong."

Such theologies of ministry are a lie. They are a denial of what grace is all about, and result in the final collapse of numerous ministries, marriages, and families. We seem to want to get as many people into ministry as possible. We ignore the numbers of ministers and believers who have been decimated by such superficial standards. Their failures are regarded as an embarrassment so they are allowed to slip quietly out the back door. Some are kicked out with righteous indignation, others let go with a corporate correctness that would make the world envious, while still others just seem to disappear, and no one knows why. There are no doubt thousands of individuals who once functioned in ministry and churches, and in due process were devastated. They were then flushed out the other end of the ministry tube onto the rubble heap of former ministers. Those who were apparent friends are now embarrassed to associate with them. Brokenness and isolation seem to be the sole and final reality.

I remember the news byte that showed Rev. Jim Bakker being lugged off to prison in chains, a weeping, broken human being. Failure had brought its total devastation. As I watched that picture, I could not help but think that the world had not seen the last of this man. To the world and many in the church, he was now nothing more than an object of disdain. The world is not expected to know about grace, but the church is! I could not help but wonder how many in the church would act as though God's grace were sufficient even for this man. The truth is that grace is always sufficient, if we in our brokenness will receive it.

I want to say to the thousands of individuals who have found themselves estranged from the body of Christ, *"It is not over for you!"* Grace is a provision that can flow into the deep crevices of any brokenness to bring a resurgence of strength and life. His strength can find a perfect work in the depth of your despair and isolation. It is okay to be weak, to admit to failures, bitterness, lust, anger, or whatever. It is *not* okay to stay there. A new day dawns when we drag our weaknesses to the light and receive his grace. Shame has been dealt with at the cross. Men and movements may despise you, but God has made an awesome provision available—his grace. This is the paradox: *There is power in weakness!*

While there may be no former friends or associates who will come along side you, there is another who will: the Spirit of Grace. He can work in your heart a day of recovery and new strength. There's enough strength to do in you what needs to be done. His Grace is sufficient and available to the weak, those who through brokenness have eaten the moldy bread of humiliation. Weakness and brokenness are the doors that lead directly to the marvelous discovery of an all-consuming love and an Omnipotent God who can impart the kind of strength that restores, lifts up, and that cannot fail.

Receive and Reign is the Reality in Romans 5:17

Grace does not flow to the proud or the strong. It is God's love provision for individuals who have eaten the bread of desolation, failures, and hopelessness. Rev. Bakker has been brought into a place of permanent humility. He, in spite of utter brokenness, found strength to keep on keeping on. Was it easy? Hardly! Our decimations are brutal in their reality. His life has been marked by "time done!" He has been humiliated, never able to forget the lessons the Spirit has taught him and thus set up by God to be a minister of grace. He can say emphatically out of his own desolation, "God's grace is sufficient!" How does he know that? He has lived to discover it for himself. He knows what it means to discover God releasing strength into the abyss of brokenness and despair. He cannot help but minister compassion versus judgmental condemnation to the broken. He knows brokenness of heart because he's been there! Now he can minister grace while his religious accusers know nothing about what he has discovered. They minister death in a graceless vacuum. I know these things of a man I've never met simply because I understand some small part of God's magnificent grace.

Any ministry model that denies grace to broken people is no ministry model at all. It has no foundation in the New Covenant. Those who hold to the ministry model that denies grace would give no room for restoration to "the likes of a Jim Bakker." There is no Covenant gospel there, but God is a God who extends recovery to whosoever will because he understands the perfect, vicarious sacrifice of Christ. Some today know that when Christ said, "It is finished," he meant everything is paid for. (And in case you think that means it's okay to go off and wallow in the pigpen of human sin and depravity, read Romans 6.) Now grace could flow to the weak, the broken, and those who have failed in this world. If we can find grace, recovery is inevitable. A new day dawns with new hope, new relationships, new courage, new vision, new possibility and new liberty from bondage springing up among the fallen. Grace is the means by which the phoenix rises from its ashes. It is no longer, "Look what you did!" but, "Look at what Christ has done!" If we have genuinely seen the cross, our ministry model will always hold out redemption and reconciliation as viable options.

God extends to every reader grace that is sufficient that if received, results in discovery of sovereign strength. Friend, life ain't over! In Christ, your weakness becomes your sole qualification for legitimate ministry of grace to other broken people. You now know what they need because you have found it yourself and can freely give it away. Remember that it was through Christ's wounds that healing and restoration became available to broken, sinful humanity. Thus it is that the healing restoration power of God can flow to others through your wounds. No seminar or book can teach us of grace in its functional reality. We must all go and read through the lines of our own failures and weaknesses, and there discover the mystery of grace that allows each to taste the power of God's redemptive love!

Chapter Four
Glimpses of Glorious Grace

Have you ever gone to a concert, found a seat, and waited for the symphony to begin? The musicians come onto the stage. They are all highly skilled, proficient individuals. Each one takes out his or her instrument and begins to tune that instrument. The strings practice various difficult sections; the brass section starts to warm up; the reed section abounds with squealing sounds that come from dry reeds; the timpani player beats the skins, bringing them into proper tension. You sit surrounded by a cacophony of sound. There is no melody, no harmony, nothing of unity or beauty; just a painful racket. Certainly, no one would pay to listen to such discordant sounds.

Then the conductor walks out on the stage and takes the podium. Upon his appearance, the dissonance instantly ceases and every member and instrument on the stage becomes subject to the man with the "stick." He taps that little bit of wood on the podium and then waves his baton. Instantly a whole different sound leaps up out of those instruments. What a few moments earlier produced an ear-grinding racket now bathes the soul and spirit with incredible beauty. It is as if the baton in the hand of the conductor is a wand, transforming the whole environment in the theater. The individual musicians no longer do their own thing. You will never see a musician stomp out of a performance because the music is not being played his or her way.

Every conductor brings his baton with him. It is his instrument of authority to which all the different members of the orchestra subject themselves. So it is with grace. Our skill must be subject to his baton. I cannot sit on the stage and play my own music. Only when the Holy Spirit is permitted to come onto the podium of our churches and interdenominational institutions will we who profess Christ become the divinely empowered answer to the culture of graceless humanism.

The body of Christ, the local church, human culture, and even the homes of believers are often much like an orchestra without a conductor. In spiritual terms the Holy Spirit is the conductor bringing the beauty of unity into disunity. What does he use to bring the various parts of the body of Christ into its intended purpose? The baton of marvelous grace! Follow the Conductor, and the symphony of God's kingdom will manifest, lovely, beautiful, and thrilling to the soul and spirit. Until the Holy Spirit is allowed the authority of grace on the stage of our lives, churches will continue to look more like killing fields than a demonstrated counter culture of love, mutual forgiveness, unity, vision, and redemption.

The only resolution for conflict in the church is to submit to the Holy Spirit who has been given the authority to provide direction in the church. He ministers the divine impulse of grace to human hearts. As divine impulses govern the heart self-absorption loses its ability to dominate the agenda. Our local fellowships begin to play the tunes of heaven and the beauty of a heavenly kingdom is made manifest. It is only to such a heavenly kingdom that the man without God is to be invited. To go on ignoring the fight and invite the world to come and dine is to play the indifferent, blind, hypocrite. The world is to be drawn to a feast, not a fight! No wonder the Spirit is so slow to convict men of sin and a judgment to come.

This may indeed sound harsh and judgmental. But I have been in a significant number of churches from different parts of the world and have found the war of the saints fully joined. The bullets are flying with the dead and dying scattered about. Grace, oh God, grant us grace that would so slam into our consciousness that our religious zeal for stoning the Stephens among us would drive us to personal brokenness; not to leave us broken, but so the glorious riches of His grace would manifest and set before the eyes of a depraved culture a jubilant alternative to hate and death. If grace does not abound among those who profess it, then grace is denied to the world. Where do we begin? With individuals recognizing their lack of grace in their lives and running to the throne of grace to receive that grace in abundance! Believer, if you have read this far, go now to Him who first and foremost died to release that grace into the earth. One thing He has promised: "My grace is sufficient for you!"

Ephesians 1:6 refers to grace as being glorious. W. E. Vine says the word glory here refers to "the exhibition of His attributes and ways." When grace is functional, God is glorified because an exhibition of his attributes and his ways has occurred. Therefore, when believers manifest grace, the character of God and the power of God are demonstrated, making the reality of God's existence visible in the natural realm. Man can perceive something that is not of natural man. The operations of grace provide proof of God's eternal existence and nature: invisible, real, but not of this world and not common to humanity, made comprehensible to those not spiritually alive (Romans 1:19-20).

When it comes to developing a working definition of grace we are faced with significant difficulties. The first is that we are trying to define an attribute of God. Now, God being God, who could hope to fathom such infinite measure? God utterly transcends our ability to comprehend even one attribute of such greatness, yet we are not excused from the call to make the endeavor. Justifying ignorance because of the immensity of the task is still destructive. The truth is that we can only "know in part" because we "see through a glass darkly" (I Corinthians 13:12), but at least we know in part and have that bit of knowledge with which to guide ourselves. It is precisely because of the immensity of God that we as mere mortals can never really exhaustively define even one attribute of God. Any so-called definition is therefore incomplete, open to adjustment, correction, and enlargement. This is why we are instructed to "grow in grace" (II Peter 3:18).

A second problem in drawing up a definition of grace (or any attribute of God) is that, as humans, we want to boil something of infinite nature down to something that will fit in a finite skin; state it in as few words as possible. I was preaching in one church that had rather large rafters and placed on the pulpit side of a rafter was this KISS slogan, telling every preacher to "Keep it simple, stupid!" We are exhorted in the spirit of modern Christianity to keep it simple. The truth is that we can get *it* so simple in our own wisdom that we lock ourselves into a beloved ignorance. Further, if *it* is true but *it* isn't simple, then we excuse ourselves from trying to understand *it*. Can the finite mind of man ever effectively take the infinite depth of any attribute of God and boil it down to a finite simplicity? It seems that we should always be seeking for greater and deeper insight if we want to be growing individuals.

A third difficulty in our particular pursuit is that grace, when it is functional, makes God visible in a profuse number of ways. I Peter 4:10 says that grace is "manifold," which, according to Webster's Encyclopedic Dictionary, means to exhibit many points, features, or characteristics of something. *Manifold* makes evident a whole having many different parts. In this case, grace as a single attribute of God exhibits many different dimensions or characteristics of God. In beginning to come to an understanding of grace there is a diversity we must grasp, but the western mind often gives up pursuit before it's even begun.

A DANGEROUS GRACE

Some years ago, I happened to walk into a home, and I found a group of highly trained professional men having a Bible study who all happily acknowledged themselves to be Christians. I was delighted at the prospect of talking with this group of intellectual believers. I have enjoyed and profited significantly from the writings of such men as C. S. Lewis and Francis Schaeffer, so I asked if any of them had taken time to read some of Schaeffer's material, thinking they would really appreciate some of his insights into culture and what he frequently refers to as "modern modern man." There was a pause. To my amazement these learned men agreed that they preferred just to study the Bible because Mr. Schaeffer was too hard to read. I stood staring at those intelligent men. Now, in grade ten, I failed five of seven subjects (passing only typing and gym), but I had read much of Schaeffer's works, torturous as it had been for me. It took me four months to work my way through only one of his books, yet here were these obviously intelligent men saying they found his writings too difficult to understand.

Our minds do not want to be driven beyond the established, long-held, comfort zone. It offers us all kinds of excuses for refusing the challenge: "That guy talks above my head," or "That's for intellectuals," or "Well, I'm just a simple man." Get over it! We have somehow let our minds convince us that they cannot really understand what's being said, so we are off the hook, but in reality, our mind loves the La-Z-Boy of its own indolence. It pleads, "Please don't require this of me." Note that in Jeremiah 31:31 God says, "I will write...on their minds," or what I Corinthians 2:16 says of the grace covenant: "We have the mind of Christ." Seems to me that with such a gift, we ought to be able to do a bit of serious thinking!

Reading through the New Testament, one soon discovers that real maturity requires much of the mind. It has to be made new and brought into a disciplined pursuit of great truths, among other things. How paralyzing it seems to have to think about the way we think, but the mind faces an inherent multiplicity in the pursuit of functional grace. A high-quality diamond can have more than one hundred facets. A facet is a tiny, smooth, flat surface on the gem that gives the stone the ability to reflect light and color, called "fire." The more facets a stone has the more light it can reflect, and the more fire it has the more valuable it becomes. A stone with one facet would be of value only for its potential. People pay dearly for a single gem with many facets that reflect fire. Are you seeing my point? Grace has manifold facets that reflect the Light of the World and the Fire of the Holy Spirit. The fire of God's multifaceted grace would attract many in the world if such were manifest in believers' lives.

A fourth difficulty lies in the fact that there is a general indifference toward discovering what grace is and how it works. Announce that there is a weekend conference or seminar focusing entirely on grace, and the hall is, for the most part, empty. Somehow grace has been perceived as being non-essential, but if we continue to treat grace as though we don't need to know what it is and how it works, then any prayer that pleads, "Thy kingdom come, thy will be done..." is just so much wasted breath. If we assume that God will move to make his kingdom evident or to express his will among us apart from grace, we have not even begun to understand either the blood covenant or the Father's heart. The following paragraphs outline a number of these facets of grace. The intent is to give some insight into grace beyond the standard definition of unmerited favor and to illustrate something of the "fire" involved. Some you may agree with, others you may question or reject outright. They are not given as though they are all inclusive nor is the intent to suggest that they are given in a spirit of final authority; they are intended as catalysts to your own discovery and understanding of this awesome provision. To stop at saying you agree or disagree is not enough. Appropriation by the individual believer is what matters.

1. Grace is an attribute of God.

Throughout scripture, God is spoken of as being gracious, as ministering grace and enabling man to find grace. He makes grace available as an abundant provision. The Christian should look and act like Christ, manifesting something of His graciousness and glory if only in a finite way. If an individual has truly come into union with God, the attribute of grace becomes evident in that life. The church should *corporately* offer the world facets of His glory, because the true church is marked by such manifold grace. Like a stone's fire, the church manifesting God's glory reflects the characteristic of spiritual fire to the world. If we are not making His grace manifest, we need to consider what we are reflecting to the world. If the world is not seeing what it needs to see in the church, how can we ever hope to offer a credible alternative?

Grace is what the New Testament is all about. Every epistle Paul wrote begins and ends with grace. We are no longer under law; we are under grace (Romans 6:14). In practical terms, this means grace is the prevailing covenant. There is no other covenant under which we are to live. Grace cannot be viewed casually when God has made it mandatory, safely relegated to a past provision that worked in our lives to bring us to Christ. It must be appropriated as a daily necessity. God always deals with man on covenant terms. If man does not live within the parameters of those covenantal terms, then relationship with God cannot exist and man should not expect life to be characterized by God's blessing or provision. It is the same with the New Covenant: to live in daily relationship with God as Our Father, there must be a willingness on our part to live life within the parameters of grace. We cannot live as we please outside the boundaries of grace and think we have a viable relationship with the Holy God. We cannot assume that because we really don't understand grace we are excused. As stated earlier, a covenant not understood is a covenant not kept.

2. Grace is the means by which God activates and maintains relationship with men.

It is by responding to His grace that we are saved and kept saved. If man does not come to God via the Grace Gate according to Ephesians 2:8, he cannot come at all. Hebrews 4:16 tells us grace is the means by which men respond to God and so find help in their time of need. Again, in II Corinthians 9:8, "God is able to make all grace abound so that in all things, at all times, having all you need, you will abound in every good work." Believers who want to experience the new life scripture speaks of must discover what it means to draw on this abundant provision. You are standing in it according to Romans 5:2 which says, "through [Christ] we have gained access by faith into this grace in which we now stand." In I Peter 5:12, Peter declares of grace, "stand in it." He does not say *stand in it if you feel like it.* His words are imperative, yet we as believers treat grace as something optional. There is no other covenantal provision. We don't know much about it or how it works, but somehow conclude that this is fine. Do you know what you are standing knee deep in? It is Christ's blood-bought, gift provision to you by which your needs are met! Do you know how to stoop down and scoop up, as it were, some of what you are standing in? If we wish to discover and experience covenantal provision, we must take the grace route.

3. Grace is the vehicle heaven uses to deliver its payload of blessing to humanity.

God's blessings are ours because grace has functioned, not simply because the Bible says we've been blessed. An expositional appreciation of grace is necessary, but it must at some point become experiential. The paradox is that grace can have its effect on our lives without our understanding it, but it cannot have its redemptive effect if it is not experienced. God through Christ overlooks our initial ignorance and by the Spirit, grace is allowed to have its way. It is not his wish that we remain ignorant of grace. How many of us on the day we were saved understood anything about the workings of grace? We didn't understand it; we just received it, marveling that we could be saved. In Ephesians 1:2-3 (KJV), Paul speaks of grace and then offers praise because, "he has blessed us with every spiritual blessing." Any blessing heaven can bestow is spiritual, and every blessing becomes ours by receiving the grace of Christ. How many of us thank God not only for such things as our salvation and his wonderful presence in our lives, but for such blessings as homes, cars, paid bills, good jobs, impossible situations changed, and the like? Heaven not only has the capacity to bless us with such spiritual fruit as love, joy, and peace, but material blessings are also in the purview of heaven to bestow. Some can even receive back their dead, and that by the power of grace!

Christ put it like this in Mark 10:29-30: "I tell you the truth, no one who has left home or brothers or sisters or mother or father or children or fields for me and the gospel will fail to receive a hundred times as much in this present age." Perhaps it should be noted here that the "hundred fold" is *contingent on what one has given up*, not on our confession of a desire. Matthew 6:33 makes it clear that "these things" are added to *those who seek first the reality of his kingdom*. There is a mindset required, and even then the reward given is not without the possibility of successive persecutions. Much could be said regarding the kinds of blessings heaven has to bestow, but the intent here is to highlight the fact that it is through operative grace that heaven's blessings are received.

4. Grace is and was always meant to be the seat of man's authority in the earth.

Most believers know that when Adam and Eve sinned, they fell from grace. Grace was the first, or Edenic covenant. Man, having been created by God, was never intended to live outside the vale of grace and has lived in an environment in which he is a foreigner since the fall. Mankind living outside grace is like a fish out of water: the fish out of water dies as the man outside grace dies. While in the state of grace, man had been given authority over all creation. Genesis 1:28-30 sets out the parameters of dominion God gave man. According to Strong's Dictionary, the word, "dominion," means to tread down, to subjugate, to prevail against, to reign and to rule over. Romans 5:17 makes it clear that those who receive the abundant provision of grace "reign in life." This is an absolute declaration of scripture, which clearly is only for those who have become righteous. What does it mean to reign? Anyone who reigns has the right to exercise authority. Strong's Dictionary characterizes the Greek word "reign" as a king reigns, carrying "the notion of a fountain of power." Here again grace leads to power.

Interestingly, God gave Adam and Eve precisely this kind of dominion over "every living creature that moves on the ground," so they had been given authority over the serpent before he made his appearance. They didn't have to listen; they just had to exercise the authority God had given them. Failing in this exercise, the serpent caused man to fall from grace. The serpent knew what the keys of grace were and used those keys against Adam and Eve to pull them from grace, and he still works the same way. Christ makes the point in Matthew 16:19 that he was going to give the keys of the kingdom back to mankind, which will be dealt with specifically in a later chapter. This fall from grace meant the loss of authority, which was then, in effect, transferred to Satan. By affecting man's fall from grace, Lucifer usurped authority over man to work in the earth. But let's be clear: he does not own the earth. Read Psalm 24:1; the earth and the fullness thereof still belong to the Lord! In coming to earth completing his ministry, Christ said in Matthew 28:18, "*All authority in heaven and on earth has been given to me*" [emphasis added]. He followed in verse 19 this by saying, "Therefore go." Christ has not only made it possible for man to come back into the state of grace, but once in this restored state he has again been given responsibility to exercise spiritual authority in the earth.

The closing shot of the Old Testament in Malachi 4:6 refers to a new and yet-to-be-instituted covenant. This new covenant would have the potential to affect the heart and so restore man's place of authority. As this new covenant provision was received it would have the power to birth a passion in fathers for their children. Blessings start with the fathers whose hearts have become flush with the fervor, wisdom, and priorities characteristic of God's heart. The healing of our children's destinies is first settled in the heart of this generation of fathers who have a genuine passion for their children and a concern for the kind of world they will inherit. How passionate are the fathers in our churches? Do we care enough to take an active role in shaping the world they will inherit from us? The generation of men who fought the Second World War cared enough to confront tyranny and understood something about the value of freedom. We tend to look back even those few decades and interpret the events of that war through the lens of modern cynicism that permeates western society. Resigned indifference may well sum up the attitude of most so-called Christian men toward the kind of world their children are moving into. If we say we love our children, then as believers we must demonstrate our love by becoming occupiers in a world grasped by a savage secularism.

We cannot genuinely care just because we know we should. There must be a working of grace that captivates the hearts of fathers, both literally and spiritually, before the blessing of God can come upon our nations. Ultimately, our children will not care if we drove expensive cars, had opulent retirement arrangements, or lived in the best neighborhood. They will measure our love in terms of the freedom they have to exercise their own genuine faith in Christ and to disciple their own children in love's redemption. Miss this gate and "reigning" as described in Romans remains nothing more than words on a page while the struggle of life goes on. Grace must first abound effectually in the hearts of a whole host of the redeemed to be the antidote to abounding sin. If only the few hear, then we fail.

5. Grace is what the ministry of the holy spirit is all about.

The Holy Spirit has been sent into the earth to minister the prevailing covenant. There is no other covenant to administer. In Zechariah 12:10, God declares that the Spirit to be poured out on the Jewish nation would be the Spirit of grace. Ultimately, the Holy Spirit will minister grace in such a way as to bring the whole nation to Christ in one day. When the Spirit ministers grace, the heart of the people will be changed, and their eyes will be opened. Seeing, Israel will repent. Apart from grace, seeing will not produce the fruit of repentance. People can even watch the miracle power work and still not come to Christ. How many people saw Christ's miracle power yet did not believe? How many people today have witnessed a miracle anointing produce heaven's evidence and yet still say they've never seen God do anything miraculous?

The Holy Spirit is the Spirit of grace. One of the factors that brings judgment upon individuals occurs when the Spirit of grace is insulted. Hebrews 10:29 makes this clear when it says, "How much more severely do you think a man deserves to be punished who has trampled the Son of God underfoot, who has treated as an unholy thing the blood of the covenant that sanctified him and who has insulted the Spirit of grace?" In Matthew, Mark, and Luke, Christ addresses the matter of insulting the Spirit of grace. In Matthew 12, Jesus is casting a demon out of a blind mute. The Pharisees attributed what was done to Beelzebub, the prince of demons. What was the blasphemy? It was attributing the work of the Holy Spirit to Satan. Mark 3:28-29 says, "People will be forgiven their sins and whatever blasphemies they utter. But whoever blasphemes against the Holy Spirit can never have forgiveness, but is guilty of eternal sin."

At this point, there needs to be a serious caution issued to many believers and ministers. Some years ago, before I had any experience with the infilling of the Holy Spirit, I had taken some members of my congregation to a Katherine Kuhlman meeting. At that meeting I watched miracles take place right before my eyes. A lady attending our church had taken her infant son to the meeting. This child had an opening of raw flesh behind one ear and doctors had been unable to effect a healing. Suddenly the mother became very animated as she looked at her son. She called me over and showed me the place where there had been only a raw open wound. Visibly, skin was forming behind the ear. The open area had been about one inch in diameter. By the time we got the child to the platform there was only a faint red dot visible. Our whole congregation knew of this miracle and most had seen the open flesh. Several days after the crusade I walked into a Bible study group where Miss Kuhlman's ministry was being assailed. The gist of the teaching being given was the Holy Spirit doesn't do miracles anymore. Having heard what the teacher was saying I interrupted the meeting and cautioned every person there to be extremely careful not to attribute the works of the Holy Spirit to the Devil. The only reason the leader of that meeting was exempt from committing blasphemy, it seems to me, was his ignorance. If genuine blasphemy of the Spirit is to occur it must be in the face of knowledge. The person attributing the works of the Spirit to the Devil must know that what is being credited to the Devil was actually done by the Holy Spirit.

We can be forgiven if we are ignorant, but to attribute a work of the Holy Spirit to the Devil in ignorance does not automatically free us of consequence. For example, I once attended a pastor's retreat where the speaker was from the headquarters of a prominent denomination. In the course of events he began to speak of the ministry of Miss Kuhlman. He openly said the miracles and healings that took place in her ministry were of a "mediumistic nature." I had only been in the ministry a few weeks, had no functional acquaintance with the works of the Holy Spirit, and still thought that if you spoke in tongues you likely needed deliverance; but when this speaker called the works of the Spirit witchcraft, I just remember being shocked. I was not accustomed to the voice of the Spirit in those early days, but as I sat there I heard, "This man will shortly be removed from his ministry position." Within a few months this man became critically ill and had to step down. I guess there are times we should be thankful that God's grace covers what is spoken in ignorance.

It astonishes me when I hear prominent church leaders speak so carelessly about the works of the Holy Spirit. The Holy Spirit is the administrator of grace. Grace leads into the administration of his power workings in the lives of believers today. Part of the grace expression of God to man brings about the activation of His gifts as outlined in I Corinthians 12. If you're going to teach that the gifts of the Spirit are not for today, then to whom should we attribute miracles and healings? Surely man in and of himself cannot cause the blind to see, the deaf to hear, or the dying to live. Then what power and authority accomplish these works? If the gifts of the Spirit have ceased, then one is hard pressed to explain supernatural phenomenon. We should be careful that we do not, even by inference, attribute the works of the Spirit to the Devil. This is a precarious place to be in before a God who will not tolerate even an "insult" of the Holy Spirit. Remember, this is right up there with treating as an unholy thing the blood of the covenant that sanctifies. Conversely, the gifts of the Spirit are not natural, human "talents." You cannot re-interpret tongues to mean "is good with people from other cultures," or prophecy as "has a gift for public speaking." To attribute the works of God to human flesh is abhorrent and falls under the purview of II Timothy 3:5: "having a form of godliness but denying its power." Be careful that the Holy Spirit is not insulted by theologies of denial.

6. Grace is central to living a supernatural experience.

None of us could experience anything of a supernatural salvation had grace not been the gateway. Receiving grace in its functional dimension activates the supernatural lifestyle, which is perpetuated by the ongoing reception of abundant grace. God activated his grace covenant in the earth in John 1:1 by sending his Word. Whenever God wants to activate grace in our lives he does so by the impartation of a word directive. For example, what word directive can be used to activate saving grace? "You must be born again" (John 3:3). Here the Word of God is giving a clear, specific directive. In Acts 20:32, Paul calls this "the word of God's grace." Responding to Word directives results in a manifestation of supernatural power. Matthew 14:22 gives us an illustration of this when Christ comes walking on the water. Peter sees him and calls out, "Lord, if it's you, tell me to come to you on the water." Christ gives him the word of his grace, "Come," and Peter obeys. He walks on water, experiences supernatural power, and Christ is glorified. We will deal with "the word of God's grace" a bit later, but our focus at this point is how grace functions as the sole gateway into a lifestyle characterized by supernatural manifestations of God's power. This grace is always and fundamentally rooted in a Word from God.

If any believer wishes to live in a dimension of the supernatural reality of God there must be functional grace. Miss grace and one misses the supernatural dimension of biblical Christianity. Christianity stripped of its supernatural dimension is not biblical Christianity. The establishment of grace itself required power: the power of the divine conception resulting in the virgin birth. In his book, *Miracles,* C. S. Lewis says that when "the core of Christianity is scraped clean of inessentials what remains for me is entirely miraculous, supernatural" (86).

7. Grace is the only means by which God's people prosper.

Any prosperity generated out of carnal ability or motive is repugnant and to be shunned, but there is an absoluteness here to which every reader must adjust his or her beliefs if scripture is to have its proper authority over Christian life and practice. Note the place the Holy Spirit gives grace in II Corinthians 9:8: "And God is able to make all grace abound, so that in all things, at all times, having all you need, you will abound in every good work." When believers learn what this means and how to receive it, grace bears its own supernatural result. Notice God makes grace abound to the place where, "having all you need" becomes a way of life. Now if people find they have all they need, "in all things and at all times," this must indicate prosperity of a divine origin. Such prosperity is a manifestation of an all-encompassing love. To love with pure love is to love to give, which can only be received by one whose heart is characterized by love. Love pours out provision on a desperate world. How do we dare say to God, "Well, I'll receive grace that sanctifies or that forgives, but now, God, you'll just have to keep the grace that supplies all

I need at all times locked up in heaven. Lord, you know I don't believe in that prosperity stuff." We cannot settle for a little grace. To argue against this provision is to argue against grace and the finality of scriptural authority.

8. Grace is motivated by an all-consuming love.

"For God so loved the world that he gave his only Son," and "God demonstrates his own love for us in this: while we were still sinners Christ died for us" (John 3:16; Romans 5:8). In dying for us, Christ paid the full price for sin and made the way for the institution of the new covenant of grace. What motivated the grace God extends to us? Love of an incomprehensible kind. It is because of his love for us as individuals that grace is always made available to us. As we receive his grace, we gratify the love passion God has for us. It is, in part, a fulfillment of Isaiah 53:11, "He shall see the travail of his soul and be *satisfied*" (KJV) [emphasis added]. Let me say it another way: the more grace you respond to, the more God's heart of love finds its satisfaction. To receive the grace of God is to step into the love of God and allow his love to flow into our hearts, homes, church relationships, ministries and the world.

9. Grace manifests itself as a result of mercy.

The heart of the Father is an all-consuming passion to love. The reality of that passion demands the extension of mercy. God loves us and because he loved, he wanted to extend mercy, so he sent Christ to establish grace in the earth. Included in the opening and closing remarks of many New Testament epistles are *grace* and *mercy*. Paul is telling us as believers that once we have received grace in the form of the new heart, our passion for those around us is now nothing less than the love of God.

Grace inevitably proves its presence by administering mercy. For believers, such ministry is mandated both by the Spirit and the Word. We don't get to decide for ourselves when to minister grace and its fruit of mercy. The question is, do we do it? Are our church relationships characterized by irrepressible mercy? How about our family and marriage relationships? Remember the servant in Matthew 18:26-32 who had received mercy and forgiveness but would not extend mercy and forgiveness in return? By the impartation of grace we are given the love-heart of God, which becomes the governing passion in our relationships, and because of this passion, we cannot help but extend mercy to those around us. Finally, we discover corporately what it means when James 2:13 declares, "Mercy triumphs over judgment." No more nasty letters or phone calls, and no more nasty gatherings of one group against another group in the church.

The implication in all this is that when grace holds its functional authority in our hearts, the church becomes a place where mercy characterizes our relationships rather than judgment. Our relationships are so adversarial in the body of Christ because, in the absence of the mercy passion, we are left with the compulsion to judge one another. Criticisms, harsh words, and judgmental hearts can only abound where grace is nothing more than a sentimental religious concept. We can read Matthew 7, which tells us not to judge, but unless grace grips our hearts with the passion of the Father's love we will continue to judge one another. We are left with empty religion and will kill one another with our words as easily as the Pharisees killed Stephen with stones. Mercy becomes the property of the congregation only when the grace gate is found. Skip the discovery of grace in its functional implication, and no credible witness of Christ's mercy remains. Is mercy really an irrepressible attribute in your heart? If not, get before God and ask for fullness of grace. If it is, ask for more!

10. Grace leads from mercy to peace.

I have ministered in churches worldwide, and what is happening is nothing less than an absolute contradiction of our profession. Some of the nastiest people on the planet are sitting in our churches, professing Christ, speaking in tongues, even prophesying, and yet they are nothing more than the personification of malevolence. Grace, mercy, and peace have eluded them, but they know their doctrine! On the other hand, the true sons of God will have discovered the divine passion that insists on peace based on the finished work of Christ rather than finding cause for controversy. Perhaps this is what Christ meant in Matthew 5:9 when he said, "Blessed are the peacemakers for they will be called the sons of God." Grace produces peacemakers. As grace asserts its influence within the believer, the world glimpses God's glory manifested in lives that demonstrate a peace not common to man, and the true light of God's nature is reflected into a dark world.

11. Grace is how the fruit of the spirit is activated in the lives of believers.

The new heart the Spirit gives us is an altogether *other* heart, beating with the desires of God and demonstrating the fruit of the Spirit as listed in Galatians 5:22-23. Failing the functional presence of grace, there can only be evidences of the sinful nature. Those evidences as listed in Galatians 5:19-21 start with sexual immorality of every imaginable kind. Try to stand against this flaw of human nature apart from grace, and the church will continue to be rocked by sexually aberrant behavior at all levels. If believers want to break the power of improper sexual passions, there must come a discovery of grace with its transforming power in the inner man. In the absence of grace, the works of the flesh manifest in many ways and situations. Idolatry, witchcraft, hatred, discord, jealousy, fits of rage, selfish ambition, dissensions, factions, and envy will not only characterize society but the community of believers! These works of the flesh are rampantly evident wherever believers congregate. (Idolatry manifests in the drive to set oneself ahead of biblical standards, while witchcraft makes itself felt through those who demand control and seek power so as to manipulate things to their desired ends.) This whole list can be found in churches in almost every country of the world. (I say *almost* in the hope that somewhere the Holy Spirit has had such ministry of grace that his fruit has found its proper expression in attitude, word, and conduct.)

The realities with which sincere pastors must contend make the ministry a gruelingly difficult task. It is because of the works of the flesh that many churches and ministries never grow or achieve the things for which they were birthed. May I ask you to consider what set of evidence you display in your church? If you are playing devil's advocate, then that is exactly what you are. Dear reader, take a few moments to get out a dictionary. What is jealousy or hatred? Are you given to fits of rage? How do you conduct yourself at the annual church meeting? For those holding staff positions in church organizations are you really there with a servant heart or are you driven by selfish ambition? Do you strengthen the senior minister or do you get caught up in behind-the-scenes divisions? Are you out to replace the pastor? How many people will you—or have you—led down the street, deceiving yourself and others that the Spirit is leading you? Be careful that you do not insult God: he doesn't treat that kind of arrogance lightly. We need to discover the grace motive, or we have nothing waiting for us at the judgment seat of Christ.

It seems that we believe in the fruits of the Spirit so long as we are not required to manifest them in difficult situations. It is precisely when someone provokes us to retaliate that the opportunity to offer the fruit of the Spirit occurs. We are faced with the necessity of delivering the fruit of love when someone, by wrong conduct and attitude, infringes on our rights and feelings. Did you ever ask yourself what the calling of a fruit tree is? It grows its fruit for someone else to enjoy. Picture this: you have been standing in your place of ministry, determined to bring honor to the Lord. There on your branches hang these lovely, tender fruits of patience. You look down and admire how they are ripening into something truly glorious. You feel so proud that you could produce something so divine. All that standing out there through those difficult times almost seems worth it. Suddenly, out of nowhere, pluck! Shock of shocks, that insensitive Mr. So-and-so just came by and casually pulled that lovely piece of fruit off your limb and gobbled it down without so much as a thank you! You vow, "I'll never speak to that jerk again!" But it gets worse. "Hey, Lord, what's that in your hand? An axe! Aw, come on Lord. Life is tough enough; do you really have to prune me quite so much? They pluck me clean and then You hack away at me? Lord, I thought you loved me!"

The truth is we no more ask a peach tree permission to pluck its fruit than we expect to see the tree eat its own peaches! Have you ever watched a peach farmer go around and ask the trees for permission to pick their fruit or go around thanking the trees for producing peaches? If anything he thanks God. We grow the fruit of patience so that when someone provokes us we respond, "Ah, wonderful, here is my opportunity to extend patience." Are you growing fruit so that others can pick it when they need it and then give thanks to *God* not *you?*

Functional grace brings us into the nature of Christ, which in turn finds expression in our ability to live out I Corinthians 13. Hmm...I wonder if we have some growing to do? If I really want to be a healthy tree, then pluck my fruit and trim that branch! Without grace, we yield only wild fruit, but with grace, as others fail to treat me right, the world sees man of another kind and kingdom. Genuine spiritual fruit is about the other guy and always the other guy. Fruit trees are always givers.

12. Grace is inherently the root source of joy in the believer's life.

When one looks at the body of Christ one can't help but ask, "Where's the joy?" In John 15:11, Christ declared his intent that his people might have the full measure of his joy within us. Not only did Christ want us to experience joy but his provisional intent was that his joy should "remain." The Greek for grace and joy are both derived from the Greek word "*chairo:*" *charis* is the Greek word for grace, while *chara* is the Greek word for joy. Joy is inextricably bound to grace. Again, God did not intend us to have one without the other. Joy operates in the same spirit dimension as grace. What does an individual look like not just having joy but being "full" of pure joy? A quick check through scriptures on joy reveals that joy has visible, outward manifestations. These outward expressions can take the form of laughter, shouting with great force, dancing, leaping, and jumping. Just watch natural man when something causes them to rejoice greatly.

One of the realities among a people experiencing the joy of the Lord is that they will be inclined to get along with others. You are not likely to find an individual full of joy who is also full of criticism, rage, faultfinding, selfish ambition, or divisiveness. A joyful person is easy to associate with and not inclined to hunt for faults in others. It is obvious that individuals are missing the grace of God by the absence of joy. Check out the joy gauge in your own heart! Look at those folks who go around critical of what is happening in the church and you will find people who have failed to operate out of spiritual joy. If you find yourself in such unfortunate and unhappy company know that you are outside the grace of God.

Nehemiah 8:10 declares, "The joy of the Lord is your strength." *Grace is the gateway into joy, and joy makes us strong.* You will find real evidences of joy where grace is being received. As a husband and wife receive grace there will be joy in the relationship, and the inevitable result will be strength in the marriage. The same reality applies to a local church. Joyful people, not being fault-focused or easily offended, will find it easier to stand in transparent fellowship. Strength will characterize their assembly, and the resultant unity will allow them to act harmoniously. God wants us to receive the grace that marks the Christian fellowship with unity and joy.

There is another reason why the grace that leads to joy produces strength. Some years ago my wife and I went through some traumatic events in which we lost our life savings, our home, and our ministry position in a church. We found ourselves on the outside of other local churches looking in. A deep sense of loneliness gripped us. We were stuck owing on a church property, and our resources were stripped bare before we finally succeeded in getting a sale after two and a half years of waiting. Just after the deal to sell the property was signed the second mortgage holder started foreclosure proceedings. I received notice in the mail, and I immediately called my lawyer. He advised me that I had to come up with a couple of thousand dollars to fight the foreclosure proceedings. I was already broke, and now I was faced with finding well over two thousand dollars. I found a source to lend me the money and got the foreclosure deferred. Everything seemed to be settled. It couldn't get any worse, right? Then, the day before the sale was to close, my lawyer called me and advised me that the deal wasn't going to go through. I asked him what this meant for us. He said something like this: "You'll be on the street owing a bunch more money I guess." What couldn't get worse just got worse! My wife sat on the stairs in tears, looking at me with deep apprehension. I was numb. I walked up to the second level in our soon-to-be-vacated home and was overcome with laughter in the middle of our bedroom. Even some of the worst TV scenarios couldn't match this! I just stood there thinking this was simply hilarious and laughed until tears ran down my face. The burden lifted, and I knew God was in control. The buffeting spirit had outdone itself. He was defeated, and my joy was irrepressible! The next day the buyers found the necessary money, and the sale closed. We were out!

Demonic spirits buffet every believer from time to time, bombarding us with every sort of evil scheme. We are all locked into a spiritual war with these dark forces. The intent of these schemes is to use any device, circumstance, or individual to cause us to yield our faith in Christ. Suppose a demonic spirit has been sent against you to work a specific strategy against your faith. You suffer through all kinds of adversity, financial difficulty, personal disaster, disease, brokenness, and betrayal, but through it all the Holy Spirit continues to minister a desire to stick with it in your heart. No matter what you go through, there wells up in your heart a new surge of determination. Just when you should start to cry in utter defeat, you receive grace that brings with it a deep inner sense of irrepressible joy, and you start to laugh. You laugh till tears run down your face. No, the outward circumstance hasn't changed a bit. The enemy of your faith is pressing in as heavily as before, but suddenly the relief of inexplicable joy grips your heart and notifies your face. The look of joy and the sound of your laughter become a dread note to that familiar spirit who has been beating you with all its might. This experience of spiritual joy signals an absolute defeat to that demon. Imagine that spirit reporting back to hell on its progress. Lucifer inquires as to how much longer before his enemy—you—are defeated. "Ah, sir, um, you see…Well, !@#$! I've done everything you've told me to do and that !@#$ Christian just keeps on singing, praising God, and to tell the unpleasant truth, I just left him laughing hysterically at me. Couldn't you send another demon for a while?"

Grace, joy, strength: what an awesome combination. His strength made perfect in our weakness lifts us out of the valley of despair into a joy unspeakable. Joy makes the pursuit of grace a wonderful quest! Missing joy? Find grace! I wonder if this might not have been what Paul had in mind when he wrote to Timothy, "Be *strong* in the grace that is in Christ Jesus" (II Timothy 2:1) [emphasis added].

13. Grace activates the human spirit to function relationally with the Spirit God.

Galatians closes by saying, "The grace of our Lord Jesus Christ be with your spirit, brothers. Amen." In writing for the believer who wants biblical principles to move from the intellectual to the experiential, I will no doubt be seen as oversimplifying a complex matter, but the complexities of grace need not be fully understood to reap its benefits. Remember your salvation? How much of grace did any of us understand at the point of our conversion?

Paul in this text to the Galatians makes it plain that the grace that comes from our Lord Jesus Christ has to do with "your spirit." It does not fundamentally deal with your soul—your mind, will, and emotions—nor does it deal initially with the body of flesh where our five senses dwell. Grace makes its first impact, and succeeding administrations upon our spirit being, because the Holy Spirit deals first with that which is spirit. He wants to bring us into spiritual life where our spirits are aware and responsive to Him. The unregenerate spirit of man can chase spiritual realities that have nothing to do with God, as it does not have a developed sensitivity or desire for spiritual things as they pertain to God. This pursuit takes many into the realm of the occult with its diverse depravity. But when the Holy Spirit brings grace to bear upon the human spirit, an awareness and desire for the spiritual realities of God and his kingdom is born. His purpose is that man might be lifted out of a soulish prison into an experience that occurs at the deeper level of the spirit being. Romans 6:11 describes this as "dead to sin but alive to God in Christ Jesus." The true biblical definition of a Christian is one whose entire existence has been impacted by grace through the Holy Spirit's ministry and carries on a relationship with an invisible, spiritual being who is Omni in every facet of his nature.

What does this mean? We live in a twofold reality. There is a natural, temporal, physical realm and an invisible, eternal, spiritual realm often referred to in scripture as the kingdom of God. The humanist declares that there is only his self-defined, material prison. Any discussion affirming the existence of a separable soul (the view that a soul—mind, will, emotion—can exist independent of the body) is considered pure folly. However, man has demonstrated throughout history that he has an insatiable interest in the metaphysical, and such complexity finds no explanation in humanism. Humanists simply choose to skirt this reality and offer nothing more than non-rational denial. For the humanists, nothing beyond their view exists. How is this accomplished? They simply declare it, opposing any other view on the basis of what they have declared. Consider the following statements drawn from tenet one of the Second Humanist Manifesto: "We find insufficient evidence for belief in the existence of a supernatural..." and, "we can discover no divine purpose or providence for the human species" (Kurtz, Wilson). The humanist is rather like the man who went to the North Pole to find canaries. He looked and looked and finally declared that canaries do not exist because he could find no evidence for their existence. In part, the humanists are right because God is not in the places they go looking for him and any evidence they found there would be lost in their determination to find nothing. Well, "as a man thinks, so is he."

In the first paragraph of tenet two, more precepts are given that help shed light on the world most of us grew up in: "Modern science discredits such historic concepts as the 'ghost in the machine' and the 'separable soul.'" In this way, all science must be made to conform to the framework set out around it. The humanist view doesn't start with the scientific method, it starts from the position that science must work to affirm atheism and discredit God and the possibility of a separable soul. Another statement from the second tenet says, "There is no credible evidence that life survives the death of the body." Argue the resurrection of Christ, and even credible evidence is simply *declared* to be irrelevant and non-credible. The only response their so-called modern science can give is to reassert their arbitrary position. It's rather like talking to a child who has decided that cats should be able to fly and keeps throwing the cat off the roof of the house. Dad comes along and tries to explain that cats can't fly. Despite the repeated evidence of the cat falling to the ground every time it was thrown off the roof, and despite the sound explanations the father offers, the child simply repeats, "Cats can fly because I say they can fly." This is precisely the kind of thinking that has gripped every cultural aspect of western society. Just because humanists say there is no God, Creator, separable soul, or life after death doesn't mean they are right. To simply say a thing with fixed conviction often enough does not make it true!

What has this got to do with grace? Humanists cannot explain grace. What's more, they insist on a world that must be graceless! The humanistic training many believers got just by growing up in a progressively secularized culture has powerfully influenced the thinking of many in the church today. In many ways we think and believe things that have no basis in truth. When confronted with truth that forces us outside what we have been taught in the past, we react not to the error of the past but to the truth, trying to get the Bible to line up with what we think we know.

As an example, on one occasion a group of Christians who had heard of my ministry in the city asked me to join them for supper. During the meal the topic turned to science and the Bible. Casually I asked those around the table, "Where does light come from?" referring to the light of day. The answer seemed obvious to all in the group: daylight comes from the sun. I asked where they had learned this. I was given rather incredulous looks. Well, it is learned in introductory science. I asked them, rather naively as it turned out, if they were Bible believers, which all agreed they were. I then asked them what God created on the first day. They all said light. Then I asked them what God created on the fourth day. There was silence. Thinking they would happily accept the authoritative statement of scripture, I said that on the fourth day God created the sun, the moon and the stars. Day one: light, day four: sun. So light does not come solely from the sun. Their reaction bordered on the hostile. Statements like, "Oh, don't give us that kind of foolishness; we all know that light comes from the sun." Don't get lost on me here: the issue isn't who's right. The issue is, *who* is *always* right?

In many ways, humanistic principles of thought have been drilled into us during formative years, training us to focus and operate in the natural, resisting that which is spirit making it difficult for many individual believers to get beyond the soulish realm. The concept of living by spiritual precepts somehow becomes non-binding. For instance, we know that as believers we are commanded to love one another, but the way we really conduct ourselves in relationships springs out of our humanistic training rather than out of the truth of scripture. This is nothing short of counterfeit Christianity!

God has given us five senses in our bodies: sight, hearing, touch, smell, and taste. Those five senses all have their place in helping us function effectively in the environment around us. Take these five senses away from a person and there may be life in his body, thoughts in his mind, emotion in his heart and a will to relate, but no media exists by which to engage the external world. People could shout at him, shoot him with spit-wads, or put a skunk in his room, but without senses, he would have no awareness of what was going on around him. Similarly, God has set within the human spirit the possibility of a lifestyle that centers on five "spirit senses." It is by these five spiritual senses that we are able to engage the reality of the spirit realm— God, angels, and the eternal kingdom of God. This is why humanists reject even the notion of God: since their human spirits are non-functional, they conclude that there is nothing of a spiritual reality. Ask any real believer about what happens to them after they die, and they all expect to see, hear, smell, touch, and taste in heaven while their bodies are turning to dust in the ground! Scripture makes it clear that these five senses are characteristic of the human spirit. For example, in II Corinthians 4:18 Paul says, "So we fix our eyes not on what is seen but on what is unseen. For what is seen is temporary, but what is unseen is eternal." We need to ask ourselves what God intends when scripture talks about the need to see, hear, taste and feel. As the five senses in your body help you to function effectively in the natural world, so it is God's intent that the five senses of your spirit enable you to function effectively in spiritual realities. The latter senses are intended to have dominance over the former. Grace impacts the human spirit to bring it to life. A living spirit is intended to have five fully functioning spiritual senses through which our true personhood is progressively discovered and liberation from a purely natural reality is experienced. The Spirit begins to apply his presence and implement inner change: change that has to do with my character, values, and thought life. He begins to interfere with my soulish commitments. He begins to open me up inwardly to another and conflicting reality. But if the Spirit is limited by our willingness to receive grace, then he is limited in his ability to quicken our spirit man. May our hearts be open and our cry be, "Lord, fill me with your grace. Let your grace be with my spirit to do what it is designed to do."

14. Grace activates divine impulses in the regenerate spirit.

Grace brings the individual into a place of inner conflict. The spirit man longs for that which is of God: the pure, the lovely, the noble; however, the carnal man is driven to nurture its own opposing passions and desires. The individual begins to experience a new and different kind of inner reality whose impulses and desires are not common to the man outside the grace experience. Galatians, Romans, Ephesians, and II Corinthians all speak of this inner warfare. A conflict exists between the spiritual nature with its God-centered impulses and the natural man screaming for its own passions to be appeased, between the desires of the sinful nature as spoken of in Galatians 5 and the desires that God the Holy Spirit implants in the heart. The spiritual desires lead away from our personal idolatries toward true worship of God, while the carnal passions insist on the maintenance of the idolatry of self. This drive toward self-centered interest manifests in many different ways in the church. Though by grace we have been saved, grace has not been allowed to continue its work over natural, self-indulgent passions. In his book *Power from on High*, Charles Finney observes, "Selfishness is a state of voluntary committal to the indulgence of the sensibility...The first act of righteousness must be to a change of heart which involves a renunciation of selfishness" (77).

There must come a willingness among believers to discern between the competing desires: does my desire for a particular thing come from God, or is it rooted in the carnal nature? We can desire good things out of the wrong source. For example, if a desire to go into the ministry does not originate in God but is rooted in a carnal desire, is it a work of the Spirit or a work of the flesh? There is a glory that attracts the carnal, self-worshipping, idolater. Again, why does an individual desire to minister in the gifts of healing and miracles, stand in the pulpit, serve in leadership, or sing a song? Is it for adulation or self-aggrandizement, or is the motive one of genuine servanthood? Why does an individual desire prosperity? Is God really generating that desire, or is it a self-generated desire sanctified by attributing that carnal desire to God? Do these desires emanate from the fallen self that wants its own gratification or the spirit man with its genuine redemptive passion? One good way to know is to watch what manifests when gratification of those desires is not forthcoming: servanthood or selfhood? At the heart of what is being done one should ask, "Is grace at work in me producing godly desires for his glory?" There must be a genuine discerning of our desires, because desires emanating from self-hood always deny the Lordship of Christ. Only one can be Lord of all! No matter how wonderful the works done may appear, if they are for personal reputation they are meaningless, no matter how much money we give away or how big the ministry is. Eternally, they are at best wood, hay, and stubble, gaining us nothing.

Can I discern my own motives or do I need help from a higher order in discerning my own heart? Are we not all cast up on the shore of desperation in ascertaining the secret passions of the heart? The discerning work of the

Spirit becomes an absolute necessity. Who better to divide asunder and bring to light the hidden motives of the heart? As stated by Jeremiah 17:9, the heart is "deceitful above all things. Who can know it?" God alone! Those who hold that the gifts of the Spirit have passed away are left to their own devices in the discovery of their motives. Nullify the discerning work of the Spirit in our lives and the supernatural help we all need ceases to be an available resource. The Spirit must reveal the hidden motives and desires of the carnal heart, and he must be called upon to lay an axe at the root of that carnal passion. This could be the bloody field of discipleship into which few are inclined to venture: a place where we discover part of what is meant by dying daily and taking up the cross. It is by grace that God wants to implant his desires in our hearts, but he is not willing for those spiritual desires to be made servant to carnal motives. Can this attitude of personally difficult discipleship really become a widespread reality in the community of believers? Only if we surrender the status quo and become truly thirsty for the manifest substance of grace!

15. Grace is the only vehicle that delivers us from the death grip of the law.

By its very nature, the law set an impossible standard, demanding to be satisfied by works. No man could live a life that would satisfy the law, the result being that every man fell short. We still do! Failure is every man's experience. We all come short, yet we persist in pointing at the failure of others around us while disregarding our own (Matthew 7:3). The reality is that even in the presence of functional grace there will be an inability to perform perfectly. This imperfection is precisely the opportunity to extend grace. Romans 3:23 plainly states that we've all failed and *continue* to fall short of God's glory. The good news is grace has been interposed between every failure of man on one side and a Holy God on the other. The next verse gives God's incredible response to the *all* who are coming short: "*By his grace* they are justified *freely*" [emphasis added]. That placement of grace was accomplished by the redemption that came by Christ Jesus. How does God cover what that individual just did? By grace through the redemption that came by Christ Jesus.

If we deny the ministry of grace to the broken around us, we are denying the very thing that Christ accomplished by the redemption. Judgment is the means by which man is sent back into the captivity of his own depravity and sin. Redemption rests in the grace that was made available to every man. Any standard of works (or how well an individual maintains an outward performance of holy perfection) is only "filthy rags" (Isaiah 64:6). Based on the work of Christ's sacrifice and the ultimate truth he represented on the cross, the demanding shouts of the law have forever been satisfied. The law has nothing to insist on anymore. The power of the Law to call for our death sentence lies forever silenced before the Christ who died. Some might surmise and even promote, "Go ahead and sin because it's okay now," but anyone who has tasted of the depths of God's grace cannot then gleefully go back to the filth of their own vomit. To suggest otherwise is ludicrous (Romans 6:1-2).

All who believe are receiving freely of grace, because Jesus purchased a way out of the death grip of the law at the cost of his life. If we hold that redemption in reverence, we are bound to offer freely to others what we have freely received. To do otherwise is to nullify the new covenant in his blood, not for the individual perceived to have failed, but for the one sitting in judgment. Every believer must discover something of the wonder of grace and then become hilarious ministers of it to others. Matthew 5:17 records Jesus as saying that he'd not come to do away with the law, but to fulfill it. Guess what? He succeeded to the full satisfaction of God. If God, being holy, is satisfied enough to extend unlimited measures of grace, how can we, being unholy, fail to offer some small measure of that satisfaction to others? Having received extreme grace at our point of need, we so often turn and deny it to others in their failure or offense! This brings to mind the parable of the wicked servant in Matthew 18 who would not pardon a small offense after being forgiven a huge debt. What was missing that brought him into such condemnation by his master? Having been a recipient of grace in an extraordinary measure he would not minister grace in light of an insignificant offense. We have received grace in astounding proportions and are called upon to realize that *any* offense by another believer is, in truth, trivial. Amazing that we who have received more than we can comprehend are inclined to minister so little to our offenders. The point here is not that others have offended you, but rather, your response. The affront triggers your call to be an authentic minister of grace—you know, the seventy-times-seven stuff of Matthew 18:22. When you are offended or perceive shortcomings, does your response mirror that of the ungrateful, ungraceful servant?

This brings me to a word of caution I would be remiss if I ignored: Do not show up at the next communion service to tell the Father that you are in right and forgiving relationship with the members of your congregation and church leadership if you deny others the mercy and forgiveness that grace extends. In plain English, don't show up with somebody else's throat between your fingers! God isn't blind or deaf! To paraphrase I Corinthians 11:30, for this reason many among us are weak in the faith, sick in our bodies and minds, and some have even died. There is no such thing as a strong church if the individual members do not actively minister the mercy inherent in grace to others in the congregation, and this includes your pastors. Similarly, all pastors have numerous God-given opportunities to both speak of grace and to model it. How is it modeled? By evident mercy! Grace is the way Christ has made that leads us out of the death grip of law and takes us into the liberty of life through faith in his blood. Grace is the great common denominator among all believers. Where Law still holds sway in the heart, judgment is never far off. But having found, received, and understood grace with its inherent and colossal benefits, the believer cannot help but look for every opportunity to lavish grace upon anything that breathes!

16. Grace is the means by which the gifts of the Spirit are activated in the life of the believer.

If we can discover what it means to receive grace in the area of the gifts, the gifts will begin to manifest, flourish, and mature in the body of Christ, becoming one of the means the Spirit uses to minister grace to both other believers and the world. Going even further, the offices of apostle, prophet, evangelist, pastor and teacher are activated and empowered by the Spirit's administration of grace. It is as the Holy Spirit ministers grace in individuals that the offices take on a supernatural dimension so as to produce supernatural results. It would seem reasonable to assume that anyone functioning in these offices should understand how grace impacts their office.

The cecessionist declares that the gifts of the Spirit have ceased. This doctrine eliminates the ministration of grace that the gifts offer to the world. Put another way, if one denies the gifts of the Spirit their biblical place in the contemporary church, then the grace those gifts can extend to the world is denied. Conversely, there is a large segment of the believing church that declares that the gifts of the Spirit are still available for use in the church today. Interestingly, in church after church where this view of the gifts is held, few have grown beyond some sporadic expression of tongues. Many strive to find the Spirit in the experience of speaking in tongues, but when you check with them a year or so later, few seem to make any systematic use of that gift that earlier was so desired. Somehow we are content that the gift of tongues has been experienced. Many then live the rest of their lives never advancing in the administration of the other gift workings of the Holy Spirit. Any call to activate them in the lives of individuals seems to be met with perplexed reactions.

One of the significant benefits grace is intended to bring to the world is a new kind of man, recreated in the image of God doing the works of God. Yes, the works of God involve things other than the gifts of the Spirit, but many of the works of God must engage the operation of the gifts if they are to be affected in the life of the believer. To think that we can accomplish the ministry of Christ without moving in the gifts of the Spirit seems to be nothing short of ignorant arrogance. Christ did not accomplish his ministry apart from the implementation of the Spirit's gift workings. In fact, the only two gifts that Christ does not appear to have used in his ministry are tongues and interpretation of tongues. Look at his earthly ministry, and you find Jesus demonstrated a continual dependence on the enabling that flows from the Holy Spirit. Do we really think that we can effectively function in the ministry of Christ and grace and not need wisdom, knowledge, faith, healing, miracles, prophesy, and discerning of spirits? If Christ needed them to fulfill *his* ministry to fallen man how do we dare be so arrogant as to believe that we can do what Christ did without drawing on the very enabling He relied on? The gift workings of the Holy Spirit are the very implements by which heaven's power is brought to bear on both the natural world and on mankind.

It seems easier to develop a theology that justifies the absence of the gifts in the lives of believers than it is to discover why they are absent and rectify their continuing absence. Once those theologies are developed, God help anyone who might suggest that the gifts are to be used by every believer. Some even go so far as to say that anyone who manifests the gifts is of the Devil. This brings us back to a dangerous border.

If believers really want to mount an effective witness in a post-Christian culture, then one unanswerable witness we can offer our cultures is a demonstration of heaven's power similar to the man born blind in John 9: "Once I was blind but now I see...Do you want to believe in Christ as well?" Think about this for a moment: if a thousand believers were ministering the gifts of healing, miracles, and prophesy to those they met week after week, what would begin to happen in that city? As it is, we speak in tongues occasionally and wait for someone to interpret, once in a while including a prophetic utterance. For the most part, we either have a theology that says that all the gifts of the Spirit are for today without a mature expression of that theology, or we deny their existence altogether. The gifts will not manifest as effective ministries from heaven until believers learn to receive ever-greater measures of grace. The world needs a supernatural witness today as much as the world in which the church was birthed. The gifts had their place then, and they have their place today.

On one occasion I sat down to chat with two Jehovah's Witnesses, and in the course of the conversation we spoke of the place the gifts of the Spirit have in the modern world. Interestingly, as I listened to their explanation, I could not help but marvel that what many Christians believe about the gifts of the Spirit is in perfect harmony with the Jehovah's Witnesses! Those in the Christian community who deny the present day validity of the gifts of the Spirit also find themselves in the company of the state church in communist China. The Communist-controlled church in China has a statement of regulations called the eight prohibitions. When Christians gather together, the rules say that they cannot prophesy, lay hands on the sick, minister healing, or speak in tongues (Danyun, *Lillies Among Thorns*, 1991, Sovereign World Ltd., Tonbridge, Kent. UK. P307). Hmm...Rather odd company for professing believers to be keeping! Imagine: atheistic Communists tell Chinese believers that they cannot operate in the gifts of the Holy Spirit. Then concurring with this view western theology also insists that they, having passed away, cannot be used. Strange bedfellows indeed!

17. Grace radically affects the nature and ministry of both the prophetic office and gift.

How has grace affected the prophetic ministry? It is easy to look into the vast array of prophetic writings, personalities, and utterances in the Old Testament and build a present-day prophetic ministry on that model. In fact, it appears that this is precisely what many have done. They look at how the Old Testament prophets saw sin and human failure and model their prophetic ministry accordingly. However, any prophetic model of ministry shaped around the Old Testament will tend to be both legalistic and judgmental. In the Old Testament, those individuals who stood in the prophetic office stood as individuals responsible for the administration of the covenant of law. Any concept of "unmerited favor" was inconceivable. Perfect performance was everyone's duty. The prophet finally thundered in response to the sin and failure of those subject to that covenant. The end of the matter was a curse, and that curse was death. No one could keep the law.

Then grace and truth came through Jesus Christ. He fulfilled every requirement of the law and took the penalty for the sin and failure of every man, changing the covenant governing the relationship between God and man. This new agreement took man out of the bondage to a law he could not possibly keep and into a new relational model called grace. By faith in Christ's blood, man now lives not out of his ability to keep the law but in Christ's fulfillment of the law. God has chosen to see and treat us as one *with* Christ based on our being *in* Christ. There is therefore now no condemnation, as said by Romans 8:1. How can that be? Man is now said to be in Christ Jesus and, being in Him who was perfect, no condemnation is possible. Understand, it is not my purpose to get into detail here on what it means to be in Christ, but I do want to point out that in Christ, the law has lost its power to condemn us based on our failure. Why? Our lives are hidden with Christ in God!

When it comes to the administration of the prophetic among those who live under grace, any model of the prophetic that hearkens back to a law-based condemnation is wrong in an absolute sense. If people are now under grace, then they must be ministered to in light of this glorious reality. To minister to people who are under grace out of a law mindset is to bring the only message law can bring: condemnation. Has some so-called prophet ever railed at you? The angry prophet tends to deal with believers on the ability to maintain a high standard of performance. If you fail to perform or live up to their declared standard, you become a second-class believer who can never know the blessings of God. Wrong! This is not what grace is all about. Condemnation, judgment, criticism, and the like have nothing to do with grace. It is by the institution of grace that mercy now triumphs over judgment. In grace, the prophetic ministry now encourages, strengthens, and comforts; it heals, lifts up, and expresses compassion to the weak. It is as grace passes into the heart of the failing believer that a new source of strength is tapped. Even if we are going to define grace as unmerited favor, then any prophetic ministry had better fit into some expression of that definition. "Not of works lest any man should boast" is an operative perspective of the prophetic ministry that has grace as its true focus.

Of course, there is occasion where individuals who are proven to be in the prophetic office will confront individuals and groups of people, but that confrontation will never be a railing, angry denunciation. It will always carry with it attitudes of grace, humility and favor. The New Testament prophet has received the Spirit's administration of grace. He or she will have understood something of the depths from which they themselves have been drawn. In the administration of the prophetic office, what the prophet extends to people must agree with what Christ, the Great Prophet, now extends. The prophet now ministers the heart of Christ to mankind. Take a careful look at the concepts found in I Corinthians 13: "keeps no record of wrongs...always protects...always perseveres." The prophetic ministry under the new covenant is not exempt from this love standard. A study of Romans 12 establishes that the exercise of the prophetic is both linked to and tempered by love. Tragically, it seems that many who are said to minister in the prophetic office have not understood that those being ministered to are no longer under law but under the blood-bought forgiveness and acceptance of God. Forget this and what is being ministered in the name of the prophetic office is neither authentically prophetic nor of the heart of God.

Grace manifests through the broken heart of the prophet. The words of the prophet minister a grace characterized by gentleness and humility. Take this a little further. Every church staff member, every elder, should remember that they are bound by covenant to live as ministers whose hearts have been tempered by grace. If, in their relationships with one another and in their contact with members of the congregation, these leaders are not ministering grace, they are abusing the office to which they have been called. It is the marvel of unconditional acceptance inherent in grace that brings the broken individual to the feet of God in worship. This is precisely what those holding ministry positions are mandated to model. Nothing else is acceptable! It is this kind of grace that helps a man taken in a fall to recover joyfully from his fall. Christ is then recognized to be awesomely "the lifter of my head" (Psalm 3:3). Every prophet and every individual holding an office in the church should reflect seriously on whether or not grace is the sole and wonderful motive of their ministry to the hearts of broken people. To do otherwise is to place oneself in the high seat of judgment, and consequently, in a place of significant spiritual jeopardy.

18. Grace is God's sole answer to culture rot.

Radical shifts have taken place in western culture over the last few decades. This shift has been led by those committed to the imposition of humanistic principles upon every segment of society. Law, politics, government, medicine, education and social theory all reflect and embody the contra-moral principles of religious humanism. If anyone wants to understand what has happened to our western countries, then an examination of the humanist manifestos and our cultures is all it will take to recognize how successful the humanists have been in their subversion of historic democracy and freedom. There, in precept after precept, the redrafting of our social ethic is outlined. Sin of every sort is championed by the depravity of humanism and finds its strongest advocate in organizations like the Civil Liberty Unions, as well as the educational and media elite. These unions are not unions designed to defend historic democratic liberties but to further the subversive efforts of humanism via the manipulation of law and language.

What is the present day reality? Sin abounds in ways and depths that cannot even be measured and has become the ethic upon which men are trying to build society. In the last four decades, the imposition of the humanist religion has resulted in the progressive destruction of the moral principles upon which the stability and freedom of western society was built. This destruction is evidenced in every segment of our once-strong cultures. True, they were a long way from perfect, but they offered a significant degree of personal freedom requiring responsible moral self-government on the part of the individual citizen. Now, instead of a growth of freedom into something even more spiritually mature, graceless humanism has progressively become the force shaping western cultures. A cursory survey of the body of Christ would seem to indicate that even we have not learned how to feed upon the bread of grace.

Every genuine believer must answer the question of Psalm 11:3: "When the foundations are being destroyed, what can the righteous do?" Note it does not ask what the unrighteous, the Muslim or the politician should do. *The weight of responsibility is placed directly at the feet of the righteous!* Now skip over to Romans 5:21 where we read, "Just as sin reigned in death, so also grace might reign through righteousness." *Grace reigns* is a singularly significant statement. If we are to answer the call that our cultures are placing on us to be authentic Christians, then we must understand God's answer to the question raised in Psalm 11:3. What is the provision that so adequately can answer the human dilemma? It is so simple that we read Romans 5:20 (KJV), pass over it, and never recognize God's answer:

A DANGEROUS GRACE

Where Sin Abounds, Grace Much More Abounds

What is God's antidote in this age where sin is not only abounding but is championed as the correct legal and social ethic? Wherever sin abounds, in whatever measure it abounds, God has declared that *grace much more* than existent sin abounds. It is because of the power of God that flows through functional grace that it is never too late for individuals or even nations, and to suggest that it is too late for our western cultures is to spurn the grace of God and the absolute truth of Romans 5:20. Truth is wonderful and absolute, but if it does not come in the context of grace, we can offer no substantial answer to our perplexed societies.

How are the righteous supposed to respond to the humanistic destruction of cultural foundations? *Discover what it means to abound much more in the grace of God!* Grace is God's all-sufficient antidote to the poison of sin no matter how much sin there may be. Further, to this we add the knowledge that not only does grace much more abound, it is sufficient for any occasion. This truth about grace meeting our need extends far beyond the narrow limits of our personal needs. It extends to human society where sin is running rampant. If the church is not about grace, it is not about God, nor is it the church. If we will not pursue God to enable us to understand and become extenders of grace, then no answer remains for our decimated world. If grace is not working within the Christian community, then we have nothing credible to offer the world. *Grace is the imperative of the authentic, relevant church!* Satan, sin, committed sinners, humanists, abortionists, criminals, bad law, supreme courts, militant anarchists, God-hating feminists, and the sages of the New Age movement combined are no match for a grace-powered church! Grace demonstrated its power to change the world in the first stages of church history, and to suggest that grace has lost its capacity to change the world in the closing chapters of human history is to discountenance the grace potential and God! Those who declare it is too late for "my" church or "my" country don't understand that grace is always God's response to sin no matter what its quantifying dimension might be. The reality is that grace received has the power to save any nation or anyone it touches!

19. Grace is a mystery.

There is a latent, unspoken hunger for an understanding of grace in the heart of sincere believers. I have had believers come to me literally in tears thanking God that they heard something revelational on grace before they died. It is amazing that the word grace appears with such frequency in the New Testament and yet discovering something of the true nature of grace is apparently very difficult. In the process of taking courses at five seminaries I never had even a single, one-hour class on the subject, yet grace holds significance far beyond contemporary understanding. Paul begins and ends every one of his epistles with grace, and throughout each, some unique aspects of grace are revealed. In reading his letters, I used to skip over his introductory and closing remarks as though statements like, "Grace to you and peace" were not much more than a spiritual way to say "hello," or "so long for now." Then one day the Spirit arrested me with II Timothy 3:16 that said he had inspired *all* scripture and that *all* of it was profitable for doctrine, reproof, and correction. I could no longer slide over the opening salutations. When Paul said, "Grace be unto you," he was making a verbal declaration involving faith. He believed that grace would indeed be imparted to those who read or heard his epistles. Under divine influence he was declaring the heart and will of God for the believers. Making such a declaration constituted an act that called upon the Holy Spirit to respond to and release a measure of his grace to believers.

Paul said to the believers in Ephesus that they had "heard about the administration of God's grace that had been given to me for you." How had he come to understand grace? It was a mystery made known to him by revelation (Ephesians 3:2-3). What grace is and how it is to be ministered is a mystery that requires a specific work of the Holy Spirit. Grace cannot be ministered as long as it remains nothing more than a vague idea. The Holy Spirit makes it abundantly clear that believers are held responsible for "faithfully administering God's grace in its various forms" (I Peter 4:10). The reality is this: few have any substantial grasp of how the components of grace work in specifics, let alone know what its various forms might be. Pastors, ask the people in your congregation these kinds of questions to test for yourselves the depth of knowledge your people have regarding the various forms of grace. Not only is grace a substantial provision upon which believers can draw, it can be ministered in a wide variety of expressions.

Grace is a powerful resource that does not originate in the natural realm. It refuses to take prisoners but rather seeks to set the offender free. Some of the saddest words people can speak are, "I'll never forgive that person as long as I live," for by these words the injured party is condemned to being a life-long victim. Grace is a characteristic imparted by the Holy Spirit into the spirit of man taking root in the natural man, changing him. It must be grasped, assimilated into his character, and ministered out of that inwardly transformed personality. To speak of grace without this inward working having taken place is to speak of nothing more than religious shadows. The conduct, motives, priorities, attitudes, and actions of the grace-filled believer are incomprehensible to the natural man. The natural man looking at the grace-filled, grace-motivated individual is driven to a contemplation of at least the possibility of a loving, personal God who can be met and known. The atheist, faced with the embodiment of a mystery originating outside his limited natural frame of reference, may choose to ignore it, to make fun of something so out of sync with the natural order, or just hate it because it reveals something that he does not want to be revealed.

Or perhaps, seeing in this grace-endued life a hope that has no known source in the natural order, the desperate atheist might find his canary after all!

The question may be asked, "Okay then, how do I come to a functional comprehension of grace?" The answer is both simple and frustrating: *The mysteries of grace are made known by the revelatory ministry of the Holy Spirit.* When the believer begins to be taught by the Holy Spirit regarding the nature and workings of grace, those mysteries are unveiled. He alone is the one who can effectively take off the blinders so that grace can be seen for what it is and how it can be applied. Grace also brings with it an ability to apply it. Discovering a working understanding of grace requires seeking the Spirit and spending time meditating on grace scriptures. At the outset there was the full realization that anything said would be inadequate and imperfect, but it is hoped that in some small measure this book might offer a place to begin. Had I required perfection, I would never have begun the undertaking!

20. Grace is something that needs to be defined beyond the term "unmerited favor."

The term "unmerited favor" is incomplete in that it does not provide the believer with sufficient input. While grace can be said to come as an unmerited favor, the term itself does not tell us what the favor is. If a friend of mine we'll call Frank does me a favor at work that really blesses me and makes my day easier I may very well go home that evening uplifted. My wife looks at me and, seeing the bright countenance, asks me what I'm so happy about. I tell her, "Frank did me an absolutely wonderful favor." My curious wife will want more information. She may be happy that Frank did me a favor, but she will not rest as long as I keep saying, "Well, honey, he did me a favor." She will persist in asking, and if I simply repeat over and over again that he did me a favor, she will soon become frustrated. However, once I divulge the details, my wife will not only know what the favor was but also be able to share in my joy. *Grace that actually becomes functional causes celebration.* (Hey! There's that joy thing again!)

Do you suppose that many have not really started to celebrate and rejoice because while they know that God has done us a favor, they as yet do not know what the favor actually is? Well, how does this thing we call grace arrive at our hearts door? God, because of the completed earthly ministry of Christ, is now free to reach down to fallen man and impart the substance that he calls grace. The effect of grace is to draw mankind out of the self-life and toward God so that slavery to the sinful nature is broken. Grace allows God to extend life and unqualified acceptance to man based wholly on who Christ is and what he accomplished. God is love. His love generates mercy. His love and mercy sent Christ. Christ completed his work of redemption and returned to the Father. The Father is now free to extend grace to man.

Illustrated, the generation of grace may look like this:

GOD ➲ LOVE ➲ MERCY ➲ CHRIST ➲ EXTENDED GRACE

This, of course, is only part of the picture. God, by the Holy Spirit now administers grace to the heart and mind of man, but once that grace is dispensed, man still remains a responsible, free-will agent. Grace places significant responsibility on the recipient. There is nothing automatic about it. I Peter 4:10 requires of stewards that they be found faithful, and according to Luke 16:2, every believer is going to be called to give an account of their stewardship. When the Spirit administers grace into our lives, it comes with having to be its responsible agents, faithful and ready to give an account.

There is a dichotomy here regarding what it means to be responsible. How does grace make or hold us responsible? Being responsible does not mean the believer or minister assumes center stage and must bear the weight of the whole world. Rather, we must learn practically what it means to be the creature versus acting like the Creator. We are invited to act like God in Ephesians 5:1, but only in the full realization that we are always the creature, hence finite, limited, and incredibly weak. It is here that we can forget that if we want to really function in the things of the kingdom we must do so in child like ways, not as masters of all we survey, commanders of all we see. There is a paradox between being responsible and the recognition that we must be as children. There is a tension between leadership and servanthood. The more one serves the more one leads, and the more one leads, the more one serves! The truth is that in grace we never get to be more than servants.

Now lets go a bit further. Grace comes in varying measures of fullness. Christ was full of grace. It is recorded of the early church that great grace was upon them all. Implicitly then, the possibility exists for every believer to be *full of grace*, living under ever-increasing measures of grace. The alternative is to *miss* the grace of God, as stated in Hebrews 12:15. Here, scripture makes it clear that the responsibility of finding grace lies within the purview of the believer. This takes us beyond an ambivalent attitude toward grace. We may be back to finding Gracie at the train station.

The results of missing the grace of God can clearly be seen in the community of believers. As outlined in this passage of scripture, when grace is missed, there will be three visible consequences.

Bitter roots will manifest. There will be grudges and unforgiveness, hard feelings and broken relationships. Distinct rifts exist in what is supposed to be a loving community.

Trouble will be constant in the local fellowship. One difficulty or discord will be resolved only to go on to another. Trouble detracts from the ministry because so much effort is spent resolving disputes that have no eternal relevance.

Many will be defiled. Strong's Lexicon says *defile* means, "to pollute, sully, contaminate, soil, to dye with another color, to stain." Things happen, attitudes manifest, and problems occur that go unresolved, which results in a death to the vitality of individuals' faith. How many believers have had their faith stained by what goes on behind the scenes of the local assembly? What is the cause of many in the congregation being defiled? Missing grace. Grace cannot be missed without due and destructive consequence. A moral impact occurs when a moral offense takes place, and individuals are negatively affected in their spirit man.

Jude 8 speaks of defilement as being in evidence when there is slander and rejection of authority. A popular television ad once showed an elderly lady looking into her burger shouting out, "Where's the beef?" Believers and pastors alike should be calling out in loud and even extreme tones, "Where's the grace?" What does this mean for ministers, elders, deacons, Sunday school teachers, husbands, wives, and members of the congregation? Dare we let these kinds of questions go unanswered? But there is more!

II Peter 4:18 confronts us with the command to "grow in grace." Compliance is mandatory! Think about this: if grace is nothing more than "unmerited favor," what specifically can one do to meet the mandate to grow? Every believer has been charged by the Holy Spirit to be growing up in the grace of God. No matter how mature one perceives himself or herself to be, the imperative still stands in its absoluteness. There is no plateau that can be reached where growth in grace is no longer mandatory. The imperative is never rescinded. How one really grows in grace will be outlined later in the chapter on the grace paradigm. The intent here is simply to indicate a problem with unmerited favor as a definition of grace. The believer may very well inquire, "Okay preacher, how do I grow in grace?" As pastors, it seems that since the Holy Spirit charges the believer with growth in grace, we have distinct responsibility to explain what that means. If we do not do this, or if we define grace in terms of things that are not grace, how can we expect the believer to effect such growth?

In Acts 13:43, Paul and Barnabas came to Antioch in Pisidia where the people were "urged to continue in the grace of God." There are a number of things that could be addressed here, but we will consider only one. Paul is urging them to continue in grace, not imploring God to pour out his unmerited favor. The direction of this statement points outward toward man, not upward toward God. By urging them to continue in grace, he is making them responsible agents. Hence the question: what constitutes continuing in grace? In the absence of a specific revelatory understanding of grace, the temptation may be to build a theology that justifies that lack of understanding. Any position that suggests, "Well, it can't really be understood so just trust that you are continuing in grace" is simply inadequate. Continuing in grace cannot be a sort of Christian mysticism. It must become in some measure explicit. The failure to continue in grace occurs in our churches, our ministries, our marriages and even in our relationship with the world. Believers are most inclined to miss grace precisely when they are being called to continue in it. Finding what it means to continue in grace is frequently downright difficult because there is no pat formula to follow. Discovery comes only as a result of a growing and intimate relationship with the Holy Spirit.

To pursue an understanding of grace beyond the term "unmerited favor," we can examine II Corinthians 8:7: "But just as you excel in everything…see that you also excel in this grace of giving." Here Paul is charging the believers to "excel in this grace." In our present context, let's first look at the word *excel* as it pertains to unmerited favor. Believers could well ask, "How do I excel in something over which I have no power? How do I excel in something I cannot earn?" It comes out as an unreasonable demand: "You can't earn it or merit it, but you'd better excel in it!" It seems to me that we should at least be giving some answers of substance to these kinds of questions. What is being stated here exceeds the narrow confines of unmerited favor. Paul was calling believers to own their spiritual responsibility. The call to excel cannot be perceived as something that flows from God in an unmerited fashion. Excelling was something required of the believers, not of God. God was very much active here, but in a measure that takes us beyond the expression "unmerited favor." If this term stands alone, it is likely to be perceived as requiring little on the part of the believer. It is as though all is left up to God.

Now, what aspect of grace was Paul urging them to excel in? The act of giving. Giving is an inevitable fruit of functional grace. If believers really tapped into grace, their giving would be just as radical as that of the Macedonian churches. The presence of functional grace can be measured by the generosity and selflessness of those giving. When grace is functionally present, there's no need to implore or manipulate giving. Rather, there may well be the need to restrain the givers in their liberality.

In wrapping this up then, there is a real need for the body of Christ to understand grace in terms that lead beyond *unmerited favor*. Why? The term "unmerited favor" is non-specific. If we fail to develop our concepts beyond such generalizations, then our practice of grace can only operate on a hit-or-miss basis. Even if God sent a revival, many would rise up and tear it to pieces simply because they do not understand his grace. The flesh wars against the spirit and the spirit against the flesh when the Holy Spirit shows up in real demonstration of power. Attitudes, motives, conduct, and speech reveal their actual spiritual state and to whom they are actually aligned. Mark it clearly: whenever the Holy Spirit moves in revival, war ensues in the pew, on the board, and in the wider Christian community. Revival is the enactment of spiritual realities by spiritual power impacting the natural realm and constitutes the presence and power of the Holy Spirit. The ultimate reason why revival seems so hard to come into does not rest in heaven, as though God is unwilling to release it. The problem is with us. Revival brings with it a variety of controversial issues. In the absence of grace, no mechanism exists by which those issues can be resolved. Unresolved issues spawn strife, criticism, in-fighting, broken relationships, and church splits. The flesh simply wins out over the spirit. Apart from functional grace, man is left to his own puny determination to love others. Why would God send a flourishing, continuing revival that would just sweep thousands of new converts into a church that is ignorant of grace and full of aberrant relational chaos? We may well pray, "Thy kingdom come," but never apart from grace! If we would pray for revival, we should first pray for grace, and grace in such measure that a genuine manifestation of the Sons of God follows!

21. Grace is the only viable foundation for our churches and ministries.

A church cannot be greater than the portion of grace upon which it rests and operates. What man calls great and what God considers great are frequently in conflict. Several things can produce what appears to be a great church: the power of a charismatic personality, powerful preaching that draws a crowd, administrative genius, a multifaceted program, entertaining services, a beautiful building, even caring ministerial staff can all be mistaken for the stuff that authenticates a church as being great. But if a church is to be truly great, it must have a depth of spiritual authenticity that validates it before God himself.

What needs to be probed is this: Why are we doing what we are doing? Christian ministry is not initially about how many people attend a church, about doing ministry, or even about getting a lot of people to say the sinner's prayer. It *is* about modeling the love of God, about loving people at your own cost because you have experienced the reality of God's love for mankind. If what I'm doing is about me apart from the passions of God's heart then the motivation is self-centered and, in final reality, is idolatry. Jesus sought Peter out after the resurrection, and they had a conversation on the beach. Peter is asked three times by Christ, "Peter, do you love me?" Each time Peter answers that he loves Christ, and each time Christ tells him to look after the sheep. The root motivation Christ is calling for here is a depth of love that serves even to death, not some kind of simulated, self-generated facade of love, but an all-compelling passion for people as people, no matter who they are, how well they perform, or what they may or may not have done. Do you remember when you first met your spouse? For most people, there was that passion of love that drove you on. It was as though you just couldn't help yourself. Well, love is like that—a love for people that causes us to keep on keeping on in ministry simply because we just can't help ourselves. *Great churches and great ministries are first measured for their greatness in the invisible dimensions of the human heart*—and God gets to be the one doing the measuring! He is looking for the mark of a supernatural love for people—his kind of love!

Kingdom building can carry with it powerful motivational factors that have nothing to do with really loving people. Position, recognition, control, and status with peers render their own deep satisfactions. Who among us in the natural does not purr at the sounds of others' adulation? How many people have ventured into some aspect of ministry only to be deeply offended, scandalized, wrongfully accused and betrayed, not once but many times? As the offenses and betrayals took their toll, the desire for ministry waned, the power of inner hurt took control, and those who once served with genuine authenticity and zeal are not even going to church anymore. Only a supernaturally generated love gripping the believer can drive him past human offenses and betrayals. You see, in asking Peter about love, Christ knew that a genuine love for God was the only device that would sustain him in his coming struggle of ministry. Romans 5:1-5 provides a profile for any great church, ministry, or minister. Read these few verses:

[1]Therefore, since we have been justified through faith, we have peace with God through our Lord Jesus Christ, [2]through whom we have gained access by faith into this grace in which we stand. And we rejoice in the hope of the glory of God. [3]Not only so, but we also rejoice in our sufferings, because we know that suffering produces perseverance; [4]perseverance, character; and character, hope. [5]And hope does not disappoint us, because God has poured out his love into our hearts by the Holy Spirit, whom he has given us.

According to these verses, by *faith* we have come into *grace*. Because of grace that actually affects our lives we *rejoice* in the fact that God will be *glorified*. Once we have come into this grace, life takes a sharp left-hand turn into adversity and suffering. Consider where grace ultimately took Peter. So much for the notion that grace leads to a flowery bed of ease! Read it like this: "Danger ahead!" Most of us hate suffering, so we spend our time pleading with God to get us out of our trouble, but God doesn't use his power to vanquish our struggle. Instead, he uses it to produce in us a perseverance that produces character, which produces hope, which in turn overcomes disappointment. We need to get a hold of this dimension of truth.

We should perhaps note that the last stage of development before the Holy Spirit starts to pour out his love in our hearts and the world is *disappointment*.

I wonder how many people have quit at the point of disappointment without realizing that they were just about to come into the manifest love of God? He has poured his love into our hearts by the Holy Spirit, and we, in turn, are to pour it out to the world. If it isn't in us first, it can't be poured out! His love can be shed abroad because it has become the deep characteristic of our own hearts.

Grace brings the church into genuine expressions of I Corinthians 13, which in turn lends authenticity to the message of the gospel and the gifts of the Holy Spirit. You remember, "Though I speak in tongues…have faith to move mountains…though I prophesy and understand all mysteries…" without love it means nothing. Grace sets supernatural love at the heart of what is being ministered. Love is the benchmark of anything that heaven considers great. How do we get there? Love is discovered in the heart by the Spirit's ministry of grace. A great church is like the church of Acts 4:33, of which it can be said, *"Great grace was upon them all."* We live in a climate of negativism; however, the intent here is not to flog the church for its failings but to flag a possible course of action for struggling pastors and those who have been wounded. If evidences of grace are not inherent in our community, the possibility of credible witness is, at best, severely limited. The measure of grace is the measure of greatness, and great grace ensures authentic witness!

I understand there is more to the gospel than grace, but my purpose is to make a case for grace! The intent is to stir people to go back to the Spirit and scripture to discover grace in more practical terms. Don't send me letters of protest. How well and precisely I have spoken of grace is not as important as a radical discovery of grace that flows in its diversity of blessing and power. Hopefully some will be so provoked that they will find sufficient cause to chase grace and share that revelation with a needy world!

22. Grace is the way truth gains its proper influence in our daily Christian lives.

The need for truth is absolute. However if grace is not administered by the Spirit and then received by the individual through an act of faith, truth will not prevail. Truth did not come alone. In John 1:14, Christ came into the world full of grace and truth. Paul puts grace and truth together in Colossians 1:6 when he speaks of understanding grace in its context of truth. Why point this out? Many believers *know* the truth but have significant difficulty *living* it. John 17:17 declares the Word of God is truth, which acts as a compass for the grace-filled heart to follow. The word of truth comes requiring a heart-centered response. If grace has not first done its preparatory work in the heart, then when the seed of the word comes, the heart can't respond to that truth and we either give up or live with guilt. Grace changes the fundamental nature of the heart so that when the seed of the word falls upon it, the heart can respond joyfully because obedience is a privilege, not an obligation. The heart lacking grace in a particular area cannot yield genuine spiritual obedience in that area. Any obedience will have been a work of the flesh rather than a love response to the Word, who is Christ!

As an example, Ephesians 5:25 says, "Husbands love your wives as Christ loved the church." The standard is clearly set for every Christian husband. Make a quick trip through the church community, and few men have ever really learned to love their wives in the way scripture commands. The traditional marriage vow carries with it a statement that says, "to have and to hold," but how about the phrase, "to love and to cherish"? To have and to hold carries clear implication of the physical dimension of the marriage relationship, but cherishing carries implications far beyond the physical. Ask most men who have been married for a few years if they know what it means to cherish their wife, and in my experience not many understand the gentle stewardship of their wives. How many husbands really strive to find the grace required in loving their wives as Christ loves the church?

Other scriptural principles, such as wives submitting to their husbands, are standards of conduct that many resist and some find outright offensive. The possibility of finding women who know and practice the biblical definition of submission to their husbands is rather remote in contemporary culture, which often includes the Christian community. We live as though concepts like "cherish" and "obey" are nothing more than nice words spoken in the wedding ceremony.

What about tithes and offerings? How many find reason to overlook this objectionable mandate of scripture?

The point in referring to these particular principles is simply to underline the critical need for the discovery of functional grace. We can know the standards scripture sets for us and can even try to bring our life practice into obedience with them, but when the pressure is on, we just can't bring ourselves into the obedience called for by scripture. While we may know the truth, as in these three examples, it may not be the governing factor in our daily lives and practice. We preach truth only to discover that people do not experience the abundance of life that Christ came to bring. If grace is not given its proper place in our teaching, then truth will neither prevail nor set us free. Why? God did not expect us to live obediently apart from grace. Conformity to Christ cannot be attained until grace becomes a functional inner reality that proves to be more powerful than external circumstances and adversities.

I had good preachers in my early Christian life that always gave clear exegesis of biblical truth. In my seminary training, the law was emphasized as the only way to straighten out what was going on in the church. In the first years of my ministry, I was never accused of failing to preach the truth. Yet in spite of my efforts to preach truth, there were constant negative reactions to what I was preaching. I thought that they didn't really want to hear the truth because they were carnal Christians, and that was all there was to it.

Then the Holy Spirit began to allow some destruction to take place in the ministry. A group of individuals rose up to get rid of me as the pastor of the church. Never once did they suggest that I had failed to preach the truth, but I was preaching truth that stood alone. I didn't understand what was really going on. Then one day while reading II Corinthians 3, I came to verse 6 that says, "The letter kills but the Spirit gives life." It began to dawn on me that I was called to be the minister of "a new covenant," the covenant of grace. I discovered that even the truths of the New Testament could be preached as law. Now if the law of the Old Testament resulted in death, how much more deadly is a New Testament law? At least in the Old Covenant you didn't die for looking at a woman with lust in your heart. How many men in our churches would be dead under New Testament law? I had not linked truth with its necessary precursor, grace, so even though I preached the truth, I was killing my congregation. I had become an effective assassin of the believer, sharpening the New Testament into a sword of legalistic truth. I could get a lot of people to the altar, shaking and weeping, not under the weight of the Holy Spirit but under the deadly arrows of truth, the weight of which could kill the most ardent believer. It was not infrequent for me to send them back to their pews thinking they had not understood and would restate the call to the duty of truth. Again, the flood to the front took place. Grace has been interposed between the Holy God and fallen man. Man dare not look into truth apart from the mercy that comes with grace. We must preach the truth, but if we miss the grace context, we will surely miss mercy. At that point we are left with bare truth, with the letter. What result do we then find? Death!

An illustration of the letter killing God's people is found in I Samuel 6:19. The Philistines had returned the Ark of the Covenant to Israel. Some of the men of Geth Shemesh had found the ark and wanted to know if Aaron's staff, the jar of manna, and the tablets of the law were still inside. They removed the mercy covering to look into the ark containing the Law and were immediately subjected to the impossible standards of the law: seventy men fell dead. Take mercy away and man dies before a holy God. Mercy triumphs over judgment because Christ went into the "Most Holy Place once for all by his own blood" (Hebrews 9:12), and thereby the new covenant, characterized by grace, mercy, and peace, was set in place. Truth must be declared in its context of grace, that in turn extends mercy, and men live. We have no other covenant to preach, no other covenant to live by. We abide in the truth by grace, or we do not abide in the truth at all. Preach as we will, if we preach truth out of the context of grace, people will not come to the expressions of life as defined in the New Testament. I've shuddered as I recall some of the things I have declared to God's people. I have sought Him for his forgiveness and to this day marvel that he did not strike me dead. Indeed, he extended his grace and mercy even to a law-preaching machine. As believers and ministers of the new covenant, all of life should succumb to the marvelous, life-transforming influences of a divine grace. There is no higher ground for us to find than life lived on the blood bought plateau of grace received and ministered, one to all and all to one! Grace is to truth what the sunrise is to the earth. It is as the sunrise of grace takes place in our hearts that truth can be properly discerned, studied, and lived.

23. Grace is the only way to come into a genuine servant motivation.

Jesus said in Matthew 20:26, "He that would be greatest among you must be servant of all." This statement strikes at the very heart of our human nature because as humans, our core motivation is to be the boss. We don't like being subordinate. The further down the ladder of subordination one lives, the greater the inclination to demean others and ourselves. Jesus said he had not come to be served but to serve, and on one occasion demonstrated this by washing his disciples' feet. He did this knowing that in a couple of hours they would all leave him to die alone. Servanthood is anathema to the natural man, and it seems to be so in much of the body of Christ. The drive to be the boss, to get ahead and to climb the ladder is just as apparent in the body of Christ as it is in the corporate world. So often staff members chafe under the leadership of the senior pastor. Discontent sets in if one's idea of proper promotion and recognition are not extended. The season of discontent only lasts for a while before it leads to an open revolt with the rebels leading segments of congregations down the road to start a new church. Only God knows how many churches have been established as a result of the rejection of the servant heart.

The natural heart cannot find satisfaction in servanthood. "Greatest" and "servant of all" is an unacceptable paradox to the natural man and carnal believer. We may offer assent to servant motives, but when servanthood calls us to climb onto the cross, the human heart cannot rise to its calling. A step down into lower tasks like cleaning the church washrooms seems best done by a paid person. If believers and individuals in ministry positions really want to be the greatest then the call is to serve all; not just the nice people who treat you right, but even the unpleasant and ungrateful. That's where the spiritual heart finds its proving ground. If we cannot stand the pressures of taking the lowest position, we cannot qualify for authentic leadership in the kingdom of God.

While scripture speaks of becoming great through the practice of servanthood, it does not explain how this principle works to make one great. Nonetheless, servanthood is a flat-out, absolute principle of the kingdom of God. If a person really wants to be great as defined by God, there is only one way: practiced, disciplined servanthood. Believers should note that it is not education, recognition, financial prosperity, or being the right race that makes one great. Are you one of the "wrong" ethnic group or economic background? There is a way to level the playing field: discover the dynamics of servanthood. Matthew 6:33 sets this out very clearly: "Seek ye first the kingdom of heaven and all these things will be added unto you." Here we find things being *added* versus being *acquired*. It's supernatural *addition* over natural *achievement*. All people, no matter what constraints they find themselves in, can determine to seek the kingdom of God and his righteousness as life's motivation, can seek true righteousness versus self aggrandizement, can seek the success of others first. There are no restrictions here. If you are looking for a way out of present difficulty, if you want to serve God in greater dimension, then remember Galatians 6:7—"A man reaps what he sows." Find someone to associate with and pour all your energies into making that person successful. Whatsoever a man sows that shall he also reap.

Servanthood, God's great key to true success and liberty, demands a fundamental change in our natures. We cannot become good servants simply because we *decide* to be good servants. There must be an administration of grace in such a profound measure that serving becomes the motivation and joy of our lives. Lots of people will line up to take a position in a church or company, but are they seen as occasions to get ahead or occasions to help another succeed? True servanthood has submission to Christ as its sole agenda. Serving to get ahead is idolatry. Grace becomes the watershed here. God knows the state of the heart. We may hide the real motivation of our hearts from those around us, but God is never fooled. Moses, Joseph, Mordecai, Esther, David, Daniel, and Christ, to name a few, all found their greatness in servant roles. Any endeavor to serve apart from a nature change is simply religious duty. The result of such self-effort can only breed conflict, hurt, disappointment, and spell the end of unity as mandated by scripture. The best way to find yourself in the flow of God's agenda for your life is to come into a servant motivation that is nothing less than an expression of a grace-replaced nature. Much more could be said as to why servanthood is the prime prerequisite for bringing God's intervention into our lives, but let me give you one illustration. Consider Joseph: it was as he exercised servanthood that God became the power behind his service, deliverance, and exaltation in a pagan environment.

24. Grace is the currency upon which the heavenly economy operates.

I made a couple of ministry trips to the tiny country of Qatar in the Middle East. While there I was paid in the currency of that country called the riyal. When I was in Qatar, I could go to any store in that country and purchase anything I needed. I brought some of that money back to Canada. If I went into a store here at home and tried to pay with the riyal, the clerk would look at me in astonishment and, in simple terms, refuse to sell me what I need. If I want to have my needs met, I have to conform to the monetary unit upon which the economy operates. No matter how hungry my children are or how much I may need groceries, if I do not pay in an acceptable currency, my need will go unmet. It doesn't mean the grocery clerk is mean, it just means I do not have the right and acceptable currency.

Grace is the heavenly currency. If we want to plug into the economy of God's kingdom, then we must discover what currency heaven trades on, appropriate that currency, learn its value and how to trade on it. Hebrews 4:16 makes it plain that what heaven dispenses is fully able to help us in our time of need. In this verse believers are directed to "come boldly to the throne of grace, that we may obtain mercy and find grace to help in time of need."

Every believer comes to the throne of grace with needs peculiar to his or her life, and yet each receives one thing and one thing only: grace. We are all invited, even directed to come before the throne of grace. There, every believer must learn the mystery of grace. What mystery? How the grace given by God is designed to meet their needs. If we do not learn what grace is and how it works, we will not know how to "spend" grace so that our needs are met. But if we do the promise is clear—it will help you in your time of need. What needs are you facing? Go beyond financial considerations and think in terms of your job, your relationships, your past, your broken heart, the fears that dominate you, your inability to express and receive love, your lack of insight to discern God's plan for your life, the need to become supernatural in working the works of Christ, or your inadequate prayer and devotional life. No matter what you fill in the blank with, one thing is certain: you can come boldly before God without fear of condemnation and know God will give you grace. Have you discovered how to receive and spend heaven's currency? It will meet your need, and in the process you will discover an intimacy with the Holy Spirit and a lifestyle that is progressively supernatural.

25. Grace is sole means by which national destinies can be directed back to God.

"Where sin abounds grace much more abounds." In every segment of western culture sin not only abounds, it is finding judicial and political authentication. Arbitrary secularism has become the guiding vehicle in western culture. All opposed to the prevailing madness of secularism must be stamped out. In his book, *1984*, George Orwell wrote an allegory that closely aligns with humanism. In this book, Newspeak is being pushed on a total society, whose aim is "not to extend but diminish the range of thought" (247), and "to make all other modes of thought impossible" (246). As the tenets of humanism become the prevailing rules by which human culture is governed, we can look to this author for the ultimate end of such a philosophy: "If you want a picture of the future, imagine a boot stamping on a human face—forever" (220).

Michael Denton wrote in 1985 what he conceived was humanism's gift to humanity when he said: "The social and political currents which have swept the world in the past eighty years would have been impossible without [the] intellectual sanction [of the Darwinian revolution]. It is ironic to recall that it was the increasingly secular outlook in the nineteenth century which initially eased the way for the acceptance of evolution, while today it is perhaps the Darwinian view of nature more than any other that is responsible for the agnostic and skeptical outlook of the twentieth century" (358). Who was Mr. Denton? An agnostic molecular biologist from New Zealand who could never bring himself to admit there was a God, but also rejected the theory of evolution, not only for its internal inconsistencies but also for its obvious fallout on a society that had accepted evolution as a foundation for its all-pervading cultural philosophy.

In every historic western democracy the historic foundations of law are being systematically destroyed. Human culture floats on the judicial whims of appointed justices sitting in their robes of authority. The dust clouds of their arrogance have systematically obscured the will of the people. Their arrogant intolerance knows no bounds, and they drag our cultures into the mire of legislated tyranny and depravity.

Millions in the third world are being swept into the Kingdom, but in western democracies—the source from which the gospel has reached the uttermost parts—spiritual leaders are left to ponder why so little is happening of the supernatural at home. We hear talk of a coming revival and of taking our nations back for God while culturally things grow darker and darker. The death mentality of savage humanism seems determined to strangle all life and hope from the population. Believers pray for revival and their sincerity is unquestionable, yet a drug-sodden population staggers on in prescribed bondage. The church continues to hold her Sunday and mid-week meetings, singing songs of conquest like "Onward Christian Soldiers" and "Blow the trumpet in Zion," but somehow our cultures continue towards the rocky shore of destruction.

Concerned leaders and believers ponder the church's apparent impotence, asking: Why don't people respond to the gospel? Is there too much wealth? Are the people of God too indifferent? Has the hour of our visitation past? Is judgment all that's left for our Western nations? Listen to some who speak as prophets and you can easily get the feeling that all is hopeless: We had better just get ready for the judgment of God! The enemy is at the gate and there is no help or hope of deliverance!

May I be so bold as to suggest why the church is impotent in the face of the ever-increasing incursions of humanistic hate? **The absence of functional grace!** The answer is so simply stated that we look for something more complex. "Oh, no brother, it must be more difficult to encapsulate an answer than just those few words." But it's right there in Romans 5:20! Read it again:

"Where sin abounds, *grace much more abounds*" [emphasis added]. (Stuff in bold print is silent shouting!).

Grace is the solution. There is enough grace for the reformation of our nations *or God is a liar!* What is wrong with or in the church is exactly the same thing that is wrong in the world. What's wrong in the family, between husband and wife, parent and child, is absolutely and fundamentally the absence of grace as a functional reality. The world, the church, and the family cannot find its redemption apart from grace. It should be noted that this scripture gives us God's perspective on abounding sin. His perspective is not the pouring out of judgment but rather abounding grace. Men declare judgment; God declares much more grace!

There is much more than enough grace to turn our nations back to God and to heal the body of Christ from her self-inflicted wounds. As long as grace is available, reformation is within the reach of grace-drenched believers. Believers who discover what it means to be full of grace are well able to redirect the destiny of nations. *Ensconced humanism can be toppled by a slight flick of God's little finger.* To the natural-eyed believer, those humanists who now appear entrenched in the places of power and authority have the look of a Goliath. How does the church stand before this boasting, arrogant, God-defying Goliath of humanism? How much do we look like the quivering army of Israelites when confronting their satanic threats and promised destruction? Oh, yes, they kept up appearances, but the truth is they were cowards. The Israelites were inspectors of the problem for sure, but they had zero capacity to understand that freedom to be true worshippers of God was at stake along with the freedom of their families and country from the tyranny of another religion.

Make no mistake: religious humanism, secularism, atheism, materialistic rationalism—whatever name you choose, is the religion dominating the social, political, educational, and judicial ethic of our western nations. We can either wring our hands in despair, overwhelmed by the Goliath of secularism, or head down into the valley of confrontation knowing that the battle is the Lord's, and he is the one who gives the victory. The notion that where sin abounds, grace much more abounds may sound straightforward, but until we are willing to confront our Goliath by our acts of faith, grace lies dormant at the throne of God. With man, the challenges posed by ensconced humanism constitute a cultural impossibility for the body of Christ, but with God, nothing is impossible. Nothing is too hard for God! The true church of Christ still has a God-given mandate to occupy until Christ comes.

Reformation—the rebuilding of foundations, national destinies, and the future liberty of our children—all are within the scope of discovered grace! Abandon grace and nothing remains but the completed destruction of freedom embedded in legislated humanism. Unless believers discover grace abounding in their own hearts, no Christ-centered response to the satanic destruction of our western cultures will appear on the scene of human history. The victories of grace that other generations of Christians have gained will become mere landmarks in history. Preachers, preach all that is on your heart, but if we do not bring the body of Christ into a functional discovery of grace, the church will fail in her biblical mandate to evangelize the world in the measure and manner He intended! We will have failed to achieve all heaven intended us to achieve, and the world will miss the full-blown witness and final reformation he intended her to have!

To the individual reader who has persevered through what must appear be wordy stuff, begin to make your own list of what grace is. Disagree with me as you please, reject whatever you wish of what I have said, but don't stop with your disagreement or rejection. Begin your own pursuit of grace. End up elsewhere, but end up somewhere in an understanding of what it means to be full of grace. Learn something as well that has to do with communicating a grace that has functional value in the lives of those around you. Throw the book away, but be stirred up to know what is meant by abounding grace that brings heaven's resources to bear on the needs of humanity. After all, it is grace we need, not the limited perceptions of one man. II Peter 1:2-3 sets out a concept that appeals to the linear thinking pattern common to the western mind: "*Grace* and peace be yours in abundance…His divine *power* has given us everything we need…through him who called us by his own *glory* and goodness." As we've noted before, the pattern is this: *grace* leads to *power*, which leads to *glory*. If we want our personal lives and our churches to demonstrate the glory of God, we must discover in practical terms how grace leads to power, which brings us into God's manifest glory. Do we want the glory of God restored to the end-time church? Then we must come via the grace gate. No other way into his glory exists, so in all of your getting, dear friend, get grace!

Chapter Five
Once More—with Heart!

Grace is the means by which the believer is empowered to live the authentic Christian experience, working from the inner most part of the new creature. It causes a passion for the world, produces the agape counter culture, transforms the vilest of sinners, is the healing power of God for the human soul, and sets the captive free! It is grace that produces the supernatural community that bears witness to the healing power of God. We are to come into the expressed reality of the kind of love that is nothing short of a manifestation of agape. Our proclamation to the world only has credibility when our declaration of love has credibility. If we fail to be the express agape counter culture we profess to be, we will fail to convince the world that God sent Christ into the world. Consider the pattern, grace to power to glory, in John 17:22-23, where glory becomes a manifest aspect of the church as a direct result of functional grace: "I have given them the glory that you gave me." Now why did He give us the glory? "That they may be one as we are one...brought into complete unity." Our unity is the manifestation of that glory! Note the next result: "to let the world know that you sent me and have loved them even as you have loved me." No matter what programs we run, the world will never really come to the knowledge that God sent Christ into the world until this manifest unity characterizes our congregations. Note as well the word "complete." Partial, self-generated, or superficial unity is not the kingdom unity scripture sets before us as the world-winning standard. Unity that is complete must be our manifest glory. We've all heard the admonition, "God will not share his glory with another." He may not *share* it, but Christ has *given* it to us as part of his grace covenant. A way into the glory of God in this present life is ours *by covenant!*

Christ set out in his Word a commandment for us to walk in love, declaring that love is the fulfillment of the law and prophets (Matthew 22:39-40). Is there a man or woman who could love with the capacity that dwells in the heart of God in and of themselves? The answer with ultimate finality is, "No!" I often ask congregations why they think God set an impossible standard, beyond human character and strength to fulfill. Grace is the only way into that place where love, supernaturally imparted by God, becomes the manifest reality in the body of Christ. How then is this single evidence to become characteristic of the relationships between believers in the local assembly, between believers of different persuasion, and between the believer and a lost, blind world?

I want to underline what I've said earlier: In reality, the so-called believing community is one of the toughest places on earth to survive, long term. We shouldn't wonder why it is so hard to win the lost when what is going on in the heart of local churches can be more a savor of hell than a foretaste of heaven! I was speaking in a church in a southern state on this concept of what the church looks like when believers miss the grace of God. The pastor of the church I was in said he'd been in a town where the conflict between a pastor and the board of the church was so severe that on one occasion, just before the pastor of that assembly got up to preach the gospel of Christ, he pulled a loaded pistol out of his pocket and laid it on the pulpit beside the Bible!

The mission statement of the much-maligned Toronto Airport church is *to walk in the Father's love and give it away.* Despite every effort on the part of that ministry to be authentic ministers of a supernatural love, believers and Christian leaders form long lines taking turns trying to destroy what God is doing through that one part of the body of Christ. War among the saints doesn't seem to bother us, and is often spun as being theologically correct! Even Judas was devastated to the point of suicide when he realized that his actions ultimately resulted in the shedding of innocent blood, yet believers having different experiences in God or holding different theological convictions are fair game for destructive thrusts of hate.

In the absence of grace, hate becomes a dominant characteristic of human relationships. Hate is practiced extensively in the body of Christ even as we sing, "He is Lord." Let me give you a bit of what Vine has to say about hate: "Malicious feelings toward others...Mutual animosity...A relative preference for one thing over another that manifests itself by expressing aversion or disregard for the claims of another." How many so-called spiritual leaders let the hate in their hearts live on their tongues under the cover of theology? Those who express hate toward others who love and serve Christ have no guts for looking into their own hearts to discover their antithetical testimony to Christ. I John 3:15 tells us, "Anyone who hates his brother is a murderer, and you know that no murderer has eternal life in him." To hold a strong and verbalized antipathy toward other believers is nothing short of the practice of hate. Such animosity is the single greatest evidence that no functional grasp of grace exists in the hearts of its practitioners, no matter where they sit on Sundays!

Somehow, our personalized theology is such that we consider ourselves exempted from pouring love on the brethren and instead feel mandated to abuse believers who are moving in different theological expressions of the same biblical Christianity. There is a brother who has carried an essential mandate of reform in Canada. He is well known for his strong, courageous, and needed witness in our nation. I received a letter from him in which he poured a volume of verbal abuse on another body of believers who are moving in a different expression of Christ.

For those who are alarmed by what you've just read, please note: grace does not imply a departure from the historic doctrines of the faith. Neither do I imply anything of a non-biblical, ecumenical nature. However, if you read many books by pastors and Christian writers, it won't be long before you find blatant expressions of thinly disguised hate. Take a hard, honest look at the definition of the word hate: we seem to be better at hating than we are at showing love, mercy, and forgiveness. The call to maintain the unity of the Spirit is rendered optional because we have mistaken our own theologies for the Word of God, and John 17:23 is rendered irrelevant when hate grips the heart.

I cannot shout on a page, but *apart from grace, there can be no true obedience to the Word!* Grace, functional grace, is the *only* remedy for the negative relational attitudes that are manifest among believers. If those who truly love Christ will go to Him seeking to be filled with his grace, then love of the brethren is the guaranteed result. Only when we have experienced God's love poured out in our hearts will the commandment to love one another find fulfillment in the church.

Let me show you why grace discovered transforms the church into a supernatural power witness and a joyfully loving culture. I often ask congregations, "Why did God create mankind?" I get answers like we were saved to serve, created to glorify and worship him, or to exercise dominion over the earth. Most of the time the answers given have to do with some dimension of man's responsibility, his duty, toward God. They all have *man* as the central focus. But the answer is simple and direct: *God created man so that he could pour out his love on him.* God's whole creative motivation was *love*. He is love and he created every individual who has ever drawn breath solely so that He could love that individual! Love was and is God's all-consuming passion when it comes to mankind, saved and unsaved alike. If we miss this passion, we miss what being Christian is all about and the Spirit of God has no mandate to empower any ministries we establish! This is true no matter how needed, noble, or theologically correct such ministry appears. Is this not what is meant by phrases like the one in I Corinthians 13 that says, "but have not love, I gain nothing"?

God created man with a single motivation in mind: He wanted someone to love! He therefore created a natural world for man to live in, fashioned a wonderful garden, and set him in that environment to live in a spiritual reality called grace. Once Adam and Eve fell from grace into sin, God, being both a holy God and a God of all consuming love, had two fundamental problems. The first was the problem of sin. The second problem was, in many ways, more difficult than the first: Man no longer had a heart desire for God. He was lost, cut off from God, and was no longer naturally inclined toward God. Do a little investigating on your own. Walk up to most people on the street and tell them you want to talk to them about Christ; or go knocking on a few doors and see how responsive the folks are behind those doors. One result of the fall has been a profound loss of sensitivity toward the very Being who offers nothing less than life itself!

So God had two fundamental problems. God created man to be a creature upon whom he could pour his love. Man, however, was perversely content to live apart from the environment of grace, and his heart was closed off to God. Left alone without the love intervention of God, man would live out his life in sin, content never to know God and ultimately finding his eternal residence to be an address in hell. God on the other hand, being the God of infinite love, could not settle for the status quo of sin. Picture it something like this: God, seeing the problem of sin, held a conference in heaven with the Son and the Holy Spirit. There, the eternal plan of redemption was considered. Christ volunteered to be the Lamb without spot or blemish, slain before the foundation of the world. In due time he came into the world, took our place and died on the cross for the sin of mankind. How much sin did Christ pay for? He in fact paid the price for the sin of every human being in our neighborhoods, our towns, cities, and nations, even if they have never been converted. So the first problem was solved, but even though all their sin was paid for, men still had no desire for God or the life that God offered us in

Christ. Time, as it were, for a second conference in heaven. Christ and the Holy Spirit sit down with the Father in the heavenly boardroom to consider this second problem. The Father God may have said something like, "Good job, Son; the sin of humanity is no longer a problem to me. However, mankind still has no desire to fellowship with us." It was agreed that the second part of the plan should be instituted and grace be imparted into the world, so the Holy Spirit says to the Son, "Well, you did a splendid job, but now it is my turn."

The Father-God says to the Holy Spirit, "Are you ready? Let's surprise Saul of Tarsus. He's the toughest case on the books. He has no desire for us. In fact he *hates* Christ and all those who belong to him." With a gleeful look in his eye the Father reaches down into his own heart of love, takes a handful of his desire, gives it to the Holy Spirit who then swoops down upon Saul as he rides along the Damascus road, knocking him off his high horse and *deposits that heaven-sent desire into Saul's heart!* Instantly, beyond the physical effects of this event, Saul's heart was made new. One moment he was breathing out hatred and murder, and the next, his heart was forever changed. What he did not desire one moment, an instant later he desired. How do we know this? Because suddenly, the man who was "breathing out murderous threats against the Lord's disciples" addresses Christ saying, "Who are you Lord?" (Acts 9:5). God had overcome the deficit of desire in the heart of rebellious man. So it is with all who have come to believe in Christ. Mankind has no desire in the heart for God, so God takes the desire of love that burns in his own heart and places it into the human breast.

This act by which God places his desire in our heart is a central aspect of what functional grace is all about. (Now watch this, because this is the source of the flow of functional grace.) God is love. He created mankind upon whom he could pour out his love. Man sinned and lost his love desire to fellowship with the God who loved him. God sent Christ to pay the penalty for sin and then sent the Holy Spirit into the world to fill our hearts with the heavenly deposit of the love desires of God. The effect of grace might be stated like this: what I did not desire one moment I desired the next. Let me take a minute and connect the love of God with the concept of desire. For those of you who have ever fallen in love, do you remember the one all-consuming characteristic of that love? Passionate desire. For lovers, no little peck on the cheek will suffice. There is a radical passion of burning desire that demands a total intimacy and is the only way that love finds satisfaction. For first love, no lukewarm expression will do.

We all know the song "Amazing Grace." The writer John Newton was a slave trader, so vile in his character and conduct that at one point, even the ship's unregenerate sailors put him off, refusing to have him on board any longer. He had no desire for God and was the perfect embodiment of abounding sin. God who had heard the prayers of Newton's godly mother for her son, decided to answer her prayers. With a gleam in his eye, the Father motioned the Holy Spirit over to the throne and quietly said, "Do you see John Newton down there on the deck of that slave ship?"

Being the holiness of God, the Spirit's initial reaction as he looked upon this vile embodiment of depravity was to shudder. "Of course I see him," was the Spirit's response.

"Let's get him right now! Look at him raging at the wind, full of depraved imaginations. Wouldn't he make a fine specimen of grace?" The Spirit's head falls back in heavenly laughter, "Indeed what a magnificent trophy; and perhaps we should even make him a preacher!"

The Father's eyes light up as he says, "My heart exactly!" With a swift movement of his right hand, a fist full of desire for heavenly things was drawn from the reservoir of the Father's heart and handed to the Holy Spirit. Instantly the Spirit moved out through the gates of heaven falling directly over the infidel John Newton and, plunk! The gift of functional grace was implanted, and the raging heart that loved depravity was shaken with an unearthly reality.

The recipient of heaven's gift stood on the deck of the ship dazed. "What's this? What has happened? Can this be possible?" The revelation gripped his heart and mind. "Mother was right. What she taught me was true. Amazing! No, Amazing grace!" A new flood of desires began to soak and cleanse the black heart of a slaver. "Lord Jesus, forgive me, come possess my heart, cleanse me and take my life. Are these really passions finding expression on my tongue? Truly, I give my life to the eternal God who has transformed my heart. He has given me these desires that burn in my heart. Grace, oh, amazing grace that saved a wretch like me!" The promise of the Father was fulfilled, the Word of Christ effected by the Holy Spirit: "I will give you a new heart" (Ezekiel 36:26).

Rev. Guy Chevreau in his book, *Catch the Fire,* writes, "It was not new knowledge that brought transformation to the Corinthians or Thessalonians but the impartation of grace" (64). It is not knowledge that will bring transformation to the express character of the church. Not even knowledge *about* grace will suffice. Please note the word Chevreau uses: "impartation." There *must* come an impartation from the Heavenly Father that finds its lodging in the human heart. What is it that is bestowed? Nothing less than the new heart. The natural heart of man is as stone, and the soft pen of the Spirit can never make its mark on such hardness. Even though he is God and all-powerful, he chooses only to write on the fleshly tablets. Without the substantive transformation from stone to flesh, functional Christianity does not appear. All we're left with are the best efforts of man striving in the strength of human endeavor to manifest what the Holy Spirit alone can produce.

Let me state it again. Functional grace at its core is this: *God by the Holy Spirit, out of his love for us, gives us a new heart marked by a desire for fellowship with himself.* He gives us the substance, by inexplicable means, of functional passions/desires inherent in and characteristic of *his* heart. We no longer live out of the low passions characteristic of the human heart, but as recipients of grace, we now live out of the supernaturally implanted desires that characterize the heart of God. A new kind of humanity appears, which finds itself driven by a whole new set of love passions that actively desire this new and other kind of reality and relationship. There is nothing earthly about the Father's heart. The new creature of II Corinthians 5 appears and manifests in the culture of a local community called the church! This organism cannot be produced by the ingenuity of human endeavor; it must totally be born from above by the sovereign act of God the Holy Spirit ministering grace. *There is no substitute for grace.* Grace and grace alone can produce a community reflective of heaven's reality. As the reality of grace transforms the foundational motivations and attitudes of the heart, the community of believers begins to bear the marks of a loving, all-powerful, creator God who can be known as Father!'

As the impartation of grace—the Father's heart—takes place, lives are transformed, and people are empowered to live out of a whole new and other set of priorities. These find their motivation not in terms of duty but in the sweetness and savor of desires implanted by the Holy Spirit. There is radical shift of passions from the human to the divine. It is as this shift takes place that a Saul becomes a Paul, produces the likes of John Wesley, whose heart was strangely warmed, or John Newton, who was struck by the majesty of amazing grace. As a leopard cannot change his spots, neither can man change his heart. The transformation of the heart from the natural to the spiritual is the sole purview of the God who rules all Creation. He can change any heart if that heart will become the depository of heaven-sent passions. The *first* heavenly passion found in the transformed heart is a passion to love God, which becomes the capacity to love even our enemies. The *second* is to hate sin, having a passion for that which is truly clean and pure. Whenever passion for spiritual holiness and love for both God and man are absent, you can be sure grace has been missed. What are the passions that characterize an all powerful, passionate God? What measures of those passions do you find burning in your own breast for fellow believers, the lost, and for a genuine imputed holiness? Has grace really captured you, or are you living in some vain vacuum of humanized religion where holiness is a manufactured work of the flesh? Check out the patterns of words that fall off your tongue in private conversations about others in, and even outside, your circle of Christian friends. Are we converts to Christ or converts to some expression of religious Christianity? The former convert loves supernaturally. The latter sheds the innocent blood of other believers with determined passion. A demon of murder lurks in the corridors of graceless Christian religion. A pseudo passion for truth holds dominance and is in no way fettered by the commandment to love one another. Here it is that the letter kills. Truth that holds sway in the heart apart from grace is ruthless Truth. It has no tone of mercy, yet finds a way to justify itself in its attitude of religious arrogance.

By what means is the solution found? Get grace! Do not rest until you discover the functional reality of a lifestyle that can be described as having great grace. The grace-conditioned heart is a heart subject to supernatural love that, being of God, must find expression. It is, after all, the love of God in the heart of man *for* man. It cannot be contained or restrained. Loving has nothing to do any longer with necessity, obligation, or what others deserve; it is all of divine compulsion. Desire has dismissed duty forever, and the heart's only satisfaction is in loving! "Walk in love" no longer represents an impossible wall, or the imposition of Christian responsibility. By grace the heart is set at liberty to love after the manner of God. It is here that the human heart discovers the only way the heart can know true joy.

Imagine finding yourself in the eternal presence of God, and your spirit being, made whole, understands that the life you lived was intended to have been one full of grace, but you never discovered such reality and lived the one life you had on trickles of that heavenly honey. Gone! *Forever* gone. Imagine having no testimony of a grace-filled life to take into eternity because you missed what God intended your spiritual experience to be. The reality before every believer is this: to miss grace here is to miss grace forever. Can any of us afford such spiritual poverty? Therefore, in all your business, in all your service and Christian activity, resolve now to get before the throne of grace so that the Author of grace might fill you with that which is fully intended to be yours in liberal measure! Resolve to be like Paul, who in I Corinthians 3:10 says, "By the grace God has given me, I laid a foundation as an expert builder…" Refuse to be the man in verses 12 and 13 who watches a lifetime of work consumed as wood, hay and stubble! Our cry to God should be, "Oh, God have mercy, for in the face of such things I find myself abjectly defeated. Have mercy oh Lord. Fill me with the wondrous impact of grace. May I in this life discover before death what it means to be full of grace! May I have been so filled with grace that upon departure from this life I will carry into eternity both the knowledge and experience of such fullness."

Some Implications of Grace

It is one thing to offer insights into grace. It is another thing to consider what possible practical applications may be drawn from those insights. Grace must be operative in the life of each believer every day when they are facing all of life's challenges, opportunities and difficulties. Someone might ask, "So, if grace is the impartation of a new heart with its accompanying new set of desires, how does it impact my life in practical ways?" How does it affect the life of the church? Grace cannot remain as some abstract theological concept that I agree with by saying "Amen!"

Throughout scripture, God puts a responsibility on the recipient when dealing with grace. Proverbs 4:23 instructs us to guard our hearts because it is the wellspring of life. We are not to guard the natural, unconverted heart but the new heart given by the Father. That is our responsibility! All the issues of our lives are affected by what is going on in our hearts. Once the new heart has been received, a flow begins. As mentioned before, one of the first rivers that manifest is the river of our words. If what is coming out of our mouths is not reflective of the nature of our Heavenly Father we have assuredly missed the grace of God. If our Christian life styles and priorities are not reflective of the Father's nature, we have missed the grace of God and failed to guard our hearts. Now let's consider a few more areas where grace produces radical change and spiritual results.

1. Discovering Effective Evangelism

How often have we heard the phrase, "It takes money to win the world." I've said it myself. While this phrase seems to ring with an air of truth it is not the final truth. If believers controlled even fifty percent of the money in the world, many would still be unsaved. A great percentage of the world could be won without spending a dollar. The early church did not win the known world to Christ because it was well financed. It was effective in pagan cultures because the individual believer knew what it meant to be a power witness. The tens of thousands being won to Christ in China today are not being won because the church in China is well funded but because the believers there have implemented the New Testament concept of evangelism, a one-on-one demonstration of the Spirit's power. If the one-on-one concept of ministering grace to the world was functional in the West, the resources of the church could be directed into the making of disciples. It is precisely because we have failed in the one-to-one practice of reaching our culture that all the other expensive alternatives of evangelism must be utilized. Yes, television and radio are wonderful tools for evangelism, for such technology helps touch hard-to-reach areas of the world with the truth of the gospel. However, the use of these tools is not the best way for our western cultures to be transformed and thus reformed. Even in the hard-to-reach parts of the world, the best method of winning the lost is indigenous: train people to reach their own!

Such an approach might be termed, "in-your-face grace!" This means that one human being gets *gracefully* in the face of another human being as the incarnate communication of redemption. I John 1:1 says, "that which we have *heard,* which we have *seen* with our eyes, which we have *looked at* and our hands have *touched*—the Word of Life." It is personal. It is hard to have a face-to-face encounter with a voice on a radio or a talking head on a TV screen. The intent here is not to denigrate technology or to demean those who use it, but ultimately, the populations of our nations can only be won in huge numbers when believers come into the grace outworking of Acts 1:8: "You will be my witnesses…" The masses will not be won until Spirit-filled believers move out into the communities in the manifest power of the Spirit. It's what Paul meant in I Corinthians 2:4 when he said that his message was not with enticing words of man's wisdom but with a demonstration of the Spirit's power. One man who had an in-your-face grace encounter with the population of an unsaved city was able to carve out of a pagan culture the church in Corinth. Remember the grace-power principle from chapter two? There is another problem that seems to go along with the techno-message of salvation. I have to wonder if the numbers crunch. Consider the United States for example. No nation on earth has ever been subjected to the techno-proclamation of the gospel like the U.S. If you went to all the ministries in every part of the States involved in radio, TV, and literature (such as tracts and Bibles) and tallied up the combined numbers of people reportedly saved in a given year, the number would be in the hundreds of thousands. Then consider that number multiplied by however many decades you choose. One decade of broadcasting means the number of thousands reportedly won in a year multiplied by ten. Go to two decades and the number of reported salvations per year is multiplied by twenty. In fact, the United States has been subjected to high-impact evangelism for multiplied decades with significant numbers of conversions being reported every single year. If we could tally up the total number of reported conversions, the whole population of the country would likely have been won several times over!

Perhaps we should take an honest look at the effectiveness of the techno-communication of the gospel. The present reality is that one believer in a hundred may win another person to Christ in a year. Should we do away with broadcast evangelism? Hardly! But if we really want to see a radical shift in the direction our cultures are taking we will have to get back to the one-on-one communication of Christ, and that in the demonstration of the Spirit's power! The ever-increasing grip humanism has on the minds of the population will only be broken by in-your-face grace! Nothing, no matter hard we work at it, no matter how much money we spend, can take the place of the one-on-one, grace-in-your-face proclamation of Christ.

Think what it would mean if only twenty percent of believers in a city of any size were to be supernaturally engaged by the Spirit in the actual implementation of all that Christ meant Acts 1:8 to be. How would this impact the local church, its ministry and its pastor? Miss the effectual working of grace and for the most part, the world will continue to drive past the church doors on their way to the country club, golf course, football game, or favorite fishing hole. There is absolutely no substitute for grace becoming operative in the individual believer. All the training courses in evangelism will never do what a powerful release of grace can accomplish. The early church did not sit down and take Evangelism 101, 102 and Advanced Methodologies for Winning the Lost. A whole different motivational power gripped their hearts, which in turn produced a church motivated to live grace-in-your-face lives. The discovery of effectual grace changes the church fundamentally so the motivations operative in the heart of the believer take on the character of Christ. Believers' attitudes toward themselves, other believers, and the lost around them undergo radical change, and Heaven's priorities dominate! The zeal of the Lord of Hosts consumes when grace abounds! It is as though one is eaten up with godly desires. Do we dare pray to the Spirit of God, "Take me there"? Where He leads is beyond understood parameters of safety. Not too many get out of the boat to follow a Peter-type believer onto the unknown waters of the mysteries of God. It just ain't safe, Bubba!

As conveyed in Romans 5:5, the context in which such love is found and expressed is this: "the love of God is shed abroad in our hearts by the Holy Spirit" (KJV). It is not the love of *man* that is shed abroad but the love of *God!* Then God-style love gets slathered on the world! *If the God love ain't in us, it can't get out of us!* Paul was testifying that something not of this world had penetrated his heart. Note the words "poured out" and then consider *what* had been poured out: God's love! The power of redemptive love cannot touch the world until it first inhabits, recreates and transforms the heart of the individual believer. There can be no pouring out unless there has been a profound and radical pouring in! Until such time as that kind of cascade is authentically taking place in the church, we will labor in the message of redemption. The fruit will be hard-won, and never in the scope that God intends. Skip over the love provision, and the great tool of our evangelism is missing. To say that we love one another and then act to assail, criticize, demean, slander, and reject other believers is to deny in practice that which we confess to be true. Regrettably, this is where much of the church lives. We are a demonstrated contradiction to the very message we smilingly proclaim to a skeptical world.

In practical terms, there is a twofold crisis in the believing church today. There is the crisis of lovelessness and a crisis of powerlessness. In short, the church is short on agape and dunamis. Let's consider the crisis of lovelessness. The lack is not so much one of knowledge but of manifestation. Believers everywhere know the commandment that we are to love one another and that a form of Godliness lacking power is unacceptable. I have traveled internationally and ministered cross-culturally, and while believers everywhere know they are called to love one another, there is far more hostility and an internalized pain in the body of Christ than the kind of love we talk about. How is this to be addressed? *By becoming the agape counter-culture!*

There can be no true evangelism until grace so floods our hearts with the Father's love that it cannot be contained. Out of the abundance of the heart our mouths speak! They are words of love that emanate from another reality. They become authentic words of good news, ringing true in the hearts of the hearers. Grace words indeed! Our words have the oil of divine love in them.

READ IRWIN MYERS

These words are seed, going down into the heart and bringing forth after their kind. They are words that minister grace, and grace is the one and only mechanism in the universe that saves to the uttermost! None are beyond the reach of such grace speech. The heart of the Father reaches the heart of the world through the heart channel of the grace-full believer!

We use the biblical term, "evangelist." This is the means and ministry of true evangelism. Believers in the grip of grace touch the world, which can then be drawn into the love grip of God. No authentic evangelism can sweep through our communities, cities, ghettos, and nations to affect the reformation so desperately needed apart from grace. Grace-motivated evangelism sets a series of things in motion that, when carried through to completion, produces a tidal reformation. The enemy of the church and the secular man cannot stop such a flood pouring out of the body of Christ like rivers of love! This is not what the world would recognize as love; it is a love generated by Him who was and is the power behind all that was made. We won't have to be told or coaxed to go. There will be no holding us back when the love of God compels us! The motive of evangelism will live in the body of Christ as an inherent characteristic of our existence. *Grace* is the great church-growth seminar.

Dear reader, take a few moments in prayer. Perhaps you can use these words as a beginning:

> *"Thank you Lord Jesus for filling my heart with the kind of love that drove you from heaven to earth, through the cross, the grave and back to heaven, there to be my advocate. I open my heart to you, Lord Jesus; fill me with the measure of grace that compels me in love to share the gospel with those around me."*

Lord Jesus, as your servant, I come into agreement with those who have prayed for your grace. Dear Holy Spirit, right now would you fill my brother/sister with that peculiar grace that compels the sharing of an eternal love? Fill each willing reader with great grace that translates into living evangelism! I agree that great grace now begins to flow into every open heart, carrying the love of God for the lost down into the depth of each reborn spirit. I believe with them that the heavenly impetus of grace is flowing into every willing, open heart. Thank you, Holy Spirit, for ministering this love compulsion into the hearts of each committed believer!

2. Liberty from Addictions, Bondage, and Perversions

In modern culture, large segments of the population struggle with such things as addictions, bondage, and perversions, some of which are open and blatant while others are secret and hidden. Finding Christ does not automatically mean that those fetters are broken. There are large numbers of people in the body of Christ who are bound by one or more of these, but because bringing them into the open is embarrassing for the church and humiliating for the individual, many live their lives as prisoners, never finding the liberty they were created to enjoy. They live their lives in secret oppression, and shame keeps them there. You will never find a joyful, well-adjusted person in the full grip of addiction, bondage, or perversion!

People struggle with addictions of various kinds. There are the obvious kinds of addictions, such as illicit drugs, prescription drugs, and certain kinds of foods, to name a few. Bondage can also exist in our lives as uncontrolled habits. The bondage can be so strong that it literally controls our lives. If polls are to be believed, pornography is a bondage that has dominion over many in the body of Christ. Then there are the secret perversions. *Perverse* is defined by Webster's as "having turned away from what is right or good, to be corrupt, or to be obstinate in opposing what is right, reasonable or acceptable behavior." Anyone who wishes has only to peruse the Humanist Manifesto to discover the careful articulation of all that is perverse. To accept humanistic values is to become the embodiment of all that is perverse, and as we've discussed, humanistic precepts form the basis of many of the prevailing thought patterns even in Christian circles. It expunges the very possibility of grace from the human condition and even does away with the historic value of language, thus promoting the destruction of civility and ordered culture. Self-government is lost, resulting in freedom becoming nothing more than a cultural artifact of history.

Because little has been done in the body of Christ to deal specifically with identifying and dismantling them, these perverse thought patterns continue to influence our behavior. Humanism has simply been amalgamated into the body of Christ. Historically and biblically, sodomy and lesbianism have been defined as perversion. Humanistic atheism has come along and systematically turned the population "away from that which is right and good." Perversions extend far beyond the sexual dimensions of life. They find expressions in our attitudes, motivations, words, and ways of treating others. The concept, "If you think you're right, then you are right," pervades humanistic culture. This kind of intellectual perversion has simply been carried over into the body of Christ, causing a great deal of conflict and destruction. People, including preachers, practice this tenet of humanism without even flinching. A large number of educators, legislators, social engineers, and media come down on the side of perversion. Perversion, to the perverse mind, is considered reasonable. Anything contrary to perversion is deemed uncivilized and is perceived as bordering on the insane. Humanistic atheism fits fully the definition of perversion, yet this perversion has become the accepted standard of conduct in society. The perversions of humanism need to be recognized and removed from the believing community if we ever hope to be an effective counter-culture. We cannot, on the one hand, be in the grip of unidentified humanistic concepts and then hope to change the world around us. Grace must have its way. We must come into the new-heart dimension of living so that those truly good and right values and ways of conduct are modeled in the church.

How does functional grace then set at liberty those who are captive to addictions, bondage, and perversions? Consider: the addict lives with an all-consuming passion for the object of his addiction. He is ruled absolutely by the desire rooted in his addiction, but upon opening his life to Christ, the Holy Spirit implants the Father's heart, complete with a whole new and uniquely divergent set of desires. Suddenly, the addict knows a powerful desire for liberty and wholeness. The desire to be free of that addiction is not just something wished for because of its negative effects. It rather flows from the heart of God, because there *is* no power of addiction in the Father's heart. The addict experiences the desire God has for him to be free. Two competing desires now function in the individual, and a choice has to be made. Both sets of desires cannot be served. Because of grace, the addict can now choose to respond to the Spirit-generated desires within. This doesn't mean that it will be easy to respond to grace, or to the inner desire for freedom. It does mean that he can choose to follow the desires that lead to liberty. Once the choice is made to go with the desires characteristic of the Father's heart, the Holy Spirit empowers that choice. In Luke 4:1, the Devil came to Christ, but Satan had no hold over him. Christ had the heart of God, and no perverse desires existed in his heart, so no temptation could overtake him. So it is with the individual on the path to a life of addiction-free living. The addict chooses to run with the deeper desires of Father's heart because the desire for Christ himself becomes stronger than any temporal thrill addiction can offer.

Let me say it a bit differently. Grace gives us the new heart. The new heart is the heart of the Father. The heart of the Father is full of desires that are positive, energizing, and uplifting. They are clean and bring a sense of wholeness and well being into the life. The Father's heart, once gained, sets within the spirit of the individual the potential to experience all that characterizes *His* heart. The individual begins to desire liberty, to choose liberty, finds empowerment flowing from the Holy Spirit, and finally, liberty wins the day. *He sets the captive free!*

What is your bondage? What perversion of thought, imagination, or conduct has enslaved you to its destructive passions? What habits do you need broken in your life? The first necessity in the fight for individual liberty is the appropriation of grace. It is not automatic. You get to do the hard work of choosing, and choosing, and choosing! Make the right choices in response to the right desires, and you will find the Holy Spirit to be a friend who will exert his power resulting in your freedom. You will find your liberty in fellowship with him. When you come into the state of liberty, you will also have come into the wondrous state of fellowship with the Spirit of God. When you find grace, you find the Spirit of God in his presence, power, and friendship. You not only come into a freedom from addictions and the like, you come into a functionally intimate relationship with the Spirit of the living God! His eternal reality permeates your daily reality, and the joy of the eternal kingdom resides in the heart. Grace does not imply a pain-free life, but it does mean a life of liberty full of purpose, hope, meaning, and love. None of these characterize the addict, the bound, or the perverse. Those so bound can never find freedom in religious humanism. The only thing they can find in humanistic atheism is a form of logic that finally surrenders to the bondage.

In ministering to needy individuals, Christians must recognize that all the effort and good intentions in the world will not suffice. All the Bible verses and biblical principles, while true, will not set the captive free unless the individual is first privileged to find and experience grace. We need to discover how to lead people into a personal discovery of functional grace, because liberty rests more with that individual and the Holy Spirit than it does with the minister. Grace is what saves and sets free, not counseling, ministry or all the might of men. Our counseling and ministries should focus first on directing the individual into a discovery of grace. Once grace begins to function, the minister progressively finds himself less and less a part of the liberty equation. The individual, instead of becoming dependent upon the minister, increasingly depends on and becomes acquainted with the God who loves him.

Our desire to minister to broken people can easily be tainted by what are ultimately selfish motives in a couple of common ways. Sometimes, ministry becomes an idol that we nourish because we get our affirmation in life based on what *we* are doing by being considered wise, compassionate, or anointed ministers. A desire for reputation can consume us, and the more grace the seeker finds, the less he needs the human instrument of ministry. As a consequence, the fulfillment of being an *enabler of noble character* diminishes. Perhaps John the Baptist summed it up best when he said, "He must increase, I must decrease" (John 3:30). Those of us who function in the ministry *are not in ministry for the sake of ministry.* We as ministers must seek to direct people to find their needs met in God, not in us. Our desire to minister can get in the way of the Spirit's ability to minister liberty to those who seek it! We are to be ministers of grace, and if we fail to lead the individual to find the sufficiency of God's grace then we have truly failed, regardless of our reputation or how many people are lined up at our door to partake of *our* wisdom and anointing!

3. Conquering the Torment of Fears

"For God has not given us the spirit of fear, but of power and of love and of a sound mind."
—II Timothy 1:7

I have heard it said that there are 365 "fear nots" in the Bible: one admonition to not be afraid for every day of the year. True or not, the scriptures state absolutely that the believer is not to be the bondservant to destructive fears, whatever their origin. I have been in churches where the song, "God has not given us a spirit of fear..." is sung with gusto, but if this topic is pursued in any given congregation, an incredible range of fears can be identified. In I John 4:18 the issue of fear is addressed: "There is no fear in love. But perfect love drives out fear, because fear has to do with punishment. The one who fears is not made perfect in love." Where fear has liberty to operate it produces inward torment. The kinds of fears that dog the human heart are almost inexhaustible. Believers can be so used to the presence of fear that life without that fear would seem unnatural. We get so accustomed to those fears that their presence simply goes unnoticed and unchallenged. Make a trip into any Christian bookstore, and you will find a whole section on the operations of fear. Despite these and other scriptural truths, and regardless of the volume of books that have been written on the subject, fear still abounds in the body of Christ.

Some years ago I visited a church, and in the time leading up to the teaching, the Spirit began to impress me that I was to speak on freedom from fear. This was my first time in the church, and I stood before the people as a stranger. I felt rather uncertain, but the leading seemed quite clear so I decided to minister on that subject. When it came time for the message, I told them I was going to speak on being fear free. One elderly man piped up right in the middle of a sentence and said, "Sonny, you must have missed God on this one. No one in this church has a problem with fear." A ripple ran through the congregation affirming this elderly gentleman's statement. Now the Lord has given me the ability to look calm, cool, and in control when inwardly I'm a wreck, so while I looked composed, silently I cried out, "Lord, are you sure I'm supposed to speak on fear? It looks like I've misunderstood you! Now what?" Instantly, the Spirit dropped a word of knowledge into my mind. Looking like I was in full control rather than flabbergasted, I responded to the elderly gentleman. "Well, sir, the Lord tells me that someone here has a dreadful fear of flying. That person will drive a thousand miles rather than take a short plane ride." My heart was pounding and inside I was saying, "Lord, I sure hope I heard you right!"

As I spoke these words the eyes of the whole congregation went in unison to the right to where the pastor sat along the wall. Everyone knew that he refused to fly for fear of crashing. (Be assured, there was a quiet inward, "Whew!" that I'm sure was heard in heaven.) Instantly several other words relating to specific fears flowed, and as I called them out people would raise their hands indicating that was their fear. The elderly gentleman then spoke up again. "Well, sonny, since it seems you know what you're talkin' about, get on with it."

Many received a touch of release that morning. One of the realities that any preacher knows is that many of God's people struggle with fears, the list being extremely long. Fear of certain diseases, old age, rape, or loss of employment are examples of such fears. Fear hates to be recognized, drawn to the light, and removed from the life of believers. Ironically, there is something terrifying about getting free of fear. Somehow, "better safe than sorry" provides an illusion of safety we are loathe to relinquish.

I John 4:18 gives us one key for the liberation from fear when it says, "Perfect love casts out fear." Love is the all-powerful tool by which fear of any kind is forcefully removed from the heart. Fear may have its foundation in the mind, but it bears its fruit in the heart. To be fear free means discovering the source of "perfect" love and plugging into it. Liberation from fear starts with the appropriation of grace. Cry out to God, "Oh, Lord, fill me with your grace." To so pursue grace is to pursue the Spirit of God whose ministry it is to operate that portion of needed grace in your inmost part. An important observation should be added here: as long as the focus stays on fear, no liberation takes place. Nor is love itself to be the focus of attention. God the Creator needs to be the focus (Ephesians 1:18). With a Spirit-birthed perception of God we discover that our case rests with God. If we can, by grace discover perfect love, fear has more than met its match, and the soul finds its rest from torment in the one who is the consummate God. Fear cannot abide the presence of such love.

At the expense of being repetitious, it is essential to understand the second component of grace to be the new heart (Jeremiah 31:33). We need to make the connection between this new, God-given heart and the impact this new heart has upon fear. The Father's heart is the source of perfect love, and because the Father's heart has been given us, the source of perfect love dwells within the breast of every believer. Perfect love comes with God's perfect heart. Dear reader, there is a wonder to be pondered here, so don't rush on too quickly.

Once we've worked our way through this spiritual terrain, an astonishing conclusion is set before the believer: He that is perfected in love *has no fear*. The NIV puts it this way: "The man who fears is not made perfect in love." Scripture would not speak of man being perfected in love if such perfection were not attainable. What overt fears lurk in the dark corners of your consciousness, paralyze your faith, and rob you of your confidence, joy and destiny? Only by coming "boldly before the throne of grace" will you be able to confront the spirit of fear. Receive the grace that meets your need!

Would you take a few moments and begin to make a list of every area where fear has a grip on your heart? Start with the most obvious. Ask the Holy Spirit to show you areas in your life where fear lurks. Ask him to show you those fears that lie below the level of your consciousness. It wouldn't even hurt to take a few days to get away in a retreat setting with a journal and let the Holy Spirit speak to you. When something comes into your mind, do not make light of it or dismiss it; add it to your list, no matter how trivial or impertinent it may seem. Remember that fear does not want to be identified nor challenged regarding its hold over your life. Its whisper is designed to get you to discountenance the still small voice of the Holy Spirit by saying things like, "Oh, that doesn't make sense," "Really now, I've never struggled with that," or, "You are doing all right just as you are." The voice of that spirit of fear will yak in your ear until you accept what it is suggesting. The tactic the Devil used to get Adam and Eve to fall from grace is precisely the tactic the spirit of fear will use to keep you from the discovery of overcoming by grace.

Once you've developed your list, sit down to talk to the Lord. Over each area of fear, a demonic being is trying to rule your life. Start with the first item on your list and, out loud, renounce that spirit of fear and command it to leave your life. Stay with this until you start to experience freedom coming into your heart no matter how long it takes. Get past wanting the instant package! In this arena of warfare, acknowledge that you belong to Christ and that *His blood has cleansed you from all unrighteousness.* Remember that you, by the operation of grace, have received the implantation of the Father's heart, where there is no fear. Tap into this, and you have, in fact tapped into the source of perfect love! After dealing with any demonic influence, it's important to ask the Father to fill you with the measure of grace designed to break the stronghold of fear in your life. Ask the Holy Spirit to begin now to minister the grace you need in the area of that particular fear. Say out loud, "Lord Jesus, I receive your grace. Fill me with that measure of grace that conquers this fear."

I'd like to pray with you now. Since I'm not sitting next to you I'm going to write down this prayer for you and ask you to agree with me that your fear be absolutely conquered by a supernatural infusion of God's grace. This is your book; write your name in it here!

Lord Jesus, I come into agreement with my brother/sister _____, that the provision of grace is the very fulfillment of why you died and rose from the dead. You died, Lord Jesus, to restore your sons and daughters to that condition of abundant grace according to Romans 5:17. Right now, precious Holy Spirit, as the administrator of grace, I ask you to begin to fill my brother/sister with a mighty flow of functional grace. Let the heart of the Father take its full place within his/her life.

Here is my profession of faith: "Be filled with the grace of the Lord Jesus Christ!" Right now the Holy Spirit is ministering the flow of grace into your life. The substance of grace—the Father's heart— is being released into your spirit. In the next few hours and days, new measures of His love will be felt at work in your heart. He has given you a new nature, and that new nature is not compatible with demonically or carnally inspired fears. You are being brought into that place where you are being made whole in the perfect love of the Father. That love will become so real to you that one morning you will wake up and realize that the fears that once marred your life have vanished! Let me pronounce it over you!

Precious believer, I declare that you are perfected in the Father's love. Fear you have been dismissed. Never return! Thank you, Holy Spirit, for being here to minister the grace of the Lord Jesus into _____'s heart. Thank you, Lord Jesus, that grace has saved my brother/sister from every torment and spirit of fear. Praise you, Heavenly Father!

4. Discovering the Connection between Grace and Faith

One of the key truths of scripture deals with the place of faith in the life of the believer. As declared in Romans 1:17, the just shall live by faith. Abraham demonstrates what the life of faith looks like and how it is to be lived out. Along with the injunctions regarding faith in James, these are not simply statements of truth. They are to be foundational in Christian experience. Ephesians 2:8 sets the two truths, grace and faith in juxtaposition for all time. "For it is by *grace* you have been saved through faith." Grace and faith are linked together in an absolute way, and each must be understood in relation to the other. A doctrine of grace that is not articulated in its relation to faith is inadequate. Why? Grace impacts the heart so that it can operate in faith, "For with the heart man believes." Grace deposits within the transplanted heart the capacity to believe God and his Word. Someone may very well know what God's Word says, but if their heart has not been impacted by the operation of grace, that person will not respond in faith to the Word. It takes a Spirit-conditioned heart to respond to spiritual directives. How often do we hear the Spirit, and even though we have a clear sense of what he wants us to do we do not do it? For instance, the Spirit may tell an individual to lay hands on a stranger who has just come into the building. Instantly the mind begins to question the directive and as a result no ministry to that individual takes place. If we are to undertake faith actions we've gotta have heart—His heart!

Similarly, any teaching of faith that is not set in the context of grace is, at least, incomplete. If believers want a biblical understanding of faith, then that understanding must be defined within the framework of grace. Every believer needs to operate in greater measures of faith. Growing in faith is progressive and comes through the continual exercise of our faith. It is by using faith in response to grace that the power of the Holy Spirit is released, and the purposes of God are discovered and achieved. If we are to have and exercise a New Testament faith, then we have to come to understand how grace impacts faith, for grace is what the New Testament's core message is about.

Faith action plugged into grace is impossible to stop. If believers can discover this connection in practical terms, radical things can happen to their exercise of faith. What is it about grace that gives supernatural empowerment to our practice of faith? Whenever we want to begin to understand any Christian doctrine in its grace context, *we must start with a consideration of how the implanted heart of the Father impacts the doctrine being considered.* We must tie the grace-impacted heart with the truth being focused upon. In this case, if faith is to be understood and practiced in its grace setting we must ask, "How does the relationship between the new heart and faith connect?"

Galatians 5:6 gives us the link between the two: "*faith* worketh by *love*" (KJV). The NIV says, "The only thing that counts is *faith* expressing itself through *love*." What causes faith to work, to swing into action? Love. Natural love? Hardly! There is only one kind of love that kicks faith into high gear: God's love. The nature of biblical faith originates in the spiritual realm where love—agape-style—is the root motivational force. This particular kind of love resides—where? In the heart of God! God *is* love. Love is the inherent nature of his heart. Remember, it is by the ministry of grace that the Holy Spirit bestows in us the heart of God. So, it is by grace that the believer reaches down into the fuel tank, if you will, of the Father's love and a deliberate act of faith is undertaken. When faced with the needs of others, a love that desires to see those needs met stirs. Action to meet those needs is undertaken. This action is faith rooted in God's own implanted love.

My wife and I rented an apartment when we were first married, and a gentleman who lived in our building went out and bought himself a brand-new, red Chevy convertible. He had no license and didn't know how to drive. We'd watch him out our living room window as he'd go out to the parking lot, turn on the radio, put the top down, sit behind the wheel looking through the windshield, hands on the steering wheel and play that he was driving. He didn't even turn on the engine. He just sat there, radio playing, going nowhere. Strange sight indeed! The power potential was there, but for that power to be released, the engine had to be on.

Faith works by love like an engine works by gas: as the gas pours into the cylinders, the firing system activates and power is released. As faith taps into that love, the spiritual fuel needed to cause a supernatural action is released. If there is no fuel, there is no power. Grace and faith have to connect if our Christian lives are to manifest power or we end up with a form of godliness, but it's powerless. We may stand guard over our powerless car insisting that it is really a car, but the fact that there is no power somehow does not really bother us. We do, after all, have a car. Some may even make weekly trips to the parking lot to sit in it. Nobody is going anywhere, but it sure is pretty! Don't tell these car guards, "Yeah but, where's the power? It really is a beautiful car, but it is useless!"

If we teach faith without showing folks how to plug into the fuel of love, we can be left without the release of power. We can teach about the marvelous engine of faith until we fall over exhausted, but no matter how well designed or powerful the engine, if it doesn't have fuel pouring into it, *there is no fire* and therefore no power! Oh, yes, the engine is absolutely the heart of the vehicle, but what folly to sit on the padded seats singing happy songs, going nowhere! I wonder what God must think when we sit in our nicely padded pews, going through all the motions, making payments on our particular vehicle of Christianity, the whole lot of us going nowhere because there is no power!

Faith is useless if it does not produce works. James 2:17 says that any model of faith propagated that does not have power (evidenced by actions) is dead. How many have been conned into a dead faith? Works by their very nature imply power. How do we come into greater faith works and power? *By grace!* Let's look at it chronologically:

Grace, ministered into my spirit, gives me the Father's heart, whose essence is love.
The love of God becomes the characteristic of my heart/nature.
The Holy Spirit gives me the gift of faith and the resource of the Father's love.
Responding to that love in faith, I initiate a deliberate faith action.
The fire of the Holy Spirit ignites and, Wham!
Supernatural power releases a movement in the kingdom of heaven on earth.

Sounds like the Lord's Prayer: "Thy kingdom come, thy will be done on earth as it is in heaven!"

Take some time for a mental exercise and think through how a grace-produced faith could affect the ministry of evangelism in your life. How would a grace-activated faith set you free from fear or break addiction, bondage, or perversion? I know that it would be easier just to skip this or have it explained, but then you'd not have to do any thinking of your own. Peruse this material on faith and grace and then consider how a grace-produced faith impacts your life. We will continue to study this as we go, but know this: when grace and faith team up, supernatural things happen!

5. Grace and the Prophetic Gift

It seems appropriate to consider the relationship between grace and the gift of prophecy as identified in I Corinthians chapters 12 and 14. Most who recognize the gifts of the Spirit will acknowledge that these gifts work by faith. Prophecy, likewise, must function in the life of the Christian through the activation of faith. We have just considered how grace sets love as the foundation for faith in the spirit of the believer. Now, tie faith and prophecy together. Romans 12:6 can help us here: "If a man's gift is prophesying, let him use it in proportion to his faith." Note the "let him," which puts the responsibility on the minister of the gift versus waiting for the Holy Spirit to do something. Paul gives an injunction to Timothy, in which he is to stir up the gift that he'd received by the laying on of hands (II Timothy 1:6). Note where the responsibility is placed: the release of the gift was to be the result of a deliberate act on Timothy's part. This act is nothing short of faith. It is a deliberate act based on biblical authority that instructs us *to use it*!

It is important to consider the impact of the statement that the prophet can prophesy, not according to some mysterious anointing that might fall upon him from time to time, but "according to their faith." *Faith* is the issue in the exercise of the prophetic gift. We can hang around waiting for God to do something and little will happen. It is up to grace-filled believers to respond to that grace and *choose* to prophesy.

Now let me demonstrate how grace and the prophetic gift tie together with grace at one end and prophesy at the other:

Grace imparts the heart of God, **the new heart.**
The prime characteristic of that heart is **love.**
Love necessitates the activation of **faith.**
By faith one begins to use, or stir up, the gift of **prophecy.**
The Holy Spirit responds to the act and **the gift manifests.**
Prophesy that is rooted in functional grace:

Makes God manifest to natural man,
Glorifies, or makes God visible,
Testifies to Christ (Revelations 19:10),
Causes the one who comes in while everyone is prophesying to declare, "God is really among you!" (I Corinthians 14:24-25).

Conclusion: grace made manifest by the prophetic gift releases grace that saves! May I offer to those who teach and insist the prophetic gift of I Corinthians 12 and 14 has passed away, that the denial of this gift is a denial of grace in one of its powerful expressions to the world.

The motive of a grace-activated prophecy is love!

Why does prophecy have such powerful potential? Why does Paul say, "I'd rather have you prophesy," in I Corinthians 14:5? Consider Luke 6:45: "Out of the abundance of the heart the mouth speaks." True prophetic utterance flows out of the heart of God, but *that abundance finds its way into human experience by the spoken prophetic word!* Agape is always its motivational force. Prophecy has power and glorifies God because it makes the heart of God known to man! So, be filled with the grace of God and stir up the gift that is within you. Functional grace will cause you to be impelled to the faith action of prophecy, and in prophesying, you become a minister of God's love! This is only one of the wonderful things that grace produces in the life of the Spirit-filled believer. Let all who would, scream, but this truth of grace and prophecy stands absolute in God's Word.

6. Grace Heals the Broken Heart

How does grace bring healing to the broken hearted? Christ said that one purpose of the anointing he'd been given was to "heal the brokenhearted" (Luke 4:18, KJV). Psalm 23:3 declares, "He restores my soul," the soul being the mind, will, and emotions. The heart has to do with our intrinsic nature. We use "broken heart," meaning something has happened to introduce a shattering or breaking of a person's nature so that he or she cannot function as God intended. Surely, the first breaking of human nature occurred in Eden. While Adam and Eve were in the garden, they lived in a state of total grace. Healing the broken spirit/nature of man requires a recovery of grace. Any ministry or practice of psychology that does not bring broken people back into the grace of God may be well intended, but restoration of true humanity is possible only in the experience of grace. Remember, man was not created to live outside the grace of God. The more critical the problem is, the more crucial the need for grace.

We in the body of Christ use the term "healing grace," but in practice, we only understand it in limited terms. The discovery of that healing grace in the breadth of its potential is still waiting to be unleashed. Grace ministered effectively can release healing for the body. However, it is equally sufficient for disorders of the troubled mind, the broken will, and shattered emotions. Admittedly, we have yet to find his sufficiency in these dimensions of human brokenness on a large scale, but Christ is the healer, and *that* without limitation. Healing administered to the soul as well as the body is one of the things that will be restored to the body of Christ as grace becomes a functional reality. People who open themselves up to the teaching of the Holy Spirit regarding grace will begin to have supernatural anointing to minister healing to those who have mental and emotional disorders. For example, an individual whose will is supernaturally restored through the administration of grace by the Holy Spirit will have divine capability to choose to walk away from that which had them bound. This is "will power" of divine origin! How about a specific illustration?

Millions of dollars are made each year in the field of weight loss and control. Grace that becomes functional can be the greatest single means of weight loss available to mankind. How can grace help in the fight for weight control? With grace comes a God-given desire that resides in the heart. The divine desire inherent in grace is deeper than the desire in the flesh for food. Once grace begins to flow into the life, there is a clash of desires. The Spirit wars against the flesh and the flesh against the Spirit (Galatians 5:17), and the individual has to make a choice as to which desire is to be fulfilled. A choice to satisfy the flesh is to sow to the flesh, but a choice to respond to the grace promptings of the Holy Spirit is an act of faith He can respond to by releasing his power that works inwardly. By making the choice to respond to the Spirit's inward motivation or desire, the believer taps into the one source of power that is greater than the flesh. I do not want to suggest that such a choice is easy, but sowing into the spirit realm can only produce life.

What is the relationship between grace and the broken heart, or the mentally ill patient? Healing grace applied to the human nature is of interest to two groups of individuals, the inwardly broken individual and those seeking to minister to the inwardly broken. *The believer ministering in the non-physical dimensions of healing must first come into a confident and revelational understanding of the sufficiency of grace.* Think about the word *sufficient* in relation to grace. Christ said that his grace is sufficient for any need faced in human existence. Sufficient for weight control, sufficient for any brokenness of heart and nature, including a sufficiency for the mentally ill and the insane. Ask yourself this question: "Do I really believe that sufficient means *sufficient*? Sufficient to heal the mental patient, the insane, the emotionally shattered victims of violence and betrayal?" *You cannot minister what you do not know*, but if you believe in the sufficiency of grace, you can reach for it when ministering to those who will be healed by no other means.

Jesus, full of grace, demonstrated such all-sufficient grace. He had it fully and could give it away fully. He met the Gadarene who was both wildly insane and demonically possessed (Mark 5). At the command of Christ, the legion of demons left for pig city, and the man, insane for years, was restored to his right mind. Picture the mother of this one who, had been running naked and wild through the local graveyard, sitting on her front porch. Glancing down the dusty road she sees in the distance what looks like the form of her insane son. He is walking very quickly toward the house. And yes, he's coming straight for the house. Instantly there is a mixture of fear and panic that flood her heart. Frozen, she stares at the distant form. She wonders how he's escaped his bonds again. What to do? Run? Hide? Call for help? A pang of deep sorrow pierces her heart. But wait; he has clothes on. He's singing one of the songs he used to sing for me as a little boy. Doubt floods her heart. "Oh, it can't be my son; he's mad!" Gradually the form becomes clear, and it is her son, smiling and waving. Shouting he says, "Hey mom, tell my wife and children I'm coming home, and I'm healed!" Can you feel anything that must have filled that mother's heart?

Dear Lord Jesus, by your Holy Spirit, fill your people with such overflowing measures of grace that modern Gadarenes might be restored to their right minds and go home whole! Touch each reader, precious Holy Spirit, with such depths of grace that they in turn might minister its healing power! Heal the Gadarene again!

One of the stories in the winter 1998/99 edition of Christian Mission magazine referred to a man in Columbia, South America. This man had suffered a mental breakdown and had spent fifteen months in a mental institution where the best psychiatrists and neurologists treated him without success. Someone took him to church, the whole church prayed for him, and he was instantly healed. He dedicated his life to evangelize in a region of

Colombia full of left-wing guerrillas. Today there are 36 gospel preachers working with him to reach the unreached in the jungles of Colombia.

How does grace bring such wholeness? With the fall from grace by Adam and Eve there was a shattering of the image and likeness of God he had placed in them. All of nature suffered incomprehensible brokenness that not only affected the external natural realm but also reached down to the very epicenter of what it meant to be human. Man apart from God became perverse and loved his perverseness. The nature that had been created to receive the love of God and enjoy his fellowship could no longer love as originally able, losing his driving thirst for fellowship with God.

I know that this kind of theological terrain is very tempting for those who want precision. It represents the kind of ground upon which genuine believers have waged war. Let's leave the war and just focus on how grace heals the broken facets of human nature. We can at least agree that there is much inner brokenness in both the church and the world that needs the healing power of grace. The whole focus of the ministry of Christ was to release the one thing in the universe that had the capacity to restore what had been lost. *The ultimate objective of the incarnation, the cross, the lashes, the blood, the death, and resurrection was to release the mechanism of grace into the earth so that what had been lost could be recovered.* If grace had not come into the world by Jesus Christ, all that had been lost would remain lost forever. Grace is not a theological option. It is the absolute imperative of human existence. Further, the grace of Christ is not a partial grace. It does not just save us from sin: it saves utterly from every dilemma imposed on life by Satan and the fall. Sufficient? Not just sufficient, but overwhelmingly so!

We need to come back to the fundamental nature of grace whereby the Holy Spirit fashions a new heart out of the resource of the Father's heart and by a sovereign mystery, implants that heart into us. I know we've gone over this before, but when we speak of that heart, we are implying that something of the essential and holy nature of God becomes supernaturally characteristic of our inner man. What do we know about this heart? There is no brokenness in the heart and nature of God. Therefore, when I receive of that wondrous heart, I obtain a new nature, which I can choose to draw upon by the Spirit's enabling. I am no longer left trying to live out of that which is imperfect, but can instead live by the Spirit's divine empowerment. I reach for the response that exists only in the unbroken nature of God. Paul declared in Corinthians, "We have the mind of Christ." There is no insanity in the mind of Christ. In Philippians he enjoins us, "Let this mind be in you which was also in Christ

Jesus." There is no crushed emotion or paralysis of the will in God's nature. Christ demonstrated what it was to choose to live out of the Father's will rather than his own in the garden of Gethsemane. Once indwelt by the Spirit of God, we also can refuse to surrender to the pleading brokenness of our fallen wills and reach into the "will well" of the Father. Once we begin that inner motion of reaching toward the unbroken nature of the Father, the Holy Spirit finds opportunity to perform his ministry. He is in us to empower us to live, by choice, out of that new and wonderfully whole nature of God.

As we make deliberate effort to place a demand upon the substance of the Father's nature in us instead of acting to satisfy our own carnal desires, the Holy Spirit empowers that spiritual choice. A new man supernaturally empowered to live a new kind of existence appears on earth. This is why Romans 8:19 says the whole earth groans. It is waiting for such manifestation of the sons of God, for indeed, all men are broken. Those in the body of Christ who struggle with the weight of their own brokenness can turn to the throne of grace, and growing in grace, can have their own supernatural return home. Remember, grace is the ministry of the omnipotent, omniscient, and omnipresent Holy Spirit. He waits for the call. Place your demand for grace upon Him, and then act in harmony with the divinely implanted desires. Seek him for that administration of grace and you will find it when you reach for it with all your heart. Grace is the antidote for the inner brokenness that drives individuals toward such things as self-pity, despair, suicide, vengeance, violence, addictions, bitterness, emotional sterility, or a paralysis of the will. For those who would minister the power of God to the inner brokenness of mankind I say, "Be filled with the grace of God!"

For those who are broken, I wish to agree with you right now and to pronounce over you what is yours by blood-bought right!

Father God, for those who find themselves prisoner of inner brokenness, fill them right now with those progressive measures of grace that bring healing to every segment of human personality. By faith I release the power of Christ's grace to effect healing in every area of brokenness. That power is working precisely as these words are going down into the good soil of the human spirit. To every area of inner brokenness I pronounce, "Be healed in the name of Jesus Christ!" On the basis that Jesus said, "All authority in heaven and on earth has been given unto me. Therefore go..." I command every demonic spirit that has usurped power and authority over your life to leave at this very moment, never to return. Go in the name of Jesus Christ! By faith I release healing grace through the Holy Spirit into every area of the human spirit and into the mind, will, and emotions of every bound believer. Father, I remit every sin that Satan has used as his "trump card" to promote brokenness in the lives of your children. Lord Jesus, I thank you right now for the miracle power that sets people free.

On the basis of Christ's shed blood, dear reader, your sins are remitted! You *are* forgiven, and *all* basis of demonic authority is broken off your life. Christ paid the price for all sin, and Satan has no more ground upon which to accuse or abuse you. *Go free!*

Summing It Up

The first part of this chapter has been given to help believers identify the essential nature of grace. The second component in God's definition of grace—the new heart—demonstrates how grace functions to bring healing to the inner brokenness of humanity. Let me state it again: The second component of grace is at its core the impartation/implantation of the heart of God into the human nature by the Holy Spirit, which we will cover in more detail later. Proverbs 4 is all about wisdom. It speaks of grace and a manifestation of God's splendor. Then in verse 23 it says this: "Above all else, guard your heart." Why? *It is the wellspring of life!*

The King James Version declares that all the issues of life flow from, or center in, the state of the heart. Think about this a bit. Above *all* else, the thing you need be most focused on has to do with the state of your heart. Now, the heart referred to here is the new heart, for all of life is intended to be framed around that supernaturally implanted nature given to us according to God's new covenant, the grace covenant. In guarding your heart, you are making choices which structure life decisions, attitudes, motives, and priorities around the new heart nature. Those inward choices, once made, are empowered by the Holy Spirit. The structure of life is then less and less like the old man and more and more of the manifest nature of Christ. In this process of choosing and being empowered, the believer discovers what it means to be walking in the Spirit. Every issue of life finds itself subjugated to the new nature by the empowerment of the Holy Spirit. It is important to understand that he is not driving himself to bring the passions, attitudes, motives, and priorities into subjection, but is choosing to respond to the new, Christ-centered set of desires.

In grace, a husband is not *obligated* to love his wife; he has a deep and profound *desire* to love her; the wife is not *subject* to blind submission, but knows the *freedom* of trust; the believer is not *duty bound* to maintain unity, it is simply his/her *nature* to do so; believers empowered by grace do not tithe because it is what the Bible demands; they tithe because it is simply their *joy* to do so. In grace, there is no, "I have to," but a "Glory to God, I *get* to, so get out of my way!" takes over. They have discovered what Paul meant when he instructed believers to "excel in the grace of giving." The standard of tithing is no longer a matter of law or obligation; the heart of the grace-filled believer is inwardly and powerfully motivated to give. Biblical conduct is an outward manifestation of a transformed nature freed from the constraints of duty and obligation. Grace is, in fact, the way of the new life in Christ. The exclamation of the grace-filled believer is "Glory to God, His heart is happening in me!"

It is a little like Scrooge on Christmas morning. There is joy, dancing, and reckless giving that fills the giver's heart with more joy. The heart of God overflows, impacting every issue that arises in human experience. Our job in guarding the heart is to insure that we make the initial right choice in keeping with the passions inherent in this new heart. The initial, inner, right choice is our responsibility. In pursuing an understanding of grace, ask the Holy Spirit to reveal the part the new heart plays, not just in relationship to giving, but in every aspect of your Christian experience. *He's* the teacher, *he's* the revealer, and *he's* the sole and exclusive administrator of grace. Grace discovered means you live out all of life from the heart, passionately! Those who are full of grace and manifest overt expressions of love for God embarrass believers who are content with minimal grace! Stony hearts cannot shout, dance, or fall down in worship! In grace, life is lived passionately and is centered in the reality of an intensely personal experience with the Holy Spirit. It becomes a passionate, Christ-centered life. It is grace that brings unity and empowerment to the various dimensions characteristic of the Christian life and community. It is by such grace manifestation that the world encounters the healed, agape counter-culture with its roots and foundation in the God of all creation. So then, grace: it starts with the heart, the heart, the heart!

Chapter Six
The Five Keys of Grace

In Matthew 6:10, Jesus directed us to pray "thy kingdom come," and later, in Matthew 16:19, Jesus said he'd give us the keys to the kingdom of heaven. If he directed us to pray for the kingdom of heaven to come, then it's only reasonable to expect such a prayer would be answered. His first message was to preach that the kingdom of heaven was at hand. The preaching of the kingdom of heaven was and should always be good news. Inherent in that good news is power that brings not just salvation, but healing for all diseases and deliverance from demonic afflictions. Power is inherently the nature of the kingdom of God. If there is no power beyond the puny efforts of man, the kingdom of God has not been manifest. Many churches recite The Lord's Prayer as found in Matthew 6:10-14, praying "Thy kingdom come." The question that comes to mind is whether or not people would recognize the answer if God decided to send it. I have asked in numerous churches how such an answer could be recognized and rarely get a clear response. It seems that we pray these powerful words in a rote fashion, never expecting an explicit response from heaven, and when God *does* answer, we don't really want the answer we get!

Would you recognize the evidence of God's kingdom on earth? If God were to answer our request to send his kingdom, there would be an outpouring of *power*! I Corinthians 4:20 makes it very clear when it speaks of the nature of God's kingdom: "For the kingdom of God *is not a matter of talk but of power.*" It cannot be said more plainly than that!

When I was first confronted by this verse, I really wanted to add the word "just." I thought the verse should read, "The kingdom of God is not *just* a matter of talk," because I wanted to make room for talking about theological precepts; however, this declaration that the kingdom of God *is not* about eloquent sermons was laid out in specific terms. Paul said earlier that he'd gone up to the city of Corinth, not with profound pronouncements of great theological depths and insight (I Corinthians 2:1). He did not bring the message of God's kingdom to bear upon the conscience of the Corinthians by the weight of his great comprehension of the mysteries of Christ, even though he, above all men, could have done so.

The church in Corinth was established because Paul's ministry was characterized by overt, visible, demonstrations of the power of the Holy Spirit. Paul clearly states that he wanted the faith of those who were to believe based not in theological precepts but in the power of God. The truth is that talk will not pierce the armor of paganist humanism that has closed over the minds of men, nor will it crush the power of the lies that hold men slaves to Satan as in the major world religions. Faith does not rest in the cradle of theoretical concepts. It is amazing how those who have given theological justification to the absence of power in their own ministries hate those in whose ministry the demonstrations of power are found. Jesus said it with absolute clarity and authority. "You will receive power when the Holy Spirit comes on you..." He didn't say *might*, he said absolutely, "You *will....*" There was no limit to any particular generation, but said that *anyone* upon whom the Spirit comes will receive power. The absence of the power of the Holy Spirit is the absence of the kingdom of God.

If people pray, "Thy kingdom come," they must understand that when God responds to that prayer, supernatural power will be released into the affairs of men. Those who argue that such practical manifestations of power passed away with the founding fathers are likely to attribute the overt demonstrations of the Spirit's power to the Devil. Then, rather than recognize and submit to the power of the Holy Spirit, some doctrine is advocated justifying the absence of power in their own ministries and lives. Those who do this cease to be Bible believers. At best this is heresy, and at most, leads dangerously close to what Christ defined as blasphemy of the Holy Spirit. (Remember, blasphemy is attributing the works that come by the power of the Holy Spirit to the Devil.) It cannot be denied that thousands of individuals who profess Christ have experienced radical and profound healings. To deny that supernatural healings occur is simply choosing to be ignorant and blind.

Clearly the kingdom of God does not change. Neither does God change. God is omnipotent—all-powerful. Further, the kingdom of God is totally, absolutely, and all-inclusively a matter of power! The kingdom of God cannot and must not be muted by the theologies of evangelical, protestant, or catholic origin. If you disagree, it's not me you stand in disagreement with: study what "not of talk but of power" really means. We must allow God's Word to stand in the place of absolute authority in our thoughts and theologies and Christian practice.

The Keys of the Kingdom

When Jesus said in Matthew 16:19, "I give you the keys to the kingdom," the clear implication was that we were not naturally in possession of the kingdom of God or his power. Christ said that there were some specific things he was going to give us, and he called these keys. In giving us these keys, he intended that there be a recovery of power. We cannot recover the kingdom without recovering power!

We cannot get into the kingdom if we do not identify and use the keys he's given. Let me suggest that there are five keys identified in scripture that unlock the grace covenant. Have you ever contemplated keys? Consider the keys to your car. What do they represent? In short they represent four things, *ownership, authority, stewardship,* and *access to power.* How likely is it that someone will challenge your right to get into your car if you walk up to the car with keys in hand? The supposition is that only the owner has keys. If they see you using keys, they assume you *own* the car. If you have the keys and own the car your *authority* is absolute. If you own the car, *stewardship* is implied. You cannot expect a neighbor down the street to keep it in good running condition. If you have the keys, you are expected to look after it. Stewardship is not optional. Finally, you have *power* to do with it what you will. You can drive it, lend it, leave it in the driveway, sell it, paint it, or just let it rust. Keys give you access to the car, and if you use the keys as intended, you can tap its power. A car that cannot generate power is useless junk! It doesn't matter how shiny it looks or how nice the interior is, it is still junk.

Two other characteristics of keys can be suggested here. Keys *unlock* and allow entry; they also *lock* and forbid entry. The one with the keys locks and unlocks at will. We might call this the power to bind and loose, to remit or not to remit. Central to all of this is the necessity of having the keys. Christ said he'd give us the keys to the kingdom. These keys allow entry into the power of God, allowing us to recover what was lost. What was lost? Ownership, authority, right of stewardship and power: all of these were held by man as an inherent part of God's creative intention. Where was it lost? In Eden! So let's go back to Eden and find out the means by which man lost his birthright.

In Genesis three, Adam and Eve existed in a place of dominion over creation by God's directive decree. We know that Adam and Eve "fell from grace," but in order to fall from grace, they first had to be in a place of grace. What was it like for Adam and Eve to be in a state of grace? Well, they had intimate, personal fellowship and friendship with God: they saw him face to face. There was no sickness or poverty, no danger or fear. There was no demonic dominion over them. Their work was fruitful, and they were successful in whatever they did. There was no strife, and their relationship was unmarred. They knew and experienced the full blessing and presence of God and understood the natural creation within the context of the invisible kingdom of God. Natural realities were always perceived in the context of spiritual, supernatural reality. They had mandated purpose and meaning.

Satan hates God, and the best way for him to demonstrate that hatred was to destroy what God loves most: man. Lucifer, seeing mankind in the wonderful blessings inherent in grace, decided to cheat him out of the place God had made for him. Knowing how we had been created, his scheme was to get man to use the five keys in ways they were never meant to be used. He wanted man to lock himself away from God outside the state of grace. He could not steal the keys from man; man had to surrender them. Thus he appeared in Eden, enticing Eve to use the first key against herself.

Key Number One: The Ear Gate

Take time to read Genesis 3:1-7 carefully. Now the serpent was more crafty than any of the wild animals the Lord God had made. And he said to the woman, "Did God really say, 'You must not eat from any tree in the garden'?" [2]The woman said to the serpent, "We may eat fruit from the trees in the garden, [3]but God did say, 'You must not eat fruit from the tree that is in the middle of the garden, and you must not touch it, or you will die.'" [4]"You will not surely die," the serpent said to the woman. [5]"For God knows that when you eat of it your eyes will be opened, and you will be like God, knowing good and evil." [6]When the woman saw that the tree was good for food and pleasing to the eye, and also desirable for gaining wisdom, she took some and ate it. She also gave some to her husband who was with her, and he ate it. [7]Then the eyes of both of them were opened, and they realized they were naked; so they sewed fig leaves together and made coverings for themselves.

What was the first thing Satan had to gain dominance over? Look at his approach, and follow the sequence of events. Event number one leads us to an understanding of the first key to grace. He said to the woman, "Did God *really* say…" What was Lucifer counting on Eve to do? Simply put, he wanted her to *listen*, to use her *ear* for something that it was not designed to be used for: to listen to Satan rather than stay in submission to the Word of God. What could Eve have done that would have defeated him on the spot? Turn a deaf ear to his voice. If she had refused to hear what he was saying, his whole scheme to bring them down out of grace would have failed absolutely. So, the first thing Satan was after was to get Eve listening to him. How did he know he was beginning to succeed against her? She tried to answer his question. As soon as she began to speak he knew he had gained access to her ear gate, and for the first time, she could no longer hear the voice of God as He had intended. In this confrontation between Eve and Lucifer, the first click of the grace combination was heard in both heaven and hell.

Ever since that fateful moment, mankind has been subjected to the rationalizations of the demonic voice and slave to the whispering voices of hell. To the captured ear, demonic logic is all that is reasonable. What comes out the mouth exposes what's gone into the ear. Things like gossip, criticism, tale bearing, and grumbling betray who our master really is. Satan can tell by our words if he is getting through or not. So it was with Eve: her words indicated that the demonic message had begun its intended destruction. Beware of the Satanic whisper from those closest to you, for we are most vulnerable to the words of our close friends in church, our buddy on the board, and even, sometimes especially, our spouses! Eve was as close to Adam as is possible, and because he listened to and acted upon the words of his wife, the entire human race reaped the fruit of his actions.

So key number one to staying in or missing grace has to do with the ear. Satan cannot take our ears; we have to surrender them to him. He does know far better than we do how vulnerable we are to what we hear. If we can learn to guard our ear gate, Satan will be immediately defeated in his efforts to draw us out of the grace place. Those of us who profess to be living within the grace covenant of Christ, take heed: our ears belong to Christ. We are repeatedly admonished, "He that hath an ear let him hear what the Spirit is saying to the church," and "My sheep hear my voice and follow me." Do you want the blessings of grace? Then we must come back into a state of grace through faith in Christ, and to stay there, *we must turn a deaf ear to satanic whisperings.*

Key Number Two: The Eye Gate

The eyes, how things are perceived, represent the second key to grace or disgrace. Once Eve began to give ear to the Satanic voice, Lucifer began the second step to leading Eve out of her state of grace. Having gained dominion over her ear gate, he now moved to get her to focus on the fruit of the tree of the knowledge of good and evil saying, "In the day you eat it, your eyes will be opened…" Note what it says next: "The woman *saw* it was pleasing to the *eye*…" What is the Satanic tactic here? He moved to provide her with a perspective different than God's. By getting her to focus on the fruit, she began to follow with her eyes what she'd heard with her ears.

The truth is we always look to confirm with our eyes what our ears have heard. Let me illustrate for you how we operate out of this connection between the ears and eyes spontaneously. Assume you are walking down a street. You crossed a major intersection about one hundred feet behind you. Two trucks approach the intersection. They are traveling at 60 miles per hour. One has the right of way; the other, a stop sign. The one with the stop sign doesn't stop, and those two trucks collide with incredible force. What is the first clue to you that something has happened behind you? The reverberating clamor of breaking glass and twisting metal! Now stop and think: when the deafening noise of that crash reaches your ear, what is your first, spontaneous reaction? Do you stop and think, "My, my, what a racket! I should turn around and have a look." Not likely! Upon hearing the crash, your head reflexively jerks backward so you can confirm what you just heard. That is how we are built. God made us that way, and Satan knows it. His scheme is to use how we were made against us. First, he speaks; as we listen, we begin to use our eyes to verify what we have been listening to. Give him control of your ears, and he will soon control how you see all of life. We've all experienced the clarity of retrospect, where every word and deed is reconsidered in light of new information. That is why listening to gossip and speaking slander is so deadly. We substantiate what we've heard with our eyes by re-evaluating events through lens of gossip. You will see and come to believe what you hear unless you bring your hearing and vision into submission under truth.

For example, how do you see the church? Do you see the church as Christ perceives her in Ephesians 5:26-27, without spot, wrinkle or blemish, holy and blameless? If you are like most of us, chances are good you perceive the church to be just as fallen as Adam. Well, has the church been cleansed by the washing of the Water by the Word or not? Is our cleansing true in the present tense, or do we relegate this description of the church to the apostolic era? The point here is simply to ask you if you see things God's way or the Devil's way. Since Eden, our focus has been built around the tree of the knowledge of good and evil, but if we allow it to stay there, we are sure to believe negatively and die. Consequently, our negative words regarding the body of Christ will not promote life, but death.

Key Number Three: The Mind Gate

With the two faculties of sight and hearing in operation something very significant is happening to Eve. As she began to focus on the tree, she began to consider and admire its fruit. Her eyes were trained in the direction Satan's words had suggested. Lucifer, standing off to one side, could tell that the second click of the combination had just fallen: he had usurped control over her ears and eyes. Tragically, she was not even aware of the keys that the adversary was using to destroy her and the nature of mankind's existence.

While the mind reaches out into the world largely through the ears and eyes, processing events and structuring decisions around the information it takes in, it is the mind that ultimately decides what to do with the information it receives. Our ears hear everything, and our eyes take in every detail, but it is our mind, through control processes, that decides what should be attended to or discarded. We once moved into a house that had a set of train tracks about fifteen feet behind our small backyard. Before we purchased the house, we asked the realtor how many times a day trains ran on the tracks, and she told us once or twice. We discovered soon after moving in that this set of tracks was a thoroughfare, and we had to listen to trains on an hourly basis, day and night. Every time a train went by, the house shook, cups jingled in our china closet, and pictures shifted on the wall. We were horrified, not knowing how we were going to live so close to all that racket. The truth is that after a few days, we didn't even notice it anymore. The mental processes quickly adjusted to the fact this was a sound that didn't need our attention. This same process must come to work on our spiritual senses: when the train that is demonic solicitation comes roaring by, it may be hard to ignore at first, but once you recognize the sound for what it is, the grace-trained mind begins to serve as a filter to its rumblings. Our destinies are tied up in how we think. Attending to wrong information leads to wrong decisions that in turn destroy our lives. In passing let me ask a question: Christian, what work have you done to identify and dismantle the secular presuppositions you were raised in and taught to believe? What secular assumptions still hold sway over your thought processes?

Eve's mind failed to recognize the roaring train of demonic deception, and she concluded two things based on her faulty information. First she saw (or thought she saw) that the fruit was "*good for food*" (Genesis 3:6). Was it? God had said, "In the day you eat of it, you will surely die." The warning was pretty specific. How can food that is guaranteed to kill you be good for lunch? The God-centered information she had in her mind was overpowered by what she saw and heard, and she came to a wrong conclusion. You might say she was dead wrong! Second, she concluded that the fruit was *"desirable for gaining wisdom."* Having arrived at a conclusion, an inordinate desire began to stir deep within her heart: she coveted that which would be her sure demise, and carnal craving was birthed in mankind. Not only did she have this death desire in her heart, she believed she was going to gain wisdom by eating the fruit. Well, in a measure she was right. James 3:15 describes the kind of wisdom she gained: "Such wisdom does not come down from heaven but is earthly, unspiritual, of the Devil."

Ever since that moment, the mind of man has been subject to a devilish "wisdom" that is no wisdom at all. This mind-set leads to death. Eve, thinking herself wise, became foolish, and Godly wisdom now took on the appearance of foolishness for mankind. Spiritual wisdom no longer made sense to her, and the Devil re-defined truth. He had penetrated her mind and taken dominion over her thought life with her full cooperation.

A third click on life's combination fell into place, and man took another step toward life outside the grace of God. As Lucifer stood before Eve in the garden, shrieks of demonic delight no doubt resounded in the dark regions of hell as mankind's intellect became the pawn of demonic strategy. Nations were about to become vulnerable to destructive deceptions. Courts, kings, educators, and religion would now propagate hell's agenda. Satanic wisdom was taking center stage, and as II Corinthians 4:4 reports, blinded the mind of man.

The tragedy born on that day with Eve was, she actually believed she was right. Opinion was born! Every man believes his own conclusions, and many even die for them. Proverbs 16:25 lays it out by saying, "There is a way that seems right to man, but the ends thereof are the ways of death." If his conclusion is that there is no God, he believes that conclusion. After a conclusion has been formed, he becomes established in his own religious framework, and all of life's decisions and outlooks are predicated on that "religious" view of the world. Romans 1:21-22 describes it well: "Their thinking became futile, and their foolish hearts were darkened. They claimed to be wise, but they became foolish."

Religious atheism illustrates perfectly the shift that took place in the thought process that resulted from man's rejection of God. The atheist formed his conclusion around a conviction that there is nothing beyond the material time-and-space framework in which men live. They sit down and write their humanist manifestos with specific tenets of faith, trusting their own conclusion. In this they are just like Eve. God said, "In the day that you eat of it you will die." With the eating of that fruit, the deadly mentality of humanistic rationalism was born.

We spoke in chapter four about the humanists' position that they can find no evidence for the existence of God and fully believe our limited dimensions to be the only reality. All information must be made to conform to their conclusion about reality. If some form of information does not confirm their conclusion, it is summarily rejected and is considered to have no validity. They set about forcing all cultural standards to conform to their own religious view of the world. Every individual in that culture is progressively forced to live within what becomes an intolerant religious view. To choose to believe something else and to live outside the specifics of imposed humanism is to be labeled a bigot or even mad.

Atheism in itself bears witness to its inherent errors. The humanist's solutions to many of the worlds' problems are abortion, euthanasia, or suicide. Their ways make death the "final solution." According to suggested figures, the earth's population should not exceed two billion people. If this is true, the worlds' population is far too large, so the population of earth has to be reduced by some four billion people! Abortion alone has taken the lives of multiplied millions, and even though they are wrong, many believe in their hearts that such things as abortion and euthanasia are right. It has even been suggested to no small acclaim that the legalization of abortion has improved the economy and reduced crime (Donahue, Levitt). Remember the "values clarification" exercises such as "life boat" where students were asked who they would throw overboard in a crowded life boat? The underlying and undeniably humanistic message there is that some life has more value than others, and where life doesn't meet a minimal standard of quality, death is perceived to be a logical solution.

Once Lucifer gained dominion over the ear and the eye gate and had subjected the thought life of mankind to demonic logic, what did demonic strategy have left to conquer? The two remaining keys basically turned themselves. He had only to step back and watch. Having come to a demonically calculated conclusion that she believed to be her own, Eve acted upon it. Because she believed the fruit was good for food and for gaining wisdom, she ate some of the fruit. What fell next to demonic dominion? The heart.

Key Four: The Heart—The Doorway to Belief

Proverbs 23:7 asserts, "*As a man thinks in his heart, so is he.*" Note the relationship between the mind and the heart. The heart does not have a brain of its own. It is totally dependent upon the mind for information. The heart believes what the mind conceives. Romans 10:10 puts it like this: "for with the heart man believes." What was Lucifer after? He needed dominion over the heart, because it is the belief center—the faith factory—of man. After his thinking becomes futile, mankind is ever prisoner of a foolish heart. As Romans 1:21 reinforces, "their foolish hearts were darkened." Satan knew what the result would be for mankind once Eve's heart succumbed to the demonic equation. He understood that for anti-grace to be effective he had to cause a fundamental shift in Eve's thought processes. He had to replace the mindset God had planted in Eve with his own, contrary mindset. Once successful at this he knew he'd captured her heart—faith center, and all future generations became subject to devilish persuasion. The last part of Proverbs 23:7, "so is he," should not be overlooked. What we become, the fulfillment of our potential, is wholly locked up in the thought/heart equation. We cannot be different from what we think, and therefore, inherently believe. A religious humanist cannot be expected to endorse biblical principles of grace and conduct. He will always judge according to those inner workings of thought and belief. Give an atheistic judge a biblical law to enforce, and he will twist it to conform to his atheism. To expect otherwise is, at best, to be naive.

God built man to act out what he believes. Satan knew this and knows it of us today. While Lucifer could not see what was going on in her heart, once she began reaching for the fruit he knew that he had conquered who and what Eve was in the inner part. The outer act evidenced what had occurred within. The fourth key of anti-grace went click. Faith in God had been replaced by faith in carnal conclusions, and the faith citadel of man fell to demonic invasion. Mankind became a prisoner to his own wrong convictions. Reference to the Word of God became irrelevant as the governing factor in the decision-making processes of life. The fourth key of the kingdom was now in Satanic possession.

Key Five: The Tongue—Doorway of Confession

As far as Satan was concerned, the last key would turn automatically by the will of man. He had only to stand back and wheeze his delight. Genesis 3:6 records, "She also gave some to her husband, who was with her, and he ate it." Note the phrase, "who was with her." Adam stood there watching what was happening and did nothing. Note as well that Eve became the active agent, not Lucifer. He simply stood back and watched the outcome of his own depraved handiwork.

Sometimes it helps us to try and picture what might have transpired. She had reached out, picked some fruit, took a few bites. Now when a person bites into a really sour or bad-tasting bit of food, they don't really want someone else to have a bite. If it tastes really delicious there is an almost automatic response: "My, this is really delightful. Try some!" Your taste buds tingle with the sweetness; you think, "This is really good," and someone next you receives an open invitation. The point in this is to understand that once something is believed in the heart, an automatic response is produced. Luke 6:45 confirms that the mouth speaks out of the abundance of the heart, and according to Romans 10:9, our very salvation is predicated upon this heart/mouth equation. What people believe in their heart will rise to the tongue. We do not know what Eve might have said upon tasting the fruit, but we know that what was in her heart found expression in her words to Adam. Her tongue became the tool of Satan. She began speaking for Lucifer. His message has forever after been on the tongue of lost mankind. James has much to say about the power of the tongue, and Proverbs 18:21 declares that the tongue has the power of life and death. What a poignant illustration we have of this in Adam and Eve. Scripture is full of repeated injunctions regarding the use of the tongue. James 3:6 says, "the tongue is a flame of fire. It is full of wickedness that can ruin your whole life. It can turn the entire course of your life into a blazing flame of destruction, for it is set on fire by hell itself" (NLT). The tongue has burned down empires and nations, and as Satan's tool, the mouth of multiplied Christians has burned down countless churches and ministries worldwide. Lucifer has only to stand back as he did with Eve and watch the conquered tongue of man do his work for him. He does not have the power to curse mankind, but must find a willing tongue. It is only because we have not regained dominion over our tongues that he continues to destroy other Christians and churches. Mark it well: if Christians took back dominion of their tongues, *the work of Lucifer in the body of Christ would be instantly and absolutely brought to a halt!*

Even when believers hear the message of the power of the tongue to do Satan's work, they continue to use it to gossip in the form of prayer requests and sometimes even in prayer itself! Criticism, gossip, and slander cannot be justified by invoking the excuse, "Well, no man can tame the tongue." This is certainly true, but we already know that doesn't mean the tongue cannot be tamed: *God* can tame it. He is omnipotent. Nothing is too hard for the Lord. With man it is impossible, but all things are possible with God—even the taming of the tongue! How is the tongue to be tamed? By the impartation of grace! Grace is, at its core, the impartation of a new heart that comes from the Father by the Holy Spirit. Remember that out of the abundance of the heart the mouth speaks. What happens to the tongue of believers who have, by grace, really been brought into the reality of the new heart? *Grace tames that tongue!* Lucifer knew that as long as Adam and Eve lived in a state of grace he would never have the tongue of mankind to work his destruction. Grace is an impenetrable fortress for men if they choose to get in it and to stay there, but mankind was drawn down out of that fortress. Had Eve's mind checked the use of her eye gate upon hearing something contrary to God's Word, entry into the heart of man by the demonic could never have occurred. Once the mind gate fell, the heart became easy prey. The faith mechanism of man fell to demonic delusion, and the tongue became the instrument of a demonic gospel. Thus, the fifth key to anti-grace was turned by the deliberate intent of the fallen heart. So it is today: believers become participants in the anti-grace strategies of hell, all the while singing, "Jesus is Lord!"

Satan knows how God made man to function. In our ignorance, we still participate in the demonic anti-grace strategy. He knows how these five keys operate and that we operate in them reactively, not out of a conscious process. All of life operates on these five keys working in the exact succession as outlined. We do not think about them. Satan is successful in using these five keys against us *because we have never recognized their importance in the scheme of grace.* In all probability they have never been expounded to many in the believing body of Christ. Christian, if you hope to live a successful, supernatural, holy, joyful, Christ-centered life, you are going to have to come to grips with how these five keys are operating in your life. Ignore them and Satan will continue to work destruction in your life, family, career, and church.

There is an illustration you can use to prove how instantly these five keys operate in every individual. (I have used this same experiment internationally and the results are always the same.) The next time you are with a group of people, hold up a piece of white paper (or any color you have at hand) and ask, "What color is this piece of paper?" Without any conscious thought, the folks in front of you will demonstrate how man was created to be a grace-oriented creature: the *eye* of every *listening* person will fall automatically on that piece of paper. *The ear gate automatically engaged the eye gate.* Instantly, the *mind* receives the information being fed it through the eye gate, processes the information and concludes, "It's white." Once the conclusion has been reached, the *heart* believes the mental conclusion. The mind and heart keys have now been engaged. Guess what comes next? Although you never ask them to speak, the answer will pop off their *tongues* like a knee jerk reaction: "White." Why? *Because that is how God made us.* You will never find someone praying, once they have determined that the paper is white, "Now Lord, give me faith to believe it is white." The heart believes it is white because that is how it has been designed to work by God.

In the garden, all Lucifer had to do was ask a simple question: "Did God really say..." With that bit of prompting, the grace structure in Adam and Eve took over and Satan had successfully wrested the keys of the kingdom from mankind. They were no longer in the reality of the grace environment God had intended for man and consequently became a slave to sin and death. Lucifer had his way with us. He had control of our ears, perception, understanding, faith center, and tongue. Truly, all of life was set on fire by hell itself.

This is the state of modern man no matter what skin of civility he might wear. Underneath, Lucifer holds the keys of fallen man and has locked us behind prison gates. Similarly, although some vestiges of grace may linger among believers, one has only to spend some time in churches to discover proof of the fallen tongue. We are not the citadels of grace we claim to be. Our tongues betray our profession. The tongue of preacher against preacher, believer against believer, and this denomination against that denomination manifests the deadly poison of anti-grace. Think about it! Anti-grace abounding in the camp of the grace-redeemed. "My people are destroyed for a lack of knowledge" (Hosea 4:6). What knowledge? The knowledge of grace: what it is, how it works, how it changes the heart, how it can be received and grown in and how it is to be ministered—*that* knowledge!

Now, let's see if these five keys can be identified in the New Covenant known as the grace covenant. Ephesians 2:8 declares that we are saved by grace. (Since our subject presently is grace, we'll leave faith for later.) We are saved by grace, and grace has five keys. How then did God move to reintroduce grace into the world? He sent his Word. Romans speaks of the foolishness of preaching. When we preach, we are appealing to the ear gate. Once an individual starts to open his ear to the message of truth being spoken, a process of examination begins. The *listening* individual will begin to examine and look for confirmation of what is being spoken. That confirmation can take many forms. It may be the manifestation of love among believers, it may be the joy of an individual, or any of a host of things, but the listening individual will begin a process of looking to corroborate what they have been hearing. If they find such evidence, the mind kicks into gear and comes to a conclusion: "Boy, this stuff is really real." Suddenly, the heart is engaged and it begins to believe what is going on upstairs in the mind. The heart, coming to believe the conclusions of the mind, prompts a response to the stimulus of what is being heard and faith comes alive. The message is believed in the heart and soon it springs to life on the tongue. That is why we so often encourage new believers to tell someone about their decision. The five keys have each played their successive part in conversion and the individual has been brought out of anti-grace into saving grace. Lucifer has then lost control of the keys of the kingdom.

Can these keys be found in New Testament scripture? Check out Ephesians 4:7: "But to each one of us grace has been given as Christ apportioned it." *Grace* has been given. Verse 15 states, "Instead, speaking the truth in love, we will in all things grow up into him who is the Head, that is, Christ." *Speaking* the truth starts the grace process.

Key 1: Activate the Ear Gate

Matthew 10:27b: "What I whisper in your ears, shout…for all to hear!"
Matthew 13:9: "He who has an ear to hear, let him hear."
Hebrews 2:1: "We must pay more careful attention, therefore, to what we have heard, so that we do not drift away."

Key 2: Activate the Eye Gate

Matthew 13:15: "For this people's heart has become calloused; they hardly hear with their ears, and they have closed their eyes. Otherwise they might see with their eyes, hear with their ears, understand with their hearts and turn, and I would heal them."

Key 3: Renew the Mind

Ephesians 4: 17-18, 23: "So I tell you this, and insist on it in the Lord, that you must no longer live as the Gentiles do, in the futility of their thinking. They are darkened in their understanding and separated from the life of God because of the ignorance that is in them due to the hardening of their hearts…to be made new in the attitude of your minds."

Key 4: Inner Transformation Resulting in the New Self

Ephesians 4: 2: "Be completely humble and gentle; be patient, bearing with one another in love."
Ephesians 4: 23-24: "Be renewed in the spirit of your mind, and put on the new man which was created according to God, in true righteousness and holiness."

Key 5: Convert the Tongue

Ephesians 4:25, 29: "Therefore, each of you must put off falsehood and speak truthfully to his neighbor, for we are all members of one body. …Do not let any unwholesome talk come out of your mouths, but only what is helpful for building others up according to their needs, that it may benefit those who listen."

Now, in the western culture, we prefer everything to be simple and linear—you know: step one, step two, step three, conclusion and application. God does not think like western man; he is not limited to linear thinking. Peruse the Sermon on the Mount in Matthew 5, 6 and 7, and you will soon discover that one passage seems to have little direct link with the next passage. Try reading through the Proverbs with an eye to making a linear pattern, and what you'll walk away with is a headache! Check out Ephesians chapter four. Many expositors rightly use this chapter to illustrate the nature of the church, but so often such exposition fails to make reference to the role of grace in fashioning the church. The linear mindset tends to ignore the restatement of the core definition of grace and three of the five keys of grace as set out in the chapter. Somehow this mindset misses the emphatic reference to grace. We can be sure of one thing: in our thinking and exposition we need to be certain that grace has been given its proper place. The church cannot be defined otherwise!

When the gospel of grace is proclaimed, men are expected to adopt a different perception of reality: they are called to see things as *God* defines them and as he says things *actually* are. Perceptions that foster falsehood, that justify lying, stealing, poor work ethics, bitterness, rage, anger, brawling, slander, and every form of malice must be rejected in light of God's Word. In order to see things the way God says they are, an entirely *other* methodology of awareness must be adopted. God said to Eve, "That tree will kill you; don't eat its fruit." She chose to see it differently and learned that what God said was true, no matter how enthusiastically she embraced the lie of the Serpent. Now, as grace abounds, we need to recover the correct perceptions of God, others and the world around us. The gospel of grace mandates a radical shift in how man perceives things around him. In Luke 4:18, Jesus referred to this as "recovery of sight."

Have you ever meditated on Genesis 3:7? If you ask most believers what the very first consequence of the loss of grace was, most do not know; however, scripture states that consequence clearly: "The eyes of both of them were opened." This at first may appear to be a bit of a curious statement. Think about what, "The eyes of both of them were opened" means. Were they blind before this? In fact, before the fall there was nothing wrong at all with their vision. What then can the meaning of this statement be? Why would the Holy Spirit bother to drop this bit of information into the biblical record? Obviously, something happened to their sight, but what? We know that it was Christ who would come down into the garden in the evening to fellowship with them. The King James expresses this in a very interesting way when it records that Adam and Eve "heard the voice of God walking." Jesus is the Word. When God is speaking to man it is Christ speaking. It was Jesus who found Adam and Eve in that state where their eyes had been opened. It was he who came that there might be a recovery of sight. What sight had been lost? What had happened to their eyes at the fall from grace?

I have no desire to argue this with anyone, but I offer this as a possible explanation. Up until the fall, Adam and Eve had what might be termed double vision. By this I mean they could see in two dimensions. They could see things in the spirit realm just a clearly as they could see a cloud, a tree, a cow, or anything in the corporeal realm. When grace ceased to be their reality, it was as if they could no longer perceive the natural world around them in the greater context of the spiritual reality, and their perception of reality ceased to extend beyond their natural circumstances. Perhaps a couple of diagrams might help. Note the placement of the dark lined circle!

Sight Capability Prior to the Fall; Sight Capability in Non-Grace Reality

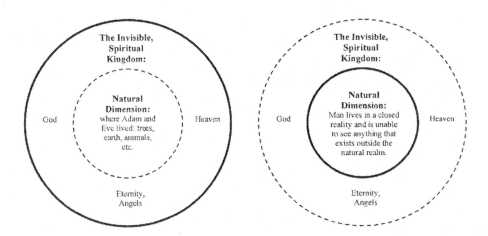

Ever since the Fall, Mankind has been locked into a one-dimensional perception of reality where all he can see is the natural world around him, and everything is judged by his present circumstances. For fallen humanity, this present existence has no greater, counter-balancing reality. When humanists declare they can find no evidence of a supernatural reality, they are admitting to the reality of non-grace existence. They are truly blind, but assert with preponderant conviction that they can see. They have no reservations about imposing their invalid conclusions of reality upon all men, by force of law and the gun if necessary. This blindness has been imposed on every facet of human existence and is reinforced by humanistic media, educators, medical ethicists, judiciary, and politicians. Thinking themselves wise, humans have been subjected to the folly of blind, sincere fools.

When individuals are reinstated into grace by the power of the Holy Spirit, certain dimensions of what life was like prior to the fall should be reflected. Grace, when it becomes a functional reality, inherently means a dramatic recovery of that which was lost. Things like intimacy with God, power, joy, success in our endeavors, health, hope, purpose, and a genuine inner sense of significance can be restored. Christ spoke explicitly of the nature of that recovered state and what the kingdom of heaven was like in Matthew 13:11-17. Here, he tells his disciples that the secrets would no longer be secrets because the knowledge of those secrets had been given to them, and explained how those secrets were to be revealed. In verse 12 he promised that if they could get hold of what he was saying, they would be given more resulting in abundance, but if they missed it, even what little they possessed would be lost. Jesus' message to them was, "Hey, guys, don't miss what I'm about to say." Do you remember the initial keys and the significant role they play in the grace-oriented experience? Well, here Christ hits four of the five keys again and again with almost overwhelming force. His purpose in such declaration was to help us appreciate that there is a reality that exists beyond the natural dimension in which we have been held prisoner since the Eden disaster.

The disciples asked why Jesus spoke to the people in parables. In verse thirteen Christ said, "This is why I speak to them this way. They see, but they're blind. They hear, but they don't listen. They don't even try to understand" (GW). Proverbs 25:2 notes that "It is the glory of God to conceal a matter." Jesus spoke in parables so that the listeners would have to think about what he was saying in order to understand. This concept is not very well understood in western Christianity, evidenced by our adoption of the K.I.S.S. approach. As it turns out, God is not really interested in expressing his concepts in bald terms that require no searching. He himself cannot be found without an intense search rooted in the heart. It seems that many believers want everything made so simple that they don't have to use their minds. Rather than respond to a challenge to think beyond what they are used to, there is a demand for teaching to fall within comfortable limits, and if the pastor doesn't reduce biblical truth down into its simplest terms, folks get uptight and critical. In truth, if the pastor capitulates, this is really boring, and soon people complain that they are not being fed.

It is interesting to find how many believers will react against God's glory. If we as believers really want to come into a functional understanding of the kingdom, then there is no alternative but to discover and use the keys of the kingdom as outlined by scripture. If we do not get hold of these keys, then clearly and absolutely the kingdom will remain veiled. How does God intend people to come into an understanding of his kingdom and get healed? In the next few lines watch the emphasis Christ places on seeing, hearing, perceiving, understanding and the heart.

That's why I speak to them in parables	v. 13	Ear Gate
because seeing they do not see,		Eye Gate
and hearing they do not hear		Ear Gate
nor do they understand.		Mind
And in them the prophecy of Isaiah is fulfilled:		
Hearing you will hear and shall not understand,	v. 14	Mind
and seeing you will see and not perceive;		Mind
For the hearts of this people have grown dull,		Heart
their ears are hard of hearing,	v. 15	Ear Gate
and their eyes they have closed,		Eye Gate
lest they should see with their eyes		Eye Gate
and hear with their ears,		Ear Gate
lest they should understand with their hearts		Mind & Heart
and turn		Result of Keys = Faith Response
so that I should heal them.		GOD'S KINGDOM MADE MANIFEST

Now in reading these few verses, a strong correlation becomes evident between the keys Satan used to draw Adam and Eve down out of the grace state and how Christ identifies the same keys as the means for discovery of God's Kingdom and a return to life in the grace of God. The word "heal" here according to W.E. Vine includes both physical and spiritual healing. Matthew in his gospel uses this word (which means "to be made whole") 22 times, and Luke uses it 15 times to refer to physical healing. If believers would seek the Holy Spirit for the activation of the keys to grace in their own lives they would discover the real meaning of "healing grace." The keys to grace are the keys to being made whole. Healing—physical, spiritual and for the soul—is inherent in this grace declaration of Christ. Those who would argue against healing as a present provision find themselves arguing against these very declarations of Christ. He could have used words such as saved, sanctified, redeemed, or blessed to define the results of functional grace, but he chose one specifically: healed!

Jesus links what he is saying to the parable of the sower by explaining how a man can hear without being changed and can see without being influenced. The word about healing goes down into the heart, but the Devil comes and snatches it away. If one jot or tittle does not pass away, then "I would heal them" cannot be removed from the biblical record. Included in the appropriation of the keys of the kingdom is the absolute promise of healing, body, soul, and spirit. Look at what Christ says to his disciples in verse sixteen. He declares them blessed. Why does he say that? It is because they *see* with their *eyes* and *hear* with their *ears*. What are the first two keys to unlocking real grace in our lives? The recovery of sight and the capacity to hear. When there is, by the anointing of the Holy Spirit, a recovery of sight (as spoken of in Luke 4:18) and an ability to hear what the Spirit is saying to the church, we begin the process of turning away from demonic persuasion to a grace mindset. Renewed thought processes infiltrate our hearts, which in turn, convert our tongues. Lucifer is defeated, and by the grace administrations of the Holy Spirit, Christ has restored us to our rightful, original place: grace!

The inevitable result flowing from the utilization of the keys of grace is the manifestation of power. Consider the Lord's Prayer: "For thine is the kingdom and the *power*..." Power! Look at Christ's words as recorded in Matthew 13:23, the man who *hears* the word (ear gate) and *understands* (mind/heart combination) the word *produces* a crop yielding a hundred, sixty, or thirty fold.

A note in passing: all seed is not intended to produce a hundred fold. Not everyone is going to have hundreds of thousands of dollars, nor can it be suggested that everyone will become multi-millionaires. One thing is sure however: the farmer whose fields are producing these kinds of yields does not live in poverty. Scripture declares that God gives power to produce wealth (Deuteronomy 8:18). The keys of grace are God's way out of poverty and into productive life styles. It is *grace before faith* that causes one to come into abundance!

The intent in this chapter is to define as clearly as I can the five keys to grace and to highlight a couple of benefits accruing from them. Is grace controversial in its outworking? No doubt! But if we are to be truly Christian in both doctrine and practice, then grace must be allowed to *be* grace in our lives to the full extent of its power! Many speak of grace in reverent tones, but they set their own narrow, harsh limits around what grace can provide and accomplish. Heavy theological arguments are pounded into the heads and hearts of believers, insisting that such manifest power has passed away. Many are left to clinging to powerless dogmas about God fashioned by men, and the omnipotent God is considered silent and uninterested in the affairs of men because we have effectively told him he is not welcome to work in our lives. To have the power of God manifest is to lose control. Oh, yes, pray for revival, but be sure to ask for an orderly one! Grace can be paid a fleshly homage, but when it activates the kingdom of God in the lives of believers, drastic measures are immediately called for by the injunction: "do all things decently and in order" (I Corinthians 14:40). The truth is, a manifest God is a God who is being glorified! Certainly, there must be believers who genuinely crave the expression of God's glory in the church. Surely, a desperate world requires a church full of believers whose lives are full of the manifest glory of God. Let me state it again: real grace brings the believer into manifest power, and once this power is released, it indicates the glory of God has fallen!

As believers begin to discover the functional reality of the five keys to grace in their lives it should be understood that there are no limits to the discovery of grace. God is, for example, omnipresent. He is everywhere at the same time. Recently, scientists at the Sloan Survey discovered a quasar some 27 billion light years from earth (Koppes). That is an astounding distance. Light, we are told, travels at 186,000 miles per second. No one can really fathom how far 27 billion years traveling at 186,000 miles per second would really be, but the truth is that God is equally present here with you as he is at that quasar. What's the point? No one can even fathom how big God really is. Therefore, when we come to consider a character attribute of God such as grace we must understand that *grace is as infinite in its nature as God is infinite!* We can never exhaustively experience all that is grace. As long as we pursue the discovery of grace, there will always be new vistas of God's providential grace to be discovered and experienced. In reaching out to experience the grace of God, we are reaching out into an infinite expanse. We should be continually reaching for more as we should be continually growing in grace.

Let's begin to draw this consideration of the five keys to grace to a close. Functional grace becomes a reality in life when our ears and eyes, by the Spirit's anointing, are turned back toward God. Take a quick trip through scripture and you will repeatedly encounter biblical characters who are either hearing God speak or are responding to what they have seen. Whole books are based on one or the other. In his first epistle, the apostle John starts with, "What we have heard, what we have seen with our eyes, what we observed and touched with our own hands—this is the Word of life!" Can anything in scripture be taken as coincidental? Is it coincidence that the disciples' experience with Christ and in Christ started with hearing and seeing? Note that John says: "What we've touched with our own hands." If grace is to produce its supernatural fruit in our lives, the exposition of grace is not sufficient in and of itself: it must be allowed to carry us into the theater of personal, intimate experience.

How do we pass into the experiential dimension of grace? The five keys of grace must become operational. There must be a restoration of hearing and seeing invisible things. Again, Paul clearly teaches this in II Corinthians 4:18 when he says, "So we fix our eyes not on what is seen but on what is unseen." At the fall from grace, the human spirit lost its capacity to hear and see beyond the natural realm and man became dependent upon the bodily senses for information. The human spirit was created to be engaged primarily with that which is invisible and spiritual, but at the fall the human spirit died and such capability ceased. The restoration of the human spirit begins at the new birth. Implicit in that restoration comes the potential to hear the voice and follow what cannot be seen in the natural. These restored capabilities are absolutely essential if we are to discover the supernatural life of Christ, the reality of God's kingdom, the presence, power and gifts of the Spirit, and the progressive discovery of God's purposes for our lives.

Ask any genuine believer about his or her death, and there is an absolute conviction that upon death they will pass into heaven hearing, seeing, feeling, smelling, and tasting. At the risk of being repetitious, let me say the capacities to hear and see in the spirit realm are inherent capabilities of the reborn spirit. God did not design us simply to experience these capabilities after we die but created us in Christ to be able to function in these capabilities while we live in the body. This concept is wholly substantiated in the scriptures.

Part of what it means to be full of grace is to be living lifestyles that are rooted in and responding to what is being heard and seen in the spirit realm. Paul said that he'd not been disobedient to the heavenly vision (Acts 26:9), so what did Paul frame his life decisions around? The things he saw in the spirit realm. His actions in the natural realm were governed by what he'd seen in the invisible realm. Peter, in Acts 10, did not base his decision to go to the home of a gentile based on natural criteria but on a hearing and seeing rooted in the spiritual reality. You can note that in Acts 11:2, Peter was criticized for taking action based on what he'd seen and heard in the spirit realm. Seeing and hearing are most controversial among those who, professing to believe, neither hear nor see. In Acts 9, Ananias undertook the risk of faith action based on a vision, but by obeying what he'd seen and heard in the spirit realm, he moved in the purposes of God, enabled the Holy Spirit to come on the scene and himself became the minister of supernatural, miracle power. That's the way it is: grace obedience will always lead the way into the manifest power of the Holy Spirit.

I realize that there are strong theologies that contradict this biblical pattern of hearing and seeing. At one point, I was seeking God for greater measures of power to be manifest in my life and ministry and openly spoke of this desire. The spiritual leadership in my denomination heard of this and came to me with the caution that I should not be seeking for more power in my ministry. Somehow it was sufficient to proclaim the doctrine of Christ. That caution became a real barrier. For the next several years, I was afraid to ask God for more power because I didn't want to "get off track."

Fear is a primal force behind the doctrine of men. Believers are given ominous warnings of spiritual disaster and demonic deception if they dare to live beyond cold doctrine. "Oh, that is not of God; it is mysticism." The doctrines of men will always keep people from seeking first the kingdom of God, which was a direct mandate given us by Christ in Matthew 6:33. Clearly, if we understand what it is to seek first the kingdom of God, we will understand that this means seeking the Holy Spirit's power. Remember what I Corinthians 4:20 says: "The kingdom of God is not a matter of talk (doctrine) but of power." Our doctrine must not militate against the manifest power of God. Believers must ask themselves if they are going to believe the scriptural patterns of truth or the doctrines of men. Certainly we need sound doctrine, but not at the expense of eradicating the power of God in our practice of the Christian life.

Wherever you are, would you open your heart to God and ask him to fill it with the full measure of grace? Grace is something God gives and something that needs to be received. He gives grace to the humble.

A Prayer for Greater Grace

> Dear Lord Jesus, I come before you asking that you begin to fill my heart with your grace on a daily basis and teach me what it means to receive it and live out of that gift. I want to hear your voice; I want you to open the eyes of my heart. Holy Spirit, come in your power and restore these capabilities to my human spirit. Thank you, Lord!

Chapter Seven
Decisive Destinies Discovered

Once we have understood the five keys to grace, the next step is to recognize how grace comes. The Holy Spirit releases it into our lives in four, sequential stages. We need to understand that biblically, grace has its own paradigm. Perhaps a few questions will help focus our thoughts:

What does the contemporary believer or church look like in the *absence* of these keys?
What appears once these keys bring functional grace into our experience?
How will these keys affect the contemporary Christian and the contemporary church?
Can we still be the people of God when the keys are not operational in our lives?
Is it possible to mount an effective witness if such grace is absent in the church?
How do the keys affect our ability to perceive reality and respond to demonic strategies?
Can we ever hope to effectively counter the destructive imposition of secular atheism on our cultures if we are negligent in regard to finding functional grace?

One of the things I've discovered over the years is that believers can be taught some of the truths pertaining to grace, but without specifically defined application those truths never make it into the fabric of their Christian practice. For example, we assent to the truth that we are to love one another, but that truth rarely becomes the governing factor at the point of conflict in the church. As soon as a point of contention arises, the mandate to love one another is abolished, and we act no differently from how the world acts. Our responses remain a manifestation of our own non-grace opinions and preferences. Somehow the dichotomy between the truths we espouse and our own graceless behavior doesn't even bother us. When ministers preach a truth such as Ephesians 4:3, "Make every effort to keep the unity of the Spirit through the bond of peace," a resounding "Amen, brother!" can be heard in the sanctuary. This makes great Sunday morning rhetoric, but let the pastor make a mistake or lead in some directive of the Holy Spirit that the people don't understand and unholy hell tears the church apart. The pastor becomes the target of the most hostile criticisms and bitter attacks.

The only answer to this demonically empowered dichotomy is the repossession of the keys of grace. Until then, we will profess vain religion and strive futilely to keep up appearances. James 1:26 tells us that if a man doesn't know how to bridle his tongue, his religion is nothing but a farce. Much of the contemporary church is in large measure proven to be a graceless organization by our carnal conduct, negative attitudes toward one another and harsh words at the point of contention. Get mad if you want, but that doesn't change what is happening in our churches.

We briefly discussed the narrative of David and Goliath in I Samuel 17, which profoundly demonstrates the differences between the people of God who know nothing about recovered grace and David, who illustrates what an individual is like when in possession of the five keys of kingdom authority. Israel's own leaders were prisoners of the natural realm, having no capacity to understand and respond to the demonic agenda. All they could see was the immensity of the enemy; all they could hear was the roaring of Goliath. Indeed, verse 11 says, "On hearing the Philistine's words, Saul and all the Israelites were dismayed and terrified." They defined the problem in terms of the natural and came to a wrong conclusion. Believing themselves right, they perceived Goliath as too powerful to be defeated, and their hearts fell victim to a wrong perception. Their tongues could only rehearse the impossible nature of the task at hand. Rather than being ruled by faith in an omnipotent God they fell victim to the spirit of fear.

With the enemy in control of the keys to the kingdom, what do we find the defenders of freedom doing? Keeping up appearances. They were sticklers for detail, lining up twice a day to march out of camp shouting the war cry. They looked like an army; they marched like an army; they shouted like an army. Truth is, however, there wasn't a stick of fighting courage in the lot. Personal safety was the dominating agenda. The implication of these challenges as to the freedom and well being of their wives and children was beyond their comprehension. If someone in possession of the five keys to the kingdom had not come on the scene, the kingdom would have been lost! The freedom to worship God would have ceased to exist, and the tyranny of another religion would have been imposed upon the people of God. The intent was to make them subservient not only to a pagan people but to a pagan religion. The wealth of Israel would have been absorbed into godless agendas. Future generations of Israelis would have lost their liberties and for all intents and purposes, God's people would have lost their identity in the world. The hope of humanity would have been extinguished. The final result would have been Satan in the seat of authority over the holy people.

It's the same today. Spend a little time examining what is going on in our present world, and you will see a direct reflection of this "pretend army" in the contemporary church. Many in the church have simply moved their tents into the Philistine camp. Secularists, over the last seven decades, have been imposing their atheistic faith on our free nations with the same intent the Philistines had purposed against Israel. Look at the contemporary church and its reluctance to understand and confront the godless agenda of atheistic humanism, and we see the Israelite army all over again. The agenda of secularists is progressively subverting the holy people of God to the tyranny of an imposed heathenism. Our political ethic, educational institutions, media, social engineers, governmental institutions, and courts are in the grip of this savage paganism and are plunging God's people to a state of total subservience. Freedom of worship for our children could become non-existent. While the church is busy fighting over its internal details and keeping up appearances, the religion of the secularist is destroying historic liberty.

If you follow decisions being imposed on our nations by the judiciary, the progressive enslavement of our populations to this single anti-God agenda is easy to spot. Millions die in abortion clinics, or "abortuaries." Adultery and fornication are culturally acceptable, while our cultures scoff at the concept of sexual purity. Suicide and murder are consistently ranked in the top 3 causes of death for youth ages 15 to 34. Suicide is the third leading cause of death in children ages 10 to 14 (Anderson, Smith, 14). The courts are progressively closing down the historic role of the church in society. Sodomy is becoming the sole and protected sexual ethic of our cultures. To speak biblically against sodomy will result in prosecution and jail. Already, various Canadian and American courts have given legal justification to sodomy. Such legal justification, as of June 2003, has been forced upon both nations through judicial activism (Gay Rights Rulings). Family and marriage are being redefined to conform to the secular definition. George W. Bush, in his 2004 State of the Union Address, disdained the action of "Activist judges [who] have begun redefining marriage by court order, without regard for the will of the people and their elected representatives." His answer to such injustice? "If judges insist on forcing their arbitrary will upon the people, the only alternative left to the people would be the constitutional process." While I agree with his assessment of the judges' rulings, I believe there is another, infinitely more effective course to be taken, but it is up to the church to take it. How easy it is for present day Christians to examine the state of our nations and fall into the same sad, unbelieving state into which Israel had fallen: the Philistines are shouting their defiance, and most won't stir from the place where we shout amen. We are virtually invisible in our witness in the theater of our daily lives.

Chinese believers place the importance of witness over freedom and life itself. For many in the West, the attitude is, "Oh, I couldn't tell folks at work about Jesus. That would cost me my job!" Thank God for the witness that does exist in our western democracies, but the individual believer in the army of God must do more than stand on the hill overlooking the valley of decision. Something must happen in the hearts of multiplied thousands of believers if the humanistic invaders of Philistine are to be turned back. Something must happen to our ears, eyes, minds, hearts, and tongues in the face of this progressive enslavement of our populations. What is that something? There must be a repossession of the five keys of God's grace.

Consider what happens in the life of an individual who has come into the functional possession of these five keys. David was a man seeking the heart of God and as a teenager had come into such repossession, even before Samuel called him from the field. His ears, eyes, mind, heart, and tongue were attuned to the heavenly reality. He had ears to hear and could discern between right and wrong. Having heard God's plan for his life through Samuel, he could believe—have faith. Sound familiar? Read Romans 10:17! "Faith comes by hearing and hearing by the Word of God." David could see beyond the immediate threats of an imposing natural reality to the ability of God to deliver victory. He was able to respond to the natural threat with a heart that had faith in God and could run to the battle pronouncing with his tongue what lived in his heart. In the quietness of being a shepherd, David had discovered the truth of Colossians 3:1-2 long before it was written: "Since you were brought back to life with Christ, focus on the things that are above-where

Christ holds the highest position. Keep your mind on things above, not on worldly things" (GW).

Now, Goliath had been defying the army of God twice a day for forty days. The Israelites were thoroughly defeated without ever drawing a sword. Why? They only heard and saw with their natural perceptions. Then David shows up looking for his brothers. He comes into the army camp of the Israelites and begins hearing the ranting of hell (I Samuel 17:23). Anyone who has subjected his ear gate to the Holy Spirit instantly recognizes the ranting of a Goliath. The situation is simply repugnant to his nature.

Notice that the Israelites were speaking into David's ear what they'd seen, and Goliath was making himself heard, but neither were having their demonically desired effect. David's response to what he was hearing is worth thinking about: he does not tiptoe over to the brow of the hill to have a peek at the problem, nor is he the slightest bit interested in the size or nature of the obstacle. He is used to acting on another voice. He has already heard and seen something far greater that has taken possession of his being. He has a true knowledge of God. Immediately upon hearing that which is contrary to God he reacts out of who he has become in God! He starts going around asking about the kind of reward to be received if Goliath is slain. He is capable only of thinking of a God who is omnipotent. The pagan ranting was his call to war, and his only mindset was victory. He was not at all concerned about upsetting the enemy or rocking the boat. He was not interested in negotiating some sort of peace or letting sleeping dogs lie. What he heard was so threatening to the freedom of the people of God that the necessity of war was never in doubt. In verse 29 (KJV), when challenged by his eldest brother, David knew how to rise above the poisoned criticism of the elder brother and asked the ever-valid question, "Is there not a cause?" David, because he had ears to hear, recognized the existence of a cause.

When mobilizing for spiritual warfare, David understood that the true nature of his weapons were not carnal, but were mighty through God (II Corinthians 10:4). He did not go in armor, with sword and spear. He already knew that the battle was the Lord's, and the victory was his. Furthermore he knew he was anointed for just such a day. He could assert the anointing, which would break the threatened yoke of the Philistines. He knew functionally that "as a man thinks...so is he." He knew about taking the kingdom of God by the right kind of force. All he needed was five smooth stones. (Interesting is it not: five smooth stones, five keys? Also interesting is that in Hebrew, five is the number of grace!) Victory did not lie in his skill with a sling, but rested in the certainty that he could launch those stones, and God would take care of the rest. Active grace permits confidence in the day of battle.

Goliath, as it says in verse 42, "*looked* David over and *saw....* " All he could see was "a mere youngster—apple-cheeked and peach-fuzzed" (MSG). He despised and cursed David, ranting, "Am I a dog?" Surely the carnal mind is death! Goliath, despite his obvious natural strength, experience and capability never rose above his carnal perceptions; he was totally under the dominion of his own wrong assessment and never perceived the deadly threat David represented. Thinking himself right, he was shortly to be proven dead wrong. Goliath, in cursing David, pronounced his own death sentence. Goliath was the blind victim of non-grace. In addition, cursing one of Abraham's seed would mean significant trouble with God!

David knew God's purpose for his life and was assured he wouldn't die that day. He was unmoved by what he heard and saw because he was moving out of another kind of sight and hearing. He wasn't daunted by Goliath's coat of armor, the size of his spear, or his sheer mass. What did he see that demanded vision beyond the natural circumstance? Note verse 46: "Today I will give..." He saw himself giving the carcasses of the whole Philistine army to the birds of the air and the beasts of the field. He saw the Lord handing Goliath over to him, saw himself striking Goliath down and cutting off Goliath's head. Goliath must have scoffed, wondering how David was going to cut off his head; the boy didn't even have a sword! David, however, was content to let Goliath bring the sword.

What is being manifest here? David knew how to see accurately, believed in his heart God would give him the victory and undertook a bold faith action, letting what lived in his heart find expression in his words and actions. It was because he knew what it meant to hear God and how to see things in context of spiritual reality that God would give him victory. David knew the meaning of, "the kingdom of God suffers violence and the violent take it by force" (Matthew 11:12; Luke 16:16). It was because these five keys were functional in David's life that he knew he would be king in the kingdom God would give him. No enemy can defeat a people moving in the functional keys of grace. This is true no matter how bad the situation may appear. Remember, "Where sin abounds, *grace much more abounds!"* Sin abounded on the side where the Philistines stood, but grace in the heart of the one man David was exceedingly more powerful. Grace is the key to the effectual release of the kingdom of God on earth. Nothing is a match for a grace-filled, Spirit-powered church. In the face of manifest grace the enemy can only suffer defeat.

A parallel illustration might be drawn from Mark 4:35-41, which demonstrates in a measure how Christ was in possession of the five keys while the disciples had not yet come into their functional reality. Here, Jesus and the disciples were in a boat, and Christ fell asleep. A furious squall came up so that it appeared that the boat was about to sink, and the disciples thought they were going to die. Luke notes that the waters were raging, the boat was being swamped, and they were in great danger. There is no doubt that this was a very real threat, even as Goliath represented a genuine threat. The disciples were experienced fishermen, and perhaps because they understood the danger such a storm could bring, responded naturally to the howling wind and surging waters. They framed their conclusion about their circumstance around what they saw, heard, and knew of the natural realm. A Goliath naturally perceived always promises death. Luke 8:24 says, "The disciples panicked." We cannot even imagine what it must have been like to spend time with the incarnate Word, to have been in his presence; however, even though the Word was present, He did not pervade their thinking. They'd heard him, but not with the ears that hear or eyes that see. They were still subject to what they heard and saw in the natural realm. Operating out of natural hearing and vision they could only come to one conclusion: "We're going to drown!"

A death mentality is the only fruit that can be grown when we draw on the tree of the knowledge of good and evil. How much the disciples acted like Israel when confronted by Goliath. The only conclusion both groups of men could draw was death. The Israelites could only look down into the valley where Goliath stood ranting and imagine (a *vain* imagination) what that spearhead of fifteen pounds would do to their rib cage. To venture down there was seen as suicide. The disciples found it all too easy to imagine a watery grave and cried out, "Master, don't you care that we are about to die here?" In both cases, fear reigned, and death was perceived as the final conclusion, but the real truth that day in the boat was that the disciples could not have died. Have you ever asked yourself that kind of question? "God don't you *care* that I'm _____ down here?" When we frame our understanding around what is happening in the natural, we cannot perceive what God is fashioning in the spiritual realm through Christ. The disciples were the foundation stones of God's eternal redemptive purposes in the earth, the first Spirit-anointed emissaries of grace to all succeeding generations. They were God's chosen, and that before the foundation of the earth, but their only focus at the moment was their human frailty, not God's omnipotent will to save.

A DANGEROUS GRACE

How significantly did David type Christ for us in such circumstances? His perception of reality had been radically altered so that he could act in keeping with God's eternal purposes without fear. Now consider Christ's response to the circumstances that the disciples thought would kill them. Christ knew the purposes of God. He knew how to interpret what he heard and saw. What he heard and saw that day did not fit in with God's eternal agenda. The furious wind and raging water posed no threat to him, as Goliath had posed no threat to David. Christ was operating in the heart and mind of God, so he could not help but speak the supernatural solution. He knew in his heart God's purpose, that this was not where he was to die, and so it was easy to know that he and the disciples were to go on living. His grace-empowered tongue defeated death and preserved life. Scripture records that Christ was "full of grace." There can be no speaking of the supernatural solution until the Holy Spirit has invested believers with the operative reality of the keys of the kingdom. The talk among many believers in the midst of the storms of life is much like that of the Israelite soldiers facing Goliath and that of the disciples on the Sea of Galilee.

It was because David knew how to live life out of these five renewed capacities that he could act decisively and do so correctly. *Unless he had been capable of acting in this manner, there would have been no one to intervene that day.* The ability of God would never have been brought to bear upon the situation. It was because he could act decisively that freedom to worship God was preserved for succeeding generations, and the pagan agendas were denied the wealth God had apportioned to his people. It was because of his conviction that his destiny in God was assured, and the kingdom promised became the kingdom possessed.

We are directed to pray, "Thy kingdom come." It is only as believers come into the possession of the keys of the kingdom that we will be empowered to experience the kingdom. It is only the grace-motivated church that can turn back the enemy of humanistic secularism. The strongholds, imaginations, the things that exalt themselves against the knowledge of God are no match for a grace-endued people. Satan can neither conquer grace nor quell the life where grace abounds. Strongholds the secularists possess in our cultures are no match for a mobilized, grace-filled church. It only took one grace-inspired teenager to effect liberty for a whole nation against the giant-led threat of the enemy. One Christ has forever delivered man from the tyranny of grace-blinded living. It is through the grace-infused church that the Holy Spirit can raise up the standard against every demonic agenda at work in our cultures. It is God's good pleasure to give us the kingdom. *GLORY!*

Do you recall how Moses sent twelve spies into the Promised Land? God would have been pleased to give them the kingdom. Everything hinged upon what the spies heard and saw. Ten were prisoners of non-grace bondage; two went in with divine sight and hearing. Natural vision articulates impossibility; grace-empowered vision says we are well able. There is no middle ground. Joshua and Caleb knew that God had declared this to be the Promised Land and their eyes looked to confirm what they'd heard *from God*. The ten, having natural eyes, saw only giants in the land, and having natural ears, heard only defeat. God had brought the whole nation to the brink of their promised destiny, but they collectively failed to hear. They had been witness to the presence, power, and provision of God but could not believe in the promise of God. There was no middle ground.

The truth seems to be this: rebellion is most likely to occur at the threshold of the grace-given kingdom. To speak or sing about it is one thing, but to actually act on it is another. Grace is the point of conflict between the true sons of God and the religious, venturing where non-grace refuses to go. Those who act on grace will always be set apart from those who are satisfied to talk it, because grace takes its follower beyond talk to power and the possession of God's promises. This is the legacy of Joshua and Caleb. Grace is life to those who are so filled; it is madness and fanaticism to the graceless, inexorably activating envy and jealousy. The Spirit of God wars against flesh that is motivated by the spirit of this world, the forces of anti-grace. Grace is the great dividing line between true godliness and Christian religion. *Nothing supernatural occurs until men have passed into the theater of grace!*

Read Numbers 13 and 14. The anti-grace crowd raged against Moses, Aaron, Joshua and Caleb. Joshua and Caleb conveyed grace in verse 9 of chapter 14 when they said, "Do not be afraid of the people of the land, because we will swallow them up. Their protection is gone, but the Lord is with us." However, this only provoked rebellion among the gathered Israelites, and verse 10 records, "the whole assembly talked about stoning them." Note again the defeat/death mindset.

If individual believers and churches want to come into the eternal purposes of God by supernatural means then these five grace capabilities must be recovered. These are the keys that bring people into genuine renewal and make the grace witness manifest in the external world. It is possible to follow for years and then come to some Jordan reality, which causes us to shrink from further pursuit of the Spirit of Grace. The stage is set for sustained revival with its accompanying warfare. God will only take the church as far as she will follow the Holy Spirit. Such was the case with the "whole assembly" of Israel: even though they had lived and been blessed under the anointed, empowered leadership of Moses, they drew back when faced with the kingdom challenge. Their failure occurred with the surrender of the five keys of destiny. *Our destinies are determined more by the measures of grace received than by the anointed leadership that God places us under!* It is easier to play it safe than it is to face the dangerous demands grace places on our lives. Who among us will dare to challenge the Goliaths of our day? Truly, grace leads in the way of danger.

Further illustrations of the five key concepts of the kingdom can be found when Joshua is faced with moving the nation across the Jordan, or when faced with the taking of Jericho. He heard, saw, understood with his mind, believed in his heart and articulated the plan of God. He then took the correct and corresponding act of faith. Consider Ananias in Acts 9, Cornelius and Peter in Acts 10, or Paul waiting for God to clarify what direction he should go in as found in Acts 16. (By way of observation, these keys to grace become integral in prophetic gifting and ministry. You can wrestle with that one on your own for a while!)

On every occasion when God's people moved as possessors of these five keys, God's purposes were accomplished, individuals were brought into their foreordained destinies and God's supernatural power found release. That's how God is glorified! These keys received from the Holy Spirit activate the power of God in our lives and circumstances. They are activated in us as a result of relational intimacy with the Holy Spirit when we obey what we've heard, seen, understood, believed and spoken! What is witnessed here is the functional demonstration of the grace/faith equation as found in Ephesians 2:8.

So then, if grace begins with hearing, what is to be heard? How does the Spirit begin to activate the ministry of grace in us? How does he reach out to us to draw us into Christ and God's power agenda for our lives and churches? Is there a grace paradigm, or model, that can be found in the pages of scripture? If so what does it look like and how does it work? Well, before we continue, I would like to pray with you.

> Dear Lord Jesus, thank you for the supremacy and unsurpassed greatness of your grace. Right now, fill each thirsty heart with the fullest possible measure of grace by the Holy Spirit. Minister the fullness of grace into their lives. Quicken their spirits so that their ears

will hear, their eyes will see, so that they understand with their minds, set their hearts on you and proclaim with their lips your loving redemption to the world. Oh, God, by your Holy Spirit, fill each life with the all-sufficient grace of the Lord Jesus Christ! Amen!

Chapter Eight
The Grace Paradigm

God has given grace a very specific model, found throughout the pages of scripture. The Spirit ministers grace in our personal lives by this same pattern. Let me begin to introduce you to the four concepts that characterize this incredible paradigm, starting with a personal illustration, which has been repeated countless times in my life and ministry.

I was ministering to a small group of believers in England. After preaching, people began to come forward for prayer. I wasn't really looking at the people I was praying for, but was simply focused on hearing any directive from the Holy Spirit, praying in general terms until some specific insights into a person's life and circumstances would drop into my mind. After ministering to several people, I came to a man in his mid-to-late forties, unaware things were about to turn traumatic. As I laid my hand on his shoulder and waited for the Holy Spirit to begin to direct my thoughts, I was shocked by the precise, clear and startling word that dropped into my mind: "Tell him it is okay to get remarried."

I had heard what I call a *Word-centered Directive:* the first phase in God's invitation into the dangers of functional grace. Immediately an inner battle rose up inside me. A whole series of contrary thoughts flooded my mind, like: "What if this is just my imagination? What if he's never been married, or worse, he's already married, his wife is sitting here in the congregation, and I tell him it's okay to get remarried? Lord, couldn't I see if he has a wedding ring on?" Any of these impulses had the potential to nullify what I'd been told to do. It is not the *theology* of grace that poses a threat, but the *call* to step into grace in its functional operation that threatens our tranquil lives.

Having received a directive from the Holy Spirit, I knew very clearly in my mind what I'd heard. I was now faced with bringing my mind and heart into submission. Jeremiah 31:33 provides biblical insight to what we are called into when the Spirit moves to bring the new covenant to bear upon our circumstance: *"This is the covenant I will make with the house of Israel after that time,* says the Lord. *I will put my law in their minds and write it on their hearts. I will be their God and they will be my people."* To obey or not to obey; to chicken out or not to chicken out, that was the question as this gentleman stood before me. There were two conflicting desires in me. The first, carnal desire was to protect myself, look good, and avoid the risk of faith. The second desire was to respond to the Word directive I'd heard. In addition to the carnal desire, I had a desire to obey what I'd heard. I call this second desire that comes up when the Holy Spirit speaks a *Word-centered Motivation*. There is always an inner conflict between these two sets of desires. That night, I had to decide whether I would act in deliberate faith and say what I'd been told, or draw back and just pray a nice, fluffy prayer. After all, no one in the room would know if I did that, but if I *was* wrong, I'd lose my credibility and reputation with this pastor and congregation. Without looking into his face, I suppressed the temptation to play it safe and blurted out, "The Lord wants you to know that it's okay to get remarried." There. I'd said it. I'd taken the plunge into the unknowable river, the mysterious ministry of grace. This response to the Spirit-placed inner motivation, I call *Word-centered Action*. The result of Word-centered action is the instant release of *Word-centered Power*. Probably not one member of the congregation realized that what they were about to witness was the result of functional grace.

Sometimes people react to the manifest power of God in unexpected ways. This man hit the floor. The release of spiritual power tied directly back to the initial word I'd heard. In just a few moments the paradigm of grace unfolded and the Holy Spirit ministered grace in the four stages of its paradigm, but the scene wasn't finished playing out. Almost as quickly, a woman in the congregation jumped up and ran out of the room shouting, "No, no, no!" Then a second lady jumped up and hastily followed her. I remember thinking as they left the room that at any moment the pastor would tap me on the shoulder and invite me to sit down; she stayed in her chair, so I acted as if I had been prepared for such an outburst and moved to minister to the next person in line.

On a visit to that fellowship about a year later, I discovered what had happened as a result of that statement. The man had been widowed about a year earlier and had no plan or even an inclination to get remarried. The word startled him, but he was instantly hit with the power of the Holy Spirit and he just enjoyed his time on the floor. At the time, I hadn't dared check what was happening with the woman who jumped up and ran out of the room shouting

"No!" It turns out she was the man's daughter and wasn't ready for her daddy to take another wife. When I spoke the word, the second lady sat there thinking what a wonderful word for such a nice man. She was surprised by such a sudden, unmistakable word and was feeling happy for the man as he fell to the floor. As she was sitting there she had a vision. A hand appeared, moved toward her with the index finger pointing directly into her face. She heard, "It's you!" (Remember ears and eyes?) She was stunned. She had had no strong feelings for the man on the floor and was shocked to *see* and *hear* such a clear *word* that applied to her. She was a single lady but had never countenanced this man as a prospective husband.

In her sense of dismay she left the room with the intent of comforting the daughter. All the while she was trying to calm the daughter, she was endeavoring to come to grips with the word that she was to become the daughter's stepmother. After consoling the daughter, the lady went back into the room as the gentleman was getting up off the floor. There was an immediate response to her in his heart. The Lord had just been matchmaker! The couple married shortly after this event. They are happy and in love, knowing that theirs is a match made in heaven. The daughter is very happily reconciled to this marriage in that the Lord's will has been done. For me, it was a big "Whew!"

Why include this narrative here? First of all, it sets up what this chapter is all about. Grace flows into our lives and circumstances in four distinct stages. It also illustrates how *hearing* and *seeing* are necessarily part of the ministry of grace. I *heard*; the wife-to-be both *heard* and *saw*; the man *heard*. If you think about it, you can see how easily someone could miss the grace of God, as Hebrews 12:15 cautions. I could so easily have dodged the Word Directive of the Spirit, but in doing so I would have missed what it meant to be a minister of grace is this particular instance. If I had not obeyed, the Spirit would not have been released to affect this specific work of grace into this potential family. Grace can be rationalized away; the act of faith called for when God speaks can so easily be dismissed.

In John 14:12 Christ put it like this: "I tell you the truth, anyone who has faith in me will do what I have been doing. He will do even greater things than these." Can you see how this one experience demonstrates and ties the five keys and four stages of grace together? In reading these words of Christ, I'm convinced there must be some believers who wonder why the greater works are not being manifest in their lives. The truth is, if we do not discover what grace is and how the Holy Spirit ministers it into our lives and circumstances then the greater works will never characterize the believer. I'm not suggesting that this event was a "greater work," but the greater works can only become a reality as grace is allowed to have its way. Clearly, Christ set one of the conditions for the release of functional grace when he said, "anyone who has faith in me *will do*..." How does the Spirit bring us to legitimate faith action? By administering grace! Let's set these four stages down.

The Paradigm of Grace as ministered by the Holy Spirit:

Stage One: Word-Centered Directive
Stage Two: Word-Centered Motivation
Stage Three: Word-Centered Action
Stage Four: Word-Centered Power

Scripture repeatedly refers to "the grace of our Lord Jesus Christ." Grace is always rooted in Christ. John 1:1 declares that "in the beginning was the Word, and the Word was with God, and the Word was God." In verse 14 it asserts of the Word-God: "The Word became flesh...*full of grace* and truth." Christ is God, and he is The Word, with a capital *W*! One characteristic of The Word is that it carries inherent grace. The Word and grace cannot be divorced. When grace comes, the Word has come in some dimension.

When God wanted to activate grace in the affairs of man, he sent his Word. This as an absolute principle: whenever God wants to activate some work of grace, he releases, or speaks a word. The word of the Lord may be some portion of scripture that the Holy Spirit quickens to our hearts, thereby calling us to some clearly understood line of action. It can also be something that we hear directly from the Holy Spirit. I hasten to add that a word heard directly from the Holy Spirit *never* contradicts the written Word: it will never bring destruction to the family or to the integrity of the living body of Christ. Anything that has to do with authentic grace is rooted in a clear authoritative word ministered to us by the Holy Spirit. You cannot cooperate with God if you cannot hear the word he speaks by His Spirit. Activating grace depends wholly upon a listening ear. Grace always starts with Word!

Next, when the word comes it will come in the form of a *directive*. The Holy Spirits knows the Father's heart as well as God's plan and purpose for our lives, so when the Holy Spirit speaks to a person he speaks directly and in the imperative. He tells us clearly and in no uncertain terms what we are to do. He does not come alongside and ask us, What do you think of this plan?" "Would you consider doing the Father's will? He is God. As far as the Spirit of God is concerned, the will of God is non-negotiable. When the Spirit speaks directively, we know with absolute clarity what he wants us to do. Whether we have heard is not in question; it is whether we will choose to obey!

When the Holy Spirit spoke to Ananias about going to find Saul of Tarsus, there was no doubt in Ananias' mind what God wanted him to do. The question was whether he'd obey or not. Now, God knows our hearts. He knows before He speaks whether or not we will do what we are told to do. If our heart-set is to negotiate with God or our predisposition is to refuse to do what we are told, then little will be heard of the Spirit. He won't waste his breath. Note that when the Spirit spoke to Ananias, the word came as a clear, authoritative directive. It all started with a *Word-centered Directive:* "Ananias, go to the house of Judas on Straight Street and ask for a man from Tarsus named Saul..." (Acts 9:11). Ananias knew with absolute clarity that God was requiring an inner submission demonstrated by an outward faith action. The Holy Spirit's intent was to draw Ananias into a significant administration and advancement of grace in the earth, which would result in the manifest miracle power of God. That is where true grace will lead. It is not at all likely that Ananias understood the immense ramifications such an act of faith would have on world history. Ananias couldn't justify what he'd heard in light of some scripture: he heard it with his spirit. Jesus put it like this: "My sheep know my voice..." (John 10:4). Ananias knew to whom the voice belonged. This is not being mystical; it is being absolutely biblical.

God, in Christ, has chosen to minister his grace to mankind through those who have ears to hear what the Spirit is saying, and he has not changed how he deals with men over the millennia. You can argue this doesn't happen today, but to suggest that hearing and seeing in the spirit realm no longer occurs is to negate portions of the Word. Throughout scripture, those who have been supernaturally directed and used of God have been hearers and seers. For example, we cannot eliminate Matthew 13:16 and still claim to believe in the Bible. If we declare ourselves to be Bible believers, then we must accept that God still speaks, and every true believer must have an ear to hear his voice in order to hear what the Spirit is saying. Further, adopting the position that God no longer moves supernaturally means slandering those who have ears to hear and eyes to see. God has an agenda of grace for those who would participate. Clinging to the stone-cold doctrines of men can only produce a stone-cold religion couched in evangelical terms. Abolish the Word-centered Directive ministry of the Holy Spirit and multiplied millions will miss the needed ministry of grace.

What comes after the directive? A *Word-centered Motivation.* Whenever the Holy Spirit speaks a directive he imparts a supernatural motivation, or impulse, to act on it. There comes with the directive an inner "want to." This is why grace is distinctly different than law. Law says you *must* because it is your religious *duty*. Grace is radically different. While the law can be spelled d-u-t-y, grace finds it's true nature in d-e-s-i-r-e. Under law, the tithe is duty, but if a person genuinely understands the "grace of giving" he doesn't *have* to tithe; he *wants* to, springing from a genuine, heart motivation. The power of God is released as believers know the joy and liberty of living out of "I can't help myself; I really want to."

Again, let's look at Ananias. Upon receiving the Word-centered directive, two sets of impulses rose up within him and he began to search for an alternative to the direction. Acts 9:13-14 records his response, which in essence was, "Lord, this doesn't really seem to be a good idea. Let me fill you in on this guy: he's a bad dude." Clearly, Ananias saw himself between a rock and a hard place, but God doesn't begin to negotiate. His very next word is "Go!" Note that God doesn't get mad at Ananias because he has to work this through in his own heart. He knew beforehand what Ananias would do: that he would work through his reservations and go, because he desired the purposes of God over his own temporal desire to preserve his life. It would appear that Ananias understood Christ's teaching about seeds: "Unless a kernel of wheat falls to the ground and dies, it remains only a single seed. But if it dies it produces many seeds. The man who loves his life will lose it, while the man who hates his life in this world will keep it for eternal life" (John 12:24-25). This is true every time the Word Directive of the Spirit penetrates our lives: to live and therefore die, or to die and therefore live! Such is the reality of functional grace. In fact, we go with one or the other. Ananias wanted to bear spiritual fruit more than he wanted to play it safe. Before the outward act of going took place, an inward choice was made. His outward going was an expression of what was in his heart, "For with the heart man believes." It was an act of faith; he believed what he'd heard, set his own safety aside, and went. In response to the *Word-centered Motivation,* he undertook the corresponding *Word-centered Action*.

Ananias, having committed himself to the Spirit-directed course of action, went to the place Saul was and lay hands on him. Without prior conversation with Saul, he called him brother, told him he knew of the experience on the road to Damascus, and declared that Saul was to recover his sight and be filled with the Holy Spirit. As far as Ananias was concerned, he'd decided he may as well go for the whole miracle—"in for a penny in for a pound." Note the next word, *"Immediately."* *Word-centered Action* was immediately followed by *Word-centered Power,* which is a consistent characteristic of functional grace. The Holy Spirit was there to implement the will of God through the bold-grace ministry of Ananias. The release of power operated to accomplish the sovereign will of an omnipotent God, not some flimsy objective of man. No pink chariot with white horses here! God's agenda for every life is that we become administrators of some aspect of His grace. What counts is that believers discover how to get involved in God's grace agenda rather than try to twist it into some materialistic bubble shielding us from the gross darkness and ugliness of lost generations. What counts for eternity, what truly satisfies, is not the degree of luxury we live in but the measures of grace in our lives and ministries. The grace ministry can often be measured better by what has been lost than by what has been gained. If we want to discover significance and a genuine sense of purpose in life, then we need to open our lives and hearts to the Spirit's administration of grace. You see, we are not only to be *recipients* of grace but *ministers* of grace. We need to get into the presence of the Spirit and allow him to give us a new heart, with which we will believe God. Having those new hearts, we must surrender ourselves to the sovereign administration of grace that flows from one stage to the next.

It is as we begin to flow in these leadings of the Spirit that we are progressively drawn into the purposes of God for our lives. The power of God becomes characteristic of our testimonies in grace-starved churches and a grace-starved world! The first stage is wholly of God. The second and third stages signify how man participates in the grace of God, and having chosen the Word-centered Motivation and undertaken the Word-centered Action, the fourth stage is back on God. God has designed this pattern to include man in the ministry of reconciliation. In its outworking, grace is neither all of God, nor all of man. Acts 1:8 power is derived "when the Holy Spirit comes on you." The result? "You will be my witnesses." Grace always leads in the way of manifest power, but it is first a matter of spirit. Paul wrote in Galatians 6:18, "The grace of our Lord Jesus Christ be with your spirit." On every occasion there must be a falling into the ground to die; the flesh must capitulate. Grace is God's method of drawing us up out of the soul realm into the spirit realm so we may discover what it means to walk with the Spirit in his all-sufficient power. Perhaps by now you understand when I use the term "functional grace," I mean the Spirit's *directives* become our *motivations*, which translate into faith-*actions*, which result in Holy Ghost *power!* Put them all together and what have you got? D-MAP.

These patterns of God's grace dealings with man are inherently characteristic of Christ and his ministry on earth. He followed the heavenly directives because that was his all-consuming motivation, acting upon that motivation even to the death on the cross, and the result was the power of God to raise him from the dead.

Examine how an individual finds salvation, and you will find the four stages of grace are inherently present. Ephesians 2:8 declares, "For by grace are you saved through faith, that not of yourself but it is the gift of God." Before the process of redemption can begin in an individual the Word of God is necessary. Christ is the Word, and he is proclaimed to the one not saved. When we meet unsaved people we start to "tell" them about Christ, how to be saved, and why they need to be saved. We speak or preach the Word, and in so doing we are initiating the ministry of grace. After an individual has been confronted with the truth about Christ and salvation, the Holy Spirit releases a second ministry-stage of grace. As the Spirit takes the word down into the heart of the listener (ear) the individual begins to think about what he has heard and starts to feel a stirring to respond. This stirring is the Holy Spirit placing the desire of God into the human heart. Now the individual is confronted with the choice to obey or not to obey. He has within his heart two conflicting desires. One is to respond to the desire to receive Christ and the other desire is to refuse. It is the carnal mind and heart reacting to the spiritual mind and heart. If the individual chooses not to respond to the inner motivation to receive Christ then that person has just refused the grace of God. If on the other hand the individual responds to the spiritual promptings of the Holy Spirit then he is responding to the grace of God as the Spirit is ministering it to him. He allows the inner motivation to cause him to undertake a faith-action. He prays to receive Christ. This act of praying is the third stage of grace, the Word-centered action. The fourth stage happens, and a supernatural work of God is immediately accomplished. Upon the prayer of faith there comes the amazing result of obeying the grace of God: power is released. It changes an individual's eternal destiny, his eternal identity, his nature, values and habits. Such is the grace of God. Whenever individuals respond to the grace of God they always come into some experience of the power of God. "To as many as received his to them gave he *power* to become the Sons of God." Power comes every time and to every individual who responds to the grace of God.

Let's look specifically at the four stages of grace in our conversion experience. There was the Word Directive about the necessity of being saved. Then at some point came a Word-centered Motivation prompting an inner desire to be saved. Then came the moment when the prayer to be saved was offered, this being Word-centered Action, and *pow!* The *power* of the Holy Spirit flooded in and we were saved: Word-centered Power. In this flow of grace we were brought into God's glorious river of life!

Consider what it means when scripture says, "But Noah found grace in the eyes of the Lord" (Genesis 6: 8). Grace is a whole lot more than finding God in a good mood. Noah demonstrates that he was, if you will, in possession of the five keys to grace. He used his *ears* to *hear* while his whole generation was deaf. God drew him a word picture so that he could *see* the ark in his *mind*. He believed in his *heart* what God had said and believing he preached to his generation for 120 years, meaning belief found expression by way of his *tongue*. The Noah narrative illustrates clearly how the five keys and the four stages of grace flow together. Have a look!

The Grace Paradigm:

WORD-CENTERED **D**IRECTIVE:	God tells Noah to build a boat.
WORD-CENTERED **M**OTIVATION:	Noah believes God and tells his family what they are going to do.
WORD-CENTERED **A**CTION:	Noah obeys for 120 years by building and preaching repentance.
WORD-CENTERED **P**OWER:	The Lord shut Noah and his family in the ark.

God was drawing Noah into his redemptive purposes. He could have simply picked Noah up and placed him above the waters. Instead he chose to work through the toil of the man. The very nature of Noah's work was a testimony of God's grace to his generation, for the Lord could have spared just Noah and his family, but he made a way for others to choose salvation. Let's examine this tremendous provision of the grace paradigm so we, too, may venture into the redemptive purposes of Christ.

Stage One: The Word-Centered Directive

Remember what is meant by the term Word-centered Directive? Christ is the Word, the Logos, and he is totally God. Ephesians 2:10 is only one place where we are clearly taught that God has created every believer with some specific set of good works in mind. One of the phrases we love to use in our evangelistic jargon says, "Give your life to Christ. God has a wonderful plan for your life." This particular phrase is familiar to believers in many parts of the world, and it is a true statement; however, I've been astonished to discover that when asked, "How many believers here know in specific terms God's plan for your life?" most people simply shrug their shoulders, admitting that they do not know. This, to me, is unacceptable. If believers have been ordained to walk in good works, how is it that so few have discovered specifically what those good works have their name on them? How important is it that you discover the answer to that question? It is possible that millions of believers will arrive in heaven having never discovered God's creative purposes for their lives. Imagine never having done what you were created to do! Have you ever wondered why on earth are you on earth? If you do not discover what those good works are, could it be said that you will have missed fulfilling your role in redemptive history? Success is not measured in how much money you made, what kind of occupation you had, or on the size of church you attended or built. It is measured in the degree to which you came into God's intended purposes for your life. So how do we begin the process of such discovery?

The key to understanding those Word-centered directives lies in discerning *what* God's purposes for your life are and then discovering *how* God intended them to be fulfilled. That discovery of God's creative purposes for life is born out of an intimate relationship with the Holy Spirit. I Corinthians 2:9 makes this statement: "No eye has seen, no ear has heard, no mind has conceived what God has prepared for those who love him." Now I understand that the normal interpretation of this verse is applied to what it will be like in heaven. I would question the completeness of this interpretation. Why? Look carefully at the next verse: "but God *has revealed* it to us *by his Spirit*." Paul is saying that the things God had prepared for those who love him have been—past tense—revealed. How? By His Spirit! The verse, "no eye has seen, no ear has heard nor mind has conceived," might very accurately describe the many believers who have never realized what God prepared for them to do. If we keep reading we discover that the Holy Spirit is doing something in the present tense: "The Spirit searches all things, even the deep things of God." It is as though the Holy Spirit rummages around in the depths of God's heart and there discovers what God has purposed for us. The Spirit then moves in a revelation of those purposes for our lives. Was Paul writing this from first-hand experience?

In Acts 16:6-10 Paul is on one of his missionary trips. He and his ministry companions are trying to go east and he records that they were "kept by the Holy Spirit from preaching the word in Asia." They try to enter Bithynia, but the Spirit of Jesus would not allow them to do so. What a radical concept: the Holy Spirit *preventing* the preaching of the Word! Why? There was no word, so there was nothing to hear; there had been no vision so there was nothing to see. They simply did not know what God had in mind at that point. Someone did, however. The Holy Spirit, being God, could search out the purposes in God's heart, hidden to man, and then reveal them to Paul. How did the Holy Spirit reveal God's plan to Paul? "During the night Paul had a vision of a man of Macedonia standing and begging him, 'Come over to Macedonia and help us.'" *Now* Paul had heard and seen and knew by revelation what was in the Father's heart. (That was how he could say in I Corinthians 2:16, "But we have the mind of Christ.") Inherent in this ministry of the Holy Spirit to Paul was a word that gave him clear insight into where he was to go and what he was to do there. The Holy Spirit didn't just give him a vision, but explained its meaning, so he didn't have to guess what the vision meant. The ear gate, the eye gate, the mind, and heart all found their role in moving in God's agenda for his life, and the tongue found its part in the program. The Holy Spirit ministered what was hidden in God's heart into the mind and heart of the one who could hear, see and respond in decisive faith action, and verse 10 records, "We got ready *at once* to leave for Macedonia, concluding that God had called us to preach the gospel to them."

Throughout scripture and church history, people discovered God's agenda for their lives as a result of a clear word from the Lord. The directives were not always welcome, and on many occasions, the individuals had to work through the challenge those directives presented. Consider how God revealed to Noah what his life's work was to be. After having heard from the Lord, if Noah had been asked, "Why on earth are you on earth?" his answer would have been, "To build a boat so that salvation might come to the human race." Word-centered directives cause the structure of your life to become Christ-centered.

Functional grace always produces a Christ-centered life. It cannot be otherwise. When God finished speaking to Noah, he didn't have to go off to pray and fast. He knew with absolute clarity what was required of him. When God speaks, he has no trouble making himself understood. Building an ark was not something Noah dreamed up. He didn't wake up one morning and decide he'd like to go sailing. It came as a startling revelation, involving a radical life-change: he went from farmer to shipbuilder. God invaded his space and, by a Word directive, extended to Noah the opportunity of cooperating with an eternal agenda. There was no big-stick approach.

Stage Two: The Word-Centered Motivation

When I use the term Word-centered Motivation, the intent is to indicate that our motivation emanates from a word the Spirit has actually spoken into our hearts. The source of our motivation is flowing into our hearts from the direct Word ministry of the Holy Spirit as opposed to some personal agenda. Psalm 37:4 puts it like this: "I will give you the desires of your heart." These desires first reside in the Father's heart and are implanted into our hearts. Grace has nothing to do with the whole range of carnal desires that cause us to be world-focused, striving for recognition and material comforts. We can frame our carnal desires in "Christianese," but in reality, we are just covering up the sad state of our own inner greed. A genuine Word-centered motivation has nothing to do with the kinds of things that stir up the natural heart. When the Holy Spirit speaks a word into our hearts, they in turn leap with enthusiasm to obey. The zeal of the Lord of Hosts becomes a consuming passion that burns in us. For example, when the Spirit drops an understanding of giving into our minds and hearts, then the contention over tithing as Old Testament law is abolished. Giving flows out of joyfully willing hearts, but only after the nature of God's heart that loves to give is implanted in our heart. This is called the grace of giving. Most professing believers do not tithe over the long term because they have not heard the Spirit speaking to them, nor have they received the "new heart" as it pertains to their money, so they cannot give out of cheerful hearts. They may have heard men saying what God has said but they have not heard what the Spirit has spoken or received divine motivation.

If you are at all familiar with how the Spirit of God speaks, you know he does so in a few sudden, precise words, and it takes only moments. If you read Genesis 6:13-21 concerning God's plan and the instructions pertaining to the ark, it might take you two minutes at most, if you are a very, very *slow* reader. In reality, God drops his articulated purposes into our minds in milliseconds, coming so quickly that their initial impact can leave a person reeling. Was Noah motivated to obey the words he heard? Did those inner realities have to overcome a lot of external and contradictory circumstances? It had never rained. He was the only one who heard the voice. He couldn't go off to check it out with the local meteorologist. Is it possible that there were some unanswered questions that might have popped into his mind during the many years of labor? He did not know *how* God was going to get all the animals into the boat; he just knew that it was going to happen. He did not know *when* it was going to rain; rain itself must have raised some curious thoughts from time to time. He didn't understand all that was entailed in "the fountains of the deep." He didn't know *where* the boat would end up. During all the time he was building, he didn't concern himself with *who* would shut them in, and God didn't fill him in on all the details. Then there was the ridicule of a whole generation. So what do you think? Did 120 years of work require some pretty powerful inner motivation? Faith had to work in the theater of unanswered questions. God neither explains himself, nor puts a gun to our heads. When God directs, he sets his motivation in our hearts by the Holy Spirit and gives us the opportunity to live out of them. Noah built the boat because God had placed a desire in his heart to do it.

Noah was truly and most incredibly a man after God's heart. We as believers today hear the Holy Spirit speak into our hearts some clear directive. When we first hear it we get enthusiastic. However, after a few days or weeks pass by, the enthusiasm starts to diminish and we start looking for another word of confirmation. We have to find another prophet to get a fresh directive from God. This repeats itself over and over and still we struggle to bring ourselves into subjection to the clear Word of the Lord. Noah on the other hand is amazing. He hears a word directive from the Lord that took no more than moments to impart. He then proceeds to live out of those words *for the next 120 years*. One word was all Noah's heart required. He could fashion the rest of his life and destiny on that one word. Everything he did for the next century hinged on that single directive that he heard in his spirit. That genuine word directive from God was not likely to change, for God is not apt to change his mind.

Stage Three: The Word-Centered Action

The action Noah undertook related directly to the Word he'd heard. Flowing out of those inner, godly motivations, he acted on what he'd heard without any visible evidences to encourage him or to confirm to those around him that he wasn't insane. Every day Noah turned what he'd heard into faith action. He externalized what the Spirit had made real to him in his heart. Noah is declared to have been a preacher of righteousness in II Peter 2:5. One thing that can be safely assumed about preachers: their tongues get involved. All five keys to grace are manifest in the life of the one who found grace. He believed God. Man believes with his heart and it is out of the abundance of the heart that the mouth speaks.

Believing does not necessarily translate into faith action. Noah could have believed God in his heart but quenched the Spirit-placed motivations so that he took no action to actually build the ark. It is easy for Christians to say they believe the scriptures but unless that believing is turned into action, we are left holding the corpse of what James calls dead faith. It is all too easy to let ourselves off the hook by doing nothing that substantiates our confession. We can believe without turning what we believe into faith action. Legitimate faith actions are founded directly in what we believe of God. If believers are ever to come into the experience of the "greater works," faith action will have to demonstrate our declared belief.

It is all too easy to sense those divine motivations stirred up in us by the Spirit, and for a whole host of carnal reasons, take no action to further those inner motivations. You know how the mind kicks into gear and suggests ten good reasons why this isn't a good time. This is how we quench the Spirit and keep God out of the picture. It is one thing to have a divine "want to" in our hearts and another thing to act on it. The outward act springing from an inward work is the only thing that makes us visible in the external world. Acting externally on that inward motivation always calls us to take risk. We can play it safe while believing, but earthly security disappears when we translate inward motivation into external action.

I heard an interesting story that illustrates this quite well. There was a period of time when daredevils would go to Niagara Falls and put a tight rope across the falls from one side to the other. To fall into that churning chasm meant certain death. One such daredevil was Charles Blondin, who reportedly came to the Falls and had the rope stretched across the roaring torrent of water. On one occasion before starting out over the Falls, he turned to the watching throng and asked, "How many of you believe that I can walk across to the other side and back without falling?" The spectators peered down into the churning waters below, thought for a few moments and said nothing. The man then walked briskly across to the other side on the rope and returned in what seemed like moments. The people were amazed. He turned to them and asked, "How many of you *believe* that I can walk across this rope to the other side and back again?" They all roared their agreement. Then the man turned and asked again, "How many of you believe I can take a wheelbarrow across this rope and bring it back without any difficulty?" Peering over the steep cliff, they decided to say nothing. Deliberately, the man picked up the waiting wheelbarrow, placed it on the rope and began his trip across and back. The audience watched in awe. Upon his return, he looked over the breathless witnesses and asked, "Now how many of you believe I can take this wheelbarrow across and bring it back?" They roared their affirmation. Again and again the man asked, "Do you really believe?" and every time, the crowd cried out that they believed. The man, having elicited such a jubilant confession asked, "How many of you believe I can put a man in this wheelbarrow, take him across and bring him back safely?" The shouting, "We believe," was so loud that it could be heard a great distance away. Holding up his hand to quiet the onlookers, the man asked, "Do you really believe I can do this?" Again they all shouted in the affirmative. The man then silenced the crowd so that not a sound could be heard but the roaring of the water and asked, "Who's first?" A stunned crowd stood in silence for several minutes until one by one they all slipped away to other sight seeing duties.

Now, let me say it again. It is wholly possible to believe without turning belief into faith action. It was one thing for the crowd to shout their belief in the tightrope walker, but a distinctly different thing to be the one who climbed into the wheelbarrow! The stages of grace must be more than believed. Grace must take us to the radical acts of faith. If we will not take our belief to its necessary expression of faith action in response to the Spirit's ministry of grace, then we are possessors of nothing more than a dead faith. Grace that is functional is designed to produce a generation of people who are wheelbarrow radicals.

It is wonderful that so many have become believers, but consider this: the man who merely believes is substantially different than the man who translates his belief into faith action. Only one will become the possessor of the kingdom promises of God. Only one can be used of God to change nations and history. Of the twelve spies Moses sent into Canaan, only Joshua and Caleb could be counted as wheelbarrow men of God. They were the only two who would write the history of Israel and affect the world. Noah climbed into the wheelbarrow of faith action and stayed there for 120 years preaching what had never been heard of or seen. He found what it meant to come into the grace of God, and he knew what it meant to stay in the grace of God. As a righteous man he understood the real meaning of, "The just live by faith" (Habakkuk 2:4). Faith action rooted in grace alone could preserve his life, that of his family and all who would find faith in Christ after him.

Stage Four: Word-Centered Power

It is possible to believe but still fall into a quasi-Christianity that is bereft of the power of the Holy Spirit. As individual believers, we must not only *hear* what the Spirit is saying, but make the "cold turkey" choice to *respond* to those promptings. When we learn to submit to the word of God's grace, the inevitable result is overt, glorious, power, which in turn authenticates our proclamation of God's eternal kingdom. I Corinthians 4:20 declares absolutely that the kingdom of God is a matter of power. Paul, in Hebrews 4:12, says the word of God divides between soul and spirit. Every manifestation of power has as its source the word of God, affecting his word purposes in the earth. The word of God sets us free from soulish demands and causes us to live in a Spirit-planted zeal for the kingdom of God and his church. In fact, contrary to embellishing our lives or satisfying our carnal, earthly cravings, such administrations of grace will probably cost us our lives!

If we want to get beyond the forms of godliness to the power of divine origin, we must discipline our souls to surrender control to the directives of the Holy Spirit. Remember the widower at the beginning of this chapter? The Holy Spirit wanted to minister grace in its inherent power to this man. It would have been so easy to skirt the issue of remarriage and just pray a nice prayer, or try to ask him a few subtle questions to see if I had heard correctly; however, I had only one option if I wanted to see the Spirit bring his power to bear on the situation. In Ezekiel 36:27, God says that he would put his Spirit in us and move us to follow his directives. He does not say he will *force* us to follow; he *motivates* us. We are not robots. Responding to that motivation, I simply said what I'd heard and the rest was done by the power of God that went to work in the hearts of two people. Their marriage is a joyful unity resulting from the release of divine power that produced a loving relationship. Every individual in that church knows the relationship between these two people is a direct result of God's supernatural power. They model grace and its inherent fruit of love, joy, and peace before the eyes of that congregation.

The word, "obeyed," brings believers not only into the manifest *power* of God, but into the manifest *love* of God. God's power and love are interdependent. Whenever power of divine origin appears, it produces its own witness of the fruit of the Spirit. If power is manifest, and the fruit of Christ's character is absent, then Christ is being missed and the carnal man on a power trip will soon show up. The character of Christ incarnate in believers manifests both power and the genuine fruit of His Spirit.

Noah, responding to the word directive of God, flowed in the first three stages of grace, and when he had finished the ark, God showed up in power. Animals came under sovereign control, God shut the door of the ark, and the rains came while the fountains of the deep poured forth hidden waters. The power of God did not come until Noah had undertaken a long-standing, determined faith action! The action of building the ark earned him a place in the Faith Hall of Fame recorded in Hebrews 11. He did not just believe. If he had settled for belief, he and his family would have died. Believing isn't enough!

Go back to picture Ananias coming into Paul's presence. God could have simply opened Paul's eyes as he had sovereignly closed them. Why didn't he? *God wants to include his people in the administration of his grace covenant,* so he moved Ananias to find Paul. He did not *force* Ananias, but *moved* him and allowed Ananias to respond to that inner motivation. The miracle power of God was brought to bear and God's purposes were accomplished. Ananias did not have to pray for the power of God to come; he just had to do what he'd been directed and motivated to do. Obedience to the word of God's grace did what it always does: it brought the power of God onto the scene and caused Ananias to discover a Christian experience characterized by power. Obedience to the grace directive led him far beyond dry ritual and empty Christian forms.

Joshua demonstrates this same truth. Upon assuming leadership of Israel, Joshua found himself at the barrier of the Jordan River. Joshua knew that God's plan was to take the people into Canaan, but how was this impossible crossing to be effected? In this river experience, he had to move in the five keys of grace. The Word-centered Directive Joshua received could be considered a word of wisdom. The Word of God is always wisdom because Christ has been made wisdom to us. The flow of the grace paradigm was released upon the nation of Israel, and the impossible was made possible. This whole experience types in what God has promised and illustrates how we are to get into the river of God's blessing, purpose, and power. Leadership, to be effective in God's kingdom, must carry these inherent characteristics of grace. It cannot be otherwise!

The word of God's grace does not appear rational in light of natural circumstances or to the carnal understanding of those circumstances. In fact, the word of God's grace most often appears preposterous. Joshua acquired the mind of God on what was to be done by a word directive. After sending in two spies, Joshua 1:2 records that he told the people "Get ready to cross over the Jordan River." He had God's mind, and by obeying, he was enabled to lead the people into the earthly kingdom God had promised. As yet he didn't know how it was going to happen. He had to base such faith action on God's Word directive. In a sense, his mind had to become unfruitful. Joshua, having been told to get ready, directs the priests to "take up the Ark of the Covenant and cross over ahead of the people." What a wild opportunity for the "Yes, but" crowd! "Yes, but the river is at flood tide. We can't do this! Get God to stop the water first, and then we'll cross over." The "Yes, but" crowd always seems to show up at the point of faith action. If Joshua had not acted on the first word directive, he would not have been prepared for a second directive, and the second would never have come. It is only as we move on one directive that the Lord gives us the next instruction. If we do not do the first then there is only silence. It is interesting that the people had decided this time to believe God and follow instructions. There were, by this time, no "Yes, but" types left in the crowd. Those guys had perished in the desert. The "Yes, but" gang always seem to miss the great moments in spiritual history.

Notice that in speaking his directives, God does not go to any lengths to explain the "why" of such directives. The second directive appears in chapter 3:8 (NLT): "Give this command to the priests who carry the Ark of the Covenant: 'When you reach the banks of the Jordan River, take a few steps into the river and stop there.'" Upon hearing God's methodology for crossing the Jordan, Joshua must have wondered how in the world getting wet feet would produce a miracle. Had the priests wanted clarification prior to obedience, all Joshua could have said was to pick up the ark and go stand in the river. He had to give directions that no one else heard and that were contrary to natural logic. He had to act, not having all the information. The skeptic could have asked, "How is standing in the river going to change anything?" The truth is that *obeying simple directives is all that God requires of us*. If we will do what we are told to do, he can demonstrate his omnipotence and get the glory.

Have you been told to stand somewhere? Are you still there? Faced with the need to cross our Jordan River experiences we can find ourselves lacking the power of the Spirit and the result is absolute: the divine purposes for our individual and corporate lives never materialize. In reality, when faced with obeying directives of the Spirit, many in our believing churches will not move until all their questions—read curiosity—are satisfied. However, God does not answer them, so they withhold their obedience and paralyze leadership. As a consequence, no power of God is manifest, and we are left with nothing more than correctly articulated Christian dogma. Any thinking person will become jaded by powerless profession. In his book, *Miracles*, C. S. Lewis states, "A naturalistic Christianity leaves out *all* that is specifically Christian" (83; italics mine). We can be quite comfortable in our Christian profession until God shows up in manifest power demonstrations. For many who profess Christ, this becomes repugnant and even frightening, and they soon join the materialistic, naturalistic crowd. There is little difference between the reaction of the anti-supernatural Christian and the unbelieving atheist. Both groups are dogmatic and hostile in their rejection of such manifestations. Nonetheless, what must be found is power! Power is not to be our ultimate objective or consuming desire, but power in the life of the believer enables the realization of God's holy purposes for our lives. In fact, if the power of God had not been brought to bear on the situation the Israelites faced, God would have been proven a liar because none of God's promises could have been fulfilled to Abraham. Powerlessness at the Jordan would have meant the end of God's purposes for his chosen people. We in Christ are a chosen people. Power is an absolute necessity in genuine Christianity.

Perhaps we need to understand that when Christ directed us to pray "Thy kingdom come," he really meant to deliver to us a kingdom reality characterized by, among other things, miracle-working power. Joshua, obeying the word directive, knew the rest was up to God. Joshua 3:15-16 (MSG) records that when "the priests got to the Jordan, and their feet touched the water at the edge (the Jordan overflows its banks throughout the harvest), the flow of water stopped. It piled up in a heap—a long way off—at Adam." What's the message here? Get in and stay in! Do not start in faith and revert to natural sightedness. Note that as soon as their feet touched the edge of the water the miracle power of God was released; however, the miracle didn't start where they were standing, but at Adam, a town about 35 to 40 kilometers from where they were. The water between the place where the water started to pile up and where the priests stood had to flow past them before the level would have started to drop. In all likelihood, it would have taken some time for them to see a noticeable change in the level of the water. The thirst for instant evidence had to be denied. Get in and stay in!

Joshua lived his life and exercised his ministry on these very principles of grace. In Joshua five and six, these same keys and stages of grace are glaringly present and operative. Joshua saw a man, who was Christ, the Word. He heard a Word-centered Directive with his ears, and understood with his mind, and believed in his heart what the mind of Christ was concerning Jericho. Then came the impartation of the inward motivation to do what he'd heard, so he spoke the directives to his leadership and the people, and by so doing, responded to Christ Himself. When he undertook the corresponding faith action, the power of God hit those walls, and they simply collapsed.

Functional grace is the means by which the Spirit of God brings believers into the flow of God's power. Consider Moses being confronted by Christ at the burning bush in Exodus 3. In Exodus 4:2, God asks Moses, "What's that in your hand?" He answered basically, "A stick." Now, watch the Word directive: "Throw it on the ground." The skeptic might well have asked, "What does throwing a stick on the ground have to do with leading a few million people out of Egypt?" Moses, however, moved in response to the directive, not allowing his mind to bear its own mutinous fruit. The directive heard, Moses made the inner decision to obey. Note the stages of the grace paradigm. Motivation produced the corresponding and God-directed faith action. This in turn brought the immediate demonstration of God's power: The stick became a snake. Then God directed Moses to reach out and pick the snake up *by its tail!* Immediately he did what he was told, and the snake became a stick. These same principles were repeated in verses 6 to 8 when God made Moses' hand leprous and then whole: power every time. The repetition helps. Recall D-MAP! It is how the Holy Spirit wants to work in the life of every believer!

If we look for the four stages in each plague, we find that on every occasion God spoke a directive, Moses obeyed, even in the presence of the most powerful human ruler on earth, and on every occasion power was released. Why did God choose Moses? Perhaps because he knew Moses' heart. God knew that he could speak, and Moses would do what he was told. The end of these grace manifestations was that Moses was enabled to fulfill his God-calling and the purposes of God for his people were accomplished supernaturally. Such is the nature of grace.

The faith response to the word directives of the Holy Spirit will transform the character and ministry of the church. Grace is apportioned to every believer. The Spirit moves to activate grace in our lives by speaking a word directive. As we respond in faith to the directives given, every believer can be drawn into the power and purposes of God for their lives. It is not in attending seminars, in listening to a thousand sermons on power, or by membership in the right church; power doesn't come by "getting it all right." Power comes when God can, by his Spirit, speak a word and find us willing and even eager to act upon what is heard. When the Spirit releases his Word-centered directives, work them through until they become the genuine motivation in our hearts. Once the desire burns in our hearts to do what has been directed, we must act accordingly. Having done so, despite the errors made along the way, the world will finally be confronted by a people who know their God in his manifest power doing exploits!

I realize that this opens the door for many people to go around saying, "God told me," when in fact they haven't heard a thing, but just because there are carnal or counterfeit Christians around does not mean that we should legislate functional grace out of the picture. If we want to discover what it means for the individual believer to be power witnesses in these last days, then we must be willing to sort through the aberrant behavior and motives of misdirected people.

At this point let me pause to make an observation. A considerable amount of material on grace has already been set before you. If you've gotten this far, the inclination is to keep plowing on. Over the years of ministry I have noticed a prevailing tendency in the body of Christ: *we are not very good at processing truth!* We enjoy *hearing* it and seem to *know* good truth when it is presented to us, yet when it comes to *integrating* that truth into our actual conduct, somehow this doesn't happen as it should. Preach a good sermon on love or forgiveness, and people will be stirred up to proclaim "Amen!" Teach what scripture reveals regarding finances and tithing, and heads will nod in agreement. Proclaim the revelation of maintaining the unity of the Spirit in the bond of peace, and there will be general assent among the members of the congregation.

I once spoke in a church on the Christian lifestyle that is meant to exist beyond the issues that come up in the life of every believer. I explained how, when those issues arise, rather than guiding our conduct and words by the biblical standards we claim to believe, we easily find in those issues sufficient cause to initiate a fight or leave the church. The breaking of trust, relationships, and responsibilities is treated as inconsequential. By our personal conduct, we act as though truth is a non-binding option and revert to our habitual, non-biblical modes of speech and behavior. Having challenged them on getting past the issues that come up in church life, the whole congregation verbalized their amens. Agreement with what was being said was very pronounced: "Amen, brother Myers, love that covers a multitude of transgressions will prevail among us! We are one in spirit. Bless the Lord!"

In a telephone conversation with the pastor of that church two weeks later, he indicated that an issue had come up in the church, and some key people in the fellowship had left. So much for amen! They *assented* to truth, but it was not *processed* as an integral part of life practice and personal discipline.

Truth must be validated and expressed in our attitudes, conduct, and speech. If truth is not binding at points of conflict and difference, then no amount of verbal affirmation will change the fact that truth has been rendered irrelevant. Satan doesn't mind it when we shout amen or nod our heads in agreement. He is content in knowing we will void the authority of truth to prevail in our lives. We can easily profess to be submitted to the Bible, but right where the rubber should hit the road in our personal conduct, we float off into the space of our own opinions unfettered by the weighty burden of truth. The "Well, I think" mentality rules the day and ruins the unity and stability of the congregation. The only absolute at the point of controversy is personal opinion, and God might just as well have remained silent.

Paul said of the place and power of grace, "I am what I am by the grace of God" (I Corinthians 15:10). Grace, for Paul, was more than just another Christian doctrine; it had so permeated his being that who he had become was a direct result of grace impacting his very nature. Has grace really prevailed on us as believers? Do we really want grace to govern our responses to life's circumstances? It's important to process the truth of grace so that it actually becomes an inherent part of who we are, not just words in a book that are read and soon forgotten.

Perhaps the following questions may help you to think of some specific incidents where these five keys have worked and what kinds of results they produced:

When the clear Word-centered directives drop into my understanding, do I respond to the grace ministry of the Holy Spirit, or have I been more inclined to miss God's grace?
What word directives has the Holy Spirit been dropping into my heart and mind recently?
Have the five keys to grace become functional in my life?
How might these five keys come into play in some of my present circumstances: in family, marriage, work life, or in my local church?

Imagine a man who has gone without food for weeks being placed before a feast. The food on the table before him may look enticing and smell wonderful, but if he doesn't eat, he will die in sight of the very thing he needs. So it is with grace: ingest it, and you will learn what it means to "live to the praise of his glorious grace." However, if all you do is admire it, sing about it, and pay it religious lip service, then you will never know the abundance Christ came to bring. The motive for everything we do in the Christian life has to go back to the desire that has been implanted into our hearts by the Holy Spirit. We do what we do as believers because we are motivated by the Holy Spirit, not because we are trying to live up to some Christian standard. The Christian life rooted in grace involves living out of His imputed desires. Duty has gone the way of the Law; desire has come by way of His wonderful grace. For the believer, fear of an angry God is forever abolished. Any appeal or call to love by personal resolution is rendered absurd. Charles Finney, in his book, *Power From on High,* observes, "To attempt to love as the Law of God requires—by force of resolution—is an absurdity" (61). So in our presentation of truth we do not call men to put on Christ by force of self-induced resolution but by the reception of grace in all its fullness. Surely we need to be careful that we have not reduced the Covenant of Christ to an absurdity.

The paradigm of grace is the only way the believing church can move into a place of active participation with the Holy Spirit. This paradigm of grace is the manner in which God moves to bring men and women of faith into the fulfillment of their pre-determined destinies as mentioned in Ephesians 2:10. Would you open your heart to the Holy Spirit and ask Him to activate you in God's pre-determined agenda for your life? It's your call! After all, He did tell us in Jeremiah 33:3 (KJV), "Call unto me, and I will answer you and show you great and mighty things that you know not of." God, the faithful one, stands ready to activate his paradigm of grace in your life and to call you into the unique journey for which you were created! Take some time to deal with the truths given us in the pages of scripture, for by grace alone can you "reign in life." May I torment you a bit? Turn to the book of Jonah and see if you can find the five keys of grace and the four stages of the grace paradigm. As well, look for the two core components God said would constitute the nature of grace. It makes an interesting study in grace.

It is true that through the sin of one man death began to rule because of that one man. But how much greater is the result of what was done by the one man, Jesus Christ! All who receive God's abundant grace and are freely put right with him will rule in life through Christ.—Romans 5:17 (GNB)

Chapter Nine
The Savage Christian

What is the proposition under consideration here? Freedom! This is the thesis regarding the nature of personal and cultural freedom: there can be none apart from grace. Once man has excused himself from the parameters of grace, he becomes subordinate to his own thought life and inner passions, neither of which make any meaningful reference to God or God's Word. In this state, he is bondservant to all he thinks and whatever his passions might be. It is only as grace is allowed its work in the lives of men and women that freedom can be experienced. Any departure from grace immediately places man in a state of slavery to himself. The first step toward a regained freedom centers in hearing what the Holy Spirit is saying. He speaks truth; however, truth spoken but unheard can never bear its intended fruit of freedom in the mind and hearts of men.

Galatians 5:1 says, "It is for freedom that Christ has set us free," but what does it mean to be free by the biblical definition? A person is actually free only once he or she discovers how to live within the context of grace. This discovery has two parts. First, there must be a regained capacity to *hear* what the Spirit is speaking and a renewal of *vision*, or as Christ put it in Luke 4:18, "recovery of sight." The second component is a thought life re-centered in the wisdom of God's Word and a recovery of the values and passions inherent in the heart of God. Romans 6:16 and 18 make a very specific statement regarding slavery and freedom: "You are slaves to the one whom you obey—whether you are *slaves to sin which leads to death or to obedience that leads to righteousness*...You have been set free from sin and have become slaves to righteousness" [emphasis added].

The culture can only reflect what operates within the individual. If the people in a culture are governed by thought lives and inner passions that ignore God, they are not only slaves individually, but their culture must reflect that same servitude, bound to those same thought patterns and inner passions. Therefore, freedom in a culture can only exist when the individuals in that culture have been set free from the demands of the thought life and inner passions that ignore submission to God.

I have observed that freedom does not seem to rank very high on the scale of priorities in the Christian community. Freedom certainly was high on the list of Christ's priorities. What role does grace play in establishing true freedom within the human heart and human culture? Freedom needs to be modeled in the Christian community, or the world has no demonstration of genuine freedom. Certainly freedom was central to God's creative intent. Man, by God's design, has always had the power of choice. Reference to freedom can first be found in the second chapter of Genesis, where God gave Adam and Eve the freedom to choose their own destiny. Adam and Eve made their choice while in full possession of their spirit senses. They could hear and see spiritual verities. Their minds and hearts had been operating as God intended. Once they decided to think and act apart from God, they became slaves to their own thought patterns and inner passions, enslaved to whatever their inner nature demanded of them. Such is the state of every individual who lives outside the parameters of God's grace. The Humanist Manifestos depict the perfect example of articulated slavery, for the "real" atheist (if there can truly be such a thing) is the perfect example of an individual who lives in bondage to his own thoughts and passions.

Freedom, finally, must be defined in terms that set man in subjection and willing submission to God. Man can only find the context in which he becomes fully man and fully free as God intended when his existence centers in a lifestyle of submission to God, living as he was created to live. Only in full submission to God can an individual find a release from the power of his ungoverned thoughts, inner passions and wrong belief systems.

Slaves?

So what is the definition of slavery? In broad terms, any explanation of existence defined apart from man's accountability to God becomes a definition of slavery. Unregenerate man, in defining freedom, assumes he is free to decide for himself what the definitions should be and does so without any meaningful reference to God. On the other hand, the believer must be sure that his definition of freedom is set within the context of scripture. Man is only free when his thought patterns and the passions of his heart have been transformed and brought into the place where they operate in subjection to

God. Subsequent to the fall, man chose to sever his intellectual connection and submission to the mind of God and began to think out of the false logic system of the knowledge of good and evil. Man has been prisoner to this inherited false logic system ever since. Furthermore, man's heart was severed from its allegiance to and passion for God at the fall. This bound man as servant to the ruling spirits behind this alternative way of thinking and believing. There is no middle ground. Either God has authority over the life, or else man, a created being of finite nature, becomes subject to the false logic system expressed as some system of religion, serving the fallen spirits behind his erroneous belief system.

No earthly dimension exists where God is absent or that Satan can't try to influence. There is no such thing as a spiritual vacuum, despite the atheist's best attempts to declare otherwise; therefore, man must pledge allegiance either as a slave to righteousness or a slave to his own inner nature. The homosexual, for instance, in declaring himself free from God's moral absolutes, becomes the absolute slave to his sin. He can neither do nor be anything else. The inner tyranny rules the person absolutely. Simply declaring that God and demonic spirits don't exist does not expunge either God or Satan. They will continue to exist no matter how many manifestos are set out to the contrary.

So, since the fall from grace, mankind has been a slave to his own self-generated passions and the demonic powers that oppose the kingdom of God. Unless man is freed first from bondage to his own thought life and heart passions, he remains a slave within himself and subservient to some demonic entity. His mind and heart are bound to function in ways they were never intended to function. The moment man supposes himself free of God, he becomes subject to the constraints imposed upon him by his inner nature and reinforced by the demonic realm. In the state of serving the sin nature, man is further handicapped as II Corinthians 4:4 explains: "The god of this world has blinded the minds of the unbelieving." The blinded mind cannot perceive its own state of slavery, so man is left to define for himself what he interprets freedom to be and then believes his own definition. The resultant definition always rejects any accountability to God and the moral principles given in scripture, but his so-called freedom is ultimately nothing more than an expression of what scripture refers to as the sin nature.

As individuals in a culture are slaves to their inner natures, so the culture follows. Laws, justice, politics, educational and social institutions will all be made to reflect man's state of slavery to what God defines as the sin nature.

This sin must be justified and covered with the cloak of rationalism, which finds expression in the form of arbitrary law. Sin must be made to appear rational and right. Even the intelligent atheist must acknowledge that man's final state apart from God results in some state of slavery.

A Surprise Encounter

It was early morning, January 1, 1986. It was very quiet as everyone in the house was still asleep. I had gone down into our family room to spend some time in scriptures and to pray about the year that lay before us, seeking God's intervention in all that would take place. It was a time of fresh commitment to the calling of the Lord on my life. I was not focused on any specific topic but sensed the presence of the Lord. I became aware that the stillness felt almost heavy. Then, without warning, I heard someone very loudly say, "Canada: a nation of slaves!" I was startled and turned to see who had invaded my quiet space. There was no human there. The stuff about sheep hearing His voice suddenly became more than just a metaphor.

Are you having the same trouble I had trying to picture the people around you as slaves? I could not imagine how Canadians could be considered slaves. People in designer clothes driving nice cars headed for the local mall did not fit my idea of slaves. Slavery had never been characteristic of Canadian history, but it was out of this verbal encounter initiated by the Holy Spirit that I began to search for what these words meant.

Perhaps one should first ask how a once-free people could be reduced to a state of slavery. The fact is that the citizens of Canada, as well as the populations of all historic western democracies, have been progressively subjected to a state of slavery, suffering the same loss of freedom. This process abolishes historic democratic freedom and replaces it with a legalized form of tyranny. Those who are slaves inwardly can never propagate an external, cultural freedom. Their passion is that all men should be slaves to the same master that made them slaves. If, for example, someone is a slave to homosexuality, that individual will be motivated to propagate that same bondage within the cultural context. Leaders of such groups then strive to gain a place of political or social power so as to propagate their particular tyranny. Laws become the weapon of enforced slavery rather than instruments of self-determination, enforcing tyranny rather than guarding freedom. Just consider recent changes in law regarding homosexuality to see how has this progression toward slavery been affected.

Demoralization

Throughout the twentieth century, a colossal shift of values has taken place in western cultures. Historic biblical values that functioned as the base for culture have been progressively replaced by the anti-values of religious atheists. This shift away from the governing values that allow individual freedom and self-government has caused sweeping and contrary changes to the way people live and communicate. Every institution in cultures so affected has had their purposes and ways of functioning radically altered. The anti-values of atheism have usurped a dominant role in framing culture and laws. For all intents and purposes, historic moral values have lost their influence in our cultures and are, in fact, becoming outlaw. Scriptures are increasingly going to be perceived as hate literature, while those believing and preaching them as absolute truth will soon be subjected to the tyranny of pagan law and very likely, prison.

In my search for clarity on the slavery issue, I was asking myself what process had permitted this shift away from our historic moral system. I began to think about morality and the place moral values had held on western cultures. I have found the dictionary to be useful in many situations, and so I began to look through some of the word definitions regarding morals. I came upon one word that aptly expresses how Christian values have been replaced by the anti-values of religious atheists: *demoralization*. The word refers to the loss of moral values and certainly we should have no difficulty in perceiving there has been an almost total loss of historic moral values that once lay at the foundation of western democracies. Based on Webster's Seventh Collegiate Dictionary, demoralization can be characterized as occurring in four stages:

Stage One: Corrupt the existing principles of right and wrong. The strategy is to attack and destroy the existing ethical system.

Stage Two: This progressive corruption enables the destruction of what has been considered the normal way of functioning. The historic criteria used in deciding between right and wrong suffers liberal revision, so that what was once considered right is gradually seen to be wrong, and what was historically defined as wrong is increasingly set out as being right, humane, and the mark of a free, progressive society.

Stage Three: As this corruption and destruction of the historic moral system advances, it produces a state of disorder and conflicting views as to what values should be embraced by the culture.

Stage Four: Those promoting the destruction and demoralization step into the void they created with the lie, "We have the answers," in order to implement their contrary set of moral principles. Enter humanist manifestos, bills of rights and the cultural implementation of religious atheism! Of course, opposition to this new anti-value system cannot be tolerated, thus the culture is finally brought to place of an imposed tyranny.

Take a trip through our museums, schools, courts, political, and social institutions, and you will find ample and conclusive evidence that our cultures have been or are being purged of any reference to our historic, Christian values. "Demoralized" increasingly defines the state of present western cultures. Religious atheists have been incredibly effective in their work of demoralizing our cultures. What's more, this shift away from the historic moral, ethical values around which western cultures were framed is fairly well complete. The moral values once held by consensus in the general population have been lost.

Reducing our once-free populations to a state of slavery is the religious atheist's grand objective. Don't believe me? Consider the introduction to Aldous Huxley's *Brave New World*, written in 1932. This book is an attempt to define, in novel form, the atheist's view of future societies: "A really efficient totalitarian state would be one in which the all-powerful executive of political bosses and their army of managers control a population of slaves" (12). In his book there is finally only one individual who believes in freedom, and he is called "the savage." Webster's defines "savage" as one who is "not domesticated or under human control." Try standing up in some social forum in most western democracies and attempt to articulate the historic moral principles that pertain to freedom. Note the response when you get on a radio or TV program: the license disappears, and the lights go out! Try to live historic values in the workplace or express them in a parliamentary setting, and in many instances, this will earn you a visit the unemployment office.

If you're still not convinced, consider this: Bertrand Russell, who was a leading atheist in Great Britain, wrote a comment for the back cover of *Brave*

New World, saying of Huxley's view of future society, "it is all too likely to come true." Check out the humanist manifestos. These documents give further insight into the intended purposes of religious atheism. All of human society is to be subjected to this single world-view and all wealth is to be conscripted to the support of this singular agenda. Laws are to reflect nothing outside this rigid, intolerant, and all-inclusive agenda. Note that those who finally will not or cannot be squeezed into this box are to be "eradicated" (tenet #8). "Eradicate" is *their* chosen word. Webster's gives it this definition: "to pull up by the root or to exterminate." Interesting agenda these humanists have. So much for freedom of conscience, religion, speech, and association! Their proposed use of euthanasia will no doubt come in handy in the "eradication" process.

Now, before you accuse me of overreacting, the drafters of the second Humanist Manifesto, Paul Kurtz and Edwin Wilson, wrote this as representative of their intention. Were they ignorant of their words, or are the Manifestos a serious attempt to set out the parameters of their worldview and cultural agenda? Do they intend the use of euthanasia, or were they just kidding? Were they kidding about abortion? If you want to understand what has been happening to western society, spend a bit of time thinking through the tenets of the Humanist Manifestos and trace how our societies are consistently being made to conform to these religious tenets. Humanism is not just some sort of passive world-view: it is an articulation of a passionate religious ideology that has become a powerful socio-political force. The more liberal a political movement is, the more it can be seen as reflecting the agendas outlined in the Humanist Manifestos, committed to redrafting the constitutional documents around which western democracies have been framed. Although several European countries have fallen to humanism and the essence of societal divisions is being played out in the United States, nowhere has this redrafting been more effectively accomplished than in Canada.

The Canadian Charter of Rights and Freedoms

With the adoption of the so-called Canadian Charter of Rights and Freedoms in 1982, religious atheism became the philosophical view upon which Canadian society and law would be based. The historic moral values that gave us a framework for freedom have been expeditiously replaced, and Canada as a nation has suffered an insidious process of demoralization. All definitions pertaining to moral values are now forcefully being framed around the single religious view of atheism.

Under the guise of the rule of law, all are going to be obliged to submit to the anti-values as articulated by religious atheists in their manifestos, and the courts have become the instruments of this religious tyranny. To believe historic moral values, such as life beginning at the moment of conception, or a biblical view that regards homosexuality as sin will soon bring the full weight of atheistic law down on the one who declares such a belief. Freedom of religion ceases to exist. Christian parents who exercise corporal correction of their children will increasingly find the free exercise of their faith curtailed by the state. In fact, this is already in effect in Canada, as propagators of atheistic definitions of family think nothing of invading the homes of Christian parents who practice the biblical principle of corporal correction. By force of arbitrary law they drag children out of their homes, and that at the point of a gun, rather like the Nazis when they decided to effect the "final solution" in Europe (*Holocaust Encyclopedia*)! Oh, certainly, it was under the guise of law, but whether it was in Nazi Germany or the present Canadian context, the only freedom that religious atheism will allow is the freedom to be atheist. People will be required to conform to the tenets of religious atheism or be seen as throwbacks to another age—savages!

So, where do those who have a passion for freedom go from here? In his book, *The Stealing of America, John* Whitehead notes, "In Nazi Germany the church, by its choice of expediency and lack of political involvement, was eventually neutralized by the state" (59). Can those who are concerned about the progressive loss of freedoms learn anything from history? History does not seem to render a positive answer to this question. How far has this neutralization of the church progressed in the various western democracies? Tragically, church leaders by their actions, or rather lack of action, have significantly helped this process of neutralization along.

Any Savages out There?

It is interesting to note a comment made in the introduction to *Brave New World*: "Only a large-scale movement towards decentralization and self-help can arrest this present tendency." (12). I cannot really help but ask where this large-scale movement should come from. Who should be the ones who understand the concept of self-help? In truth, self-help is the only expression that Huxley could use, being an atheist. The real concept in this should not be one of self-help but self-government centered in an empowerment coming from God. It is time for religious atheism to be confronted by a host of savages.

So, what has all this got to do with grace, and what has grace got to do with setting the prisoner free? Let's begin by examining why slavery is unacceptable to God. God made man; therefore, man belongs to God. God did not create man to be owned by or subjected to the will of another; neither was he created to live in some kind of enforced servitude to himself or others. There is something in man that demands freedom. It seems that those who most thirst for freedom are those who have none, while those who have some measure of freedom treat it as a sort of self-propagating entity that needs no oversight or defense. It also appears as though we are satisfied with transferring the responsibility for maintaining freedom to God, or mistakenly trust that our governments will guard our freedom. One such phrase that encapsulates this concept of abdication is found in the Canadian national anthem: "God keep our land." It is rather like saying, "Okay, God, you look after it. I'm busy making a living." It is too easy for the believers to abdicate their role in maintaining freedom.

Truth: The Instrument of Freedom

Freedom is God's creative intent for mankind. True freedom then, must acknowledge the existence of a binding Truth. There must be correct, verifiable moral absolutes to which man holds himself accountable. That God wants us free is made evidently clear in Galatians 5:1: "It was for freedom that Christ has made us free," and John 8:36: "Whom the Son sets free is free indeed." Jesus declares that he was sent "to proclaim freedom" in Luke 4:18, and in John 8:32, Christ identified the instrument by which freedom comes: "Then you will know the truth and the truth will set you free." Imparted truth is the instrument God uses to establish freedom for men, but it is not sufficient to know *about* truth, truth must be *known*. Many people know about things without really knowing them. For example, many people know about airplanes, but they couldn't fix one or fly it in a jam. Similarly, *acknowledging* the existence of truth is not the same as *submitting* to truth.

Are there any savages out there who thirst to discover and live in the dimension of real inner, moral freedom? Are there any who would still ask, "What must I do to be free, to be the new breed of savage?" The first essential concept scripture sets out regarding freedom is, "Whom the Son sets free is free indeed." Jesus said of himself in John 14:6, "I am the way, the truth and the life. No man comes to the Father *except by me."* Apart from Christ, there can be no freedom. Next, the instrument Christ uses in the process of setting men free and keeping them free is propositional truth: the absolute, unchanging Word of God. Finally, the Holy Spirit works to take the seeds of truth into the minds and hearts of men. He is the agent of freedom in the earth.

How does the Holy Spirit work to set men free? Believers are repeatedly enjoined, "He that has an ear to hear, let him hear what the Spirit is saying to the church." The Holy Spirit is actively speaking truth to mankind. This takes us right back to the first key of grace: the ear gate. Do we have ears to hear the truth the Spirit is speaking to us? It is only as we hear and respond to the truth that we can come into Christ. Once there, we must submit ourselves to the mind of Christ and those passions that rule our lives must progressively reflect the passions distinctive of the Father's heart. At last we have come to the centrality of grace in establishing true liberty. Men are not free because some constitutional document says so; they only come to true freedom when God the Holy Spirit sets them free and that by the integration of grace!

No chart perfectly sets out the concept of freedom versus slavery, but it may provide a place to start in developing a framework. The first core concept has to do with the biblical definition of a slave. A slave, in God's perspective, is one who is inextricably fettered to his own thought life and the passions of his heart. Such an individual can only be externally what he is internally in his mind and heart. Only God the Holy Spirit can liberate man from the prison of his own thought life and from the driving passions of his heart. Man, in and of himself, cannot deliver himself from who he is: a slave to his inner reality. Follow the progression laid out here, and modify it however you might see fit.

	THE PROGRESSION OF FREEDOM	
HOLY SPIRIT	STARTS WITH A SLAVE	
	Rom 6:16 (MSG) You know well enough from your own experience that there are some acts of so-called freedom that destroy freedom. Offer yourselves to sin, for instance, and it's your last free act. But offer yourselves to the ways of God and the freedom never quits…	
TRUTH: WORD OF GOD	THE WORD IS SOWN	
	Mar 4:3b-9 (MSG) A farmer planted seed. As he scattered the seed, some of it fell on the road… Some fell in the gravel… Some fell in the weeds… Some fell on good earth and came up with a flourish, producing a harvest exceeding his wildest dreams.	
GRACE IMPARTATION	SPIRIT OF GRACE	
	Zechariah 12:10; Hebrews 10:29 (MSG) "… I'll pour a spirit of grace and prayer over them. They'll then be able to recognize me as the One they so grievously wounded…" "What do you think will happen if you turn on God's Son, spit on the sacrifice that made you whole, and insult this most gracious Spirit?"	
THE INDIVIDUAL	THE TRANSITION BEGINS: The New Mind, New Heart	
	II Corinthians 5:17 (GNB) "Anyone who is joined to Christ is a new being; the old is gone, the new has come." How does it happen? Jeremiah 31:33 "This is the covenant I will make with the house of Israel after that time," declares the LORD. "I will put my law in their minds and write it on their hearts. I will be their God, and they will be my people."	
CONVERSION	FREED FROM SIN AND DEATH	
	Romans 8:2 "…because through Christ Jesus the law of the Spirit of life set me free from the law of sin and death."	
FREEDOM	FROM THE CARNAL MIND AND HEART	
	John 8:36 "So if the Son sets you free, you will be free indeed."	
SELF-GOVERNMENT	THE NEW NATURE	
	Galatians 5:22-23, "The fruit of the Spirit is …self-control." By this means the believer fits Romans 13:1-7 (GW) ¹Everyone must submit himself to the governing authorities, for there is no authority except that which God has established… ⁵Therefore, it is necessary to submit to the authorities, not only because of possible punishment but also because of conscience…This believer can control his own inner man!"	
THE DECALOGUE	DEFINES THE NEW MAN	
	Exodus 20:1-17; Romans 13:9 (GW) ⁹ The commandments, 'Never commit adultery; never murder; never steal; never have wrong desires,' and every other commandment are summed up in this statement: 'Love your neighbor as you love yourself.'" The believer with the new heart and new mind is empowered to live out of the Decalogue.	

This new creation, this new man, does not see in the Ten Commandments some kind of standard toward which he must strive. Neither do they represent some kind of bondage that must be thrown off. Instead, he finds these declarations to be a definition of what he is like. He worships God alone because that is his new nature. He finds the concept of idols repugnant. He cannot even broach the possibility of using the Father's name in vain. Neither is it his nature to steal, commit adultery, murder, or covet. The Decalogue is now a description of what he has become through the Spirit's ministry of grace. He has become not only new, but has been freed from all the old inward thought patterns, passions, and corresponding bondages that once characterized his life. The free man is a self-governing man. He has the inner power to make the right choices simply because they are the right choices. Further, the moral absolutes of God are a delight to him through the impartations of the Holy Spirit, and he models what it means to be truly free as he lives by those moral principles. This new man is no longer a slave to the cravings of the inner man. He has found power over the sin nature, and as he lives this new nature out within the cultural context he is viewed as Huxley's "savage."

A Grace Awakening

This phrase, currently being used in contemporary evangelical circles, accurately describes what is needed in our culture. Unless there is a deep and genuine stirring of grace in the body of Christ, the populations of western democracies will ultimately be subjugated, and that slavery will be the only legacy our children will stand to inherit. The only antidote for the cultural disintegration that is taking place around us is a revelatory recovery of grace among believers. Do we care enough to pursue God for those increased measures of grace? Paul understood the importance of grace as he stood in the midst of the pagan cultures of his day and expressed it succinctly in Romans 5:20, when under the Spirit's direction he wrote, "Where sin abounds, grace much more abounds." There is only one antidote to the poison of religious atheism and to the slavery it imposes on humanity: grace! It is only through a functional grace that man is liberated from the bondage and power of the sin nature. Humanistic religion binds man to his sin nature, reinforcing that bondage in the form of arbitrary law, and freedom ultimately becomes outlaw. Free people will be seen as a breed of savage, and the propagation of truth will be singularly perceived as the propagation of hate.

Anyone living in the western democracies should learn from the lessons the religious atheists are teaching us. Historic constitutional documents are progressively being subverted and reinterpreted to say what they were never meant to say. Secularists, while they call on the population to be tolerant, are themselves dogmatically, militantly, and viciously intolerant.

The words I heard that January morning in my family room indeed describe the state of the Canadian citizen and many in the historic western democracies. If we neglect to challenge the secularists, then the singing songs like, "God Bless America," or as in the Canadian national anthem, "God Keep our Land," are reduced to nothing more than sentimental throwbacks to another age. Secularists are totally committed to relegating entire populations to the prison of secular atheism. Culture, shaded around Huxley's *Brave New World*, will be the only reality. Nothing else, no other values, are to be allowed. "If you don't like it, to the ovens with you! If we don't value you, off with your head!" Extreme? Consider the fate of the unwanted unborn! "So long, and by the way, we need your baby body parts first." Once secularism has usurped legal supremacy in a society, it becomes the full embodiment of religious tyranny. The only freedom allowed will be the freedom to be atheistic or the freedom to die. I cannot help but ask the question David posed to his elder brother: "Is there not a cause?" If there is a cause, what resource do we have at our disposal as believers? I can say it in a single word: *Grace!*

It is recorded of the church in Acts 4:33 that, "great grace was on them all." The early believers were able to affect the surrounding pagan culture precisely because they had been filled with the Spirit, and grace was something that bore influence upon their attitudes, motives, and conduct. The early believers had discovered the power of grace to set them free. It was not something that they would easily surrender. It was in grace and the freedom it brought that they found courage to face torture, arenas, and death triumphantly! Can we even comprehend that kind of response?

I trust you can stand the repetition, but there must be a discovery of functional grace in the lives of tens of thousands of believers if there is to be any kind of sustained reformation with a resultant freedom in our societies! Believers must continually bind their minds to the mind of Christ. There must be a willingness to reject the machinations of the carnal intellect and submit to the moral principles God has set before us in the pages of scripture. We must bind our heart-passions to the heart-passions of Christ. Sayings like, "America for God," "The United Kingdom for the King," or "Canada for

Christ" are meaningless if the body of Christ does not become the agape counter culture. Unless we faithfully learn to appropriate grace in its functional dimensions, then there is no escape from slavery and as Christ tarries, our children will progressively become the outcasts and new serfs in a society governed by intolerant, hateful atheism.

The Three R's of the Christian Mandate

The sequence of *renewal, revival,* and *reformation* can be considered the Three R's of the Christian mandate. *Renewal* cannot occur nor be sustained if grace is not functionally present, because believers will not have the mind or heart for the struggle without the inward transformational work of grace. Neither can their fellowship with God be of sufficient depth to sustain them in the struggle. Consequently, *revival* cannot occur or be sustained when grace is functionally absent. Any definition of revival must include the concept of the surrounding culture being affected by empowered believers. If grace-motivated believers do not permeate their surrounding cultures, then the possibility of *reformation* can only be seen as preposterous. Believers must therefore discover and move in the grace administrations of the Holy Spirit. To move in these administrations means that believers learn practically to hear the voice of God, welcome it inwardly, discover the inner freedom truth brings, and then do what they hear!

As believers speak the truth of God and act upon it in our contemporary western cultures, they will increasingly be perceived to be the savage as defined by Huxley's humanistic perspective. There will be an ever-deepening hostility toward those who practice and proclaim the absolute truth of God. The world will love its servitude and be unable to tolerate genuinely free men! But there is a second reality about these free men that will further fuel this hostility. These free men and women will live lives that bear non-refutable evidence of a type of vision that is incomprehensible to the general populations around them. Imagine people who not only "hear voices" but also "see things!" Surely such free individuals will be perceived as fitting the psychological profile of mentally troubled. But whatever the world's perception of such grace activated people *might* be, let us become the vision-mission people we are *called* to be!

Vision-Mission Savages

Those individuals who have discovered the transition from inner slavery to being morally free are now positioned for the next dimension of functional grace: a lifestyle centered in and reflecting spiritual vision. Only free people have the capacity to understand and operate out of "recovery of sight." The recovery of spirit-sightedness is central to discovering and living the life God intends his children to live. Jesus said in John 5:19, "I only do what I see." In Luke 4:18 he declared that he had been anointed by the Holy Spirit to bring, among other things, "recovery of sight." This is *not* a referral to the healing of natural blindness, but a recovery of spirit sightedness that was lost in Eden. If Jesus declared that he was anointed to bring "recovery of sight" there must be a need for sight to be recovered.

Proverbs 29:18 (KJV) records, "Where there is no vision the people perish." Clearly, the lack of spiritual vision equates to death. Conversely, the presence of spiritual vision equates to life. It's that simple. The first question that needs to be asked is whether or not God's people have actually recovered their spirit-sightedness. A second question that needs answering is whether or not scripture mandates spirit-sightedness. What did Jesus have to say on the matter? Does vision operate in two distinct dimensions? Look at the words of Christ in Matthew 6:22: "The *eye* is the lamp of the body. If your *eyes* are good, your whole body will be full of light. But if your *eyes* are bad, your whole body will be full of darkness." There can be no doubt that Jesus taught that vision functions in two dimensions—the natural and the spiritual. If you are still not sure, consider what Paul was declaring in II Corinthians 4:18 when he said, "So we fix our eyes not on what is seen but on what is unseen." Believer, are you a Holy Spirit-powered seer yet?

If we as God's people do not reacquire spirit-sightedness, our ability to demonstrate genuine freedom to the world around us will never materialize because our lives, words, and conduct will contradict our confession! A meaningful translation of Proverbs 29:18 is found in the New International Version: "Where there is no revelation the people cast off restraint." If the people of God cast off spiritual restraint because they lack revelation or vision, what is left of our message and mission? The attribute that kept the Apostle Paul focused on his mission was his capacity for vision. In his testimony to King Agrippa recorded in Acts 26:19, Paul said that he had not been disobedient to the heavenly vision. It is possible for us to be God's people and yet neglect to restrain ourselves because we have failed to recover our spirit-sightedness.

A clear illustration of the relationship between lack of vision and lack of restraint is found in Numbers 13 and 14. In these chapters we find God's people who, lacking vision, cast off the restraint of spiritual principles and spiritual leadership. They are unrestrained despite all God has done for them, despite the presence of incredibly powerful spiritual leadership, and despite the still-present pillars of fire and cloud. The lesson here for the contemporary body of Christ is profound. Tragically, it is a lesson we are not likely to heed. Even though the Israelites had repeatedly experienced the power of God to save and provide for them, they had no capacity to *see* how God could successfully bring them into that which he had promised. They functioned out of the "bad eye" of Matthew 6:22, rendered totally captive to natural sightedness. All that God had done for them, all the demonstrations of His mighty miracles, all the benefits of powerful, spiritual leadership counted as nothing. The result of this lack of spirit sightedness filled the whole body of Israel with darkness, resulting in their continued enslavement to their lack of vision, seeing only death before them in the desert. Returning to Egypt, the environment from which God had delivered them, seemed entirely reasonable. It got to the point in Numbers 14:10 that God's people were ready to murder Moses and Aaron. Joshua and Caleb stood up in the middle of this unholy commotion and identified the root problem when they said, "Do not rebel against the Lord" (v. 9). What was the end result of all this? Well, what you see is what you get: no vision meant death! They died in the desert, never coming into the promised provisions of God.

How easy it is to look at the body of Christ today and see the apparent evidence of a lack of vision and revelation. Rather than being restrained in our words, conduct, and attitudes, it seems that personal perspectives prevail. Do we actually walk in love, maintaining the unity of the Spirit in the bond of peace, seeing with the good eye so that the local body reflects fullness of light? Who is light but Christ? Note the statement Christ made: "The *whole body full of light.*" We really need to get this, because it is in seeing that we become the free men and women that God intends us to be. Do our local fellowships bear authentic witness to being people of vision?

The clear absolute here is this: the end result of missing spirit-sightedness always leads to some death reality. People so bound cannot authentically live as free men, but must act out their true condition, as the people of Israel did. Failing to see things as God declared, they reflected their slavery and cast off the restraints of God's moral principles and leadership. Even though God had delivered them from the state of slavery, they remained slaves to their own inner natures and passions. Reflecting on how far along we've actually come makes me want to ask the question children unfailingly ask their parents on a road trip: "Are we there yet?"

Recovery of Sight: The Second Key

What kind of sight is Christ referring to when he speaks of "recovery of sight?" As we went over in chapter six, Genesis 3:7 reveals the first recorded result of sin: "the eyes of both of them were opened." Up until the moment of sin Adam and Eve had sight that saw the creation in the context of its true nature. The natural, visible reality was perceived in its invisible, spiritual context. However, at the moment of sin they could no longer see the natural in context of the spiritual, and their vision became subject or open to the much narrower reality provided by a single viewpoint: their own. Immediately after they lost their ability to see in the spiritual, invisible dimension, they became prisoners of natural reality and circumstance. Their eyes subsequent to the fall saw only that which was of the material, natural realm, ergo, they could no longer see their natural world in its greater, eternal, and original context. Christ found Adam and Eve in this state of blindness when he came looking for them in the garden, and in Luke 4:18, he pronounced healing for this greater blindness!

There can be no doubt that Christ intended this recovery of spirit-sightedness. In Matthew 13:11-17, Christ declared that believers would be given knowledge of the secrets of the kingdom of heaven. He quotes Isaiah's prophecy, "You will be ever hearing but never understanding; you will be ever seeing but never perceiving," referring to the fact that the people could neither hear nor see in the spirit dimension. Then Christ, speaking to his disciples says, "But blessed are your eyes because they see, and your ears because they hear." Christ was referring to the recovery of spirit-sightedness once lost in the garden.

Paul refers to this spirit-sightedness in Ephesians 1:18 when he said, "I pray also that the *eyes of your heart* may be enlightened..." He is not praying for the eyes in the *head* to be enlightened but for the eyes of the *heart* to be enlightened so that the believers might "*know* the hope to which he has called you." Christ spoke of coming to a knowledge of the secrets of the kingdom of heaven in Matthew 13:11. The disciples were to come into this knowledge by having eyes that could see accurately into the spirit realm. There is a direct link here between spiritual sight and spiritual knowledge.

I know that this kind of teaching flies in the face of much contemporary theology and practice. I know as well that in saying this kind of thing, the door is opened for all kinds of potential quackery to come along. However, the overwhelming truth is that recovery of a spirit-sightedness is both explicit and implicit in scripture. If we say that scriptures are the final authority upon which we base all Christian life and practice, then we must allow the truth set out by scripture to be the framework for what we believe and how we live.

Have you ever meditated on what would happen to biblical revelation if all that had been given via vision were removed from the Bible? Vast portions of scripture would be lost if spirit-sightedness had not been recovered by the inspired writers. For example, what would happen to the book of Isaiah if spirit-sightedness had not been functional? What about the book of Daniel? Paul himself, though blind in Damascus, was shown all that he must suffer (Acts 9:18). If spiritual vision had not been functional in the apostle John's life, there would be no book of Revelation. Paul framed his whole ministry and life decisions around what he'd seen in the spiritual realm. In II Corinthians 12:1 he declares he would "go on to visions and revelations from the Lord." In Acts 2:17 Peter is declaring some of the results of the Spirit of God being poured out, and under divine inspiration says, "your young men will *see visions*." He goes on in verse 25 and repeats King David's words, "I *saw* the Lord always before me." It is recorded in Hebrews 11:27 that Moses could keep going because he "*saw* him who is *invisible*." Consider that even a man as uniquely called as Moses required eyes that could see in the invisible dimension to fulfill his God-appointed responsibility.

While there may be a substantial number of evangelicals who would scorn recovery of spirit-sightedness, what they truly are denigrating is that which is biblical and genuinely spiritual. It is one thing to bandy about verses such as, "Where there is no vision the people perish." It is another thing to minister this concept of vision so that the reality of it begins to function in the lives of believers. I remember how astonished I was the first time I noticed the scripture that said while Peter was on the rooftop waiting for lunch, he fell into a trance (Acts 10:10). I had always thought of trances (a visional experience) as being solely occult and of the Devil. But there it was: Peter fell into a trance. Interesting word, "fell." Falling inherently involves a loss of personal control, and oh, how we hate to lose control! In most evangelical circles if someone fell into a trance, that individual would probably be ushered out of the church or rushed to the hospital to pay a visit to the psychiatrist. In some Pentecostal circles (and I use the term in the broadest sense of the word) the individual may well be subjected to deliverance ministry. Perhaps this was the reason God waited for Peter to get away from the believers downstairs. Regardless, while in this trance, Peter *saw* and *heard* (v. 11). God was activating a grace ministry to be expressed through Peter. For this ministry of saving grace to be ministered by Peter to Cornelius and his family, a supernatural vision capability was necessary. Take away the vision Peter had and what action would he have taken toward the salvation of that little group of gentiles? The Holy Spirit does nothing spurious. He knew it would require something strong to get Peter past his religious upbringing in not only associating with gentiles, but also preaching the gospel to them! In God's economy, vision was and still is essential for effective grace ministry. He does not change, even if the biblical concepts of sight and sound are inconvenient to our current theological models.

Under Demonic Dominion

The antithesis of grace is subjection to demonic dominion. Why does the lack of vision always lead to death? Simple. To rebel against God is to submit to Satan and the satanic agenda, which is always to steal, kill, and destroy everything the body of Christ should represent and do. People who lack spirit sightedness cannot be led in the purposes of God, for where there is no revelation the people cast off restraint. No vision means rebellion. Rebellion invites the incursion of demonic spirits. The demons can observe our conduct and speech, know that we have cast off the restraints of Christ's Lordship, and upon such observance close in for the kill. No revelation means the only thing that can be perceived is death, the demonic perspective.

To allow rebellion to go unchecked is to hand control of our churches and ministries over to Satan. When this kind of thing happens in our churches, it spells the end of effective ministry. It has happened and is happening in literally thousands of churches around the world. All the while, those in rebellion sing, "He is Lord!" Indeed, but the song is in many instances being ministered to the lord of darkness, not the Lord of Light! A couple of blind people in places of leadership are all it takes to incite a rebellion in the pew. In the case of the Israelites, ten spies got several million of God's people infected with the deadly virus of rebellion. Why? They were determined to make their voices heard and have their wills enforced!

Most who join a rebellion are as blind as those leading it. There is only one fruit to rebellion and those who succumb to it eat of its fruit. Those who rebelled in the wilderness died as prophesied. The church, rather than flourishing in the purposes and power of God, can die a painful death while the rebels place the blame on proven, spiritual leadership. The abundant life Christ spoke of never comes. Hmm...right back to the garden! The "Me? Never!" denials of Eden rise again. God willing, may ten thousand church rebels read this and repent so that they might live life in the inheritance God intends.

Do we need to recover the spirit-sightedness of which Christ spoke? Without it, the truth of Proverbs 29:18 still prevails regardless of the songs we sing, or what kind of church we attend. No vision = no life. GET A LIFE!

Some Biblical Illustrations

Consider the Israelite army facing Goliath. The whole army, to a man, could only look down into the valley and see death. Not one of them ventured down into the valley of confrontation because they had no capacity to see that it was God's purpose to deliver Israel. They could not see God coming on the scene, nor see how God could intervene to deliver them. They had no capacity for spiritual sightedness, and the thought of victory didn't even enter their minds. Then David arrives. He's had a revelation of God's plan for his life: he knows he is appointed and anointed to be king. That being the case, he moves in knowledge. (Note the relationship between revelation and knowledge, activating the eyes of the heart.) He could venture down into the valley of confrontation with all confidence, knowing that he *couldn't* die that day. He could therefore cooperate with God by faith because *he knew God would do what he said he'd do!* He understood the reality, "The battle is the Lord's" (I Samuel 17:47), and there was no doubt about the outcome. He could look down into the valley and instead of seeing fifteen pounds of brass piercing his rib cage, see Goliath with his head severed. He understood what the real weapons of warfare were all about. Ultimately, David's ability to correctly perceive was the deciding factor between freedom for the whole nation and enslavement to a pagan religion.

Remember the disciples in the boat? The disciples demonstrate the consequence of the lack of vision. They did not perceive things as they really were. Jesus, however, had the revelation of God for his life and remained undisturbed by the storm's commotion. He could see that this was not the time, the place, nor the manner by which he was to die, so he could rebuke the wind and the waves with authority. The disciples had no revelation of God's plan and purpose for their lives and even though they were Christ's by God's choosing, they still had not come into the discovery of spirit vision. Lacking that vision in the midst of difficulty, the only thing they could see was impending death. What they saw in the natural they believed, and what they believed in their hearts came out of their mouths: "Don't you care that we are about to die?" (Mark 4:38, GNB). The fact remains that they were in no danger of dying that day. God had a different plan for their lives, but because they had no revelation of who they were, they cast off the restraint of faith. Faith places its own kind of restraint on our perceptions of reality, on our conduct and speech. Note in verse 40, Christ rebuked them for their lack of faith. This same lack of vision and confidence gripped the whole army of Israel when confronted by Goliath. Had the disciples *seen* what God's plan for their lives was really all about they would not have lost their faith in the crisis, just as if the army of Israel had understood their place in God's design, they would all have had the heart of David and could have said to the Philistines with David: "I come against you in the name of the Lord Almighty...Then the whole world will know that Israel has a God!"

You see, faith is all about being confident, certain about what is not seen in the natural (Hebrews 11:1). David did not cast away his confidence because he knew who he was and knew God's purposes for his life. He had a revelation that allowed him to maintain his confidence, making him stable, courageous ,and victorious. He could spend his life in the purposes of God and live to serve his generation. The disciples discovered the same reality later on and blew out from behind locked doors to change the world!

If the church in these last days is to be the kind of church God intends her to be, then there must essentially be a recovery of revelational, spirit-sightedness. Recovery of this sight alone will enable us to know who we are. Then and only then will we be able to stand with confidence in the knowledge of God's power and plan for our lives. We cannot simply settle for singing nice songs about grace or paying it some sort of meaningless verbal homage. We must discover effectually what it is, how it works, and then grasp it so that we in fact become living demonstrations of grace-filled believers.

If freedom is to be defended against the progressive incursions of humanistic tyranny, then some of God's people must begin to hear, see, and obey. It was only as Moses responded in faith to what he'd heard and seen that he could become the deliverer God intended him to be. It was by adding faith to what he'd heard and seen of God that the people were delivered from slavery in Egypt. Surely, it is still in the heart of God that men should be free.

The humanistic agenda is to forever seal men and women off from the liberty truth brings, and they are bent on enslaving the whole world to their own ideal and its accompanying demonic doctrine. If our children are to be free to worship God, then having heard and seen, some among God's people must venture into the conflict for such liberation! Why does the humanist define the true Christian as a savage? It is because the true Christian cannot be tamed to serve any but God alone. As in Huxley's *Brave New World*, the savage is ultimately locked up in a prison because he cannot be made to serve anything but freedom. Tragically, we too may have to agree with Bertrand Russell's statement, "It is all too likely to come true." What then our cry? Lord, that we be not tamed!

The Savage Breast

Oh, that God would give that savage breast
that knows its freedom
in divine submission
to all that is true and noble.
That my heart might sing upon the battle line,
"The victory, it is already mine!"
My mind and heart agree:
Great grace has captured me.
I find in Him my great desires
So fully quenched, I lay,
satisfied before the throne.
Freed at last and nothing yield,
My God, what joy, this savage breast
To You!

Chapter Ten
Blood-Blind Believers

Imagine! Blood blind believers gathered at the communion table of Christ, celebrating, as it were, the Passover while violating the very Spirit and meaning of *Passover*. What a travesty! Could it be possible? "Surely not, Lord!"

Throughout the Book of Malachi, every time God confronted his people through the prophet their violations of specific spiritual principles, they denied it. It seems they had neither the capacity nor the willingness to recognize and confront their transgressions against the Lord and his plan for them as a people. In contemporary terms, their response might be summed up as, "Well, I don't see how that applies to us." Even when their own sinful violations were pointed out specifically, they did not respond in repentance but continued in their stubbornness. They chose to resist the word of his grace and the prophetic truth that was meant to heal, deliver, and spare them the judgment of God.

It is very easy for believers to read through the Old Testament and pinpoint the specific sins Israel committed against the Lord. It is almost inconceivable to us that they would not face their obvious sins. However, a present-day prophetic word can be equally difficult to hear and respond to, yet believers of today are violating the Covenant of Grace in parallel ways and are bringing those violations directly to the communion table. In the contemporary church, we seem to be unable to recognize how we violate the prevailing covenant. When I make reference to a prophetic word, I am not talking about the individual spouting the lingo of a prophet who proceeds to tear the body of Christ apart in keeping with his own judgments. A true prophetic word will always be in keeping with the spirit of grace. Yet it is also true that apart from a prophetic word there can be little to make us aware of the kinds of things from which we need to repent. If we could discover these violations and genuinely repent of them, we would come into a significantly greater manifestation of the freedoms, power and blessings that are meant to characterize the body of Christ.

One of the most serious ways we violate the covenant of grace is in the way we treat one another. There seems to be a refusal to meet head-on the attitudes that lurk in our own hearts, bringing us into a direct confrontation with the Lord at the communion table. We continue having our communion services, professing that we are walking in love toward one another, when all the while the church resembles a war zone instead of a demonstration of the kingdom of God. If what is going on in many churches is representative of the heaven we proclaim, then God help the poor sinner who comes into our spiritual shoot-outs!

We need to stop acting as though everything is as it should be. What you are about to read has to be something more than information to be added to your already overfed theological grid: *Relational violations are a direct contradiction of the grace covenant.* Hebrews 10:29 tells us God takes offense when his children live and act carelessly before him, especially when it comes to how we treat the blood of Christ's sacrifice, his broken body and his Holy Spirit! There is a direct link between our relational failures and the blood of Christ. One of the verses that believers have referred to extensively when focusing on a move of God for our nations is II Chronicles 7:14—"If my people, who are called by my name, will humble themselves and pray and seek my face and *turn from their wicked ways,* then will I hear from heaven and will forgive their sin and will *heal their land."* Certainly there is a clear recognition that our nations need the supernatural healing that only God can impute. So why is it we can recite this verse, hold prayer meetings, have times of fasting, and call for repentance but still witness no move of God in the magnitude necessary to win the lost of our nations?

The central premise of this verse is that *the people of God are violating the holy nature of God.* Typical of the Holy Spirit, he identifies the core problem with incredible simplicity: "their wicked ways." The fruit of humbling ourselves, praying, and seeking God's face means that we must come face to face with *our* wicked ways and be broken before God in genuine repentance. The communion service is all about personal repentance—it must be marked by genuine repentance! If we as God's people want to see a profound move of the Spirit that in fact heals our nations, then we need to ask ourselves a couple fundamental questions: "Who, me?" and, "What wicked ways?" I have been in meetings where the leader, with good intentions, ordered people to get on their knees and start repenting. Repenting of what, however, was not identified. The assumption by the leader was that some secret sin of the people present was holding back God's move in the nation, thus everyone present was required to pray out loud prayers of repentance regarding their own personal sins. The problem with this is that even repentance must be something that flows in response to the Spirit's ministry of grace in our hearts or it fails to be the kind of repentance that will move God's Spirit. There is a brokenness of heart that precedes repentance, which can only take place after the Holy Spirit has shown us the ugliness of our own sin as opposed to someone else's sin. So, we move to the second question: "What wicked ways?" Note that the word "ways" is plural. There is about our "ways" that which God perceives to be "wicked." That is to say, when our conduct, speech, attitudes, priorities, and motives as expressed in our relationships fail to reflect the covenant we live under.

Any church or individual believer really wanting to be used of God in affecting the history of nations—you know, that "heal their land" stuff—must first have identified what those "wicked ways" are *in specifics*. It is the Holy Spirit who comes in to reveal how we individually are involved in wicked ways and *he* who convicts us of sin. General, religious prayers of repentance will not suffice. It is, among other things, about brokenness of heart and the recognition of how we have crucified Christ in one another. *There is a direct connection between crucifying Christ in one another and our attitude toward his shed blood!* One of the main areas in which wickedness among believers is apparent to God has to do with our conduct toward the blood of Christ. Hebrews 10:28 makes it clear that if we carelessly violate the sanctity of His blood, then the effectiveness of Christ's sacrifice is nullified. Putting it bluntly, there is a widespread violation of the blood of Christ in the body of Christ today. This violation has to do with "trampling the Son of God underfoot" by treating the blood of the covenant as though it was any unholy thing. Sitting there, you can almost hear the question, "How have we violated the blood of Christ?" or again, "Who me?" It is that Malachi malady: Christ is trampled underfoot when we demonstrate a callous disregard for his shed blood. (Read the first chapter of Malachi. God rebukes the priesthood for defiling worship by using animals they wanted to get rid of and believing that God would be all right with getting the castoffs. We do the same when we mistreat fellow believers and think that God will just overlook it because we're no longer under the law.)

Despite our frequent trips to the communion table, our verbalized regard for Christ's sacrifice, and all our songs about his blood, there is an almost universal disregard and violation of the sanctity of the blood of Christ in the whole span of the church. It is out of this disregard that our wicked ways find expression in the body of Christ! Certainly we come to the communion table with deep sincerity, sing our songs with great affection for Christ, and listen with devotion to sermons about the blood and sacrifice of Christ. It is not our theology that is in question here, but how our attitudes, motives, words, and actions contradict that theology. We say and sing one thing and live and act in "ways" radically opposed to what we profess. This contradiction between our confession and our conduct does not go unnoticed by God, especially when we gather around the grace table. *These* are the ways God calls "wicked."

If we don't get it right at the communion table, then the rest of what we do is nothing more than the practice of vain religion. It is because we violate the essence of the communion service that there is absolutely no hope of any kind of sustained, widespread revival. If there is no widespread turning to God, there can be no foundation for effective, nation-changing, history-making reformation. Yes, we can use our eschatology to dismiss any possibility of reformation, but to do so is to refuse to face our violation of Christ and his sacrificial blood. Nothing is too hard for the Lord. He can bring effective, long-term spiritual awakening to our nations, opening the way for genuine reformation. Reformation is the act of God by which he heals our land. If we believe it is too late in the day for reformation, then we had better stop preaching II Chronicles 7:14, and prayer should be limited to things other than the rebirth of righteousness in our nations.

As long as we are in the age of grace, his grace is sufficient—even for revival that will in turn affect the moral and institutional structures of our nations. If it is too late for real reformation, then the battle for the unborn is lost; euthanasia and every sort of vile conduct cannot be stemmed; the generation of young people raised without the benefit of a truly defined morality is already lost to us; and we might just as well give way to wickedness and hide in the leafy bushes of escapist theologies. We do not have to tolerate the satanic wickedness of legislated atheistic humanism: evil is overcome by good. From what source can genuine revival and reformation flow? The epicenter lies squarely in the spiritual integrity of our communion services. There is a direct link between the spiritual soundness of our communion services and the present and future state of our nations, because in the final analysis, if we get it right at our communion services, God will affect the history of our nations for good!

So, have you figured out what God means by our *wicked ways?* In short, we violate Christ, his blood, insult the Spirit of grace, and crucify Christ afresh in our churches and this most particularly in our communion services. If we violate one another relationally, then our communion services constitute a contradiction to the very meaning of the atonement of Jesus Christ! Sometimes the truth is an offense even to believers, but the purpose here is not to offend. We must allow truth to have its proper authority in our lives even if it is painfully unpleasant. The need for genuine revival and reformation far outweighs either our individual or religious sensibilities. Before you turf the book, I would invite you to think through the concepts being set out here, not because my ego needs a boost, but because there is a dire need for revival to change the direction in which our nations are being driven if our children are to inherit the legacy of freedom.

Surely, if some possibility exists that believers are violating the grace table, we need to understand how it is taking place and what we need to do to remedy it. Remember, God's Word says that *his people* were involved in what *he* termed "wicked ways." If such a possibility exists in the believing community, then we must have the courage and determination to face and confess what those violations are as they pertain to Christ's atoning work. To repeat: If we don't honor the grace table then the rest of what we say and believe loses credibility with both God and a lost world.

In I Corinthians 10, where Paul is urging us to learn from Israel's history, he goes directly to the communion service. In verse 16, he speaks of giving thanks for *"a participation in the blood of Christ."* We cannot be participants in the blood of Christ while simultaneously trampling it underfoot! He goes on to speak specifically about the Lord's Supper in chapter 11, a passage routinely read at communion services. Note that in speaking to the believers regarding what is happening at the Lord's Table in verse 17 he says, "I have no praise for you, for your meetings do more harm than good." Can you picture it? Communion services that are destructive, that do more harm than good? Be careful that the response to such a statement doesn't invoke a "How have we?" or "Not our communion services, Lord!" There were some serious violations showing up at the Lord's Table that Paul addressed in a very uncomplimentary manner. If the believers had chosen to take offense at his rebuke, then the meaning of the Lord's Table as they participated in it would have been reduced to an empty religious ritual with deadly side effects (v. 30).

His first topic of concern focuses on *"divisions among you." Full stop!* One of the most prominent characteristics of the community of believers today is that there are *divisions* among us. These divisions thrive on hate, venom, and verbalized death and are often justified by our theologies. The relational devastations in the body of Christ are epidemic, yet despite the presence of those divisions, we insist on having our communion services the first Sunday of the month. The general approach to dealing with divisions in our churches is simply to ignore them.

Have you ever looked up the definition for the word hate? Webster's defines it this way: "[1] to feel extreme enmity toward [2] to have strong aversion toward [3] to detest [4] active hostility [5] moral condemnation [6] disgust and intolerance." Would anyone be hard pressed to find these kinds of attitudes in our churches? Listen to how one preacher speaks of another preacher, or spend a little time on the board of a church or as an elder. Get into some staff responsibility, and pretty soon some or all of the above becomes an operative reality in what are supposed to be love relationships. Check out the Sunday school operations, the choir or worship team. Clearly our manifest attitudes, motives, priorities, conduct, and speech more often fall within the definition of hate rather than Christ's definition of love. The relational reality in our churches is frequently appalling and more representative of hell than heaven. Yet we insist that we have our "love feast" the first Sunday of the month. Truly, hate is more often characteristic of what's going on in our fellowships than is agape. We pay lip service to I Corinthians 13 and to the blood of Christ, yet our attitudes, hostility, unwillingness to forgive and aversion toward others in the body of Christ rage on unchecked. We have separated our confession from our conduct. If our confession is right, then it seems our conduct ceases to be something we need to confront and correct! Those who insist with unrelenting forcefulness that we get our theology right may often be the ones who excuse themselves from Christ-like attitudes of heart and target those believers holding a different theology!

Forget It!

Now consider God in heaven watching his children gather around what we dare call "The Lord's Table." *His* Table! Is it possible that he is blind and deaf to our love for the carnal, for our practiced unforgiveness? Is it possible that he is indifferent to our grumbling, criticisms, infighting, or lack of gentleness and regard for one another? Is he at all affected by the fact that we come to the communion table holding strong aversion toward others—a pastor or elder, a husband or wife? Does he simply ignore our hostile attitudes and speech, or does God see such carnal realities as trampling Christ underfoot, as treating the blood of the covenant we are supposedly celebrating as an unholy thing? Is it still possible today that the Holy Spirit is concerned about the divisions that exist and operate among believers in full view of God? By ignoring our relational wars and going ahead with our communion services, is it possible that we are insulting the Spirit of grace? A shoot out at the O.K. Corral seems an unlikely place for a love feast!

God takes our communion services seriously even if we somehow overlook the very things that grieve the Spirit and nullify functional grace. Can we really expect the Spirit to empower our witness to the world if the world is only to find itself drawn into the same vortex of hate that it thought it was escaping by coming into the church? How can we expect the blessings of Christ on our churches, lives, marriages, and ministries if we continue to ignore the hate that exists between believers? I do hope the word *hate* jerks your chain! Remember, that definition was not something I made up, twisted, or manipulated to serve my literary purposes. We may think that God doesn't scrutinize our hearts and attitudes when we participate in a communion service, but you can be sure he is watching! What do we think I Corinthians 11:27-30 is all about? Let's read it:

[27] Therefore, whoever eats the bread or drinks the cup of the Lord in an unworthy manner will be guilty of sinning against the body and the blood of the Lord. [28] A man ought to examine himself before he eats of the bread and drinks of the cup. [29] For anyone who eats and drinks without recognizing the body of the Lord eats and drinks judgment on himself. [30] That is why many among you are weak and sick, and a number of you have fallen asleep.

In the Message, these verses read as follows:

[27] Anyone who eats the bread or drinks the cup of the Master irreverently is like part of the crowd that jeered and spit on him at his death. Is that the kind of "remembrance" you want to be part of? [28] Examine your motives, test your heart, come to this meal in holy awe. [29] If you give no thought (or worse, don't care) about the broken body of the Master when you eat and drink, you're running the risk of serious consequences. [30] That's why so many of you even now are listless and sick, and others have gone to an early grave.

Remember, God expects spiritual authenticity on the part of every participant at the communion service even if we are content to let divisions exist among us. *Thinking* we take it seriously is not enough. Holding hate in our hearts while participating in communion is colossal, arrogant hypocrisy! Our conduct, speech and manifest attitudes are the real measure of spiritual sincerity! God expects us to apply grace to our conduct, to conform to the Word, and thus represent an authentic, visible likeness to Christ. Pastors must hold their congregations accountable for the veracity of relationships whether the people like it or not. The agape-walk is not optional.

Look at verse 27 in reference to "wicked ways." How wicked do you think sinning against the body and blood of the Lord is? Who was Paul speaking to? It wasn't to some religious hypocrites or pagans on the street, but to born-again, Spirit-filled believers. Who can be in danger of sinning against the body and blood of Christ? Believers! If we don't esteem the communion table as believers, then we are sinning against the body and blood of Christ. What does the Word say? Guilty! Sorry if this offends religious sensibilities, but if we are going to conduct communion services they must be done in a way that pleases God. Time spent before the grace table must be acceptable to God. Personal sincerity will not act as a substitute, satisfying God that we are indeed living as we profess to be living. The communion service is no place to act as though everything is okay when the characteristics of hate exist in our hearts and manifests in the relational contexts of our churches.

Paul is not finished yet, but continues in verse 28: "A man ought to examine himself before he eats of the bread and drinks of the cup." This is not some kind of option the Spirit is offering us. This is imperative! In plain English, it might be put like this: "Hey, you'd better take stock of your own issues before you insist the pastor conduct a regular communion service. How are you treating your wife? How are you treating your employees or your employer? How righteous are your finances? Do you think God doesn't know about those X-rated movies you tune into, or the web sites you log onto? How about those attitudes and words you speak in front of your children criticizing the pastor, your church leadership, or those Christians with whom you have found fault? Do you then dare to show up on communion Sunday and act as though God is deaf and blind?"

God has his eye on every communion service that we as His church conduct. He weighs them in the balance to discover whether or not our relationships are really reflective of the Spirit of love. How do you talk about your husband when you get together with the women's prayer fellowship? What messages are you sending into the church through your husband? Do your children see you hold your husband in a place of respect so they can learn how to conduct themselves toward God's appointed authority? "Oh, yeah, but you don't know my husband!" True, but God does! Abraham wasn't the best of husbands, putting his wife in another man's bed on two occasions, yet it is said of Sarah in I Peter 3:1-7 that she "obeyed Abraham and called him her master." If you can get a revelation on that, you will cry out for more grace and mercy as it relates to your own state before God!

Whether we are men or women, we all face relational challenges to our spirituality. We can't decide to accomplish this by some dint of self-effort. We seek the Spirit of grace to find grace, which helps us in the places we need help. *We cannot use our interpersonal difficulties as excuses for copping out of fellowship and Christian responsibility.* My oldest daughter tells the story of an encounter she had with God in her driveway. She and her husband had been in several ministry positions, where they had been sorely wounded. They had moved away from ministry and were working in management. One day as she got in her car to go to work, she heard a question from the Lord:

"Do you love me?"

"Of course, Lord, more than anything!" she quickly replied.

"Then love my people."

She sat for a minute absorbing the concept of risking her heart to people, who were not perfect, over God, who is.

"Lord, I love you, but people—they aren't trustworthy," she contended.

"If you love me," he insisted, "then you must trust *me* to guard your heart."

They went back into the ministry within a year, and met some of the worst trials they had ever encountered, but God gave them grace to not only face their circumstance, but to fight the true battle that lay before them, not engage the people they were sent to serve.

Many just miss the grace of God, finding it easier just to pick up their Bibles and go home, no longer interested in participating in the life of a local fellowship. The world is full of copped-out Christians! We must recognize interpersonal conflicts as God's call to find and appropriate more grace. John 12:24 describes the kind of grace we are called to: "Except a grain of wheat fall into the ground and die." The call of grace is the call to death—death to our own perceived rights. But what are the results? We produce eternal fruit, and we are no longer alone.

Let's move on to verse 29. Our initial response to reading this particular passage may be, "Now Lord, isn't this getting radically extreme?" But remember, "Every part of scripture is God-breathed and useful one way or another—showing us truth, exposing our rebellion, correcting our mistakes, training us to live God's way" (II Timothy 3:16, MSG). In this passage in I Corinthians is some of the strongest New Testament language we find the Spirit using to address the believer, but honestly, if a believing Christian eats or drinks without recognizing the body of Christ, then that person is bringing damnation down on his or her own head. This term damnation doesn't mean a really bad day, but means the offender is assigned to hell! While such a concept may be a powerful motivator to examine ourselves, the key focus in this verse is not damnation, but rather a failure to "recognize the body of Christ." If we fail to discern the body of Christ, we are dancing on the precipice of Hell. How's that for danger? It reminds me of Exodus 4:24, where God moved to kill Moses on his way down to Egypt.

Here's the point: the folks in the fellowship are not *like* the body of Christ they *are* the body of Christ. That's how Christ sees the believers around you. What was Christ's first question to Saul when he knocked him off his high horse? "Saul, Saul, why do you persecute *me*?" Who was Saul imprisoning and putting to death? Believers! Have you made the connection between the believer and Christ? As far as Christ is concerned, the believer cannot be separated from His own person. You know, "whatsoever you do to one of the least of these my brethren you have done unto me" (Matthew 25:40). So, dear reader, how have you been treating Christ lately? What attitudes are in your heart toward Christ that contradicts your confession? What hate lies hidden in your heart? Take a moment and go back to the definition of hate. Don't just pull the Malachi question: "How have we despised you?" What conduct, what words have you unleashed against the body of Christ? You'd better examine your relational attitudes toward the body of Christ before you show up at the communion table! If we fail at the communion table, we can forget about the kind of church mission that bears the marks of the Spirit's power, because quite separate from the eternal implications, there are some deeply personal consequences to be suffered in this present life.

To discover the specific consequences, look at verse 30. What happens to those who fluff over the directives Paul has given and just partake of the elements? Remember this is New Testament! "For this reason"—now watch the next word—"*many,*" Did you get that? Not a few tormented individuals, but *many* among the believers had suffered three effects arising from "common-union" abuse. Some were weak, some had fallen sick, and some had even died. The *many* fall into three categories: weak, sick, and *dead*! Why? They had been careless at the communion table! They saw no need to get their relationships, attitudes, motives, words, or conduct right. They just showed up drinking the cup and eating the body of the Lord carelessly! "So what if I'm critical; so what if I'm _____?" Fill in your own blank. Listen: *God is weighing our hearts and spiritual veracity whenever we show up at the communion service!* If you don't got it right, then get on your knees and get it right! How? Ask God for the grace to change what needs to be changed. Call hate, hate! Face it and get free of it! The change that God expects is a change that inherently takes place in the heart, instilled in us by the Holy Spirit.

Concept: as Our Communion Services Go, So Go Our Nations

Now, I've stated previously that what happens in our communion services affects our cultures, but what is the connection that impinges on our capacity to affect our national destinies? There is a threefold progression that flows out of our communion services that starts with the individual believer who is in violation of the covenant stipulations and carries those violations into the local church. The local church subsequently suffers corporate infection, which causes a successive loss of power to impact the world around us. If an individual believer shows up at the communion table ignoring the need to be in right relationship with the rest of the members of the congregation, sooner or later one of three things will happen to him: he will end up weak, sick, or even dead. Ananias and Sapphira are New Testament illustrations of this reality, and they weren't even *at* a communion service. Lets examine these three conditions more closely.

1. **Weak:** An individual cannot habitually be careless in approaching the grace table without affecting the quality of his own faith: you cannot insult the Spirit's ministry of grace and long stay strong in your faith. So, the first consequence for careless communal participants is that they become increasingly weak in their faith. They are always in need of being propped up, and their capacity to participate in the faith life of the fellowship dissipates.

2. **Sick:** This needs no explanation, but let me give a caution here. Every Christian who struggles with sickness cannot be considered to have violated the sanctity of the Lord's Table. Shouldn't have to say that, but if it's not said some goof will come to this kind of foolish conclusion. Clearly, however, one consequence of careless participation in the communion service is sickness. Some disease or infirmity from the Devil finds its way into the life of that believer through the open door of carelessness. This kind of sickness even the prayer of faith and the anointing of oil cannot heal! God is not the only one who can recognize communal violations: the Devil takes opportunity at our

inconsistency. The spirit of hate capitalizes on hate. If believers persist in relational violations and continue to come to the Lord's Table acting as though everything is all right they are putting themselves in jeopardy.

Listen, among other things, *the Lord's Table represents the heart of our confession before God.* When we come to the table, we are in effect confessing to God, "See, God? All my relationships with my fellow believers are grace-oriented. I have examined myself and discerned my relationship with the rest of Your body. Thank you for your great sacrifice that sanctifies my fellow believers as well as myself. Thank you for the grace that enables me to love the brethren and for giving me deliverance from the carnal impulses of hate." Hey, you might look good to the members of the congregation and to the pastor, but who cares? How do you look to Christ at His grace table? He knows. No, don't skip the table; get to the table acknowledging your carnal failings, asking for forgiveness for what's in your heart and what's been on your tongue. Cry out for delivering grace. Get your heart right, particularly with those believers you feel have offended you. We cannot safely violate Christ, his blood, or the Spirit of grace.

3. **Dead:** There is no doubt that when various translations say "asleep," they mean dead. In fact, many modern versions, like the one we looked at earlier, do translate it this way. God does not take the grace table lightly! He'll let Satan kill you if you persist in carnal, self-indulgent participation in the communion service. We can be thankful that His mercy endures to a thousand generations, but that does not excuse us from keeping the directives of scripture.

Another dimension of existence that falls between sick and dead is territory we might call spiritual indifference, complacency, or being lukewarm. So, between sick and dead physically, dead here carries the implication of being spiritually indifferent to God, his people and purposes in the earth. When life is focused on temporal reality despite a profession to the contrary, prioritized in terms of work, money, or pleasure and characterized by unchecked carnal motives, conduct and speech, then our profession becomes vain and meaningless. Things like going to church, giving to the Lord's work, teaching Sunday School, or participating in building a local ministry all lose their relevance. Remember that in Matthew 8 when Christ was talking about the cost of discipleship, one of the examples he gave was of a man who wanted to follow Christ, but when Jesus said, "Follow me," the man replied, "First let me bury my father." He didn't want to follow Christ at that moment; he wanted to wait a bit till his father died. Jesus then responded,

"Let the dead bury the dead." The living were deemed to be dead before they were indeed dead! Is it possible that *you* are already dead, you just don't know it? How astute are the dead in recognizing they are dead?

Remember, these are the consequences the Holy Spirit warns us will come from a failure to govern our relationships with other believers while we continue to participate at the grace table. Here is the question: how can anyone who is weak in the faith, sick in body, and spiritually indifferent be an effective witness in the surrounding culture? What kind of witness will a person in that condition be at work? Go ahead, send some turkey out door-to-door, but how effective will someone who is weak in his faith, sick in his body, and/or spiritually indifferent be in changing his community? The truth is you have to have a significant carrot to get him out there on the street in the first place.

It is important to note that these principles do not solely apply to those that sit in the pews on Sunday. Frankly, I would imagine that there are pastors who are in right standing with the Lord in regard to their own flock and those of their own particular denomination, but when it comes to maintaining biblical attitudes toward other believers and pastors who do not fall into their particular theological or denominational niche, they are guilty of offending the Holy Spirit and of demonstrating a profound disregard for the blood of Christ. While they serve communion to their own congregations and partake of the elements themselves with all due reverence, their attitudes and words toward those outside their circle of doctrinal fellowship are harsh, critical, unloving, and judgmental. The elements of Christ's body and blood stand for a complete salvation for all who hold to the basic and historic doctrines of the church, even if our practice of the faith may differ considerably. For example, if the blood of Christ avails for the Baptist, it must also avail for the Pentecostal, the charismatic, the Lutheran, and the Roman Catholic who truly understands and believes in Christ! We must allow the atonement to work equally for others who are similarly trusting in His blood and had better see to it that we exercise due diligence in how we regard them, for they have been placed under the same blood benefits by a sovereign act of God!

In the exercise of our communion services, believers must examine themselves to assure that they are in right relationship with all other believers. Similarly, pastors who host the communion services must assure that they are in right relationship with the spiritual leaders of other movements and denominations. Let's go for the whole ball of wax while we're at it! Staff members do not escape the requirement to live and minister in right attitudinal relationship with other members of their ministry organization. Neither are denominational leaders exempt in their dealings with the pastors under their spiritual oversight. There is no hiding behind the office. None are exempt from personal responsibility and accountability to God when it comes to the communion table. *None!* The communion service is designed to keep us straight and honest in *every* relationship. It must never be reduced to some kind of somber religious ceremony. Skip this stuff simply because you are a pastor or in some leadership role and you may find yourself in serious jeopardy! Some aspect of corporate responsibility does not give us leave to violate the blood atonement. We cannot celebrate the blood of Christ and simultaneously trample it underfoot. We must refrain our words and hands from working against others whom God considers benefactors of Christ's blood covering.

Let's be bold enough to face the reality of what is going on in our churches and between our Christian ministry structures: we are more like combatants than representatives of heaven. A whole lot of books and sermons should be withdrawn and repented of before the next communion celebration. Read I Corinthians 11:17,18 and 22, and note the three words in succession: *directives, divisions,* and a *despising* of the church. If someone falls into despising the body of Christ, that person cannot then minister a communion celebration with impunity! To treat with indifference the biblical *directives* regarding how we conduct ourselves, so as to take no notice of the *divisions* among us, is to ultimately *despise* the church. These are tough concepts, but if an individual violates the premise scripture sets out for the communion service, then weakness, sickness, and spiritual deadness creep in. Ultimately, physical death can occur, and anyone who participates in the communion service without correctly discerning his own conduct has only cursed himself.

Two things prevent an honest personal evaluation of our own spiritual state. The first is *pride*. We cannot imagine how we could be at fault. The second has to do with a *victim mentality*. We see ourselves as the ones offended rather than as the offenders. Both pride and the victim mentality present strong inner arguments for focusing on the other guy. Those who have locked themselves into one or both may very well be among those in Matthew 7:22 who cry, "Lord, Lord did we not...." This reality exists not only in the pew but in multiple pulpits. Pastors, we should not kid ourselves—the biblical injunctions apply to us with equal force. We can skip over the state of our own hearts with the same facility as the failing members of our congregations. A pride-blindness or a victim mentality can allow us to use our office as a screen to hide our own wrong attitudes and habits. Ultimately, however, no matter who it is that offends the Lord's Table, in *every* case the most extreme result of our failure to discern our own state is death at the individual level. Unfortunately, the repercussions don't stop there. Let's follow this sequence from a personal level to a corporate one.

From the Individual to the Congregation

Just as an individual can violate the biblical injunctions regarding the blood of Christ and the Holy Spirit, so can a congregation. Now if a congregation violates these biblical injunctions regarding Christ's body, the consequences outlined can become the corporate reality. The congregation can be characterized by:

A weakness in the faith
Sickness that can permeate the fellowship, affecting both the physical and the soul
Spiritual indifference that becomes its prevailing characteristic

What does this look like? Most of the folks sittin' around doin' nothin'! How can a congregation so affected become an effectual witness to their surrounding community and culture? Sooner or later, if the biblical injunctions regarding the conduct of our communion services are continuously violated, that congregation will lose its spiritual zeal, and there will be little if any real spiritual life left there. Certainly the forms and programs will be there exuding religious fervor, but no zealousness will exist for the kind of righteousness that brings genuine spiritual unity and that exalts a nation. Instead, just below the surface of religious Christianity lie all sorts of divisions, controversies, and conflicts. If it spreads to individual congregations from the hearts of individuals, then where will this kind of spiritual inertia go next?

From the Individual to the Congregation to the Denomination

Whole denominations and movements can succumb to the same set of spiritually induced consequences. If enough believing fellowships fail to honor the grace table, then that portion of the corporate church becomes ineffectual, suffering from weakness, sickness, and a fatal lethargy. When such is the case, there is no hope of that group being effective in stemming the tide of destruction affecting our cultures' moral and spiritual fiber, which affects millions of families and kills millions of pre-born human beings. If we really care, something radical must happen in the spiritual substance of our communion services. *Only* if we succeed there will God be stirred to begin the movement necessary to effect moral and spiritual righteousness in our nations. Understand this: our wars against one another testify against us before both the God of our salvation and a watching world. We may choose to overlook the interpersonal violations that exist among us, but God sees the hypocrisy that is perpetrated at the communion table, and to put it lightly, he gets upset!

Several years ago, the Holy Spirit gave me a startling insight into how our communion services are frequently nothing more than a religious sham that came out of the story of Ham and Noah. I was partially awake early one morning waiting for the alarm clock to go off when the Spirit spoke clearly and with such force that I was startled awake: "Would you like to know what Ham's sin was?" Now, this was not something to which I had given much thought. I had simply accepted the teaching as to what this particular portion of scripture in Genesis 9 was saying. Somewhat stunned, I replied, "Of course!" The short explanation was this: "As a son, he did not cover the transgression of a righteous man." Then the whole portion of Genesis 9:20-27 unfolded in my mind in a flash. If we can understand this portion of scripture, we will get a very significant insight into I Corinthians 11:23-31. Remember, the statement referring to damnation is an incredibly strong statement addressed to seemingly sincere believers gathered to celebrate the love feast. If we fail in the way we discern the body of Christ, the rest of the communion service ultimately becomes an instrument of damnation for those so gathered! So what does the narrative in Genesis 9 have to say to us about our communion services?

First of all, God distinguished Noah as being a righteous man. Interesting, is it not, that he found *grace* in the eyes of the Lord (Genesis 6:8). By God's standards, he was righteous and living in a state of grace! Now here's the rub. He experienced an exceedingly real failure. He got drunk, staggered around his tent completely naked, and then passed out. What kind of things would happen in most believing fellowships if the word got out one week that the pastor had gotten into the booze, got stone drunk, was seen to have been staggering around his home stark, raving naked, only to pass out on the floor, and there to be found by one of the church elders? I'll leave the result to your imagination. What's the first point here? Righteous people who have been genuinely brought into a state of grace experience real spiritual failures. Somehow, failures are only acceptable among the believing community as long as they remain theoretical or theological, but if someone suffers a real spiritual failure, then all our theologies regarding personal failure take wing and fly away. The cries go up, "Get that pastor out of here!" or, "We can't tolerate this kind of behavior! It will destroy our reputation in the city!" Meanwhile all the gossip circuits are in overload, and the controversy rages on in the fellowship. Warfare among the saints heats up once again with this new fodder as fuel. Let this sink in! Noah was: a righteous man according to God's measure, and he was a man who had come into the *grace of God!*

Doesn't that sound a bit like what it is for us who have found Christ as Savior? Being righteous and in a state of grace does not mean we no longer fail; it means we have a wonderful and significant method of dealing with failures of all kinds. Galatians 6:1 defines the biblical methodology of dealing with failures. "Brothers, if someone is caught in a sin"—note the word *sin*—"you who are *spiritual* should restore him" [emphasis added]. Did you get that restoration idea? Restore him, how? *Gently!* There is no sense here in which we can go on TV or radio and blast the individual for his failure. This truth might even hurt various book sales!

Simply stated, non-spiritual people do not have a heart to restore those who fail. There is nothing gentle about the non-spiritual believer or preacher! They are fault-focused, and their words, attitudes, actions, and heart motivations are judgmental and without mercy. Think back to what you heard or what you yourself said when some famous preacher was taken in sin. When unspiritual individuals, thinking themselves to be spiritual, act corporately in a congregation, church splits and contention become characteristic of the fellowship. Scripture holds no authority over their carnal motives and actions. Usually the fault-focused, strife-breeding individuals, though bereft of any grace understanding, are the first to demand a communion service the first Sunday of the month.

Well, let's look a bit further at Genesis 9: Noah is in the final state of his failing, out cold on the floor of his tent, naked in his failure. Then, in comes a member of the family, of the bloodline. What's the connection? We who are in Christ are all members of the same family and partakers of the same bloodline: *His!* Ham types the carnal believer for us, coming into his father's tent and finding dad naked, passed out drunk on the floor of his tent, focused on the failure of a man declared by God to be righteous: a man who had found grace! Now watch what it says in verse 22: "Ham, the father of Canaan"—a nation cursed as slaves—"saw his father's nakedness." Ham was fault-focused, and he did what every fault-focused believer does: he ran immediately to those closest to him in the bloodline. He'd likely have used a cell phone for quick and easy access if he'd had one. Upon discovering his father's failure he went and told his brothers. Ah, how the carnal tongue loves to dwell on the failure of another believer! What he did is repeated thousands of times every day in the believing community. Someone misses the accepted standard, another one finds out, and immediately the phone lines begin to light up; those closest to the discoverer are the first to hear, but it's not long before the news spreads throughout the whole congregation.

You can be sure the spirit of Ham will always be lurking about when a righteous man is found in his failure. The point here is not the existence of a Ham among the believers, but what those believers do when Ham pays them a visit with his or her juicy news. It is so significant that this failure-focus Ham lived with brought damnation upon not only himself but on all his posterity. *The children of faultfinders are put in significant jeopardy along with their parents.* Further, when Noah awoke and learned of Ham's action he cursed his own son, making him a slave to his failure.

Take a minute on this thought: the failure of a fellow believer is our call to respond in grace. Look at it this way. Noah had one failure. Ham's failure opened the door to innumerable failures. It could have stopped at one. It's the same in any church or ministry situation. The real sin lies not with the first failure but with the one who learns of the failure and fails to cover it. Noah's curse on Ham is reflective of God the Father's pronouncement of damnation/judgment in I Corinthians 11:29. But scripture does not leave us without a proper and effective model for dealing with the very real failures of others close to us. First ask yourself this question: was Noah's failure a tangible failure or was it just theoretical? Assuming that a real failure actually took place in time and space, take a close look at Ham's two brothers: when Ham came to them, their whole response is radically different. Because of their response, the blessings of the Father came to rest not only on them, *but on their children.*

The next part is absolutely wonderful reading: "But Shem and Japheth took a garment and *laid it across their shoulders,* then they *walked in backward* and *covered their fathers nakedness. Their faces were turned* the other way so that they would not *see* their father's nakedness." Think about this for a few moments. The two spiritual brothers respond to the very real failure of a righteous man, as the bloodline should. *They took a garment with the intent to cover.* What is the prime function of love? It covers! Proverbs 10:12 makes a truly radical statement when it says, "Love covers over all wrongs." The King James puts it like this: "Love covers a multitude of transgressions." Not just a few, but a multitude; not just little slights but actual transgressions. I heard one definition of transgression as being "deliberate willful sin with eyes wide open." Love, the first fruit of the Spirit, covers an array of deliberately willful sins committed by individuals who know full well what they are doing. So what was the motivation of Shem and Japheth? Love! They knew how to walk in love, cover a real failure and avoid the controversy of the tongue.

What did they do next? They walked backwards. How desperately the body of Christ needs people who know how to walk backwards. How many marriages would be affected by some backward-walking spouses? What might this mean for us as believers in the grace of Christ? The natural way of walking is forward; the spiritual way feels unnatural, as it is opposite to the natural. The two brothers who loved were totally prepared to walk in love, because love motivated them to walk in the spirit as opposed to the flesh.

In walking backward, what did they assume? *Personal responsibility* for that failure. They did not pass off the responsibility for Noah's failure to a slave, but put the garment on their *own* shoulders. We cannot expect the world to be about covering those willful-sins-with-eyes-wide-open; that's the business of the spiritual believer. What have we seen when some believer is taken in sin? Preachers going on the TV and radio, decrying the failure to the masses. No gentleness, no restoring or grace-generated mercy; just the voice of the faultfinder who thrives on the failures of others and brings that poison not only to the world, but to as many believers as can be reached via the media. We might at this point reiterate Paul's question to the Corinthians: "Do you despise the church?" What happens in the local assembly when it is discovered that an elder, a pastor, or a member is caught in sin? Most of the time, we act like the Pharisees who brought the woman taken in the act of adultery before Christ, demanding justice for her failure based on law. There was no love in their hearts, no covering, no mercy, only a self-righteous demand for a justification of their own depravity.

What's the last thing to be noted in the brothers' response to Noah's failure? *"Their faces were turned the other way—so that they would not **see** their father's nakedness."* Do you get the parallel here? Which way do we as believers face when someone has failed? When someone in the bloodline of believers experiences a real failure and is found out, how do we tend to respond? I'm not asking for a theoretical or theological response. I'm asking how we *actually* respond. How have *you* responded in the past? What happens to your words? Who do you confide in? I know you know the right answer, but that doesn't count. Do you look on the failure full faced and give it your full attention? Do you go over it, refining every detail, or do you do what Shem and Japheth did? Do you refuse to be fault-focused and instead assume personal responsibility, walking in the Spirit and in love, acting to cover? The truth is, if we really did this, there'd be no cause for controversy in our churches.

Remember, we are still working on the "damnation" concept as found in the context of the communion table. We know and call the work of Christ the atonement because atonement means covering. Why did Christ cover our sins? Because he loves us. What does he cover us with? His holy blood! We are all familiar with the phrase, "under the blood." We can use that phrase because it is exactly what Christ has done: he assumed personal responsibility choosing to walk in love by the Spirit and spread over us a very precious garment, covering our nakedness and all our transgressions with his blood. Look at those with whom you have a controversy. Are they, by faith, recipients of the benefits of Christ's shed blood? Are they justified by faith in God's sight because they have come under the blood provisions made available to all men? Has Christ spread the corner of his garment of atonement over them? If so, then the truth is this: justification is no longer a matter of performance but one of faith, and faith in the blood of Christ. Read Romans 3:21-27 for yourself!

Now, let's make a final trip back to Genesis 9 for one more question: if Ham got cursed because he chose to focus on Noah's failure, what would have been the consequence if he had gone back into the tent after his brothers had covered Noah and pulled back that covering? Would he not have been violating the garment of love? If Christ has covered our nakedness with the covering garment of his own blood, then the nakedness is no longer visible. However, if we ignore that fact and go on *re*-exposing one another's failures, what have we done to Christ's atoning work, his blood, and the Spirit of Grace? How much trouble are we in if we come into another man's tent and pull back that covering, making his failure the corporate focus of our eyes, speech, attitudes, and actions? Listen: Christ *has* come into the tent of our own failures and covered us, and what Christ has covered—our willful sins with eyes wide open—is meant to *stay* covered. This is, in part, what the love feast is all about. To show up at the communion table fault-focused and ignore the fact that Christ has covered our fellow believers with the blood is to be worse than Ham, uncovering what God has dearly and forever covered. No wonder people get sick, weak, and die, "for by fire and by the sword will the Lord plead with all flesh" (Isaiah 66:16, KJV). No wonder damnation waits for those who despitefully treat the blood of Christ with disdain and thus despise the church! Blood-blind indeed!

The fig leaf of theology cannot hide us from the God who commands us to love one another, nor can it be considered a suitable substitute for the blood of Christ! If you are trusting in the power of Christ's blood to atone for your own failure, how can you then deny the dispensation of the blood covering to another brother or sister in Christ? You are *both* under the atoning blood! You see, when God looks down at a believer who is under the blood, he does not see the believer alone, but first sees that believer through the sinless blood of Christ's sacrifice. The lens of the blood translates that believer as sinless. Shem and Japheth type the ministry of Christ and the Holy Spirit in covering and refusing to see our faults. In doing so, we have become that righteous man. Here's the question: *What are your sight habits with other believers?* Do you see the blood, allowing other believers the privilege of the blood covering, or do you, by your perception, attitudes, and words, act as though there is no blood covering, insisting that some believers' failure be taken into the public arena of the local congregation or to the spiritual leadership? Take it a bit further. Are you sinless, without spiritual failure? To be a fault-focused believer when it comes to other believers not only violates the blood of Christ's sacrifice but attempts to deny the functioning of the blood of Christ to another brother or sister. In reality we are all desperately wicked (Jeremiah 17:9) and in desperate need of that incredibly precious blood covering every moment of every day! Can we possibly deny the benefit of the blood of Christ to other frail, imperfect believers and then presume to come to the Lord's Table in a selfish attempt to appropriate the benefits of that blood solely for ourselves?

When God was speaking to Moses about the Exodus and about sparing the Israelites from the judgment that was to come on Egypt he said, "When I see the blood, I will pass over you" (Exodus 12:13). If God passes over us when he sees the blood, what should be the habit of our conduct? Then there is the blood that Christ took into the heavens that cries mercy before the throne. When God sees a believer, who by faith has come under the provisions of Christ's blood, his response is three-fold:

He sees the blood
He passes over
He extends mercy and grace.

    Dear believer, do you truly see the blood when you look at other believers, or do you go directly to the judgment seat? Blood-blindness is evidenced when expressions of mercy are missing. Oh, yes, mercy is there theologically and theoretically and even manages to find its way into our hymnology, but does it really appear on the stage of real human failures? When functional mercy disappears, judgmental words, attitudes, and contention are all we have left. *Every* believer has been invited to come boldly to find both mercy and grace. How is this possible? Christ has made a new and living way into real grace and real mercy through his blood. Consider this: if a *holy* God is willing to extend grace and mercy based on the blood of Christ to "whosoever," then perhaps we'd better find the grace capacity to do the same for those frail believers around us, rather than measure our spirituality by how much contention we can stir up.

    If you realize you have violated the blood covering put in place over other believers, don't despair. Acknowledge it, and repent before God. *He* is the one we offend at the communion service. Remember that love covers, so ask him to give you his heart of love, real love. Don't try to do this on your own. Go to God and in Christ ask Him to give you grace by the Holy Spirit, and stay there until you genuinely receive the gift of his heart for the believers around you. When you get *His* heart, then and only then do you have the heart that can fulfill the commandment to "Love one another as Christ has loved us" (John 13:34). Leave the covering in place, and when a brother or sister is found in a fault, let the Father's heart to restore gently be the motivation that rules in your heart.

    Certainly what Ham saw was a problem, but how did he respond? He took the judgment he'd made on his father and turned that inner judgment into words. What was in Ham's heart came out his mouth. We need to discover by revelation what it really means to minister grace to one another in our conversation. Why? When you've got it in your conversation you've got it in your heart. Truly, out of the abundance of the heart the mouth speaks! When the Holy Spirit had Paul write Ephesians 4:29, he was not laying it out as an option we could choose to obey or ignore: ministering grace in our conversations is imperative. The concept of conversation here deals not only with our words but also with our whole demeanor and conduct toward others. Let there be an end to individual and corporate blood-blindness! If we continue our relational wars while holding our so-called communion services, we are simply inviting, sooner or later, a God-imposed damnation. This disaster does not fall upon the one who failed, but upon the one who refused to honor the blood of Christ. The curse of slavery did not fall on Noah, the one who failed, but on Ham who failed to cover. As long as we have these relational violations among believers—hateful words, critical attitudes, church splits, and divisions—we are neither having communion with one another, nor are we in right communion with God the Holy Spirit, and our communion services are nothing more than religious farce. They indict us before the bench of the Great Eternal Judge. There will be no fully vibrant churches, no nation-changing, history-making churches until our communion services hold genuine spiritual integrity in the sight of God. Blood-blind equates to disaster! Just weak, sick, and dead!

Have you understood in practice what it means to discern the body of Christ? Discerning the body of Christ involves a personal examination of one's relationship with all other believers to assure that those relationships actually reflect biblical standards. Such discerning means the believer can openly declare before God that he/she is in right relationship with all other believers. There is nothing hidden in the heart contradicting Christ's love mandate!

Now let me ask a final question that every believer should consider the answer to: if God, who is infinitely holy, is fully satisfied with the power of the blood of Christ to atone for all our sin, then why does it appear insufficient in our relationships with one another? The concepts in this chapter need to stand alone because of their significant importance to individual Christian practice and to the body of Christ as a whole, but there are some critical associated issues to examine. Our witness to the nations is at stake!

Chapter Eleven
Mark the Sky

Long after an airliner disappears over the horizon, the white contrails it leaves behind are clearly visible and easily seen, allowing you have eyes to see. The congregation that has been penetrated by the functional grace of God will leave its own visible contrail. Such a community of believers will functionally demonstrate the agape counter-culture. There will be a clear correlation between the confession of love and the demonstration of a love that is supernatural in its origin and outworking, because the revelation of the blood of Christ will have penetrated and captured the heart.

When believers gather around the grace table, they are professing to God that they are in right relationship with all their fellow believers, not just a chosen few. What does *right* mean? Heart right: right in attitude, motive, conduct, and speech. As has been pointed out, far too often we gloss over our relational failures as though they are somehow unimportant to God. On one hand, we decry the world for its rejection of moral absolutes, but when faced with I Corinthians 11:28, we sense no weight of obligation to examine ourselves. It is at the grace table that God expects believers to hold themselves accountable for their own conduct, attitudes and speech. However, God leaves us free to choose otherwise, rather like Adam and Eve when it came to the tree of the knowledge of good and evil. That terrible freedom of choice still remains for every individual in the body of Christ.

Grace that works interpersonally sets the Christian congregation apart from any other kind of religious assembly. Grace carries the believer to the tree of life and away from that death tree where we operate out of our own innate knowledge of good and evil. Grace is solely indigenous to biblical Christianity. It cannot be found in Buddhism, Islam, or any other religious philosophy or cult. New Age proponents may talk of grace, but they have no inkling of what it means; they use the word and simply redefine its meaning to suit their agenda. Sadly, many believers live their whole lives without experiencing the impact grace can have upon the human heart and relationship. We get to salvation and somehow stay there the rest of our lives. Developing a lifestyle reflecting the power of grace to conform us to Christ seems still to be some remote destination to which few ever depart.

You might get the feeling that this is re-hashing what has already been said, and the question may be running through your mind, "Why so much repetition?" Fair enough. Here's why. I have methodically set this concept of the covenant blood covering and blood-blind believers before congregations internationally. Everywhere I've gone, people have nodded their heads in agreement and shouted amen, seeming to give whole-hearted assent to the blood of Christ being our covering, affirming that now, by love, the multitude of transgressions are covered. Tragically, all of this supposed reverence for Christ and one another lasts not much past the end of the communion service. Within days, the lists of issues, offenses, and differences rise and become so much the focus that covering, loving, forgiving, and serving are proven to be nothing more than optional theological niceties. Quote I Corinthians 13 about how love endures, how it keeps no record of wrongs to the issue-oriented believer or theologian, and there is absolutely no apparent practical regard for the blood of Christ: teeth sink through the Blood, coveting to taste the flesh beneath.

Paul speaks forcefully to all those who come to the communion service and show disdain for the very things to which the communion service attests. In I Corinthians 11:17,18 and 22, he is incredibly explicit. This might be termed the three D's for desecrating the communion table and marking our religion as vain.

The First D: Directives

"In the following directives I have no praise for you, for your meetings do more harm than good" (v 17).

Can this be a word we need to take to heart about the spiritual quality of our own services? We need to be careful of any "Malachian denial" here. Denial is easier than the pain of honest, personal examination. The communion service is intrinsic to the context here. There were specific directives regarding the communion service that were not being followed. Such departure from biblical directives always produces a demonically inspired departure from truth. With any departure from the biblical directives the enemy finds entrance to destroy. So, not feeling obliged to stick to the directives, a church goes automatically to the next D.

The Second D: Divisions

"There are divisions among you" (v. 18).

Throughout the gospels and the whole of the New Testament, such things as love and unity among believers are set before us as non-negotiable standards. The existence of divisions make it clear that violations of the biblical directives have occurred. Mark it clearly. Wherever we find divisions, there has been a departure from the directives by which Christ intends us to govern ourselves. If divisions are allowed to fester because we do not want to hold ourselves to the biblical standard, then we must let Paul's evaluation prevail. The result is inevitable.

The Third D: Despise

"You despise the church of God" (v. 22).

It's no great mystery what Paul would say about our communion services if he saw how we treat one another. The Corinthian Christians were Spirit-filled people holding communion services, and yet it seems they felt not one twinge of conscience about how they humiliated and mistreated other believers. When we examine the body of Christ, we find mistreatment of believers and a breaking of God's communion directives. What? Believers gathered around the communion table who in actual practice, despise the church of God? Yep! That was and is exactly his point! Where divisions are not brought into subjection to the directives about love, mercy, forgiveness, and maintaining a spirit of harmony in our relationships, a place has been found where people despise what the church is really all about. Webster defines the word, "despise," as, *to look down on, to hold in low esteem or regard, to have contempt and aversion in one's heart toward another*. Let me say this as plainly as possible: if we violate the biblical directives about how we treat one another, if we insist on being divisive, critical, ugly and vindictive in our attitudes and then show up at the grace table as though everything is fine, we are in fact despising the church of God. The number of people who have departed from the local assembly and sit at home despising the church is incredible. If you are an issue-driven individual, you will be a person who spawns divisions in your church. Your speech will betray you, your tongue will be hell's fire, and if you have the gall to sit piously at the communion table, your religion will at best will be vain and void. How do we get the victory over the carnal man?

A DANGEROUS GRACE

The real believer as described in the New Testament is one who genuinely demonstrates the very nature of Christ. The challenge before us is the recovery of that which was lost in the fall from grace. What was lost in the fall? The image and likeness of God! Grace that has become personally functional produces a new kind of human being who progressively moves into a recovery of the image and likeness of God. True humanness is found only in the express recovery of God's image and likeness. I'll let the theologians struggle with the meaning of image and likeness, but here is a simple definition for our purposes: image implies something seen and likeness describes something in one's nature. The church is called upon to so feast on the grace of God that the world can look in and see the image of God and the manifestation of the God nature. It is Christ's nature to love, cover, forgive, extend mercy, bless, and pray. No contrary nature options are common to him. Grace is the only way to manifest that new Christ-man! Paul summed it up quite nicely in I Corinthians 15:10 when he said, "I am what I am by the grace of God." We cannot be what God intended us to be in nature apart from effectual grace. If Paul's transformation had its root in grace, dare we look anywhere else or settle for anything less?

There must be more to our Christianity than a right preaching and profession of the facts. The new-natured individual, who by grace is being restored in nature, is one who finds himself in possession of something not common to man: mercy! Fallen man is not inclined toward mercy but rather toward judgment and revenge. Mercy has its root in a love of supernatural origin. Real love demands of itself mercy in the face of transgression. Is the love feast not also inherently a place where mercy triumphs over judgment as written in James 2:13? Mercy gives life to the needy: "God who is rich in mercy *made us alive*" (Ephesians 2:4) [emphasis added]. Judgment, on the other hand, takes the life of the offender, gets even, and fights for its own turf. It loves to pronounce sentence!

One of the central concepts of the Lord's Table is the mercy of God extended to sinful humanity. In partaking of God's mercy; the communion participant is called upon to be merciful in like manner. One of the great works of grace is that it creates in us the passion of mercy. What a great place the church is designed to be: a living well of love and mercy extended to other believers and the world! I can almost hear the cynical snort, but if we could find the grace gate, we'd find it leads to the manifest mercy of God from one believer to another. What a sight that would be! Paul opens the first epistle to Timothy with this wonderful salutation: "Grace, mercy, and peace from

God." Thus the two are linked together not just in scripture but also in the very nature of God.

Grace that has produced mercy is authenticated by peace proving our profession as participants in genuine Christian community. The unity of the Spirit is maintained because of the strong demand that peace has placed on our hearts. We become a people captive to the mandate to be keepers of the peace. Remember the Beatitude of Matthew 5:9, "Blessed are the peacekeepers." Grace sets mercy at work in our hearts, and our hearts then work the work of peace! A genuine regard for the church of God suffuses the believing community, even parts of the church that believe a little differently, and corporately find their faith growing in new directions expressed in their experience and worship of Christ.

How the vicious pen and tongue of biblical scholars betray their profession of love for Christ, His Word, and His Church. It seems they would give verbal assent to loving their enemies while their tongues are laced with hate for others who serve Christ as Lord but know him in different terms. The very words flowing from their heart demonstrate that they despise the church of God! One member cannot say to another, "I have no need of you" (I Corinthians 12:21). What is it that Luke 6:45 says about the tongue? It makes manifest what's in the heart! It would appear that a good number of ministers find in the ministry a cloak for the bitterness and hatred that lurks in their own hearts. Try this question on for size: if God who is infinitely holy can be at peace with such as we are, by what model of truth do we as the hardly holy condemn, criticize, and vilify others with whom that same God has made peace? (By the way, peace that is both biblical and spiritual and that finds expression among the body of Christ is no submission to an evil ecumenism!)

Scripture gives no latitude to the true believer. Either we are brought by grace into a place where we are empowered to live life as a demonstration of the directives, or we miss grace and fall into the pit of divisions ending up in a place where we despise the Bride of Christ. If His heart has become our experiential reality, it is wholly impossible to disconnect from the local body of believers, because we are drawn to one another as Christ is drawn to us. Perhaps a visual comparison between a sanctimonious Christian community and the authentic agape counter culture of Christian community would help.

Religious Christianity	Authentic Christianity
Ignored Directives ⬇ Divisions ⬇ Despising	Applied Grace ⬇ Mercy ⬇ Peace

The incredible reality in all of this is that many who have come into the place where they despise the body of Christ don't even realize their condition! They have moved away from any involvement with or commitment to the local church, but think themselves safe in Christ. These individuals can be found sitting in their living rooms, on the golf course, watching TV, or just sleeping in on Sunday mornings. When they speak to others either about the local church or about one that they used to attend, the words are full of criticism, and they have manifestly rejected playing any responsible role in a local congregation. The sad reality is that there are tens of thousands—if not hundreds of thousands—of these disillusioned believers who want nothing to do with their local church. Suggesting that their spiritual destiny cannot be realized outside the relational dimension of a local assembly is offensive to them.

Yes, the abuses have come: the betrayals, the manipulation, and disappointments have fallen on their heads, but disastrously, these have become the molding factors of their lives instead of truth. Why disastrously? The Word has lost its authority over their lives, and most of these dearly departed brethren do not even realize that its power has been supplanted. Offenses come to all of us in the body of Christ, but in God's economy such wounds are prods meant to drive us deeper into grace, deeper into the heart of God and make us even more desperate to find one another, not drive us from fellowship.

Over the years I have been asked to identify who Christ was referring in Matthew 7:21-23: "Not everyone who says to me, 'Lord, Lord' will enter the kingdom of heaven, but only he who does the will of my Father who is in heaven. Many will say to me on that day, 'Lord, Lord, did we not prophesy in your name, and in your name drive out demons and perform many miracles?' Then I will say to them plainly, 'I never knew you. Away from me, you evildoers!'"

Well, here is one possible answer. A brief look at this passage makes it plain who gets into the kingdom of heaven: "He who does the will of my

Father." Well, what is the Father's will? Christ summed it up very succinctly when he said, "Love one another" (John 13:34-35; 15:12 and 17). Love means to desire relationship with, to keep no record of wrongs of, and all the rest of I Corinthians 13, not "disassociate yourself." To do the will of the Father is to maintain unity in the bond of peace versus getting destroyed by involvement in divisions that end up causing us to despise those for whom Christ died. Say, "Lord, Lord," all you want, but if doing His will does not take precedence over your hurt feelings and carnal responses, then the will of the Father is not paramount in your heart. Take a hard look, and that terrible four-letter word in verse 22—*many*—and note as well who used it!

In the last four decades, a radical explosion of spiritual phenomena has taken place. Multiplied thousands of individuals have prophesied, have used the authority in the name of Jesus to cast out devils, have laid hands on the sick, and witnessed miracles and seen the power of the Holy Spirit fall on people with profound effect. Yet after a time things did not go as they hoped. They were misunderstood, passed over by leadership, mistreated by authority, wrongly accused, slandered, and even demonized by their critics. In turn, they became critics of the church. Now they stand off from the call to corporate relationships and find no joy in the larger family of believers. They settle into a pattern of life that serves nothing more than their own narrow interests and priorities. Verbal venom lies just under the crust of civility. What a catastrophe!

There are two parts to this catastrophe. First, they have missed the call to find greater grace and succumbed to the conclusions and attitudes characteristic of the carnal mind and heart. Second, they have no inkling that they have turned from the will of the Father. In their garden testing they did not find the grace to pray, "Not my will but your will be done." They have fallen back into the soulish realm, and because of their past, they fail to recognize their state before God. Doing the will of God is simply no longer likely. "Me go to church? You've got to be kidding!" And so it goes with untold numbers of once-upon-a-time believers whose hearts were aflame with passion for Christ and service. Do with this what you will. Play doctrine if that's your gig, but one thing is for sure: what Christ said he meant! *Many who once prophesied, cast out devils, and ministered in the miracle power of the Holy Spirit stand in great peril because doing the will of God is no longer their food and drink.*

This clearly makes reference to individuals who were once involved in what has been called the charismatic movement and other ministries oriented around the gift ministry of the Holy Spirit. You won't find cecessionists prophesying, or casting out demons, or ministering the miracle power of the Holy Spirit because in their understanding, all this kind of thing ceased with the death of the twelve apostles. This passage in Matthew 7 speaks most clearly to those individuals who have been involved in Pentecostal, charismatic, and neo-charismatic movements. Dear reader, if at some point you were involved in circles that moved in the miracle power of the Holy Spirit but now find you are a turned off, bitter individual who wants nothing to do with the body of Christ, you should get ready to hear, "*I never knew you. Depart from me!*" No one can profess love for the brethren and then withdraw from them. You cannot build loving relationships with the believers down at the local house of worship while you sit alone in your living room. Love causes us to draw near with a joyful passion. It hates the separation that divisions bring and happily covers a multitude of personal injuries and misunderstandings. It will simply not be separated from the brethren, for such is the heart of the Godhead. Severing relationship is antithetical to the very fundamentals of grace. Think about it: despite all the offenses we have heaped on our God, He has never withdrawn. Grace carries its own redemptive fruit and annihilates the likes of anger, bitterness, separation, criticism, or vindictiveness. The true fruit of grace lives on the tongue and speaks only life and peace, making way for the passions characteristic of the heart of our God. Fellowship must be characteristic of those divine passions or we fail to be authentic and missed the practical impact of grace, namely mercy and peace. Should we miss mercy and peace, our verbalizations about winning the lost and about the church being a loving community reflective of heaven becomes a macabre, black comedy. Instead of leaving a divine contrail of heavenly reality for men to see, our communities are more reflective of a 747 jetliner plummeting toward earth in a gigantic fireball. No wonder the world doesn't rush into our midst! Life is tough enough outside the gates. Why come inside the supposed parameters of grace only to hit the earth at warp speed with a bunch of spiritual pretenders?

The fruit of appropriated grace, on the other hand, paints the heavenly picture we long to hang in the foyers of our collective congregations. *Grace* manifests a genuine *mercy* among believers. His *peace* then marks our corporate reality. These three scriptural hallmarks are the Spirit-born essentials that authenticate the church, constituting the definitive plum line by which God measures every heart and every fellowship. If we miss the grace gate, both mercy and peace lie beyond human reach. What is then left to us but to be spiritual contortionists doing our best to look like something we can never be?

May the Lord bind the power of a spirit of delusion and renew the gift of his heart in you, moving you to the place where doing the Father's will is the highest and most important priority in your life. May the Holy Spirit at this moment bring the revelation of grace afresh to the one who has been deceived and fallen victim to the spirit of delusion. May he deliver you from the spirit that says a correct profession of the truth is all that counts; that whispers, "It's okay to separate yourself from the rest of the body of Christ, because God understands the things you've had to endure in churches, and he's given you special permission to quit getting together with others who love Christ." May God deliver the one who has fallen prey to the adversary of our souls, for whom hate has replaced love for the brethren and the Samson symptom progressively envelops your whole reality: you will go out as before not knowing that the anointing is no longer functional. You have departed from the faith and played with a Delilah of your own making. Yes, you may have in your history pulled off the gates of Gaza and carried them up into the mountains, throwing them down at the Hebron seat of faith, but now the natural cords of man bind you from your destiny. What are those natural cords? Things common to man: bitterness, unforgiveness, greed, lust, anger, despising, slander, railing, criticism, and self centered determinism. The very thought of being an active part in a local gathering of believers is like rotten meat between your teeth. There is only one entity in creation that feels that way about the bride of Christ, and it may well be that your passions agree more with that terrible fallenness than with the expectant Bridegroom.

Long after we as individuals have left planet earth, what contrail will we have left behind as markers of the eternal reality for the next generation? Will that marker look like the 747 plummeting to earth as a great fireball of disaster, or will it bear witness of a great, all-powerful Redeemer who in truth became the answer to the dilemmas of our generation? One thing is sure: our children will read whatever testimony we've written in the sky of our own confessions.

Chapter Twelve
The God Mind

Here we need to focus on the new mind of the Christian. Grace can be understood as having five keys, being a paradigm which functions in four stages, and as operating on two components. The two components are declared to be so by God in Jeremiah 33:31-33. The two core components of grace are the new God-given heart and the renewed mind. The writer of Hebrews repeats this essential core definition of grace in Hebrews chapters eight and ten. Hopefully by now something better than unmerited favor as a definition of grace has been understood. Any effort to articulate matters of truth or faith not countenancing the implications of grace will be, at the very best, an incomplete effort.

How important is it then that our understanding of grace be deep enough so that truth does not function like a wild horse? Apart from the governing influence of grace, truth can be made subject to ungoverned interpretation and, even worse, manipulation. Truth is always truth, but it must be tethered to grace or it can very easily become unfettered imagination where every individual lends to it his or her own interpretation. This perhaps may be the reason why there is such wide diversity in the presentation of truth in the body of Christ: some of what passes for truth is just wild, unbridled, imagination. That being said, what is the essential second component of grace? God, in scripture, sets out with incredible clarity and absoluteness the nature of the new covenant. If we are going to give some definition of grace, we must start with the specifics God has given *His law written on our minds:* "This is the covenant I will make with the house of Israel after that time," declares the Lord, "I will put my law in their minds and write it on their hearts. I will be their God, and they will be my people" (Jeremiah 31:33; Hebrews 8:10, 10:16).

Notice, the Law was not to be abolished, but was to be written on our minds. If we are to understand grace in practical terms and experience, we must be drawn back to a consideration not only of what it means to have a new heart but also what it means to have the law of God written on our minds. So then, the two characteristics of this new covenant concern the new heart and the reprogramming of how man thinks.

Understanding the Gift vs. the Process

The new heart comes as a gift God said he would give; however, scripture makes it clear that gaining the new mind is very much a process for which the believer is responsible. In dealing with the second component of grace, then, the purpose of God is to rewrite or rewire the way the mind works. Renewing our thinking has always been God's purpose; if we fail in the process of rewiring our thought processes, we cannot succeed in the life of grace and will miss the life he intended redeemed mankind to discover and experience. If we miss the grace influence on our thought life individually, then it follows that our corporate life will mirror that same lack.

If we do not bring our thought lives into conformity and subjection to God's Word, then the grace covenant ceases to be a full possibility. Rewiring the mind involves a process that takes place as we open ourselves to the ministry of the Holy Spirit, looking to him for a transition from the carnal to the spiritual mindset. Romans 12:2 attests to this necessity when we are given the following directive: "Do not conform any longer to the pattern of this world but be transformed by the renewing of your mind." In Ephesians 4:17 Paul writes "You must no longer live as the gentiles do, in the futility of their thinking. They are darkened in their understanding and separated from the life of God." He goes on to point out that the believers were taught "to be made new in the attitude of [their] minds" (v. 23). The King James gives the injunction that the believer is expected by God to renew the spirit of the mind. One of the toughest things the believer has to do is begin thinking effectively about the way he or she thinks. Most people think they think correctly, just because they think!

When we begin to piece the scriptures together that deal with the mind, two things become apparent. First, the necessity to change how we think is imperative. The call to change the spirit that is in control of your mind was not offered by Paul as a good suggestion. Second, if we fail to actively involve ourselves in this process we will continue in some measure to be like "the gentiles," separated from the life God intends us to portray. We will miss the fruit that God has designed grace to produce in our inner lives, in our homes, fellowships, and communities. We will look more like the world than a representation of heaven's reality. We may well have preached our sermons on the topic of the renewed mind and written our books on the subject, but the question we must ask ourselves is this: are we actually doing what God has required of us? How many believers consciously involve themselves in the discipline of reprogramming their thought lives? Proverbs 23:7 (KJV) says, "As a man thinks in his heart, so is he." If we think like the old man of Ephesians 4:22, we will not only *act* like the old man, but will continue to *manifest* the old nature. Conversely, if we think like the new man we will manifest the new man, the new creature.

If the old man seems to be in preeminence, what is required of us? How about a discovery of functional grace? You remember, God writing his law on our minds! If we fail here, our choices will reflect our failure. Furthermore, when we try to grapple with the fundamental issues of life, the definitions we endeavor to live by will be inadequate, if not outright wrong. What are some of those fundamental issues that we must have a clear understanding of? Here are three: *being, knowledge* and *values*.

<u>BEING</u>:
- Being has to do with the issues of worth and life: Who am I, what is life really all about?

<u>KNOWLEDGE</u>:
- The struggle in the area of knowledge has to do with how we can know that we really know. Can man really know things about himself and his world with certainty?

<u>VALUES</u>:
- In the area of values, the mind and heart struggle with defining governing principles, for man must have some system by which he determines what is right and wrong.

It is with the mind that man struggles with the issues of his being, knowledge and values. Here, man is confronted with an absolute reality: he *must* develop definitions in each of these three areas. Every social context operates around some definition in these three areas, and further, every man lives with some inherent definition in each of these three areas. Do you know what your presupposed definitions are in each of these areas? The consequence of not having these things in correct perspective is that the body of Christ will manifest a false picture of what the believer and the church look like and how it behaves.

In western culture, we had a historic definition of each of these three categories, but over the last several decades, there has been an abolition of the foundation from which our definitions were drawn. In its place, another totally opposite system of definitions has been imposed. This latter system operates under several names, with one system essentially the same as another. In short, in each of these three areas, the definitions of religious atheism have replaced those founded in Scripture.

How are atheists accomplishing this transition from biblical definitions of being, knowledge and values to those set forth by religious atheism? Every individual, in every area of human existence, is now being trained to think solely within the parameters of the definitions of religious atheism. In school we are taught to think apart from God and scripture. History, language, science, social studies, and geography are taught apart from God. For example, I attended a Baptist university, majored in history, and in four years of study I never even had a one hour class devoted to the person of Jesus Christ or his place in western history. The implications of this kind of academic bias can hardly be articulated. Surely an honest presentation of history must include a significant reference to the influence Christ has had upon western law and culture. So much for academic honesty!

Secularists have claimed the minds of men to be their private domain. Over the last several decades, religious secularists have shown their total intolerance toward the Christian worldview. Our educational system has been redesigned to become the instrument for the repudiation of our historic cultural values and the propagation of the religion of atheism. Any possibility of adequately defining being, knowledge, and values has been eradicated. Religious humanists now insist that all men settle for their arbitrary, expedient concepts in each of these three areas. Our cultures have been subjected to their intolerant ideology. Summing up their worldview might be put like this:

You are [being] what we say you are;
Knowledge is what we say it is;
Values are what we dictate them to be!

We need to ask ourselves how being raised to think and believe as secularists affects those who subsequently have become Christian. Up until people give their lives to Christ, they have been trained to think and believe apart from God. Their definitions of being, knowledge, and values have been framed around the secular agenda; however, just because we have given our lives to Christ and know what it means to be converted does not mean we automatically start to *think* like Christians. We may very well be Christian via the new birth, but unless we move substantially to change the principles by which we think, we will continue to live and act out of those ingrained secular definitions pertaining to being, knowledge and values. What we end up with is a flock of people who have experienced the new birth in Christ but live out of a set of contradictory principles, betraying what they have experienced of Christ in both word and conduct. The possibility of a continuation of such intellectual folly among believers is made clear when Paul tells the Ephesians not to continue in the futility of their thinking. We must ask ourselves if we have made any substantial effort to abandon such futility and seek to discover what this process of renewing the mind involves.

There are two parts to the process. First, there is the absolute necessity of recognizing and casting down every secular thought pattern that holds sway in our minds. Second, we must consciously train our minds to operate out of biblical truth. We must force our minds to shift from old, humanistic principles to the place where our thought lives flow out of an absolute adherence to biblical Truth and that in every area of life.

The Weapons of Our Warfare

II Corinthians 10:4-6 describes the conflict that must take place in the thought lives of believers who would live effective, supernatural lives.

⁴For the weapons of our warfare are not fleshly, but mighty through God to the pulling down of strongholds, ⁵pulling down imaginations and every high thing that exalts itself against the knowledge of God, and bringing into captivity every thought into the obedience of Christ, ⁶and having readiness to avenge all disobedience, when your obedience is fulfilled (MKJV).

When it comes to conquering the inner thought life, God has given us the instruction and the mandate to do so; however, he has placed the responsibility on those of us who have received Christ and want to live effectively in the power of His grace. There is nothing automatic here! If we fail to come to grips with such scriptural injunctions, we can only fail in discovering the Christian life as God intended. To continue in a place of passive indifference toward the call to renew our minds is to choose to remain under the spiritual jurisdiction of Satan. The implications here for the believer and the body of Christ are immense. Look at verse five and consider these phrases:

A) *"Pulling down imaginations."* The word "imaginations" implies a departure from correct reasoning. Any perception of life and reality pertaining to being, knowledge, or values that is not rooted within a scriptural definition is an imagination. The word "pulling" implies that this is not easy work!

B) *"And every high thing that exalts itself against the knowledge of God."* Note the word *every*. Every what? Every high thing! Any knowledge that operates apart from God and does not refer back to God is a high thing. Every humanist definition is a high thing! How many "high things" have we been taught in school? Every high thing, *every* one of them has to be identified and cast down!

C) *"Bringing into captivity every thought."* Now if that doesn't present a challenge to the believer, nothing does. Think about what is being said here: every single thought that trundles through your mind must be examined as to whether or not it is in obedience to Christ! If you have a rather queasy feeling in the pit of your stomach about the challenge that lies before you, that is probably a positive indication that you are getting the message. Some expletive might well erupt upon realizing the task that God, by the Spirit of grace, is calling us into. It truly is a daunting concept. Every thought must be brought into obedience to Christ!

Perhaps you'd allow me to make an observation at this point. Since Eden, man has operated out of an inherent sense that causes him to act as his own god. The New Age movement encourages its adherents to proclaim, "I am God." Here is my observation: the spirit of the New Age has thoroughly infiltrated the body of Christ in a number of ways. For example, the scriptures tell us to love one another, to prefer one another ahead of ourselves, and to maintain the unity of the Spirit in the bond of peace; however, when an issue arises, rather than conduct ourselves according to scriptural principles, the "I am God" mentality rears its fat head. Our opinion has such force within our hearts that it must be fought for and expressed at the expense of love, peace and unity in the body. We are called to live in a spirit of humility. The first evidence of that humility should be a submission to scriptural mandates, but this is not what we see in the body of Christ. We profess truth and insist that it be preached while the family and church are torn apart by a corrupted set of mind principles. Tough stuff, eh?

The "I am God" cry of the New Age also manifests itself as believers in the multiplied hundreds of thousands are running from church to church looking for a place that will minister to their needs. Folks, the church does not exist to meet your needs; it exists as God's instrument of grace to a lost world. Believers visit our service stating that they have come to see what our church has to offer them. My response is often, "Not a thing!" Instead, I ask, "What have you got to offer the world?"

D) *"Having a readiness to avenge all disobedience."* Can we even come to grips with this concept? Avenge? All? Whoa! Sure would be cool if we knew how to take revenge on the disobediences of our own thought life rather than target the failure of others. What is the result of our failure in all of this? The Church is in disarray. How's I Corinthians 1:10 for a mind-blower? "I appeal to you brothers, in the name of the Lord Jesus Christ, that: all of you agree with one another, so that there may be *no* divisions among you, that you may be perfectly united in mind and thought.

The Eden Tree

What is the root of all the discord and controversy in the body of Christ? In Adam, we all made the choice to eat of the tree of the knowledge of good and evil, so when we as believers operate out of our own inherent sense of good and evil, we have opted for a form of knowledge that makes no final reference to God. In truth, we operate out of the satanic mind-set. God clearly spoke to Adam and Eve telling them that they could eat the fruit of any tree in the garden except the tree of the knowledge of good and evil. They were even free to go to the tree of life, the true source of wisdom, but there in the center of the garden was this one peculiar tree that God had named the tree of the knowledge of good and evil. Think of it: an ability to define the knowledge of right and wrong totally on your own! This is the essence of every form of atheism.

Listen to the fights, the arguments, and the reasoning used in the body of Christ to justify divisiveness, and it always comes back to someone saying, "I am right, and you are wrong!" Thus the lines of battle are drawn, and it doesn't matter how many casualties there are along the way. The cry goes up, "We are right, so let the fight begin!" As with every war, everything is in shambles when it's over; destruction is everywhere. Trying to quote I Corinthians 1:10 to these rebels is like pouring water on a duck hoping he'll get wet! Proverbs puts it like this: "A rebuke enters the heart of a wise man more than a hundred lashes a fool." Those who have opted to live out of their own knowledge of right and wrong are impervious to the rebukes of wisdom. Imagine the church being perfectly united in mind and thought. What a concept! But is she perfectly united when faced with those issues that inevitably crop up in every congregation? Hardly!

Let's get real: the root of all discord and judgment in the church lies in our commitment to live out of the knowledge of good and evil. It is a knowledge that operates independent of God, accountable to no one and nothing but our own petulant pride! We feel totally free and justified to define wisdom for ourselves according to our own set of standards. The attitude might be summed up like this: "What is wisdom? Just ask me!" The apostle James sets us straight on this subject: "But if you harbor bitter envy and selfish ambition in your hearts, do not boast about it or deny the truth. Such wisdom does not come down from heaven but is earthly, unspiritual, of the Devil. But the wisdom that comes down from heaven is first of all pure, then peace loving, considerate, submissive, full of mercy, and good fruit, impartial, and sincere" (James 3:14-17).

Scripture refers to two kinds of wisdom. One manifests the Devil; the other manifests the true knowledge of God. The principles that control our thought lives frame our destinies and dictate which spirit will direct those destinies. Remember, we are directed in Ephesians 4:23 to renew the spirit, or attitude of our minds. As long as believers operate out of the knowledge of good and evil, the spirit controlling them is demonic. It is only when we understand that we must reject the whole impulse toward self-generated knowledge and submit ourselves to the absolutes of scripture that we can break free of the demonic dominion Satan holds over our lives and congregations. Accurate concepts of being, knowledge and values, can never be derived if the mind has not been freed from the power of the tree of knowledge of good and evil!

Life or Death

To say that what is at stake is life and death is not an exaggeration. That was the choice before Adam and Eve. Christ came that we might have life and have it in abundance. That abundance of life is dependent upon how we think. Paul states the issue succinctly in Romans 8:5-6: "Those who live according to the sinful nature have their minds set on what that nature desires, but those who live according to the Spirit have their minds set on what the Spirit desires. The mind of sinful man is death, but the mind controlled by the Spirit is life and peace."

Upon reading or hearing such declarations of truth, Christians are very good at acknowledging them, but woefully inclined not to be changed by them. The result is that we continue to profess Christ while living out of a devilish wisdom. The evidence of this dichotomy is found in what goes on in our homes, congregations and denominations. Are we in the least brought low in tears of repentance when confronted by such reality? Satan is not given to repentance, and when he is the spirit in control of our minds, we are not much given to repentance either!

Let's be very clear: only the mind controlled by the Holy Spirit can find the life and peace that Christ came to bring. If we will not commit ourselves to the process of bringing *every thought* into captivity to Christ, then Satan holds onto his dominion in our lives. Sing all the songs you want, give all you want, prophesy all you want, go to church a dozen times a week; all that is fine with Satan so long as you keep thinking like he does.

Where Satan Leads

The knowledge of good and evil encompasses the whole field of knowledge carrying the satanic definition. All evil progressively is defined as good, and all good is progressively defined as evil. Consider what has happened to the child in the womb, to the roles of male and female, or to chastity and purity; redefinition according to the knowledge of good and evil is clear. Where does the knowledge that defines evil as good lead? Away from a true knowledge of God, away from the possibility of any absolutes in life. It is in this way that meaning, hope, and purpose are lost to humanity. This knowledge holds God responsible to explain himself to us. It demands that before we offer him faith he must explain to us what he's up to. His Word must first conform to my understanding before I offer obedience. In short, it maintains the "I am God" theology. If things happen in life that I don't like, the knowledge of good and evil holds *God* accountable and makes *Him* the fall guy. "Well, God says he is all-powerful and all-knowing. If that's true, why didn't he intervene? He could have, but he didn't. Well, I don't need God if that is what he's like!"

Thus, the second aspect of wrong knowledge has become manifest. Man not only chooses to define his own standards of evil, he insists on defining his own standards of good. The knowledge of the Tree is not just a knowledge of evil, but carries its own inherent knowledge of good defined apart from what God distinguishes as good in the scriptures. The knowledge of good that we inherited from the tree is just as deadly as the knowledge of evil. If we live out of a good defined apart from God, it leads us to the lethal reasoning. "Well, if I'm good enough, God will *have* to let me into heaven." Unfortunately, in this definition of good, man refuses to acknowledge that he is a sinner who acts against God and doesn't recognize why Christ needed to die in his place. It is a good that doesn't require the creature to submit to the Creator. It is a good that requires no humility, but stiffens its victim in the death grip of his own unyielding pride. He mistakenly believes he is good enough to compensate for his own faults, sins and failures, and his heart and mind rebel against both God and the scriptures when confronted with his own fallen condition. It is incredible how many people hope to gain acceptance by God because they believe their good works will outweigh the bad ones. They operate out of their own definitions of good and evil, impervious to their rejection of God's definitions in these areas, thinking that if they can somehow just achieve a 51% on good works, that will be sufficient.

Before I received Christ, a dear missionary told me, "All your righteousness is filthy rags in God's sight." I sat there for a few moments and then said, "Well, if I'm not good enough in and of myself, then I guess God will just have to send me to hell." My inherent definition of good was just as deadly as my definition of evil because they both justified my rejection of Christ.

All individuals and believers, if they want to come into the true knowledge and life of God, must examine where they have pitched their tents in the fields of their thought life. Are they camped out beneath the tree of the knowledge of good and evil, still eating its fruit, or have they moved their tents into the shade of the Tree of Life, Jesus Christ? You cannot pitch your tent in two places at the same time: you are living in the shade of one of these two trees! Your values, attitudes, priorities, habits, and speech give you away!

What Must I Do to Be Saved?

It's time to take stock. What mindset have you been living out of? Examine the passages of scripture we've looked at in Romans, I Corinthians, Ephesians, and James with an eye to recognizing the root concepts upon which your thought life is built. Then ask yourself if you have done anything substantial in renewing your mind. How sweet is your own opinion to your soul? How hard have you fought, and how many casualties have there been as you determined to have your own way in your church, family, and various other relationships? Paul could say of himself and those with him, "We have the mind of Christ" (I Corinthians 2:16), because this transition led him to put down his own life's priorities and agenda and to take up another set of life priorities that radically reflected an altered thought life. It affected how he related to others, igniting a passion in his heart for Christ and his people. This passion was strong enough to keep him pressing on even though it meant years of struggle, imprisonment, rejection, shipwreck, snakebite, and finally death. It is not difficult to determine which definition of good carried authority in Paul's thought life and practice.

Once we have come to recognize that we have not dealt the deathblow to the carnal mind, we need to find the grace of a genuine repentance. Why repent? Because if we have persisted in the carnal mindset, we have rebelled against the blood by continuing to submit our lives to the powers and agenda of darkness and have undoubtedly left many wounded behind us. If we will not engage ourselves in the process of renewing our minds in substantial terms and everyday experience, there will always be an echo in our hearts and habits that can be summed up, "I am still God, you know. Forgive? Why? I did nothing wrong!"

Here's one that will stir up the Old Man: money! Your attitude toward money serves as a good gauge of the unconquered mind. Jesus did not come to do away with the law, but we will conjure as many arguments as necessary to hold on to our money. Matthew 23:23 makes it clear that Christ did not do away with the tithe. His intent was that the law of the tithe be fulfilled in our lives out of the impartation of the new heart and the renewed mind, not out of obligation or duty.

If we can at all find the grace of God in our hearts to grieve over our rebellion and repent for having defied God, we then must find the courage and faith to renounce our complicity with Satan. As long as he maintains his subtle dominion in our minds, we will never yield what needs to be yielded! What must we do? We must resign the right to decide for ourselves what is right and wrong, and take up as the standard those definitions that God has declared. God must be wholly God, and we must assume our creature role. Submission is not only required but must be perceived as both fully reasonable and a joy to the converted heart and mind! What God's Word says about being, knowledge, and values becomes the pillar of the believer's thought, life, and practice.

The Appeal for Grace

"Father, according to your own declaration, would you write your law on my mind? Holy Spirit, bring the Word of God, the scriptures, to my understanding as they bear on my life. Lord, your Word is a lamp to my feet, and a light to my path. Now, by the Holy Spirit's empowerment, let your Word have full authority over my thought life. Let me be transformed so that I may find my heart and mind gladly in submission to what it says! When I find myself thinking one way and the Word of God directs me to think and act another, let there be no altercation between what your Word is calling me to and my own preferences."

Now you can find safety in submitting to the authority of his Word. The battle is won, and Satan has been defeated. The mind has found its true foundation and is saved from its own madness. "Whom the Son sets free is free indeed," becomes the daily reality. The rebel mind has been vanquished, pounded into submission on the anvil of truth with the hammer of grace. Christ is now established as the true Lord of life. As Martin Luther King proclaimed on one occasion, "Thank God Almighty...free at last." How true this can be for the believer who has won the battle for his mind.

Here, clarity of mind sets the foundation for the rest of life. Clarity of purpose, meaning, hope, faith, joy, and achievement in life come up like the sun on a summer morning. The new man is born and steps into the pages of human history. Grace proves adequate, and a human being appears who bears the stamp of an eternal, omnipotent, all-knowing God. The leopard cannot change his spots; neither can fallen man change his habits. But God can change both. He does not choose to change the leopard's spots, because that is God's design for him; however, man was made in the image of God, and man's sin has taken him on a journey far away from his intended design. Why does God declare himself against any and every sin? Because every such act carries man further and further away from the image and likeness man was created to bear. Grace granted by a risen Christ, however, means recovery of that which was lost. As one sinner sang to succeeding generations, "Amazing Grace, how sweet the sound that saved a wretch like me!"

What does grace mean to us as men and women? It means life can be restored to the splendor of heaven and is fully worth the pain. It means that man can rediscover who he really is. He comes into the fountain of pure knowledge and is gripped with the value of all that he is and all that is around him! Oh, that you might find this matchless gift of God taking root in your heart and gaining dominion in your mind so the god of this world would find himself foiled in his attempts to blind you. A vision of reality fashioned by God causes the spirit of man to soar into the high adventures for which he was created and finds power sufficient to minister Christ to the garbage dump of man's continual depravity.

Grace stands singularly alone among all the provisions God made for man. Its cost cannot be calculated. But this we know: where sin abounds, grace and grace alone is the sole and divine antidote that sufficiently answers to abounding sin. The great need is for the God-man with the God-mind to make his forceful appearance upon the stage of human history!

What shall we cry?
"Oh, God, grant me grace!"
And how shall we cry?
With incessant fury!

Chapter Thirteen
Warning: Danger Ahead!

I must warn you: if you are going to follow the "word of God's grace" per Acts 20:32 then you must know that you are being led into demon-infested territory. Grace, once it becomes functional, will lead you into danger. Grace by its very nature is dangerous. Grace will turn out to be about losing your life. Risk-free Christianity does not exist. Any concept of Christianity that is geared to play it safe is only a mirage. Those who stepped up into God's presence and purposes moved beyond the pale of safety and security. If we will not risk, we will not discover the high ground of spiritual adventure God planned to be the experience of each believer. The extent to which we find and step into this spiritual adventure defines the testimony each will take with them into eternity.

Failure to risk leaves a void in life that we will then be driven to fill. Some strive to fill the void with the materialistic security and comforts of this world. Many believers develop a mindset that the church exists to fill the void and the local assembly becomes the substitute. The truth is, however, that both these strategies will fail: material possessions can never fill the God-need and the local congregation was never intended to be the source of spiritual fulfillment for the believer. Yes, it is a place of inspiration, salvation, and restoration, but never a substitute for fellowship with "the voice of God walking." It is designed to be a community that accepts the risk and dangers of spiritual living. It must be a place where people live beyond themselves and beyond self-interest in a shared endeavor with all parties, braving the ramparts of hazard. It is intended to be a community that lives beyond the confines of being safe and comfortable.

I rather believe that upon conversion we carry our narcissistic cravings over into our Christianity. (Narcissism is being consumed with or governed by one's own self-interest.) I sometimes wonder if we have not made church our idol, striving to fashion it after our own preferences and pet theologies.

The result is disaster. One group in the church wants it one way, and another group wants it another way, each insisting on their own perspective. If for some reason the leadership or pastor will not follow the design set forward by one or other of the groups, the group whose design has not been followed finds some spiritual excuse to justify either their exit or the forced exit of the pastor. The cover here frequently sounds like, "Well, God is leading us out. Frankly, Pastor, I'd be ashamed to bring any of my friends to this church!" This narcissism breeds rebellion, which is nothing short of idolatry. In fact, this rebellion could be classified as witchcraft! How is this witchcraft? When an individual or group within the church finds that the church does not exist to meet their demands for satisfaction, they rebel against the head of the church (not the pastor, but Christ), cast off restraint, and reject the God-placed spiritual authority. I Samuel 15:23 clearly states, "Rebellion is as the sin of witchcraft." People involved in witchcraft are set on having their own way. If the church leadership does not serve their desired objectives, they resort to manipulation and strive to gain control.

Numbers 14 gives a clear biblical illustration of the rebels' motivation toward spiritual leadership, for it was here that the Israelites banded together against Moses and Aaron after they'd sent spies into Canaan, vying for new leaders. When the church is perceived as not serving the objectives or viewpoint of the rebel, biblical imperatives cease to be relevant. God's purposes for his people and the world do not register on the scale of personal priorities. Who then is left to care about maintaining the unity of the Holy Spirit or about being bound to maintain peace? What of the lost in our cities and towns, or the loss of freedom and the moral depravity that is engulfing our cultures?

Are you getting my point here? Church can become our substitute for the adventure of hearing God's voice and following Him. Hearing and following is where the challenges and the fulfillment of spiritual living are found. Paul noted in II Corinthians 12:1 that he intended to go on in visions and revelations. It is in stepping through the portal of God's revelatory purposes for our lives that life is worth living. It is easy to read, "My sheep hear my voice and follow me," and treat Christ's words as nothing more than idealistic rhetoric. The question is this: *Do you hear his voice?* The ability to hear his voice functions as the very point of departure to spiritual destinations. The true Christian life is about hearing Christ via the voice of the Holy Spirit and following his divine direction. It's difficult to speculate how many Christians are framing their lives around following the voice of Christ. Of those who say they do, how many have any ability to discern between their own imaginations and the true voice of God? In Genesis 3:8, He is the voice of God walking in the evening, and in Revelation 1:12 he is the voice of God walking among the candlesticks. Christ is still the voice of God walking!

Consider this: when Christ began to activate his ministry, he simply walked up to the unsuspecting men and said, "Follow me." Scripture notes that *immediately* they left all. That's a hard reality to fathom! Immediately? We'd be entreating Jesus, "Now, Lord, let's be reasonable. Could you please explain how this is going to work?" But not so much as a whisper rose from their lips. Notice the result of moving in response to the word of grace, the voice of God: they paid with adversity, cold, hunger, shipwreck, persecution, imprisonment, boiling oil, all sorts of torture, and generally, a gruesome death. So much for most of what passes for modern discipleship!

Such is the nature of the word of God's grace. Play it safe, and you'll have to engineer the church to suit your own perceived needs. But when it fails or those in the church somehow do not measure up to the demanded expectation, someone else is to blame for the disillusionment. Let's get real: the local church is *not* what your life is all about. It is simply a vehicle where, in association with other radical people, you can hear God's voice in your own heart and lay down your life and die! There is no other way into God's purposed adventure for your life: you must hear His voice. If you hear and begin to follow as He directs, your thirst for natural security will be trashed. Remember, they left all and there was no old age pension, no benefit package covering dental and medical and no life insurance. No, they left all, and that immediately. When Christ spoke to Matthew, it does not even appear that he stopped to close the cash register, count the day's receipts and make one last trip to the bank. True discipleship must have hearing Christ at its core and the corresponding faith-action. It's not about rules and regulations; it is about discovering the miracle and danger of His functional grace reaching into our hearts and minds so that we find ourselves risking it all. Throughout scripture, this point is made with incredible force.

Think of all the questions Abraham could have asked following the Voice out of Ur to an undisclosed destination. Or the questions Sarai could have demanded answers to from Abraham. "Where are we going to live when we get there, wherever 'there' is? And how do you plan to make a living? Lord [remember, she called him lord], do you mean I have to leave my family behind? What about my favorite china?" Consider Joseph receiving a single dream in the middle of the night: "Get up and take the child to Egypt."

Immediately, in the middle of the same night, he woke Mary, left home, and headed to Egypt. Can you think of a few good reasons she could have mounted so as to postpone the trip? "Shouldn't you finish the contracts you have down at the shop? It will give us that bit of extra money! Well, the baby is sleeping, so we should let him be well rested for such a trip. How are we going to make a living in a place where people don't like doing business with us? You know those Egyptians hate us, and besides, the last time some Jews went down there it was over 400 years before they got out! We really need to postpone this until we've had confirmation from the Lord, dear!" We need to understand how the kingdom voice works: He speaks, we get to leave all—*immediately*—and follow!

In Acts 20:32, Paul was commending the Ephesian believers to God. The means of that commendation was via "the word of God's grace." Notice this phrase implicitly necessitates having an ear to hear. What needs to be heard? The Word spoken by the Holy Spirit! Hearing in turn necessitates a faith response that calls for a heart that will believe in spite of every apparent, natural reality. All the various aspects of grace are implicit here.

What specifically does this phrase, "the word of God's grace," mean? It means that God the Holy Spirit speaks, giving a specific directive the purpose of which is to bring us into compliance with the heart and purposes of God. How does it function in real life so as to bring us into a place where we find commendation before God? First, it builds the believer up; second, it brings the believer into his/her inheritance; and third, it calls us into a fellowship with all those who are declared by God to be sanctified.

The risk of grace is real. I have often said to congregations that if they will come into the place where the Spirit ministers the grace word to their hearts, they may be scared to the bone, but they will cease to suffer from boredom! Plummeting over the precipice of faith-action rooted solely in the word of God's grace is somewhat like jumping over a 5,000 foot cliff without a parachute: God had better show up, or you are in deep trouble! Truth be told, we would all choose to have the parachute strapped firmly in place before we jump because then the jump would be a thrill, and we all like thrills, even if it's just the taste of ice cream. The word of God's grace does not allow the mindset that says, "I get to pull the release handle; I get to be in control." It does not even come with the guarantee that you will survive the leap!

Quite frankly, grace makes a sharp left-hand turn into adversity, risk, and suffering. Only perseverance, faith, and character can keep us on the pathway of grace! You will have to risk it all, trading in your thirst for security and the knowledge of how God is going to work things out for you. One of the things that grace does is put the question *"how?"* to death. Abraham could have asked God, "How are we going to know we are on the right track?" Joshua could have asked, "How will our shouting bring down the walls?" Gideon and Moses could have asked *how* in a few dozen ways! Even when Mary asked how she was going to conceive and Gabriel answered, she still didn't know how it was really going to happen. Peter asked, "Is that you out there on the water, Lord? If that's you out there Lord tell me to come." Jesus spoke: "Come." Peter could have asked *how,* but without details, he went.

Check out the word of God's grace as it came to the widow of Zarephath in I Kings 17. There we read that the Lord commanded a widow to feed Elijah. Notice that God did not open a dialogue with her to find out how she felt about feeding a guest prophet. She and her son were starving through a famine and on the verge of death. The prophet Elijah shows up, demands that he be fed first, requiring what little she had. How unreasonable the word of God's grace can appear to be. God doesn't negotiate; he commands, in spite of our natural circumstances. Think about this for a minute. On one hand she had an unknown prophet asking her for the last bit of bread while she had a starving son on the verge of death. Do you think it possible that she might have had a few doubtful thoughts at this point? "What if I only *thought* I heard God and this guy is here to rip me off? God, this does not seem fair. How can you ask me to deny my own son for this guy I've never met?" Oh, yes, we can drop her into some class of super sainthood thinking she had no humanity about her, but that's not realistic. If Elijah was a man just like us, how much more would this dear nameless widow be found in her humanity in the face of such a command from God? While motherhood has suffered a deadly blow in our Godless culture, for this widow, being a mother was the great fulfillment of her womanhood. With what powerful, protective instincts might she have wrestled? Can we even imagine her conflict?

Did she not have to be willing for the risk? What happens if nothing happened? She could not even play it safe with the little that she had. We need to understand that when Jesus said his sheep would hear his voice, God expects us to do just what the widow did: hear and follow. Nothing of the kingdom provision would have been hers had she opted for a logical, natural course of action. Having the mentality, "Lord, make the meal increase first," wouldn't work; it never does! Nothing of kingdom reality occurred in the lives of the above noted individuals until they simply followed the voice of God. That's the biblical, spiritual principle. That's the life!

The truth here is that many believers have very little and rather than risk the little they have, they hold on to it with all their might. Not so the widow. She took the risk even at the potential cost of depriving her own son. How many of us can tap into God at a level like this? How many times do we hear his voice and shrink back because we don't have all the answers, or count the risk too high. "Put my house or career on the line? Lord, that doesn't sound like you. Give that guy my last ten dollars? Lord, that's not even good stewardship!" I wonder if this was not what Christ was driving at when he told the rich young ruler to sell all he had and to come and follow him. "Sell something or sell part of, sure, but Lord, sell all?" Following can cost you all! That's the nature of grace.

Christ in his life called twelve men; this rich young ruler would have been number thirteen, but he never signed up. He hadn't the heart for the stuff of the kingdom. He failed where the widow succeeded. Have you ever meditated on what this nameless young man missed? Imagine: he was called to follow Christ. The voice, the opportunity, was there, but the word that would have led him into the experience of functional grace was missed. I cannot help but wonder how many believers never get on track with God's eternal agenda for their lives because they hold on to "what little I have."

Let's go back to the widow again. She had the word from God. Do you remember D-MAP? The *directive* was given, the *motivation* stirred in her heart, she responded in logic-defying faith-*action*, and the *power* of God to provide became her reality. The fruit of responding to the word of God's grace as noted in Acts 20:32 is highlighted in her life. Note the three results of responding to the word of God's grace as outlined in this verse.

> She was built up in her faith,
> She gained a twofold inheritance in that her son did not die, and her testimony has stood for thousands of years, and,
> She can stand shoulder to shoulder with all those sanctified saints in eternity.

She stepped through the portal of grace and discovered a kingdom that is not of this world. What would have been her fate had she not been willing to risk all to respond to the word of God's grace? What about us? Are we a sleeping giant or have we simply missed grace? We cannot come into the purpose and provision of God apart from the word of God's grace. There are many who have been drawn to the portal of grace by the voice of God but looking through it into the unknown and unexplained, knowing that all must be left behind and seeing the risk, have drawn back. The grace portal can look more like the eye of a needle than an invitation to join God in an eternal adventure. People who have drawn back may still be in the local fellowship, but they are trying to make that assembly serve their needs. "Well, this church doesn't have all the programs I want, so the Lord is leading me somewhere else." Then, after a time, they realize that no local congregation will ever meet their needs and, becoming disillusioned, disassociate themselves from any real involvement in the corporate nature of being Christian. The issue might be summed up like this: serve or be served. Which is the biblical imperative? Where do many believers put the emphasis, and more to the point, which assumption have *you* been operating under?

Grace is like an intersection in the road. Go left, and we can play it safe; go right, we leave it all, not knowing. We can take the left turn, and God will still love us, but we will never find the high adventure of kingdom living. The matter of making history passes to those who have taken the other path. Taking the path on the right will strip you of all that the path on the left offers, but you will experience God in ways those who play it safe will never know. You will know what it is to suffer, to lose your reputation, to have to persevere and to find the character of Christ resident in your own heart and values. To the world—and much of the church—you will look the fool. "Sacrifice a brilliant career, lose all those wonderful opportunities? He must be crazy."

The truth is that once you start down the highway of God's functional grace, life will repeatedly call you to "take the road less traveled." Time and again you will hear from heaven and be called to take new risks, to encounter more losses in the natural realm, to face new uncertainties, and dangers. Can you stand the grace pathway? Find out what grace cost Paul. The grace life cannot be lived because you know about grace; it can only be lived because God has given you the heart for the battle. A song from a musical song puts it like this: "You've gotta have heart. Miles and miles and miles of heart!" Whose heart? God's heart! His heart is the only resource that will keep you going, counting the cost of those new visions and revelations as acceptable. This grace adventure happens progressively and is life long!

We need to understand Paul's declaration of II Timothy 4:7: "I have *fought* the good *fight*; I have *finished* my course" [emphasis added]. How many of us will be considered members of the "Three-F Club" because we passed through the grace gate into the unknown? The heart finds its highest calling in the perils offered by grace, and there is a sense in which the heart of a man is designed for grace in ways that can threaten the heart of any but a truly spiritual woman. Consider God showing up and commanding Abraham to take Isaac to an unknown mountain, and once there, kill him and then set him on fire. When God spoke to Abraham he found himself at a crossroad in the walk of faith. Would he take the safe route to the left or the dangerous route to the right? Can you imagine him chatting this over with Sarah to get her opinion and approval?

"Honey, I just heard from God."

"That's nice, dear." She continues to chop the veggies for supper.

"Well, honey, I think I need to discuss this latest word with you."

"Oh, okay, dear, what might it be?"

"I have to take Isaac to a mountain God will show me, kill him with a knife, and then set him on fire!"

Is it any wonder he snuck out of camp early next day? Isaac was her child of promise! Guess who would likely have got a knife buried in his chest?

The Spirit of God showed up in our church in an evening service on the April 7, 1975. I heard the words, "Have the people stand," so I asked them to stand. Inwardly, not knowing what to do next, I asked, "Now what?" Clear as a bell I heard, "Lift your hands and start to pray." Seemed simple enough, so thinking the benediction was a good idea I started to pray. I didn't have a clue as to what he was about to do, but as I lifted my hands and started to pray. The power of the Spirit began to fill the room. Inside three minutes over 90% of the congregation was on the floor, out under the profound power of God. People started to repent, get healed, get saved, and some couldn't get up for hours. As people were falling over and slipping under our nice, hardwood pews, I remember whimpering, "Lord, this is the end of my ministry in the denomination." Without missing a beat the Spirit responded, "Well, you can always stop praying!" There, directly before me, was an intersection in the road of my spiritual destiny. It was a directive to "Choose you today whom you shall serve" (Joshua 24:15). He made it my choice. Not knowing what lay ahead I just kept on praying! The Spirit had something in mind for me other than conformity to the prevailing denominational paradigm. God was speaking to my own heart and calling *me* through another portal of the word of His grace, not telling me to take the *denomination* in a new direction. It was a new and threatening "eye of the needle" challenge. Repeatedly, the intersection in the road has popped up and usually in unexpected ways at unexpected times. Sometimes the voice has been incredibly clear and other times only a whisper, but the challenge has always been to make the choice to follow His voice. The emphasis has to be on "not knowing" because grace does not lead through the way of the intellect, but over the precipice of faith.

Life must be an adventure if it is to really be the life God ordains. It may very well lead you away from houses and lands, away from the cocoon of personal security, and into unknown territory. You will have to stop looking to a church or pastor to satisfy your needs and get on with meeting the needs of others at your own cost. This poses a real challenge to the nesting instinct. What becomes the guideposts of life? What do you hold on to when there are no familiar landmarks by which to navigate? Faith in the God who said He'd never leave us, faith in the one who is the Good Shepherd, faith in the one who has declared his everlasting love for us, faith in the one who has promised to provide all our needs, faith in the one who has said that the steps of the righteous are ordered of the Lord. In the process of responding to the grace initiatives of the Holy Spirit, life becomes a full declaration of the Lordship of Christ. Only then has he found true disciples! It is here at this crossroads of spiritual experience that many men have missed the calling of God, either by the choice of their own heart or by a wife who would not hazard such a journey. In either case, an eternal loss has been evoked; an eternal testimony was not written, and the world was robbed of some administration of grace!

Making God-ordained choices means an ever-deepening intimacy with the Godhead, which moves the grace-oriented life further and further away from the old paradigms that conform to the natural world. Those who respond to the grace initiatives of the Holy Spirit become increasingly radical in the practice of the Christian lifestyle. It must be radical. A non-radical, don't-rock-the-boat Christianity is not biblical Christianity. Grace, fully followed, relentlessly produces radical believers.

At different times in the first years of the ministry I had a number of individuals in ministry chastise me for being too radical. I actually had one individual at a ministers' conference walk away from the lunch table we were sitting at, asking me why I had to be so radical. On another occasion when in company with a group of pastors, one of them asked, "Read, why do you always have to be so radical?" I left the meeting wondering what this disease was that had place in my life. I had never tried to be radical; I did not see myself as being radical so what was this thing that seemed to be so offensive to other ministers? Arriving home I went into my office and picked up my dictionary to look up the word *radical*. I felt I needed help to get my life in line so I should at least know what it was about being radical that needed adjustment. Opening my trusty Webster's, I read the following: "to pertain directly to a root philosophy, to govern one's decisions and actions by that root philosophy; to be seen as extreme; to seek a cure." I've got to tell you, I did a jig around my little office. Yes sir, I was a radical! I *wanted* my life to orient around the root philosophy of God's Word; I *wanted* my decisions and actions to reflect that philosophy; I was *certainly* viewed as extreme, and I was *wholly* committed to effecting the cure of the cross!

As I meditated on the concept of being radical, I understood that only radical individuals change history. Throughout the scriptures, every hero of the faith was radical. Finding and walking in God's grace through the power of the Spirit brings us into God's purposes. The religious crowd then marks the follower as extreme. The greatest demonstration of radicalism is God stretched out on a cross. Paul and the apostles were radicals; early Christians were extreme in their faith, willing to die rather than compromise. They were gripped by the power of truth in their hearts, and thus they lived out of a set of principles and priorities that made them non-conformists. It is only a spiritual radicalism in Christ that will bring the cure of the cross powerfully before lost humanity. Surely, as we ponder the state of contemporary culture, we must conclude there is great need for more power. We must finally find a spiritual radicalism that is at least comparable to the inverse radicalism of the evil around us. Who then would face the great dare to danger by confronting the weak god of atheism presently ensconced in our cultures? A. W. Tozer notes in his book, *Paths to Power*, "God works as long as his people live daringly" (35). Are we willing for grace to so fully grip us that we dare the death to which the gospel invites us? Consider the fate of every apostle who committed his life to serve the grace of God in their generation: "Others were tortured and refused to be released, so that they might gain a better resurrection. Some faced jeers and flogging, while still others were chained and put in prison. They were stoned; they were sawed in two; they were put to death by the sword. They went about in sheepskins and goatskins, destitute, persecuted and mistreated—the world was not worthy of them. They wandered in deserts and mountains, and in caves and holes in the ground" (Hebrews 11:35-38).

What lies before us? The perils of dangerous grace! *You don't survive this mission!* Any volunteers? How many among us will sign up for this journey? How many spouses will joyfully follow? How many of us really even care about a "better resurrection?" Remember the old hymn, "Where He Leads Me, I Will Follow"? The road is narrow, and only those whose hearts have been conquered by the incomparable grace of God will be found thereon.

Chapter Fourteen
The First and Second Voice

Responding to the voice of God activates our recovery of grace. Any time you mention hearing the voice of God, the question frequently asked is, "How can I know I've really heard God?" First of all, there is no formula that will tell us with certainty that we have heard the voice of God, but the believer can spend a bit of time meditating on those portions of scripture where God shows up and speaks to men. It is critical that believers understand that there is a first Voice and a second voice, and in addition must know how to discern between the two. There are numerous instances that can serve as a place to begin: God speaking to Adam and Eve; the voice giving directives to Abraham, Moses, Gideon, Samuel, Elijah, and Elisha; the books of the prophets; Zacharias regarding the birth of John the Baptist; Christ and the disciples; Ananias and Saul in Acts chapter 9; Peter in Acts 10; Christ to the churches in Revelation. In studying these different passages of scripture look for the kinds of things that characterize God's communication with man.

One thing we know: Christ is a communicator, and He still speaks today. Under modern atheistic philosophy, if you admit to hearing voices it is assumed that you suffer from severe mental difficulty. Certainly there are those who hear voices that do not belong to God; however, there is still the Divine Author who said, "Blessed are your ears because they hear" (Matthew 13:16). Modern atheism must vilify anyone who says they hear God because if there is a God who actually communicates, the case for atheism is dead. How important is it that men have a capacity to hear with ears that identify the voice of God? If the individual man cannot hear God speaking, then the revelation of God's purpose ceases to be a possibility.

What do we learn from scripture on this matter? Adam was created with a capacity to hear God. The God he heard and conversed with did not come down in physical form as many might assume, for until Christ was conceived in Mary, God in physical form did not occur. Adam communicated with God because he could hear "the voice of God walking" in the spirit realm. If man cannot hear in the spirit realm, the revelation of God and the words of Christ about hearing are rendered meaningless.

It is possible to settle for a form of Christianity that excludes the possibility of individual communication with God, but that forces us to question the authenticity of scriptures themselves, for if the writers of scripture could not hear in the spirit realm, then we do not have an inspired personal revelation of God, by God. There is a further implication that must be considered: if we are going to hold that the individual cannot hear God, then we must also take the position that the voice of the demonic cannot be heard. The fall has not only isolated man from a communicating God but also isolated him from demonic communication, because hearing in the spirit realm ceases to be a possibility. If the latter is true, then Lucifer defeated himself in Eden!

Any concept of Christianity that says the individual can no longer hear God or the Holy Spirit as the "My voice" of both the Old and New Testament represents a complete departure from both explicit and implicit biblical truth. Indeed, salvation itself hinges upon our ability to hear, for Christ declares, "Behold I stand at the door and knock. If anyone *hears My voice* and opens the door, I will come in to him and will dine with him and he with Me" (Revelation 3:20). Ask anyone who has received the new birth about their experience, and they will speak with undeniable conviction. At the core of their being, deeper than intellect, exists a bedrock of knowledge that they have been saved and are eternally alive.

So it is that man's capacity to hear must essentially be something that God intended to be restored. If hearing is not restored to the believing community, then grace and the paradigm of grace is rendered powerless. What's left? Works! Man is dependent on his own effort, and Christianity takes on a form of godliness bereft of power.

When considering the narrative in Genesis chapter three, there are clearly two voices that play upon man and the choices he makes regarding his destiny. The first is noted as "the voice of God" and the second as the voice of the serpent, Lucifer. Thus, we have the first and second voices that play on the ear, mind, heart, and tongue of man. The first Voice endeavors to bring man into grace while the second voice endeavors to lead man away from grace and fellowship with God. Our destinies are framed around the voice to which we respond. It is only in a state of grace that man can truly know God personally, contend with his own sin passions, discover his true identity, and fulfill a revealed destiny.

So what can we learn of these two voices? Are there criteria that might be used in discerning between the Voice and the anti-Voice, between God and Lucifer, between truth and a lie, between true good and real evil? You can only discern spirit things in your spirit, but the following characteristics may help you to begin in the discerning process.

Characteristics of the Voice of God

When God speaks, he speaks with absolute clarity. If a man has heard from God, he does not have to go away and pray about whether or not he has heard from God because the individual knows exactly what God has said and directed. The only question that needs to be answered is whether or not the individual will obey. If a person is uncertain about whether or not he has heard from God, then he has not heard from God. For example, when Christ told Peter, "Come," Peter knew exactly what he was called to do. He did not have to go away and pray for clarification. He did not have to seek counsel from the rest of the apostles. All he had to do was decide if he was going to obey. So it was with Abraham leaving Ur, Moses going to Egypt, or Jonah going to Nineveh: they knew with absolute clarity what God was saying.

When God speaks, He does so suddenly and unexpectedly. Moses was not expecting to find a burning bush, much less hear the voice of God coming out of the bush. One moment there was just a bush, life as usual, the next, the bush was ablaze. One moment Peter and John were washing the nets, the next moment Christ the Word spoke, saying, "Come, follow me." Check out Saul riding along to Damascus: now, *there* was a sudden and unexpected conversation!

When God speaks, he is not inclined to use a lot of words. God's directives tend to be short and to the point, probably because he knows how easily we get confused. Further, he does not negotiate. For example, consider the few words He used in his conversation with Noah regarding the ark, or Peter when calling him to walk on water.

When God speaks, he does not provide all the details. The first Voice does not come with a bucket full of details. He just speaks. If he were to give full disclosure, we'd be excused from faith and could hold God hostage to the carnal man. God did not give full disclosure to Moses, Gideon, or Jonah. He simply instructed them in what they were to do. They were called to act beyond their understanding. In Hebrews 11:2 God said, "By faith we understand." Which comes first: faith or understanding? The order here is not coincidental. There is something in the order that God wants us to grasp. How easy it is to say, "If I understood how this was going to work I'd do it." The "I" in "I am God" waits, putting off obedience to the Holy Spirit. Faith-action precedes understanding. Understanding the ways and purposes of God follows the act of faith. The mind must become servant to the Spirit. When the Spirit directs some course of action, he is calling us to come up into the spirit realm. We go with what we've got versus what's missing! (Mark 4:24-25 gives an interesting study on this topic.)

When God speaks, it can be startling. Clearly, Peter was surprised to hear God tell him to go minister to a bunch of Gentile in Acts 10. He was even more surprised at the result. At the crossroads which came April 7, 1975, I was surprised to hear God give me the topic of the evening message: Binding Sin. (My inward reaction was, "These nice people, God?") After speaking, the directive came that altered my destiny, my standing with the denomination, and the very nature of my ministry: "Lift your hands and start to pray." The result? Shocking, unexpected power.

When God speaks, the individual is called to a logic-defying, faith action. There is no way that what he is requiring of us can be fulfilled naturally, and a sense of being overwhelmed by the challenge is not uncommon. He calls us into the impossible! The false logic system we inherited from Adam must be superseded by the wisdom of God. The carnal mind must be subjected to the Word of God. Proverbs 3:3 directs us to another way of living: "Trust in the Lord with all your heart and lean not on your own understanding; in all your ways acknowledge him, and he will make your paths straight." How hard it is to depart from our own understanding! When God speaks, the carnal mind must die. We are being called out of the soul realm and into the spirit reality, to participate with God in his eternal purposes.

When God speaks, he frequently calls us to break the normal established patterns of our everyday life. The voice of God will shatter our comfort zone. Our habits have to be surrendered. We must leave the familiar for the unknown, thinking in dimensions we've not thought in before, acting in ways that make us uncomfortable. Again, imagine Paul's experience from the moment he finds himself on the ground beside his mount, looking rather silly. What did that look like to his traveling companions? Paul was called to break with what had been the normal pattern of his life. How did that call look to the onlookers? What impact did obedience to this voice have upon his comfort zone? Could you go there? This same paradigm shift takes place when God speaks to a congregation (often through the pastor) under leadership of the

Holy Spirit. Guess what? When God speaks, our pride suffers! God only gives grace to the humble, and often *He* is the one who humbles us.

When God speaks, what he is requiring can be so far out that it is preposterous. How preposterous must it have seemed when Noah built a boat before there was such a thing as rain, when Moses went on his way to humiliate Egypt, when Joshua proposed destroying the walls of Jericho with a lot of noise, or when Gideon set out to defeat the Midianites with only three hundred men armed with horns and torches! When looking back on these amazing events, it's easy to simply accept the result. However, when *you* are the one in a place where the voice of God is leading you to perform some incredible course of action, it can seem overwhelmingly preposterous. The directives of the Holy Spirit frequently call us beyond our human capability. If God called us to something that we could accomplish in our natural strength, we'd have no need of God and could even take the credit for it. Have you been invited to Preposterous City? Did you go, or will you make the trip?

When God speaks, the first Voice is immediately followed by the second, dissenting voice. There were two voices in Eden that played upon the mind and destiny of mankind. The first said, "Do not eat of the tree in the middle of the Garden," and the second offered an alternative interpretation: "Did God really say...." The question is, to which voice do we most often and most easily respond, the one that calls us to faith action, or the one that seems to offer the more rational course of action? One of these two voices is the controlling spirit behind our minds; thus we are directed to do something radical: "renew the spirit of your mind" (Ephesians 4:23). When we follow the second voice, the assembly looks more like a pack of wolves hunting than a herd of sheep following. We need to be prepared to go with the voice calling us to risk, loss, and the crucified life. It calls us to a life of active trust in the head of the church, Jesus Christ. After all, we are called to be like sheep who hear and follow His voice.

When God speaks, He is presenting a door of opportunity for the hearer. In speaking, God sets possibility before the believer. Unfortunately, we are much better at finding a reasoned impossibility, meaning we look for a reason not to do what we've been told to do. We so easily opt for the impossibility mindset rather than the possibility mindset. Here's the point: when the Holy Spirit speaks, look for the possibility. Remember Ananias in Acts 9? Upon hearing the words of the Holy Spirit, did he focus on problem or possibility first? Did he jump with excitement that he'd heard the Holy Spirit speak to him about the conversion of the deadliest foe of the new church? Did he grab his hat and head for the door of possibility, or halt at the bench of improbability? Was his attitude, "Wow, the gift of miracles is about to be activated in my life!" or was it more like, "God, do you *know* what you are asking?" Only one perspective will result in the fulfillment of God's heavenly agenda for our lives, our congregations and our nations.

When God speaks, an affirmation comes to the individual who obeys. Affirmation for faith-oriented obedience may or may not occur in the earthly dimension, but an affirmation is always entered into the heavenly record when we do what we are told. How did affirmation work for Moses, Esther, or Nehemiah? God affirmed these people before men. Acts 2:22 points out that God accredited Jesus with miracles, wonders and signs. This accreditation took place *before* men *for* men. Those listed in Hebrews 11 were all accredited by the power of God before men, affirmed for their faith by God. Though not seen or affirmed by man, they were seen and affirmed in the heavenly record by God! There is a pure intoxication in the human spirit when a man or woman recognizes that the God of the universe has just affirmed and accredited them. There is no comparison between the affirmations of man and the affirmations of God. The affirmations of man are often no more than empty enticements to pride. How we need to have a heart to live for the affirmation that declares, "Well, done, good and faithful servant" (Matthew 25:21). As much as carnal man craves for fame, may it be that God's people crave the bread of an eternal affirmation: famous in heaven, unknown on earth! The means to such affirmation rests in obedience to the voice of God!

When God speaks and we obey, he is able to activate the priesthood of the believer (I Peter 2:9). Whether or not this is understood, *God believes in the corporate priesthood of believers.* The priesthood is not just a matter of profession; it must be the active proof of a realized redemption. God intends for every believer to participate in the ministry of the new covenant instituted through Jesus Christ. Ephesians 4:11-12 sets the paradigm for this new covenant in order to build up the body of Christ by assigning some to be apostles, others prophets, evangelists, pastors, and teachers. God, through Jesus Christ, has given specially equipped individuals as trainers to the body of Christ, the *members* of which are mandated in turn to do the work of the ministry. The world is desperate for the day when the work of the ministry is placed into the hands of the anointed believerhood! It seems that the God-appointed trainers have had a hard time letting the believers occupy the field of play. The trainers need to train and then set the believer-player loose on the field to do the things that Christ did. This is an all-encompassing concept of the new covenant. The believer is called to do the work of the ministry of Christ. We are not saved to sit in church and watch a trainer do his stuff. If the trainer is doing the job right, then those being trained must do the supernatural and replicate Christ in the market place. I have often said in churches where I've ministered that if the priests of the Old Testament conducted the ministry of the priesthood like the New Testament priesthood conducts itself, the Old Testament priesthood would have died instantly before an angry God. Thank God for grace and mercy! Leaning ignorantly in grace and mercy, however, is not the biblical agenda for the believer.

I have had the privilege of being accompanied by a ministry team from my home church on several trips to Trinidad. While there, the individuals who come with me are given full opportunity to do the work of the ministry. I do my part and set the team members free to minister in other places on their own. Guess what? God honors their endeavors equally with mine. They have seen the power of God being released. They cast out demons, minister healing, teach, and love the body of Christ with supernatural enabling.

On a ministry trip to Trinidad with a team from our fellowship there was a rather profound demonstration of the Spirit's gifts and power. A couple of our team members went to the home of a family in the church where we were ministering. During the ministry time one of the women on the team suddenly ran out to the house into the back yard. She ran up to a very large tree in the back yard and started to break the power of a curse over the property. The family came out into the background in astonishment at the warfare she was in. They then explained that the family who had lived in the home prior to their moving in had pronounced a curse over the property. They had slaughtered a pig and buried it at the base of this tree pronouncing the property to be under a demonic, permanent curse. The team and family members simply agreed and then went back into the house.

The family came to the service the next evening with an astonishing story. When they had gotten up in the morning they happened to look out into the backyard during breakfast. There, laying flat on the ground, was this huge tree. There had been no storm, no wind, no rain. It had just fallen over in the night. This became both a personal and a wonderful testimony of God's love and grace for the whole family. It was a powerful testimony to the members of the congregation, as most of them knew of this tree. Now, either that blows your spiritual paradigm apart, or you can only marvel at the greatness of our God! He still works his gifts and power in this present generation!

Ah, what a blessing! On every occasion, on these kinds of trips the saints act and are accredited as the priesthood by God. Did I know they were going to do everything right? No, but I knew that God believes in the priesthood of the believer and that I could trust him fully to look after things. He did! He will! Believer, *you* are the priesthood, called to be ministers of God's awesome grace to a hurting world! Listen and you will hear heaven speaking to activate you into a royal expression of heaven's priesthood!

When God speaks, we must frequently face the "fear factor." Often, we succumb to fear because we do not understand how God is going to move. When the Holy Spirit spoke to Ananias about his impending trip to see Saul, he had to conquer a spirit of fear. He knew full well the nature of the man God was directing him to deliver. The first Voice will entice us to move into that which is beyond our understanding, and instantly we are faced with a litany of dangers. It can be fear of failure, fear of rejection, fear of looking stupid or ridiculous, fear of getting off track, fear of criticism, fear of losing a job or reputation: the list goes on. The truth is that often the first Voice will knowingly call the believer into dangerous places. It has been estimated that 160,000 Christians have been martyred every year since 1990, which is almost one person every three minutes (Trifkovic). This demonstrates that there are not just imagined fears, but real dangers to obeying the inner call of the Holy Spirit. You only have to consider the history of missions to understand the dangers of becoming ministers of grace. The question on those occasions when the Spirit speaks comes down to this: "Will I save my life or lose it? Will I be the kernel of wheat that falls into the ground and dies or will I abide alone?"

When God speaks, you will be required to rely on supernatural provision. God wants to bless and prosper his people. He can, for example, call upon them to activate a skill that he's planted within them. He does so by releasing a Spirit directive. Upon hearing the directive they often look to the resource at hand and wonder how that resource can possibly be adequate. When God speaks, you need to identify the provision you have on hand. God does not want you to act because you have the money; he wants you to commit yourself to an act of faith. The Christian life is not about money or some other resource, it is about faith. It will usually appear so small and inadequate that you will be inclined to ignore it. It's that proverbial mustard-seed concept. The resources Moses had in hand when God told him to go to Egypt must have appeared significantly inadequate. Remember in Exodus 4:2 when Moses was wondering about this, God's question to him was, "What have you got in your hand?" In the natural, all he had was a stick. Up until the encounter with God, it wasn't even a very impressive stick. From man's perspective, it was significantly insufficient. God's perspective, however, was, "That will do!"

We must recognize that *it is not the resource that is going to win the day and make the way!* To look to the resource is to take our eyes off God and misplace our confidence! Our faith focus on God gives God the opportunity to act, so that the resource we have and use proves sufficient. But even as the resource proves sufficient, our faith must never be transferred to the resource. Moses could not start looking to the stick as the source of power. The resource you may have may be a skill, an idea, a passion, an invention, or just a basement as a place to start, but when the first Voice gives you a directive, *use what you've got, and use it in full dependence on God.* It is as we trust that the barriers to life's blessings can begin to be overcome one at a time. The word-directive of the first Voice is all the resource you need to begin the journey to your Egypt. Remember what Mary said to the servants in Cana of Galilee in John 2:5? "Do what he says." What was the question when Christ told the disciples to feed the throng? He asked them what they had. When they did not understand this principle, Jesus illustrated it for them. Find what you've got, use it, and trust God for the rest! And remember, it is not the resource that brings the supernatural result, but the God behind the resource that we use!

When God speaks, a shift from the natural into the spiritual must take place. To the natural man, there is something non-rational here. *Watch the emotions!* It is incredibly difficult to move beyond the soul man and act out of the spirit man, especially for those of us trained in the thought processes of western man. God will not strike a bargain with your pride or your emotional demands! In II Kings 5, Elisha told Naaman that if he wanted to be healed of his leprosy he should dip himself in the Jordan River seven times. Upon hearing these instructions, Naaman went away angry because he thought it should happen some other way. The carnal mind can trigger carnal emotions. As Jesse Duplantis put it, "Seven ducks in a muddy pond" don't do much for one's ego! The spirit man must respond to the directives that come into the heart and mind as the first wave, the first Voice. It was only when Naaman conquered his anger and did what he was told that he was healed. Paul put it like this: "The man without the Spirit does not accept the things that come from the Spirit of God, for they are foolishness to him" (I Corinthians 2:14). Yes, it is dangerous! Grace will put the carnal man to the sword every time, and death does not come without some kind of emotional reaction.

When God speaks, those closest to you may not understand or support you and may even criticize you.

The Holy Spirit does not pay much attention to the religious sensibilities of the human heart. Be assured, however, that religious people will become your adversaries, your critics, or abandon you altogether in favor of the company of others that "have their theology right." Peter had his theology all wrong when he ventured off to Cornelius' house in Acts 11:2; after all, Gentiles were unclean! The circumcised believers (the crowd that had it "right") criticized him. The reality is that you have to be prepared to stand alone. In speaking about the person who knows how to stand alone, I am not referring to the head-case who will not subject himself to genuine spiritual authority. Such an individual goes off telling people that God has told him to do exploits, when in fact heaven has been silent. (You know, the kind of guy that will go off and prophesy over a dead cow, but will not live in subjection to any kind of valid, spiritual authority.) The kind of standing alone I'm referring to here takes the course of action as directed by the first Voice. If you read the record of what first happened when Moses got to Egypt, things did not go very well. It was bricks without straw, and not too many in the crowd demonstrated a lot of confidence in Moses. He had to stand alone. Jesus, in Matthew 4, heard the Father's voice and then had to face the wilderness alone. Ultimately, he had to face the cross alone. The first Voice will lead you to the place where you are invited to "eat my flesh, and drink my blood." Be prepared: you may well have to traverse the valley of the shadow of death alone. It is at this place that many will turn away and find a nice comfortable pew or Sunday morning TV minister. Standing alone means obeying God without the support or company of man. God, however, is to be found in that lonely place.

Are you getting the idea about what it's like to recognize the voice of God? It is important to recognize that in rendering obedience to the first Voice, there is only one solid foundation: we must act on the basis of the finished work of Christ and that in accord with the Spirit of the written Word. You cannot presume to render obedience based on personal strength or some kind of imagined spiritual superiority. We are never competent in and of ourselves. Jesus alone is our confidence and our competence comes from him alone, given to us as a gift.

So often when the Holy Spirit renders a directive, the person receiving it is immediately confronted with his or her own lack of qualification. I can remember feeling uncertain about my own call to the ministry. I felt completely overwhelmed by my own lack of strength, wisdom and ability to be a pastor. There were also a good number of believers who did all they could to foster this uncertainty. Then came the day that the Spirit whispered into my heart, "Your weaknesses are your qualification for the ministry." I was instantly put on ground that required me to wholly trust in the provision and power that Christ would exert through the gateway of my weaknesses. This proved to be unfortunate for those who could see nothing but my weaknesses, because they dismissed the possibility of Christ in a pastor's life. Fortunately, because of my weaknesses, I was forced to put my trust in Christ and have found Him to be totally sufficient for over thirty years.

Saint, when you hear the first Voice invading the quiet of your own life, God is calling you to look beyond your abilities—or lack thereof—to the full sufficiency of Jesus Christ. He is well able to find in your weakness His greatest opportunity and in the end, the glory is His alone! Weakness is the doorway of opportunity, for it is then that Christ becomes the functional foundation of whatever ministry starts to flow out of your life. The strength is of heaven, not of man!

How about a few characteristics of the second voice? This is not about the ramblings of the carnal mind, but the second voice that showed up in Eden. How can we possibly discern the whispers of the enemy? The second voice will set itself in enmity to the first Voice by trying to:

Counter the first Voice
Offer an apparently more reasonable alternative
Find a good reason to avoid the pending risk
Appeal to the desire for safety and security ("What about your job/reputation?")
Attack your apparent lack of qualification
Major on the lack of available resource
Offer a good reason why you should avoid action at this moment
Strive to neutralize your realization of the "priesthood"
Put no demand on God's anointing in your life
Discourage any call you might make upon the power of God
Suggest that you alter the directive
Prompt you to put off any decision for the moment
Whisper, "What will others think if this doesn't work?"
Remind you of past attempts in which you failed
Encourage more counsel from your friends before you act

I have no doubt that you have had your own experiences and can add a few points to this list. The important thing is to realize that there were two voices in Eden, and the fact that they exist impacts every believer's life. One leads into the wisdom and power of God and the discovery of our destiny in this life. The other voice leads us to live out of the inherent knowledge of good and evil we inherited in Eden. The song, "I Did It My Way," sums up this latter alternative.

Have you ever considered what character qualities mark those who hear and respond to the first Voice as opposed to those who hear and follow the second voice? Those who hear and follow Jesus Christ as directed by the Holy Spirit will demonstrate one clear set of characteristics while those who have followed demonic whispering will manifest a completely different set of character attitudes. In the following random list, which set of attitudes most characterize your spiritual life?

THE FIRST VOICE	THE SECOND VOICE
Doers	Watchers
Faith-action	Want an explanation first
Servant heart	Expect to be served
Those who are judged	Those who judge
Those who love	Those who find fault
Joyful	Negative, unhappy
Peace-makers	Divisive, argumentative
Active in Church	Absented themselves
Sacrificial Commitment—giving	Personal agendas—buying
"What can I do for you?" attitude	"What can you do for me?" attitude

How did you do? Life is found only in obedience to the first Voice. Jesus spoke about the two kinds of builders in Matthew 7:24-26. One builds his house on the rock and stands the test of adversity, while the other builds on sand and is overcome when adversity strikes. The wise man hears the words of Christ and puts them into practice while the foolish man hears the words but does not act on them. Hearing the first Voice is the way through adversity into the wisdom and life of Christ. Hearing and responding to the first Voice enables the Holy Spirit to bring believers into that place of abounding grace. It's only in the grace place that we recover our Edenic inheritance.

Chapter Fifteen
Truth in Tension with Truth

"If we are to do His work we must do everything in both grace and truth. Truth without grace is what the enemy brings when he comes as an Angel of Light." Rick Joyner

The concept of grace cannot be separated from truth, nor can truth be separated from grace. Truth exists in tension with other truth. If we are to arrive at a correct understanding of truth, then we must understand how one truth impacts other truth. For example, the truth of mercy must be understood in the context of other truth such as holiness or how the truth of judgment is affected by the truth of grace. A correct exegesis of the doctrine of faith cannot be found if that doctrine ignores other aspects of truth.

To start with, we should consider the absolute relationship between grace and truth. We need to understand the tension that exists between these two doctrines. All that is expressed as truth must finally be seen through the lens of grace or we fail to communicate that which is fully truth, and instead, subject it to manipulation or misinterpretation. We end up with a cacophony of voices that claim to be declaring truth. Truth is then reduced to someone's religious opinion of various Bible verses, communicated in deep tones of conviction. Put another way, when truth is not founded in a solid understanding of grace, truth devolves into a multiplicity of divergent theologies.

Consider a few concept questions. Don't just read them, but try to think about the possible answers.

If you take the truth of grace out of any truth being presented, do you have the truth as God intended? What has then been done to scripture? How often is truth presented without tying it referentially to grace?

In practical terms, what does "full of grace" really mean? Consider Christ. Jesus said of himself that he was Truth. He, as Truth, was the Word and inherently full of grace. If we do not understand the concept *"full of grace"* as it pertains to Christ, do we have an accurate understanding of Christ as God intended? Is it enough to simply assent to the statement?

If we, in ignorance, disregard grace in the declaration of truth, have we diminished the power of the Word to save? What is left? Duty? Formula? Law?

If we adopt a concept of truth that is devoid of a developed understanding of grace, has man's ability to receive help from God been affected? Has our ability to help men been affected? (Take a look at Hebrews 4:16.) How then do we explain that grace meets human need? How many believers know how to find their needs met in God's grace? How does grace meet the need inherent in the whole human dilemma?

I do not want here to presume to answer these kinds of questions. I do, however, think that our ability to answer these kinds of questions is imperative if we want an accurate exegesis of truth! Here is an absolute: neither Christian truth nor life can be effectually defined or experienced *apart from grace.*

The New Testament was written with a two-fold presumption about its readers and its would-be practitioners. It first presumes that there is an understanding of how grace works and second, that grace has become functional in the believer's life. When Christians are called to demonstrate the nature of God in their congregational community, marriages, families, etc., it is presumed that they are responding first of all to the grace of Christ as ministered into their natures by the Holy Spirit. When we read through the Sermon on the Mount, this presumption becomes clear. Christ was not calling fallen humanity into a standard and practice of life that was a higher concept of legalism. The standard of the New Testament is far beyond the capability of human effort. In saying the things He said, it is logical to conclude that He wanted people to discover the power of grace by which they could be freed from a performance of the law and thus be brought into a power-demonstration of godliness! The Sermon on the Mount was not a call on man's fallen nature to try harder. Christ had something else in mind: Grace! The resource for the new life cannot be found in the heart of fallen man. Something completely otherworldly had to invade that twisted nature and cause a powerful inward transformation so that man's whole approach to life and relationships became a manifestation of God's nature.

Clearly the New Testament presumes a new kind of man living out of the new heart and new mindset as worked within by the Holy Spirit!

The Presumption of Grace

We may have discussed some of these areas before, but I want to illustrate how grace is a necessary prerequisite to obedience. "Blessed are the pure in heart..." (Matthew 5:8). Is it at all possible that fallen man could achieve purity of heart on his own? How about this one? "Rejoice and be glad." When? "When people insult you, persecute you and say all kinds of evil things about you falsely for my name's sake." Looks good on paper and sounds good in sermons, but go ahead and see if you can honestly rejoice when you are insulted, persecuted and slandered. You are not just to rejoice in such situations, but be genuinely glad.

This is not an isolated directive. James adds this challenge: "Consider it pure joy when you face fiery trials" (James 1:2). Fiery trials, pure joy? How's *that* for a foreign concept? Only grace could make the event of such a dichotomy an opportunity for pure joy. Might I suggest that if anyone is to experience "pure joy" in the midst of "fiery trials," grace is going to be a functional necessity, or pure joy in *any* trial will be impossible to come by!

Peter poses a similar challenge when it comes to how we handle life's adversities: "In this you *greatly* rejoice...though you suffer grief in all kinds of trials" (I Peter 1:6) [emphasis added]. What a dichotomy: suffering, grief, and all kinds of trials in tandem with greatly rejoicing? Little beads of sweat, anybody? What necessity of grace will you face trying to rejoice greatly in the midst of suffering, grief, and all kinds of trials? It might be suggested that there is a significant need to discover how grace impacts the believer who finds himself suffering, grieving and facing all kinds of trials.

What about James' references to taming the tongue? It doesn't appear that we've had much success with this particular challenge. If we consider ourselves to be okay in Jesus but don't keep a tight reign on our tongues, we are simply deceiving ourselves and our faith is worthless (James 1:2, 26). How can God expect us to keep such a reign on our tongues when, as the inspired writer says in James 3:8, "No man can tame the tongue"? If our discussion of taming the tongue is without grace, then it is ceases to be a discussion and becomes a slaughter.

Then the Holy Spirit inspires II Corinthians chapters 8 and 9 about our money and where our treasure is to be found. How do we know where the heart is? We know where our hearts are finally anchored by whether or not we can give the Lord His tithe! Whoops, did you feel that? Our treasures are no secret: the treasure map is the heart! Whenever the New Testament speaks to the money issue, it presumes that believers have discovered how grace affects our giving. People who do not know what grace is experientially cannot give their money or do anything else that the believer is called to do with the appropriate attitude.

How about these ones, guys? "Anyone who looks on a woman and lusts after her *in his heart* is guilty of adultery." Or when scripture directs husbands to love their wives as Christ loved the church, there is a profound presumption that grace has invaded the heart and brought with it a supernatural capacity to love. Why supernatural? Simply put, because Christ's love for the church is supernatural in its nature and outworking. Guess what, guys? The biblical expectation is that you discover how the grace of Christ works so that you can love like he loved. Appropriated grace is the end of stuff like abuse and adultery!

Try suggesting this to ladies who do not know what it means to experience real grace: "Wives submit to your husbands." An incredible negative reaction is to be expected from the ladies if you divorce grace from your conversation of submission. One must play upon the other.

Then there is Philippians 2:3, directing believers to humbly esteem others as better than themselves rather than the internal congregational warfare that so often characterizes our fellowships. There is a clear assumption in scripture that grace must become the motivational reality of the human spirit. Check out Galatians 6:18 where Paul concludes, "The grace of the Lord Jesus Christ be with your spirit, brothers." Can we even contemplate the possibility of "brothers" if we fail to be partakers of such grace? To make things even worse, Christ goes on to say things like, "love your enemies." Sure, pal! We can't even live out our commitment to love the rest of God's sons and daughters, let alone our enemies!

Let's go a bit further. When Christ directs us not to judge, there is a profound presumption that grace has borne its powerful effect on the inward man so that even the inclination to judge has been abolished from our hearts. Christ's injunction about not judging others puts to a quick death the concept of the so-called prophet whose purported anointing is to pronounce "judgment on the people of God." Get over it! The tension between grace and judgment must be inherent in our practice.

All these admonitions in scripture assume the necessity of a grace that has gone beyond understanding to conquer the heart. Only then will our responses to life's adversities and challenges reflect these biblical standards! This, not because we force ourselves to live up to such standards, but because it is in our nature to do so! Miss the functional empowerment of grace and the Christian life as prescribed by the New Testament can never be attained. The result? People live their whole lives without discovering how to live life in the dimensions for which Christ died! Many in the body of Christ never get beyond the vain effort to conform their lives to the standards of the Law dressed up in New Testament language. This equates to death!

Now, let's consider further how scriptures set grace and truth in juxtaposition. We need to tie our understanding of truth into grace something like we tie a ship to a dock. Here the ship is truth and the dock is grace. If the ship is not tied properly to the dock, it can slowly drift away from its intended position and either cause damage to other ships or founder on the rocks along the shore. Either way, trouble is inevitable. We've noted that every epistle written by Paul begins and ends with grace while referring to grace periodically. He is anchoring truth to grace!

Well, whenever the ship leaves one dock it is always headed toward another dock. The ship may be altogether wonderful, but once it leaves one dock it is always en route to another dock. Truth is an entity in its own right, but it is only kept on track when it proceeds from one aspect of grace and concludes in another aspect of grace. That is irrevocably the New Testament pattern as demonstrated in the Epistles, and it is how Paul wrote the Epistles. If we ignore this pattern in our exposition of scriptures, then truth is set adrift like a ship sailing without a destination. The captain may well be on the bridge shouting his orders, but the crew on board have no destination (or destiny). In the absence of grace, people are set adrift to believe whatever they consider truth to be, as opposed to being obliged to acknowledge the truth God has declared. When reference to grace is absent or ignored, there is little difference between the secularist who makes up his own mind about what truth is and the believer who operates the same way.

The New Testament presumes in the absolute that believers have grasped the fundamental relationship between grace and truth. Both life and truth must find their definitions within the context of biblical grace. All declarations of truth and exposition of Christian doctrine must be framed around an accurate understanding of grace. If what is put forth as truth violates the principles of grace, then it is only a partial and inaccurate presentation of that truth at best and may well be nothing more than an attempt to manipulate the hearers. Truth that ignores its root of grace is the kind of truth that II Corinthians 3:6 terms, "letter," and the letter kills!

Remember Christ forever linked grace and truth together in both His deity and His humanity. John 1:14 records that Jesus Christ came "from the Father full of grace and truth," and verse 17 reasserts the concept by noting, "Grace and truth came through Jesus Christ." We perhaps should ask, "Is this combination coincidental, or does it reflect a clear pattern that runs throughout the New Testament?" A high view of scripture demands that this connection is part of the divinely precise intent: nothing in God's Word is coincidental. All scripture is infinitely precise by Divine inspiration! So, if grace and truth are inextricably bound together in Christ, and every believer is mandated into the likeness of Christ, doesn't it follow that grace and truth must also be inextricably bound together in the believer? Absolutely!

This being true, the inward working of grace in the heart empowers the believer to live the truth, not just know about it and pay it verbal homage! What is the result? Believers discover what it is to be like Christ in everyday life. He did not abolish the moral standards of the law but, being full of grace, was able to fulfill those moral standards. Contrary to what many believe, conforming to the moral standards of the law should not mean we are bound to a works or performance mentality. Instead, it is to discover the inner power to appropriate the moral nature of God because grace has had its work in our hearts. Remove the inner presence and power of grace, and Christianity is reduced to a code of religious practice that can never be attained. Believers are then faced with impossible demands, which are beyond human ability to fulfill. So much for an easy yoke!

My purpose here is not to introduce some new kind of doctrine. You can very easily set this book down, pick up any exhaustive concordance, look up the word, "grace," and begin to make a list of all the references where grace is linked to some other truth. Your list will be a couple of pages long. Then you need to take some time and meditate upon the relationship between grace and the specific instances where truths are set in the context of grace. Simply ask yourself a few questions. For example, why does scripture associate grace to the truths of salvation, peace, mercy, justification, prosperity, faith, or money? Then meditate on answering how each area of truth relates to grace. For instance, the Bible speaks of weakness in I Corinthians 12:9, but how is weakness overcome by the presence of functional grace? Giving assent to this truth does not mean we understand how grace works in helping us to overcome our weaknesses. Is such understanding optional or imperative?

On my first time through *Strong's Concordance*, I compiled a list of fifty-five instances where truth was directly tied to grace. These ties, being specific in the pages of scripture, clearly demonstrate that the affiliation between grace and other dimensions of truth cannot be dismissed. I then made a list of thirty-five areas where grace, though not explicitly mentioned, was necessitated.

Those thirty-five categories were just a preliminary listing and could easily have been close to one hundred. May I simply suggest that this material be a place from which to begin? You are under no compulsion to agree with me. Whether you agree or disagree is of little or no consequence. What is important for every believer, minister, ministry, and church is that a clear biblical perspective be developed on the grace/truth paradigm. If we esteem scripture, and scripture consistently sets grace in juxtaposition with various aspects of truth, then it would seem that serious-minded believers are under obligation to understand those various truths in the context of grace.

This chapter would be far too long if it were to look at all the places where some aspect of truth is joined to grace in the New Testament, so I will take a few examples from the scriptures and try to demonstrate how grace and truth are connected.

A Snubbing Post

Truth must have a snubbing post. Not very many people know what a snubbing post is or how important it can be. I was raised around riding horses. Some horses are easier to break than others. Some are downright wild. One thing I learned very early in my exposure to horses was that they are very powerful animals that tend to have a mind of their own. If you are going to tame a horse so that it can be ridden, various methods can be used. If the horse is really wild, and you can't get near it, you need two things: a lasso and a snubbing post. A snubbing post is a post set deep into the earth in the middle of a corral. The person taming the horse first throws the lasso around the horse's neck. Immediately that horse starts to react against the tension on the rope. As soon as that rope drops around the horse's neck the trainer loops his end of the rope around the snubbing post. How important is the snubbing post? If there is no snubbing post, the person on the end of that rope is in for some very interesting moments. It's the power of a wild horse against the strength of the trainer! Guess which one wins? The man without a snubbing post is very much subject to the power of a wild horse. Talk about dusty trails! However, if there is a snubbing post, the trainer simply loops his end of the rope around the post and the horse's strength has found a match. Slowly the rope can be shortened and the horse brought under control and made useful.

Are you getting the picture? You'd better not lasso that wild horse without it! It is important that our understanding of grace is deep enough so that truth does not become like a wild horse.

Grace is to Truth what a Snubbing Post is to the Horse

Have you ever heard wild, unbridled truth? Apart from the governing influence of grace, truth can be made subject to unfettered imagination and personal interpretation. Truth is absolute. Our theologies, however, may not be, even if we believe they are. When truth is not tied into grace, it is subjected to the opinion or theological persuasion of the one presenting it. The wide diversity in the presentation of truth as seen in the body of Christ could be due, at least in part, to the absence of a functional revelation of grace. The snubbing post of grace is not there to *diminish* the strength of truth, but to *release* it. Unfettered truth will never serve the Kingdom of God as it is intended to do. If there is anything God's people need to be conversant with, it should be the covenant under which we live and by which we relate to God, each other and the world.

Is there more that can be learned of grace? Are we finished yet or have we just begun? While it is not my intent to do so in this present writing, I would suggest that there are at least three more areas of inquiry that need to be addressed in some considerable detail.

Every scripture that makes reference to grace must be exposited. Then and only then will we know what the Bible teaches specifically regarding grace. Check out *Strong's Concordance* for the listing of scriptural references on grace. In doing this kind of exhaustive study may I suggest that the five keys, the four stages, and the two components of the grace paradigm as identified in Jeremiah 31:33 can be helpful in such exposition. Use these concepts as a kind of overlay in understanding and interpreting the grace scriptures.

There is a need to understand the relationship between grace and all other biblical doctrine. For example, what is the relationship between in each of the following truth equations? How do the two truths interact? How do they play upon each other?

GRACE AND OTHER BIBLICAL TRUTHS	
Grace and the Kingdom	Matthew 6:10 & 13
Grace and Faith	Romans 4:16; 5:2
Grace and Giving	II Corinthians 8:7
Grace and Prosperity	II Corinthians 9:8
Grace and Reigning in Life	Romans 5:17
Grace and Stewardship	I Peter 4:10
Grace and Peace	Galatians 1:3
Grace and Mercy	I Timothy 1:2
Grace and Salvation	Ephesians 2:8
Grace and Holiness	Acts 13:43
Grace and Discipleship	Matthew 28:19
Grace and Power	II Peter 1:2-3
Grace and Glory	I Peter 5:10
Grace as the Abundant Provision	Romans 5:17
Grace and The Ministry of Christ	II Corinthians 3:4-6
Grace and our Conversation	Ephesians 4:29; Colossians 4:6
Grace and The Sufficiency of God	II Corinthians 12:9
Grace and Human Weakness	II Corinthians 12:10; Hebrews 4:16
Grace and Miracles	Acts 14:3
Grace and Church Mission	Mark 16:15
Grace as 'bookends' to Paul's Epistles	Why?

There needs to be an understanding of how grace applies to everyday life, to church community, to human culture and civilization. For example, what is the relationship between grace and the following areas of human society?

Grace and work life
Grace and human sexuality
Grace and our economies
Grace as the antidote to poverty
Grace as the necessary ingredient for effective civilization
Grace and law and order within a society
Grace and freedom in a society
Grace and government
Grace and cultural values
Grace and personal worth of each citizen
Grace and violence in a society
Grace and the role of truth in society

Grace and the definition of equality
Grace and the definition of roles and responsibility
Grace and the media, the free press

Grace is the only provision God has given man upon which to govern human society and by which that society can be kept from the tyranny of another set of religious presuppositions. Biblical principles properly understood and applied to human culture are the only foundation that exists to keep man truly free. Conversely, a progressive tyranny is guaranteed for the citizens in the state where grace has been abolished. Such is the case in our western democracies.

How About a Pop Quiz?

We have covered a significant amount of ground on grace, but reading and retaining are two different things. Applying a principle means understanding the concept behind it. Try these on for size:

Why is "unmerited favor" an inadequate definition?
Why does grace require the gift of discernment?
How does grace impact our speech?
How has grace affected the prophetic?
What is the motive behind the ministry of grace?
What differentiates grace from law?
What is the core definition of grace? Where is it found?
What are the five keys to grace?
Define the paradigm of grace.
Explain how grace works through weakness.
How does grace activate and necessitate the gifts of the Holy Spirit?
How does grace bring us into a revelation of God and truth?
How does grace work to activate the power of God?
How does grace enable us to "reign in life?"
Why can our Christian experience not exceed an understanding of grace?

If you cannot really answer most of these in some degree, how well are you prepared for the genuine Christian experience?

A Necessary Fusion

Webster's Dictionary gives this definition of the word, "fusion:" "a merging of diverse elements into a unified whole." You don't have to be an expert to understand that the body of Christ is not yet what God intends it to be. There is a considerable contradiction between our conduct and our confession. We confess that we love one another, but our demonstrated character can frequently contradict our creed. While we know about our mandate to manifest the new creation, many times what we see in the body of Christ is the old creature. How is this dichotomy to be resolved? Trying harder doesn't work. What is God's provision so that this rift between our conduct and confession is resolved? Grace that has conquered the mind and heart of the believer is the only means by which a fusion occurs, causing our creed and conduct to become unified. Once this grace-activated fusion takes place within the believer, the believer becomes the whole creature manifesting the new man, the replication of Christ!

A Final Comment

I want to add this final commentary just in case some would misinterpret what I've been trying to say of the nature of grace. I do not want in any way to imply that man is relieved from the duty of biblical, moral obligation. We are still called to live within the defined parameters of righteousness as set before us in scripture. There are two parts to the covenant of grace that Christ set in place for the salvation and benefit of mankind. The first part has to do with the work that God alone could do. No man could pay the price for humanity. God, on the other hand, cannot repent as man is meant to repent. Repentance is man choosing to respond to what God has shown, said, and done.

I was ministering on grace in a church in Miami. After speaking on the freedom and accountability set upon us by grace a lady approached me with the following question. "Now that I'm free can I still live with a man who is not my husband?" I couldn't believe my ears. My answer? "Lady, Paul put it like this: 'God forbid'" (Romans 6:15).

Grace can never be interpreted as having absolved man from submission to the moral principles God has set out for us in scripture. Rather, it means that we, by choice and by enabling power from the Holy Spirit, keep and rejoice in those moral standards. The reality is this: when grace abounds within our hearts and minds, sin is utterly repugnant and contrary to our very nature.

A DANGEROUS GRACE

Calvinist or Armenian? Truth exists in tension with other truth. True exegesis must balance one truth with a corresponding truth. Note the list of corresponding truths as previously shown. Can any one of those areas be correctly understood if grace is ignored in our effort to correctly define our doctrine regarding such subjects? Can we really come to an accurate knowledge of what Francis Schaeffer terms "true truth" if grace is ignored? In an absolute sense, discipleship cannot be divorced from its context of grace, nor can grace be emptied of its impact on discipleship. Faith must have as its reference point grace, and grace must be allowed its true impact on the definition of faith, because faith cannot be accurately defined if it is defined without reference to grace. Grace must function as a counterbalance with other truths so that we arrive at a point of accurate biblical exegesis.

Grace must be allowed to play upon our understanding of mercy, and mercy must be allowed to play upon our definition of grace. Love must be allowed to play upon our definition of holiness, and holiness must be allowed to play upon our concept of love. Both love and holiness must countenance the implications of grace. Obviously, the lady mentioned above had no grasp of this dynamic. If our understanding of one truth is divorced from other truth, then in all likelihood our understanding of truth is wrong! Heresy will be the result, and truth becomes the manipulated instrument of man.

In matters of salvation, sanctification and the Christian life, God must be allowed his chosen role toward man, and man must be held accountable for his choices toward God. God extends grace; man, by an act of will, responds to grace. The two truths, the grace of God and the will of man, exist in tension with one another. Both must be allowed. Let's go back to Rick Joyner's statement: "Truth without grace is what the enemy brings when he comes as an angel of light." Any truth divorced from its context of grace is in danger of becoming an instrument of the enemy.

How about a final analogy using the barrel of a gun and its bullets: the barrel of the gun is likened to grace and the bullets to the truths of scripture. If someone has bullets and no gun barrel (grace) to deliver them, the bullets cannot hit the mark for which they are designed, and in fact can do great harm to the one holding the weapon. The bullets are still bullets with the capacity to function as bullets, but there is no gun barrel to be used. Grace is to truth what the barrel is to the bullets. You can fire the many bullets of biblical truth accurately only through the barrel of God's grace. Note as well, the bullets must be of the caliber of the gun barrel. You cannot fire .45 caliber bullets through the barrel of a shotgun. As the barrel dictates the caliber of bullets to be used so grace dictates the nature of truth to be declared. There must be a match between grace and the truth being presented! Going further, if the barrel and bullets are to be useful, there must be a marksman, who knows how the two function as one. He must be the workman approved. If there is no marksman, then the target of the human dilemma will never be affected by that which saves. The picture is indeed one of warfare.

Finally, grace understood and lived leads us to the danger of the cross; grace not understood leaves us in danger of demonic deception. How then shall we pursue this thing called grace? What shall be said of Grace, our "beloved enemy"?

Epilogue

Beloved Enemy
A Monologue in Prose by Read Irwin Myers

The great design agreed upon
By God, great Three in One,
And what was not was soon to be
Of light, of sky, of land, and sea,
Of plants that live to bear forth seed.
The stars, the sun, the moon
Were cast across an endless void,
While in a moment life became—abundant
Of fish and birds and creeping things
To fill the thing that God had made
And yet the work was incomplete.

Unseen wisdom bent down to stir
What only had been dust,
A strange and awful sight appeared
And lay in silent form—unseen before.
He then stood back to view the thing of dust
That lay upon earth's floor,
As if waiting for some wonder yet to come.
And come it did, at last, in a moment—
The thing that God called breath,
Forced its way through nostrils
Made by God—so life might come
That living souls should rise and stand
And take the place that God had planned,
A perfect place, a perfect man
And perfect state of grace.

READ IRWIN MYERS

He called it good what He had made
But more was yet to come.
The plan to be complete
The one made two
The two made one
And now the work was done.

The state of grace—The state of man
And this was meant to be.
The whole and only place
Where man was meant to be,
The perfect state of grace.

A darkened shadow
Slid across the earthly floor—
Its own and other way to bring.
Through ear and eye his words deceived.
Enticement worked its dreadful chore.
The perfect state was lost.
And strange new creatures driven forth
Upon the earth—to face the deadly curse
Subject, it would seem,
Forever to that dark and ugly force.

Despair, and want, and violent war
With pain so deep and unrelenting;
Broken, crushed, the image lost
While death owned every man,
But first found glee to make him pay
For having turned away
From the perfect state of grace.
A victim now—forever chained to shame
Unable to go free.

A DANGEROUS GRACE

Repeatedly, Creator God
With passion unrelenting,
Reached out in ways of love
To touch and change the heart of man
Who, living and so fully lost,
Refused the ways by which he might return.
His heart and mind forever fixed
And set in sin against his God.
Dark hate had won the heart and day.

But truly God as God,
In love so great
Would move to have His Way
Descend—in human form,
As wisdom far beyond the mind of man
The one called Christ
Conceived by Sovereign will,
Stood forth upon the earth
The Second Man,
Embodiment of yet a greater plan
Unique.

A perfect man and perfect God
The second death for sin the plan,
Repeatedly God's men had failed
To conquer—this ancient foe and
Death subdue.
And so he sent Himself
To do what only perfect God could do.
A cross, and blood, full death, a tomb
And hell
Were made to serve this greater plan
For God and love would have their way.
The tomb and death soon lost their prey
And grace once more was set by God
To be the only way, and that by faith
Expressed toward The Perfect Man
And perfect God.

READ IRWIN MYERS

So now to soulish man we turn
Whose hope to grace has turned
Expecting wonder and burden light
But finding that this ancient grace
Determined in its end to kill
Repentant man.
What's this?—God's grace that kills its man?
Where then this peace profound
Of which He spoke?
If grace has come to pierce
Its victim through
To find another death?
No! No mercy seems to mark the sky
And war instead of peace.
My inner man to rage against my inner man!
For part would seek an earthly peace
That leaves me as I am
Unchanged, unyielding, loving only who I am,
And that apart from grace.
But love, unyielding in its drive,
Stalking, stalking, ever stalking me—
Relentless foe, amazing grace
Sweet enemy—that beckons me to die.
For grace has come to draw my blood and life
That I might find the place of death:
A cross—the way to life!
But will I go across such barrenness?

So thirsty, lost, and broken,
My desperate heart cries out its
"Yes" to pain and inner death
That all my passions bleed and die
To honor Him
Who rose and lives beyond the sky,
And there has made a home
Eternal,
For those who eat the bread

And drink the blood
Of His amazing grace.
Beloved enemy—by which I die,
And only then to live.
Recovered all that had been lost
To live again a perfect man
And in that perfect state,
And thus the great design is made complete
And God?—Magnificent!

Bibliography

CHAPTER ONE
1. "The Grace Awakening" Charles R. Swindoll. Walker Publishing, Large Print. 1992.
2. "What's So Amazing About Grace" Philip Yancy. Zondervan Publishing House Grand Rapids, Michigan. 1997

CHAPTER TWO
1. "True Spirituality" Francis A. Schaeffer. Tyndale House Publishers, Wheaten, Illinois, 1971.

CHAPTER FOUR
1. Strong's Exhaustive Concordance of the Bible. Abbington Press, Nashville. 1977.
2. Ibid
3. "Miracles" C.S. Lewis. Geoffery Bles – The Centenary Press. London. 1947
4. "Power from on High" Charles G. Finney. Victory Press, Sussex, England. 1975
5. Strong's Exhaustive Concordance of the Bible, Abbington Press, Nashville 1977.
6. "Expository Dictionary of the New Testament" W.E. Vine. Fleming H. Revell Co. New Jersey. United States. 1966.
7. Quote: H. G. Wells. "Source Unknown"

CHAPTER FIVE
1. "Expository Dictionary of the New Testament" W.E. Vine. Fleming H.Revell Co. New Jersey. United States. 1966.
2. "Catch the Fire" Guy Chevreaux. Harper Collins Publishing. 1995
3. "Webster's Seventh Collegiate Dictionary" G &C Merriam Co. Springfield, Mass. 1969.

CHAPTER SIX
1. "Expository Dictionary of the New Testament" W.E. Vine. Fleming H. Revell Co. New Jersey, United States. 1966.

CHAPTER EIGHT
1. "Miracles" C.S. Lewis. Geoffrey Bles * The Centenary Press. London,
2. England. 1947.
3. "Power from on High" Charles G. Finney. Victory Press. Sussex. England. 1975.

CHAPTER NINE
1. Webster's Seventh Collegiate Dictionary. "Demoralization" G&C Merriam Co. Springfield, Mass. 1969.
2. "Brave New World" Aldous Huxley. Triad Panther Books, Granada Publishing Ltd. London. England 1985.
3. Webster's Ibid.
4. Quote: Bertrand Russell. "Brave New World" Ibid
5. Humanist Manifesto II, 1973. Tenet # 8.
6. Webster's Ibid
7. "The Stealing of America" John W. Whitehead. Crossway Books. Westchester, Illinois.1983
8. "Brave New World" Ibid
9. Quote: H.G. Wells. "Source Unknown."
10. Quote: Bertrand Russell. "Brave New World" Ibid

CHAPTER TEN
1. Webster's Seventh Collegiate Dictionary. Ibid.

CHAPTER ELEVEN
1. Webster's Seventh Collegiate Dictionary. Ibid.

CHAPTER THIRTEEN
1. "Paths to Power" A.W. Tozer. Christian Publications Inc. Harrisburg. Pa. U.S.A. * Note date indicated for publication.

CHAPTER FIFTEEN
1. "The Final Quest". Rick Joyner. Whitaker House. New Kensington. PA. U.S.A. 1996
2. "Strongs' Exhaustive Concordance of the Bible" Ibid
3. Ibid
4. Webster's Seventh Collegiate Dictionary. Ibid.
5. "The Final Quest" Ibid

Works Cited

Adler, Richard; Jerry Ross. Ya Gotta Have Heart. 1957.

Bush, President George. State of the Union Address, 2004. 20 Jan. 2004. Accessed 18 Dec. 2005. <http://www.whitehouse.gov/news/releases/2004/01/20040120-7.html>

Chevreaux, Guy. Catch the Fire. 1965. Harper Collins Publishing.

Danyun. Lilies Amongst Thorns: Chinese Christians Tell Their Story Through Blood and Tears. Sovereign World Ltd., Tongridge Kent, UK. 1991.

Denton, Michael. Evolution: A Theory in Crisis. 1985. London: Burnett Books.

Donahue, John J III; Steven D. Levitt. The Impact of Legalized Abortion on Crime. The Quarterly Journal of Economics. May, 2001. (available at <http://repositories.cdlib.org/cgi/viewcontent.cgi?article=1009&context=blewp>)

Duplantis, Jesse. Seven Ducks in a Muddy Pond. Video Recording.

Finney, Charles G. Power From on High. 1975. Victory Press. Sussex, England.

Gay Rights Rulings in U.S. and Canada Fuel Marriage Battle. Arthur W. Diamond Law Library, Columbia Law School. Updated 24 Feb. 2004. 17 Dec. 2005. <http://www.hrcr.org/hottopics/marriage.html>

Holocaust Encyclopedia. *Final Solution.* United States Holocaust Memorial Museum. Washington, D.C. Accessed 12 Dec. 2005. <http://www.ushmm.org/wlc/article.php?lang=en&ModuleId=10005151>

Huxley, Aldous. Brave New World. 1946; 1985 Ed. Triad/Panther Books, Granada Publishing Ltd. London.

Joyner, Rick. The Final Quest. 1996. Whitaker House. New Kensington PA, USA

King, Martin Luther, Jr. *I Have a Dream.* Delivered on the steps at the Lincoln Memorial in Washington D.C. on August 28, 1963. The Peaceful Warrior, Pocket Books, NY 1968

Koppes, Steve. Sloan Survey Astronomers Identify Most Distant Object. The University of Chicago Chronicle. 19-16, May 11, 2000. < http://chronicle.uchicago.edu/000511/sloan.shtml>

Kurtz, Paul; Wilson, Edwin. The Humanist Manifesto II. 1973. American Humanist Association. <http://www.american humanist.org/about/manifesto2.html>

Lewis, C.S. Miracles. 1975. Geoffrey Bles-The Centenary Press. London, England.

Newton, John. Amazing Grace. Public Domain, 1779.

Orwell, George. Nineteen Eighty Four. 1977. Harcourt Brace Jovanovich, San Diego CA.

Schaeffer, Francis. Escape From Reason. 1968. InterVarsity Press, Downers Grove, Ill.

Schaeffer, Francis. True Spirituality. 1971. Tyndale House Pub., Wheaton Ill.

Strong, James. Strong's Exhaustive Concordance of the Bible. © 1890; 36th reprint, 1977. Abingdon. Nashville, TN.

Strong, James. Strong's King James Hebrew and Greek Lexicon. 1977. Abbington Press. Nashville.

Swindoll, Charles. The Grace Awakening. 2003. Thomas Nelson.

Tozer, A.W. Paths to Power. Christian Publications Inc. Harrisburg, PA, USA.

Vine, W.E. Expository Dictionary of the New Testament. Fleming H. Revell Co., New Jersey, USA, © 1940, 17th reprint, 1966.

Webster's Seventh New Collegiate Dictionary. 1970. Springfield, Mass., G. & C. Merriam Co.

Whitehead, John. The Stealing of America. 1983, Westchester, Ill.: Crossway Books

Morrow, Lance. I Spoke...As a Brother. Time Magazine. January, 1984. <http://www.time.com/time/archive/preview/0,10987,952295,00.html>

Unless otherwise noted, the version of the Bible used in this book is the New International Version (NIV). Other versions are credited using the following notations:

- Good News Bible (GNB)
- God's Word (GW)
- King James Version (KJV)
- The Message (MSG)
- International Standard Version (ISV)
- New Living Translation (NLT)